Humanity's Children

Sonja C. Grover

Humanity's Children

ICC Jurisprudence and the Failure to Address the Genocidal Forcible Transfer of Children

Springer

Sonja C. Grover
Faculty of Education
Lakehead University
Thunder Bay
Canada

ISBN 978-3-642-32500-7 ISBN 978-3-642-32501-4 (eBook)
DOI 10.1007/978-3-642-32501-4
Springer Heidelberg New York Dordrecht London

Library of Congress Control Number: 2012952298

Printed on acid-free paper

Springer is part of Springer Science+Business Media (www.springer.com)

This book is dedicated with great respect and love to the memory of my parents Gina and David Gazan and that of my brother Albert Gazan. It is offered in the hopes that in some small way it may lead to the assistance of surviving direct and indirect victims of the 'genocidal forcible transfer of children' and contribute to both prevention and prosecution of this grave international crime.

Acknowledgments

My sincere thanks is extended to Dr. Brigitte Reschke, executive editor of law for Springer for her expert advice and support of this book project and to the anonymous reviewer for the encouraging words. I also extend my appreciation to Anke Seyfried and Manuela Schweitzer for their technical assistance and to the entire Springer production team especially Mrs. R. Krithika; project manager for their excellent work. As always, I acknowledge the love and support of my husband Roshan and daughter Angeline who seem to make all things possible.

Contents

Part I Introduction

1 Reconsidering the Legal Concepts of Genocide and the 'Genocidal Forcible Transfer of Children' 3
1.1 Children as Targets of Genocide 3
1.2 Genocide as a Separate Category of Grave International Crime 9
1.3 Children as a 'Protected Group': Implications for Our Understanding of 'Protected Group' 11
1.3.1 The Genocidal Forcible Transfer of Children and Children as a 'Protected Group' 16
1.4 Additional Points Regarding 'Protected Groups' 20
1.5 'Restrictive Interpretation' of Genocide Provisions: Implications for the Notion of Children as Persons 22
1.5.1 Restrictive Interpretation That Favours the Intention of the Parties Versus What Is Expressed in Text 24
1.6 Foreseeability, Perpetrator Accountability and Rome Statute Article 6(e) 28
1.6.1 The Nullum Crimen Principle and the Genocidal Forcible Transfer of Children to an Armed Group or Force 30
1.6.2 Evolving Conceptions of What Constitutes a Protected Group 34
1.7 The Rome Statute Article 6 Protected Group "As Such" Terminology 37
1.7.1 'Forcible Displacement' *vs.* 'Genocidal Forcible Transfer of Children' 38
1.7.2 Genocide's Special Targets and the Destruction of Future Generations 41
Literature, Materials and Situations/Cases 47

Part II ICC Prosecutor Case Selection and Charging Decisions

2 Gravity and Interests of Justice Considerations 53
2.1 Ambiguity of the Test for 'Sufficient Gravity' Regarding Admissibility of the Case 53
2.2 The Situation in the DRC: Case Selection and Gravity 55
2.3 The Situation in Darfur: Case Selection and Gravity 58
2.3.1 Parallels Between U.N. Peacekeepers and Children as 'Protected Groups' 60
2.4 Legal Characterization of the Facts and the Assessment of Gravity 61
2.4.1 'Relative Gravity' and the 'Genocidal Forcible Transfer of Children' 63
2.5 Children's Right to Justice and Legal Empowerment 64
2.6 Truth and Reconciliation Mechanisms and Child Victims 67
2.7 An Additional Note Regarding Child Soldier Victims of the 'Genocidal Forcible Transfer of Children' 69
2.8 Child Soldiers and the Question of Potential State Criminal Liability 74
2.9 'The Interests of Justice' and ICC Case Admissibility 77
Literature, Materials and Situations/Cases 80

Part III Selected ICC Cases Illustrating the Failure to Address the Genocidal Forcible Transfer of Children

3 Case 1: Prosecutor v. Thomas Lubanga Dyilo (Hereafter Also Referred to as *Lubanga*) 85
3.1 The War Crimes Charges: On Why They Were Insufficient 85
3.1.1 The Confirmed Charges 85
3.1.2 The Prosecution's Closing: Selected Issues Arising 86
3.1.3 The Context of Armed Conflict in *Lubanga* 94
3.1.4 The Common Plan and Genocidal Intent 97
3.1.5 Gender Crimes and the 'Genocidal Forcible Transfer of Children' 106
3.1.6 The Legal Re-Characterization of the Facts Controversy in Lubanga 113
3.1.7 On the Short Training Afforded FPLC Child Soldiers: Implications 137
3.1.8 The 'Continuous Nature' of the International Crimes Perpetrated Against FPLC Child Soldiers 138
3.1.9 The Defence Closing and the Prosecution Reply: Selected Issues Arising 146
Literature, Materials and Cases 197

4 Case 2: Prosecutor v. Germain Katanga and Mathieu Ngudjolo Chui 201
4.1 Confirmed Charges 201
4.2 The Prosecution Opening Statement 202
4.3 Charging Sexual Violence Crimes Under the Rome Statute 203
4.4 The Genocidal Forcible Transfer of Children as "Child Soldiers" 208
4.4.1 The FNI/FRPI Appropriation of Children as the 'Genocidal Forcible Transfer of Children' 208
4.4.2 Cruel and Inhuman Treatment of FNI/FRPI 'Child Soldiers' 214
4.4.3 Mens Rea and the Appropriation of Children to the FNI/FRPI 217
4.4.4 Genocidal Forcible Transfer of Children; Nationality and the Protected Status of Children 218
4.4.5 More on Outrages on Personal Dignity 219
Literature, Materials and Cases 220

5 Case 3: Prosecutor v Omar Hassan Ahmad Al Bashir 223
5.1 Background 223
5.2 The Prosecutor's ICC Application for an Arrest Warrant Re Omar Hassan Ahmad Al Bashir (14 July, 2008) 224
5.2.1 On Whether Darfur Involved 'Autogenocide' and Whether Correctly Answering that Question Matters 224
5.2.2 Motive, Genocide and Child Soldiering 225
5.2.3 The Targeting of So-Called 'Arab' Children of Darfur for Child Soldiering as an Act of Genocide 228
5.2.4 Sexual Violence as a Vehicle for the Genocidal Forcible Transfer of Children 232
5.2.5 The Recruitment and Use of Child Soldiers by the GoS During the Time Period Covered by the Al Bashir Case (March 2003 to July 14, 2008) 236
5.2.6 Report of the Secretary-General on Children and Armed Conflict in the Sudan (5 July, 2011) 237
5.3 The Interests of Justice and a Judicial Remedy for Child Victims in Darfur 242
5.4 The Standard of Proof in Regards to Establishing the Offence of Genocide in Its Various Forms 244
5.4.1 The Struggle to Confirm Genocide Charges in the Al Bashir Case 244
5.5 The Standard of Proof in Regards to Establishing the Offence of the Genocidal Forcible Transfer of Children (Warrant Stage) . . . 245
5.6 On Identifying Genocide in Darfur 248
5.7 The Genocidal Forcible Transfer of Children in Darfur 253
Literature, Materials and Cases 257

Part IV Conclusion

6 The Genocidal Forcible Transfer of Children: A Crime Well Established in International Law; Yet Still Not Prosecuted by the ICC . . . 261
6.1 Introduction . . . 261
6.2 Gravity of the Crime as an ICC Admissibility Criterion . . . 268
6.3 The Interests of Justice: Insights from the ICC Pre-Trial Judgement in *Kenya* . . . 269
6.4 The Somali Situation and the Matter of Impunity for Perpetrating 'Child Soldiering' . . . 270
6.4.1 Introduction . . . 270
6.4.2 Background to the Somali Situation and Child Victimization . . . 271
6.5 Gravity of the International Crimes Perpetrated by Al Shabaab Against Children . . . 276
6.6 Pursuing the Accountability of Somali Perpetrators . . . 278
6.7 The Situation in Chad and the Matter of Impunity for Perpetrating 'Child Soldiering' . . . 283
6.7.1 Reports by Amnesty International and the UN on the Situation in Chad . . . 283
6.7.2 Chad and the U.S. 'Child Soldiers Prevention Act of 2008' . . . 287
6.8 Acknowledging Existing International Norms that Protect Children from Genocidal Forcible Transfer . . . 289
6.8.1 Gaps in Children's Access to International Justice . . . 291
6.8.2 Genocidal Context and the Recruitment and Use of Child Soldiers . . . 293
6.8.3 Genocidal Forcible Transfer of Children Through Sexual Victimization . . . 298
6.8.4 ICC independence and Impartiality and Prosecuting Grave International Crimes Perpetrated Against Children . . . 301
6.8.5 The ICC and the Interests of Child Victims of Genocidal Forcible Transfer . . . 303
6.9 PostScript: The Syrian Regime's Genocidal Targeting of Children in Particular . . . 308
Literature, Materials and Cases . . . 313

Index . . . 317

Part I
Introduction

Chapter 1
Reconsidering the Legal Concepts of Genocide and the 'Genocidal Forcible Transfer of Children'

1.1 Children as Targets of Genocide

> Aside from ...general kinds of cruelty, perpetrators reserve certain cruelties for certain specific members of targeted peoples or groups ... Perpetrators often target two such kinds of victims, women and children, with specific horrors – though their [perpetrator] deeds are little recognized, and not conceptualized and analyzed as specific instances of cruelty...This failure reflects the general lack of attentive analysis given to perpetrators' acts ...*manner* of killing, *general* treatment of the victims, and other acts. Yet, it also reflects women's and children's general invisibility as distinct victim groups. Women's and children's *particularity* cannot rightly be ignored by subsuming them under the general category of victims, or by treating them as no different than men. The perpetrators' particular treatment of and cruelty toward women and children, perhaps even more than general cruelty, has not been focused upon probably for another reason: Doing so reveals the hollowness of so much existing analysis [of mass atrocity].[1]

The purpose of this book is to explore through selected case examples from ICC jurisprudence how the ICC has dealt with the matter of: (a) the special targeting and particularly heinous treatment accorded children as victims of mass atrocity and with (b) the international law implications of this special targeting and selective treatment. This author is in accord with Goldhagen that the extraordinarily cruel treatment typically inflicted upon women; especially pregnant women and children in the context of mass atrocity has to date been largely ignored as of any particular analytical significance in assessing international crimes:

> ...the perpetrators' treatment of children is not focused on, let alone appropriately highlighted, even though they [perpetrators] immensely brutalize children and kill them, often most gruesomely. This failure...effectively excludes or greatly reduces such acts' enormous descriptive significance from the recounting of events, and their analytical centrality from the inquiry into the events' causes and meanings.[2]

---

[1] Goldhagen (2009, p. 451, emphasis added).

[2] Goldhagen (2009, p. 145).

S.C. Grover, *Humanity's Children*, DOI 10.1007/978-3-642-32501-4_1,

It is here argued then that the targeting and special cruelty accorded women and girls; and children generally; in the context of mass atrocity is highly revealing with respect to: (a) the specific nature of the international crimes committed in such instances, (b) their gravity and (c) whether ICC prosecution of the perpetrators most responsible would best serve the 'interests of justice' where the crimes committed fall under the jurisdiction of the ICC. This work then endorses Goldhagen's view that attacks on children and women as particular targets for extreme cruelty during mass atrocity have special significance. The latter notion is applied in an assessment of ICC jurisprudence with respect to evaluating the validity of ICC determinations regarding the nature and gravity of the crime and the appropriateness of the charges and prosecutions in certain situations where children and women are special victim targets. The contention is advanced here that where women and girls and children generally are special or prized targets for extreme atrocity; crimes against humanity and war crimes morph into genocide or at least meet the criteria for genocide as well. The central focus of this book, however, is on the genocidal forcible transfer of children by various means during armed conflict and the deficiencies of ICC jurisprudence in addressing this specific grave international crime.

The need for a broader view of what is meant by a genocidal attack which constitutes an attack on 'humanity' and not simply the immediate victims is also a central focus in what follows. It is argued that genocide is not simply conduct directed to denying humanity the rich diversity that is represented in the various categories of the largely socially constructed restrictive list of 'protected groups' specified in the Genocide Convention (GC)[3] and subsequently incorporated into the Rome Statute[4] under the article dealing with genocide. That is, genocide cannot simply be reduced to an attempt to create a monolithic ethnic, religious, so-called 'racial' or national identity. Rather, at its core, *genocide is even more fundamentally about intentionally destroying future generations of humanity in the most general sense*[5] by a variety of acts inflicted upon targeted victims in the present; most particularly, though not exclusively, women and children. On the current analysis, in the context of mass atrocities and genocide, both the indoctrinated children of the perpetrator group and the children belonging to the targeted group of marginalized 'others' are the victims of genocide (though depending on the circumstances different acts of genocide). In essence then it is in reality children *per se* who are amongst the specially targeted victim groups in the context of mass atrocity and genocide and not simply the ethnic or other perceived 'protected group' as listed in the Genocide Convention[6] (religious, national or 'racial' group) slated for destruction in whole or in part. Consider in this regard, for example, the circumstance of the Holocaust perpetrated by the Nazis. It is here contended that German youth and

[3] Genocide Convention (1951).

[4] Rome Statute (2002).

[5] The means of 'destruction' of children is not confined to the mass murder of children but can include, for instance, the genocidal forcible transfer of children to the perpetrator group and other means of destroying the children's personal identities and psychological health.

[6] Genocide Convention (1951).

children indoctrinated with Nazi anti-Semitic propaganda were the victims of the genocidal forcible transfer of children from mainstream German society as originally constituted to the Nazi machine as an entity unto itself. Indeed, arguments were made in certain cases before the International Military Tribunal at Nuremburg to the effect that indoctrination of German children and youth with Nazi anti-Semitic propaganda constituted a violation of the Nuremberg Charter[7] and thus an international crime. For instance, the Prosecutor in the Julius Streicher case presented evidence during the trial that Streicher had, over the period of 25 years, published materials which included children's books and certain newspaper articles specifically targeting German children and youth for Nazi indoctrination.[8] This was done with the express objective of inciting hatred toward the Jews and perpetuating this hatred inter-generationally for time immemorial.[9] Addressing the Nazi indoctrination of German children and youth during the Streicher trial was, however, apparently "an afterthought by the Prosecution" as is apparent from the fact that Streicher had not been indicted for indoctrination of the German youth nor was this allegation contained in the Prosecutor's filed brief.[10] Streicher also advocated that such indoctrination occur in German schools and that non-Jews only be allowed to teach in the schools.[11] Eastwood who has written on the case of Streicher and the issue of indoctrination to so-called 'racial' hatred, states that the International Military Tribunal (IMT) at Nuremberg "lost an opportunity" to create a precedent and prosecute indoctrination of hate toward a targeted protected group as a specific international crime that can lead to genocide (where indoctrination is thought of as closely linked to; but yet separate in some ways from incitement to genocide).[12] On the analysis here, in contrast, indoctrination to hatred of a targeted *perceived* identifiable discrete group (to the point of desiring that group destroyed in whole or in part) is not only a means to incitement to genocide; but is part and parcel of the genocidal forcible transfer of the children so indoctrinated to the perpetrator group.[13]

In this case then the perpetrator indoctrinating German children and youth with Nazi anti-Semitic propaganda viewed this in the best interests of Germany and also ostensibly of the children targeted for indoctrination. This was the Nazi perpetrator fallacious claim also in regards to those non-German so-called Aryan looking children in Nazi occupied States who were the victims of genocidal forcible transfer to Germany for appropriation by German authorities under the Lebensborn

[7] Nuremberg Charter (1945).

[8] Eastwood (2011).

[9] Eastwood (2011, p. 1293).

[10] Eastwood (2011, p. 1292).

[11] Eastwood (2011, p. 1296).

[12] Eastwood (2011, p. 1300).

[13] Arguably, viewed from this perspective, the indoctrination of children and youth in genocidal hatred might have been classified as a form of enslavement and persecution (crimes against humanity) under the Nuremberg Charter (1945).

program.[14] Thus, children of *various* ethnicities, national origins and/or religious affiliations are most often the victims of genocide in any particular singular context of mass atrocity and genocide. The victimization of children in a genocidal context thus cannot be reduced to the perpetrator-defined child group targeted for physical destruction (i.e. the destruction of Jewish children as a group). It is the disregard also for the fundamental right of children to their humanity; to their personal identity;[15] to their ties to biological family and home community and the values of civilized society that serves as one of the key markers for genocide (whether carried out through the mass murder of children of a targeted victim group and/or other means such as the genocidal forcible transfer of children to the perpetrator group). Thus, genocidal intent is present in instances of the forcible transfer of children to the perpetrator group committing mass atrocities notwithstanding any alleged concern for the best interest of children who are the victims of the transfer. Indeed, those who perpetrate the genocidal forcible transfer of children are well aware that to accomplish the objectives of this crime the children's psyche will need to be destroyed and re-shaped in a fashion envisioned by the perpetrator group. This is well illustrated by the facts regarding the *Hitlerjugend* as it is in more contemporary examples of child soldiers 'recruited' by armed groups or forces committing conflict-related mass atrocities and/or genocide.

In regard to the Nazi genocidal forcible transfer of German children and youth, note that: "By early 1939 about 82 % (7.3 million) of eligible youths within Germany belonged to the Hitler Youth" and that from these ranks were selected certain candidates to join the SS and others to become military officers.[16] In 1943, the 12 SS Panzer Division *Hitlerjugend* "a fully equipped Waffen-SS armoured division" was established as a military reserve force and had adult officers commanding enlisted youths ages 16–18.[17] This SS division comprised of Nazi so-called child soldiers was known for its ferocity and willingness to fight to the death consistent with the vision of Hitler's youth indoctrination common plan and practice.[18] That ambition to destroy the humanity of German youth through genocidal indoctrination is reflected in the following quote of Hitler's words to Hermann Rauschning:

> We shall educate a youth before which the whole world shall tremble, rough, exacting, cruel youth. That is what I want. Our youth must possess all these qualities. It must be pitiless before the sight of suffering. It must be without weakness or softness. I want to see the glint of the wild animal in their eyes.[19]

---

[14] Grover (2011a).

[15] The denial of the children's personal identity is accomplished by: (a) transforming children into but cogs in the perpetrator's machinery (this occurring most often if the children are members of the perpetrator so-called 'racial', ethnic, national and/or religious group); or by (b) classifying the children as subhuman if they are members of the victim non-perpetrator group targeted for destruction in whole or in part.

[16] Eastwood (2011, p. 1293).

[17] Eastwood (2011, p. 1293).

[18] Eastwood (2011, p. 1293).

[19] International Military Tribunal Trial of the Major War Criminals (1946, p. 616). Cited in Eastwood (2011, p. 1293).

The Prosecutor in the Baldur van Schirach[20] case before the International Military Tribunal (IMT) at Nuremburg quoted the above Hitler speech as evidence of "…youth morally corrupted with the obscurantism of the Hitlerites."[21] The Prosecutor went on to note the following

> The part played by the Defendant Von Schirach and his participation in the common conspiracy, in war crimes and crimes against humanity, *are characterized best of all by the behavior of German youth brought up in Hitlerjugend during the war…* [For example]…in the territory of Lvov [a witness testified to] the inhuman cruelty of the members of the Hitlerjugend against young children, whom they used as targets for shooting practice.[22] …Schirach himself did not, of course, shoot, did not set on fire; but he did arm the German youth, morally corrupted them and prepared them for the perpetration of every atrocity.[23][The *Hitlerjugend* executed all assigned duties to facilitate a war of aggression and to perpetrate international crimes including, for instance, respectively creating fifth columns and deporting for slavery children aged 10–14 from the occupied territories].[24]

The concept of 'genocide' as a notion defined in law was, as is well known, not yet formulated at the time of the Nuremberg trials as was also the case, of course, in regards to the legal concept of the genocidal forcible transfer of children of the group to another. The trial transcript quoted above in respect of the *Hitlerjugend* reveals, however, that the IMT Prosecutor in the van Schirach and Streicher cases argued vehemently that the indoctrination of youth into the Nazi mind set and the use of child soldiers to participate in the Nazi mass atrocities was itself an integral part of the overall common plan. That common plan involved the perpetrating of all manner of grave international crime including crimes against humanity (as well as what we today would term genocide). The IMT Prosecutor in fact, on the view here, indirectly laid the groundwork (through his arguments and the evidence presented at trial in the aforementioned cases) for the notion that: (1) the Nazi indoctrination of German children and youth and (2) the use of *Hitlerjugend* as child soldiers to perpetrate conflict-related mass atrocity in themselves constituted grave international crimes. For instance, the use of child soldiers violated the customs and laws of war (a war crime), the use of child soldiers and their indoctrination to commit mass atrocity was part of a common plan to wage a war of aggression (thus arguably in themselves constituting crimes against peace) while the Nazi indoctrination of children and youth and their conscription into the *Hitlerjugend* can be considered as a forced mental and physical enslavement (each of these categories of international crimes being stipulated in the Nuremberg Charter of 1945).[25]

---

[20] Baldur van Schirach was head of the Hitler Youth from 1931 to the end of WWII.

[21] International Military Tribunal Trial of the Major War Criminals (1946, p. 615).

[22] International Military Tribunal Trial of the Major War Criminals (1946, p. 616, emphasis added).

[23] International Military Tribunal Trial of the Major War Criminals (1946, p. 617).

[24] International Military Tribunal Trial of the Major War Criminals (1946, p. 617).

[25] Nuremberg Charter (1945).

The argument is made here thus that the recruitment and indoctrination of children as child soldiers with a view to their use in armed hostilities by an armed group or force perpetrating mass atrocities and/or genocide constitutes the genocidal forcible transfer of children. However, as we shall discover, ICC jurisprudence has failed to adequately address and properly charge this grave international crime perpetrated against children. Instead, the ICC prosecutions concerning the recruitment and use of child soldiers for active participation in hostilities have ignored the implications of the context of mass atrocity and/or genocide (which have been a feature of the broader situation in the child soldier cases to date) for the articulation of the case. Consequently, the ICC Prosecutor has framed the crime of recruitment and use of children for active participation in hostilities *only* in terms of the war crime of recruiting and/or using under 15s for active participation in hostility.[26] The latter then as opposed to dealing also with the genocidal forcible transfer of children under 18 to the perpetrator group as child soldiers to serve as a support and/or direct participant in the perpetrating of mass atrocity and/or genocide.

It is here argued that the concept of genocide, though not currently thus understood under Lemkin's definition as commonly interpreted, does not require that the victimized children 'belong' to any particular protected group (i.e. religious, ethnic, national or racial). Ultimately all children generally belong in any case to a number of *overlapping* such socially constructed categories including political categories (the latter perpetrator perceived children's group affiliation arising through the political associations of the children's parents). The targeted perceived group is destroyed in part or in whole in no small measure through the loss of some or most of their children consequent to the mass murder of children; assimilation or other forcible transfer of the children to another group or some such factor (in short, due to some devastating physical and/or psychological harm done to the children of the targeted group).

Children in and of themselves belong to a special protected group (under international customary law and humanitarian treaty law) that is owed special care and respect in times of armed conflict (for instance as per Protocol I[27] and Protocol II[28] Additional to the Geneva Conventions; Article 77 and Article 4(3), respectively). On this analysis then terrorists who at some point in their terror

[26] Such a war crime involving the recruitment and use of under 15s in hostilities can occur in the context also of internal or international conflict where (1) the parties are not engaged in perpetrating mass atrocities and/or genocide; (2) the child soldiers are not forced or expected to commit atrocity and are not subjected to cruel and inhuman treatment during training; and (3) the child soldiers are not regarded as property belonging indefinitely to the recruiting armed force or group such that the children's bonds with their family and community are intentionally severed.

[27] Protocol I Additional to the Geneva Conventions.

[28] Protocol II additional to the Geneva Conventions.

campaign *specifically and deliberately target children*; such as do the Taliban associated with Al Qaeda and other extremists when they carry out school attacks[29] or use children as suicide bombers for instance, are committing genocide. Future generations are destroyed in whole or in part in the most direct way via such targeted attacks. Selective especially brutal attacks on children, and women (especially pregnant women) are well understood by the general populace for their symbolic significance as an attempt to wipe out future generations of the despised target victim group (i.e. the dissident population comprised of those who would defy authoritarian extremist Taliban dictates for example, ethnic or religious minorities or some other targeted civilian group). So, too, parents and communities understand that children appropriated by terrorists to, for instance, the Al Qaeda cause are a lost generation for those affected families and local communities. Put in other terms; the children thus targeted are the victims of the genocidal forcible transfer of children to these terrorist groups.[30]

1.2 Genocide as a Separate Category of Grave International Crime

The question arises as to whether the distinction in law between the concept genocide versus that of crimes against humanity is a legitimate and useful one. The distinction is made typically on the grounds that crimes against humanity involve a widespread systematic attack while genocide can occur even when only one victim is targeted as long as the specific intent requirement is met (that intent being to destroy a Genocide Convention defined 'protected group' in whole or in part). However, consider that, for instance, a terror attack on one civilian or a considerable number of civilians which attack is not part of an organized systematic widespread campaign nonetheless has a widespread systemic effect on the victim civilian population (the entire civilian population feels threatened). This parallels the situation in which an act of atrocity occurs against one or a small number of members of one of the Genocide Convention[31] protected groups based on the group membership of the targeted individual or individuals. That is, the latter acts of atrocity are also perceived as threats to the larger group (i.e. ethnic, national, religious or 'racial' group).

---

[29] Grover (2011b).

[30] Security Council Working Group on Children and Armed Conflict (2005): The use of child soldiers is now understood to threaten peace and security in the regions affected. It is for that reason that a U.N. Security Council working group was established in 2005 to address reports on the incidence of children's involvement in armed conflict globally and to make recommendations to the Security Council on needed measures to better protect children.

[31] Genocide Convention (1951).

Another argument for maintaining the distinction has been that genocide involves *discriminatory intent* (against certain protected groups; namely those listed in the Genocide Convention[32]) while crimes against humanity allegedly do not necessarily except in cases of persecution for instance.[33] However, the perpetrators in both instances (with regard to genocide and crimes against humanity; separable crimes under international law) distinguish between those to be victimized (those who allegedly deserve to be subjected to atrocity) and those not so. Hence, the perpetrators of both of these categories of international crime have constructed separable groups based on a certain discriminatory criterion (those committing crimes against humanity often targeting the victim groups based on their perceived political affiliation. Political affiliation could, in some instances at least, be considered an aspect of culture/ethnicity if it characterizes a certain people in the main and correlates with other traditions and cultural features of the particular group).

The distinction between 'genocide' and 'crimes against humanity' is often problematic in part given the difficulties with interpretation of the four protected groups listed in the Genocide Convention (the protected group categories being duplicated nonetheless in the articles dealing with genocide in the Rome Statute[34] and in the enabling statutes of several international criminal tribunals). Consider in this regard the fact that the categories listed as protected groups under the Genocide Convention[35] are neither immutable (i.e. national and religious groups) nor necessarily scientifically legitimate constructions (i.e. so-called 'racial' groups) and certain categories have no universal definition and are therefore ambiguous (i.e. ethnic groups). Note that notions of ethnicity have often been more related to colonial or other *imposed* arbitrary distinctions as opposed to what might be considered genuine objective distinctions in culture (especially where the groups that are allegedly ethnically distinct have intermarried and coexisted with much interaction for decades if not longer and share basic cultural characteristics in common). Consider, for instance, the perceived distinction between Hutu and Tutsi:

> The fact is that the Tutsi and the Hutu do not constitute at first glance distinct ethnic, racial, religious or national groups. *They have the same language, culture and religion*, as well as basically the same physical traits. In *Akayesu* the ICTR Trial Chamber emphasized that the two groups were nevertheless distinct because (i) they had been made distinct by the Belgian colonizers when they established a system of identity cards differentiating between the two groups... and (ii) the distinction was confirmed by the self-perception of the members of each group.[36]

---

[32] Genocide Convention (1951).

[33] See Article 7(i)(h)(3) of the Rome Statute (2002) pertaining to persecution as a crime against humanity.

[34] Rome Statute (2002).

[35] Genocide Convention (1951).

[36] UN Commission of Inquiry on Darfur (2005, p. 126, para 498, emphasis added).

Consider also that one's particular political affiliation may be longstanding and, in some cases, reflect an intergenerational characteristic of a family or community. In the latter situations it is likely that political orientation is associated with a particular well-established familial and/or predominant communal cultural world view and set of values. That is, political orientation, in certain instances, may arguably be considered an aspect or dimension of ethnicity. At present, a political group is not considered to constitute a 'protected group' as that term is understood in respect of the Genocide Convention[37] nor is political affiliation considered as an aspect of ethnicity. The latter, on the view here, are errors resulting from an under-inclusive faulty interpretation of the genocide provision of the Rome Statute.[38]

While the distinction in international law between crimes against humanity and genocide is, in many respects, clearly problematic theoretically; it will be relied on here but only in certain respects. For the purposes of the present inquiry then genocide will be considered as an attempt to destroy a targeted group in whole or in part by the means described at Article 2 of the Genocide Convention directed at individual members of that targeted group.[39] However, any such identifiable targeted group is here considered protected; particularly any child group.

In the next section, we will consider children as a protected group *as such* (in their own right) under the Genocide Convention.[40] The argument will be made that such an interpretation [children as a protected group under the Genocide Convention (GC)][41] is in fact dictated by: (1) aspects of the text of the GC itself and by (2) the special privilege accorded children under international law.

1.3 Children as a 'Protected Group': Implications for Our Understanding of 'Protected Group'

Recall that children are a *special protected* group under international law in times of armed conflict and in peacetime. As such, they are owed a high duty of care and protection on account of their age and vulnerability as reflected, for instance, in international humanitarian law (i.e. Protocols I and II Additional to the Geneva Conventions);[42] human rights law (i.e. Convention on the Rights of the Child[43] and its two Optional Protocols namely the Protocol dealing with children in armed

---

[37] Genocide Convention (1951).

[38] Rome Statute (2002).

[39] Genocide Convention (1951).

[40] Genocide Convention (1951).

[41] Genocide Convention (1951).

[42] Protocols I and II Additional to the Genocide Conventions (1977).

[43] Convention on the Rights of the Child (1990).

conflict[44] and that addressing the sale of children, child prostitution and child pornography);[45] international criminal law (i.e. the Rome Statute criminalizes the conscription or enlistment and use of children under age 15 for active participation in hostilities)[46] as well as customary law. This high duty of protection owed to children is also evident in the child-specific provisions in the Genocide Convention[47] concerning: (1) the absolute prohibition on the genocidal forcible transfer of children of the group to another group and (2) on the prevention, with genocidal intent, of births in the targeted victim group.[48] In fact, under international law, *all* children *as children* are automatically members of a 'special protected' subgroup of any general population. Under international law thus children, both in times of peace and during armed conflict are, in many respects, owed a higher standard of protection than that due the adult civilian population. This is the case even where the children are correctly or incorrectly considered to be non-civilians as evidenced by certain special protections included in the Additional Protocols to the Geneva Conventions[49] for children considered to be direct participants in the armed conflict (i.e. protection against the death penalty for grave violations of the laws and customs of armed conflict or other significant conflict-related international crimes).[50]

The special protected status under international law to be enjoyed by all children is independent of the children's other perceived group affiliations and whether or not those perceived affiliations are or are not based on objective fact [such other group affiliations would include, but are not limited to, being a member of a particular perceived ethnic, 'racial', religious or national group or political group (in respect of the latter affiliation what is referred to here are children who may be perceived as having a political group affiliation by virtue of their parents, for instance, being members of a particular political party or resistance movement or other social reform activist group)]. Children[51] then as individuals or as a group *as such* (in their own right) (regardless of their other perceived group affiliations;

---

[44] Optional Protocol to the Convention on the Rights of the Child on the involvement of children in armed conflict (2002).

[45] Optional Protocol to the Convention on the Rights of the Child on the sale of children, child prostitution and child pornography (2002).

[46] Rome Statute (2002).

[47] Genocide Convention (1951).

[48] The latter prohibition, of course, also affords women special protection against certain actions such as forced sterilization or compelled abortion where there is genocidal intent.

[49] Protocols I and II Additional to the Genocide Conventions (1977).

[50] This author has argued that child soldier recruits to armed forces or groups committing mass atrocities and/or genocide are in fact civilians and continue to hold the status of civilian as victims of genocidal forcible transfer to an unlawful belligerent State or non-State armed group or force.

[51] Children are here defined as persons under age 18 consistent with the age criterion for child incorporated in the Rome Statute (2002) elements of the crime regarding the genocidal forcible transfer of children and the exclusion of ICC jurisdiction over children (persons under age 18 at the time he or she committed an international crime) set out in the Rome Statute (2002).

or the size of the child group; or the extent of homogeneity of the child group in terms of religion, 'race', ethnicity or nationality or some other dimension),[52] are, on the analysis here, entitled to *special protection* under the Genocide Convention as members of a protected group.[53] Given the fact that children possess an entitlement to a special privilege of protection *in their own right* under international law as children: (1) the attempt to destroy a child, or more commonly a group of children, *as such* or (2) the attempt to destroy a child, or more commonly a group of children as symbolic targets for the destruction in whole or in part of some larger other group to which the children belong ('racial', ethnic, national, religious or other) is, on the view here, a genocidal attack on humanity generally.[54]

It is the case thus that children, *as a group in their own right*, are entitled to a high level of special protection under international law; including under the Genocide Convention (GC).[55] At the same time, any identifiable separable group of children belongs to multiple perceived wholly or partially socially constructed and/or objectively defined larger mixed age groups (defined in terms of religious, ethnic, racial, national, political dimensions etc.). It is here argued, however, that the intentional targeting of a child group *as such* for destruction in whole or in part by any of the means listed at Article 2 of the Genocide Convention[56] constitutes genocide *regardless of the children's larger group affiliation(s)* since children as a group are, as discussed, a protected group under the Genocide Convention. In addition, of course, genocide occurs where children are being targeted as a means of destroying some other perceived group of which they are a part. On the analysis here that larger group may be an ethnic, religious, political, national, so-called racial group, a group defined in terms of being comprised of same-sex parents or any other identifiable group.[57] Put differently; it is not logically possible (or indeed

---

[52] The perceived group affiliations of children may or may not be derivatives directly or indirectly from their parentage, and/or be objectively real, and may or may not involve groups that are amongst those listed as protected under the Genocide Convention (1951).

[53] Genocide Convention (1951).

[54] This is not to say that such conduct may not also be a genocidal attack on a particular targeted larger victim group perceived as of a particular 'racial', ethnic, religious or national group or, on the view here, whether defined in other terms. Where women and/or men *of any identifiable group* are targeted in an effort to wipe out future generations of *any* identifiable distinct group (as when women are gang raped and thereafter unable to bear children or men and women are sexually mutilated, or kept apart to prevent procreation and then in many instances killed etc.) such mass atrocities also, on the view here, rise to the level of genocide.

[55] Genocide Convention (1951).

[56] Genocide Convention (1951).

[57] Genocide can occur in instances where there is but one or a small number of victims targeted as well as where there are masses of victims if the destruction of each individual is, *in effect*, a genocidal attack on the group of which the victimized individual is perceived to be a member. For instance, where small or large numbers of children are killed or suffer any of the genocidal acts described at Article 2 of the Genocide Convention (1951) because they are *as individuals* imaginatively thought to be witches or to be possessed in some fashion as has occurred in some regions of particular African States; this too, on the analysis here, constitutes genocide. Any child

legally supportable) to interpret the Genocide Convention (GC)[58] as stipulating that the protected groups under that Convention are restricted to the four explicitly listed in the text of the GC. To do so would be to exclude, without any legal support or justification in international law, certain child groups from the full range of special protections owed all children (i.e. protection against the acts listed at Article 2 of the Genocide Convention in a context where the children are being targeted based on their membership in a group not explicitly listed in the Genocide Convention).[59] Thus, for instance, some children may have homosexual parents; others may have parents who are political dissidents etc. such that these children may be perceived as affiliated through their parentage with larger groups that are targeted for destruction in part or in whole. In order for *these* children to also receive the special protection to which they are entitled under international law[60] in such contexts; the targeted larger groups to which they belong, though not explicitly listed in the GC, must, contrary to current general practice, also be considered as 'protected groups' under the Genocide Convention.[61] Thus, on the analysis here, all perceived groups [not just the four explicitly listed in the Genocide Convention[62](GC)] intentionally targeted for destruction in part or in whole *as a group* (through any means listed at Article 2 of the GC) are protected under the Genocide Convention.[63] This is the necessary conclusion if international humanitarian law and customary law as it applies to children being entitled to special protection is to be internally consistent in actually providing, as it must, that special protection to *all children* across all relevant treaties including the Genocide Convention.[64]

---

is potentially at risk in certain regions if declared by community elders as a witch but especially so children who had unusual births, children who exhibit unusual behaviour, disabled children, children born with albinism, orphaned children and certain others such as twins (Cimpric 2010). These children so targeted are thus victimized as individuals first and foremost though their destruction or expulsion from the community is considered a vehicle also for eliminating some larger imagined or real group of which they are perceived to be a member [respectively a so-called witch group or some group characterized by a physical or behavioural feature or life circumstance (Cimpric 2010)]. Children being denied life-saving treatment and let die because they are severely disabled is a phenomenon that has occurred also in 'developed' countries even where some of the children involved would have, with the needed medical treatment, survived for shorter or some times long periods (Sobsey 2007, p. 378–384). In such instances also the children are being targeted firstly because of who they are as individuals though the ultimate effect is to reduce the overall population group comprised of severely disabled persons. Such medical non-treatment of certain categories of severely disabled children also arguably constitutes genocide though alleged defences regarding the children's anticipated abysmal quality of life are generally raised.

58 Genocide Convention (1951).

59 Genocide Convention (1951).

60 That special protection owed all children equally under international law must include, among other things, of course, protection of the child group *as such* from destruction in whole or in part regardless of how the perpetrators perceive or define the child group in question.

61 Genocide Convention (1951).

62 Genocide Convention (1951).

63 Genocide Convention (1951).

64 Genocide Convention (1951).

It is thus simply not possible in any logical or legally supportable fashion to essentially attempt to define away as instances of genocide for *any* group of children (all of whom have special protected status under international law as children regardless of their larger group affiliation) the grave child-specific international crimes involving: (1) forcible transfer of children of the group to another or (2) the prevention of births in the targeted victim group where the intent is to eliminate or destroy in whole or in part future generations of that targeted group *regardless how defined or perceived.* Likewise, other acts of genocide (i.e. the killing of children, causing children severe mental and physical harms, and deliberately inflicting on children conditions of life intended to destroy the children as a group in whole or in part) cannot be ruled non-genocidal based on the children not belonging to a larger mixed age group targeted for destruction in whole or in part based on that group's perpetrator perceived 'race', ethnicity, religion or nationality (the group being targeted for annihilation in part or in whole instead based on some other perceived characteristic attributed by the perpetrator to the larger mixed age group of which the children are members).

As discussed, on the analysis here: (1) the child-specific provisions in the Genocide Convention[65] and (2) the general international law recognition of the special protected status of all children as children, renders children a protected group *per se* under the Genocide Convention.[66] Thus, the intentional targeting of any identifiable discrete group of children for destruction in part or in whole by any of the means listed in the Genocide Convention[67] at Article 2 constitutes genocide regardless whether: (1) the child group is internally homogenous with respect to any particular feature or combination of features such as, but not limited to; religion, 'race', nationality or ethnicity or (2) the children are victimized as part of any particular larger group of origin targeted based on sometimes highly ambiguous characterizations in terms of 'race', ethnicity, religion and/or nationality or some other alleged defining characteristic. Thus, in the final analysis, ironically it turns out that it is through our children that we can come to realize that the Genocide Convention (GC)[68] affords protection to individuals from the acts lists at Article 2 of the Convention as members of *any identifiable group* targeted for destruction in whole or in part *as such.* Thus, the protection of the GC extends beyond protection of the four groups explicitly listed in the Genocide Convention[69] to all groups that are groups in their own right and targeted for annihilation in part or in whole "as such" through the means articulated in the Genocide Convention at Article 2.

---

[65] Genocide Convention (1951).

[66] Genocide Convention (1951).

[67] Genocide Convention (1951).

[68] Genocide Convention (1951).

[69] Genocide Convention (1951).

To recap then; it cannot be a correct interpretation of the Genocide Convention[70] (or of the notion of 'protected group' in the duplicated definition of genocide in the Rome Statute[71] Article 6) that genocide only occurs if one or more of the four so-called protected groups explicitly listed in the Genocide Convention (GC)[72] are targeted for destruction in whole or in part as is the traditional interpretation. Referred to here are the explicitly listed groups mentioned in the introductory line at Article 2: "In the present Convention, genocide means any of the following acts committed with intent to destroy, in whole or in part, a national, ethnical, racial or religious group, as such."[73] That erroneous traditional interpretation would mean that children not targeted on the basis that they belong to one or more of the aforementioned four groups explicitly listed in the GC (or at Article 6 of the Rome Statute[74]) would not enjoy the special protection under international law in respect to a grave international crime; namely genocide (most would contend the gravest of international crimes) to which protection certain other children are entitled. This due to a *circular definition* of what constitutes a 'protected group'[75] under the Genocide Convention.[76]

1.3.1 The Genocidal Forcible Transfer of Children and Children as a 'Protected Group'

Only the Genocide Convention and the Rome Statute at Article 6(e) include *a child-specific provision* addressing the grave international crime of genocidal forcible transfer of children of the group to another group[77] (a crime that can be accomplished, as has here been discussed, by various means such as mass rape of children; recruitment and use of children as child soldiers to commit atrocities against their own people and others; transfer of girl children to the perpetrator group to serve as sex slaves etc. though the latter crimes may *also*, in many instances, meet the

[70] Genocide Convention (1951).

[71] Rome Statute (2002).

[72] Genocide Convention (1951).

[73] The current author has argued here that the Genocide Convention (1951) in fact also lists children as a protected group by articulating child-specific acts of genocide at Article 2 (d) and (e).

[74] Rome Statute (2002).

[75] That circular definition amounts to the following: 'A group targeted for destruction in whole or in part by the means specified at Article 2 of the Genocide Convention (1951) is a protected group *if the context is declared genocidal* and the group targeted is *not* a protected group where the context is not declared genocidal.' Thus, for instance, in the case of the Rwanda genocide, the ICTR arguably worked backward from the recognition of the fact that a genocide had occurred to a construction of ethnic distinction that was, on the view here, erroneously perceived as a precondition for affirming that the context of the armed conflict had been genocidal.

[76] Genocide Convention (1951) Article 2.

[77] Genocide Convention (1951) Article 2(e).

criteria for other international crimes such as war crimes or crimes against humanity). Hence, the exclusion of any group of children from this child-specific protection provision would mean generally weaker protections in this regard than are provided via other child protection provisions of international law (i.e. the relevant provisions of the Additional Protocols to the Geneva Conventions[78] dealing with the protection of children during armed conflict).[79]

The proposition that only *some children*; namely those belonging to a specified limited set of groups can benefit from the Genocide Convention's (duplicated at Article 6(e) of the Rome Statute) child-specific clause[80] regarding forcible transfer of children of the group to another group is not viable or reasonable.[81] This is the case as *all children* as a category in themselves enjoy a special protected status under international treaty and customary law regardless their other group memberships. Put differently, it makes no interpretive sense to consider that **all** children as children[82] (that is as a distinct group or category of persons recognized under international law) should have special protected status under the Additional Protocols I and II to the Geneva Conventions[83] (which have arguably taken on customary law status); but that some children would be exempted from the protection afforded by the child-specific protection provision concerning the forcible transfer of children of the group to another group (would not be considered part of a protected group in regards to this grave international crime).[84] It is relevant to note at this point given the aforementioned argument concerning: (1) the internal consistency that should exist in international law in respect of regarding children as a special protected group in their own right and (2) our consideration of the Genocide Convention Article 2 (e)[85] in light of the special protected status of children (reflected for instance under the Protocols I and II Additional to the

[78] Protocols I and II additional to the 1949 Geneva Conventions (1977).

[79] This since protection from recruitment and from use for active participation in hostilities as child soldiers is afforded under the Rome Statute (2002) Article 8 and the Additional Protocols I and II to the Geneva Conventions (1977) to all children regardless of their larger group affiliations (though granted only in regard to children under 15 making any under-inclusiveness in protection under Rome Statute Article 6(e) especially detrimental to child soldier victims of genocidal forcible transfer aged 15 and over who are not protected under Rome Statute Article 8).

[80] Genocide Convention (1951).

[81] Note that Article 32 of the Vienna Convention on the Law of Treaties (1969) does *not* contemplate that the proper interpretation of treaty text would lead to a "manifestly absurd" or "unreasonable" result. Recourse to other sources of law are then said to be necessary to rectify the unreasonable textual interpretation.

[82] There are no exclusions to the special care and respect owed children during international or internal armed conflict under the Additional Protocols to the Geneva Conventions based on the particular nationality, religion, ethnic group or 'race' of the children in question.

[83] Protocols I and II additional to the 1949 Geneva Conventions (1977).

[84] The same applies in regards to the need to consider all unborn children protected from attempts to prevent their existence motivated by genocidal intent and the unborn children's affiliation, through their parentage, to some targeted group.

[85] Genocide Convention (1951, Article 2(e)).

Geneva Conventions[86]); the following proposition advanced by the Preparatory Working Group on the Definition of Crimes for the Rome Statute:

> The Working Group noted that with respect to the interpretation and application of the provisions concerning the crimes within the jurisdiction of the Court [the ICC), the Court shall apply relevant international conventions and other sources of international law. In this regard, *the Working Group noted that for the purposes of interpreting [the provision concerning genocide]it may be necessary to consider...other sources of international law.*[87]

Consistent with the Preparatory Working Group on the Definition of Crimes for the Rome Statute having opined that reference to sources of international law outside the Rome Statute might be necessary to interpret the Rome Statute provision concerning genocide; the current author found it necessary to look to other sources of international law (i.e. here the Protocols I and II Additional to the Geneva Conventions; specifically provisions therein according *all* children special protected status during armed conflict regardless of nationality, ethnicity, religion or race) to properly interpret and consider the application of Article 6 (e) of the Rome Statute[88] (reflecting Article 2 (e) of the Genocide Convention).[89] Note that Article 32 of the Vienna Convention on the Law of Treaties (1969)[90] contemplated that recourse might need to be made to the preparatory work regarding a treaty where the textual interpretation of a provision of the treaty led to a "manifestly absurd" or "unreasonable" result (here reference is made in this regard to the Preparatory Working Group for the Rome Statute's recognition that properly interpreting the provision on genocide in the Rome Statute might require reference to other sources of international law). Note that Article 21 of the Rome Statute[91] in fact lists other sources of international law as one possible guide to interpretation of the Rome Statute where there is ambiguity.

Genocide then is better understood as an attempt to destroy *any perceived* group in whole or in part with *discriminatory intent* by the means listed in the Genocide Convention.[92] Arguably, the Genocide Convention[93] as written (and Article 6 of the Rome Statute[94] mirroring the Genocide Convention Article 2) is ripe for such an interpretation for the reasons previously explained; where the explicitly listed protected groups are taken to be examples and not a definitive list of protected groups and the latter approach is taken to be in accord with the drafters' intent.

---

86 Protocols I and II additional to the 1949 Geneva Conventions (1977).

87 Schabas (2010, p. 122–123, emphasis added).

88 Rome Statute (2002, Article 6(e)).

89 Genocide Convention (1951, Article 2(e)).

90 Vienna Convention on the Law of Treaties (1969).

91 Rome Statute (2002).

92 Genocide Convention (1951).

93 Genocide Convention (1951).

94 Rome Statute (2002, Article 6).

Thus, the Genocide Convention (GC),[95] on the analysis here, if properly interpreted, is without restriction as to which groups are protected under the Convention. This is a supportable interpretation in that genocide is fundamentally about the destruction of future generations of any targeted group through the elimination of some or all individuals belonging to the targeted group by any of a variety of means as listed in the Genocide Convention[96] at Article 2. Hence, whether there is, for instance, forcible transfer of children from a politically dissident group to a genocidal perpetrator group attempting to quash the aforementioned political group through mass atrocities, or whether the transferred children were targeted primarily or exclusively because of their perceived 'ethnicity', 'race', nationality or religion[97] (a combination of factors causing the targeting being the more typical case); genocidal intent is present in all these instances and further the *actus reus* is the same (involving the conduct described at Article 2 of the Genocide Convention).[98]

It is well understood by perpetrators and victims alike that the forcible transfer of children from one group to another group (the appropriation of children by the perpetrator group) destroys in whole or in part the children's group of origin and as such is genocidal in its intent and consequence (i.e. reduced reproductive capacity of the children's group of origin, the infliction of severe mental harms on the children transferred, on their immediate families and on the communities from which the children originate etc.). This genocidal aspect of the forcible transfer of children to another group cannot be adequately captured by the concept of 'crimes against humanity' which reduces such acts simply to another feature of the widespread systematic attack on civilians and does not take into account the very particular *mens rea* of the perpetrators in regards to: (1) destroying in part or in whole the children's *particular* perceived group of origin; (2) destroying the children's original personal identity and affiliation with their group of origin however defined (i.e. local community etc.) and (3) appropriating the children for an indefinite period, if they survive, into the perpetrator group as 'children of the enemy' (the term 'enemy' here referring to the perpetrator group appropriating children).

Genocidal intent is thus formulated in terms of the objective of destroying the specified victim group(s) in whole or in part and, on the analysis here, is not a function to any degree of the nature of the group(s) targeted (individuals are victimized only because they are members of the group(s) targeted and not in their capacity as individuals). On the view here then the proper reading of the Genocide Convention (GC)[99] is that the groups listed in the GC (duplicated in

---

[95] Genocide Convention (1951).

[96] Genocide Convention (1951).

[97] 'Ethnicity' and 'race' in particular are considered in the scholarly legal and social science literature to be highly contentious concepts.

[98] Genocide Convention (1951).

[99] Genocide Convention (1951).

Article 6 of the Rome Statute)[100] should not be considered an exhaustive list of protected groups under the GC but rather as examples of the perceived characteristics/dimensions upon which groups are arbitrarily defined and targeted by the *genocidaires*. Thus, despite the fact that the Genocide Convention (GC)[101] is silent on various further potential protected groups under the GC such as political groups (due to compromises and negotiations in the drafting of the Convention); this cannot legitimately be taken to mean that the groups listed constitute an exhaustive list rather than being simply exemplars of groups commonly targeted for genocide.

1.4 Additional Points Regarding 'Protected Groups'

There is generally an overlap between perceived groups explicitly listed in the Genocide Convention[102] and certain others not listed (i.e. between perceived ethnic and political groups; the former listed in the Genocide Convention[103] explicitly as a protected group and the latter not so). In regards to the issue of objectively real political groups and their overlap with *perceived* ethnic and other protected groups under the Genocide Convention; recall that the UN Commission of Inquiry on Darfur rejected the proposition that the Sudanese government was responsible for a genocide. The Commission of Inquiry contended instead that though the widespread systematic attacks on civilians by Al Bashir forces and allied militia likely involved war crimes and crimes against humanity; these attacks were allegedly solely politically motivated (and therefore not genocidal). This was the contention even though the UN Commission of Inquiry on Darfur acknowledged that the attacks targeted persons belonging to perceived particular ethnic groups. Arguably it is not at all clear if perceived ethnicity was a proxy for perceived political group in the Al Bashir attacks on the targeted victim groups or vice versa or neither. The UN Commission of Inquiry on Darfur recognized the overlap between the specific perceived ethnic groups targeted by the Al Bashir forces and allied militia and the perceived political affiliations or loyalties of these victim groups. Nevertheless; the Commission of Inquiry declined to consider that genocide had occurred in Darfur in the relevant time period thus essentially arbitrarily confounding genocidal intent to destroy a targeted group in whole or in part with potential political motive:

---

[100] Rome Statute (2002).

[101] Genocide Convention (1951).

[102] Genocide Convention (1951).

[103] Genocide Convention (1951).

> In a vast majority of cases, victims of the attacks belonged to African tribes, in particular the Fur, Masaalit and Zaghawa tribes, *who were systematically* ***targeted on political grounds*** *in the context of the counter-insurgency policy of the Government.*[104]
>
> Recent developments have led members of African and Arab tribes to perceive themselves and others as two distinct ethnic groups. The rift between tribes, and the political polarization around the rebel opposition to the central authorities has extended itself to the issues of identity. *The tribes in Darfur supporting rebels have increasingly come to be identified as "African" and those supporting the Government as "Arabs".*[105]

The ICC Prosecutor, however, charged genocide in the Al Bashir case despite the overlap between perceived ethnicity of the targeted victim groups in Darfur and their perceived political affiliations (i.e. as rebel loyalists). Those charges were confirmed on appeal with the reversal of the ICC Pre-Trial Chamber's initial decision to refuse confirmation of the genocide charges against Al Bashir. The Pre-Trial Chamber ultimately issued a second warrant of arrest for Al Bashir which included charges of genocide along with various counts of crimes against humanity and war crimes.[106]

The distinction between 'crimes against humanity' and 'genocide', it would appear, is often blurry. Both concepts are circular and descriptive as currently defined in international law such that their application in any particular situation is largely a matter of idiosyncratic judgment in interpretation. This is especially the case as the 'protected groups' explicitly listed in the Genocide Convention (GC)[107] most often *overlap* with perceived political and other groups not listed in the GC as protected. Hence, for this reason and others, as discussed, it is not feasible logically to delimit the protected groups to those explicitly listed in the text of the Genocide Convention.[108]

It would seem that a distinction between crimes against humanity and genocide is still possible with a more inclusive approach to the notion of 'protected group.' Such a distinction may be, for instance, that crimes against humanity are conceptualized as involving individuals *per se* as the intended civilian victims (in a widespread attack on the civilian population); while genocide is framed as targeting individuals as mere vehicles for destroying an identifiable discrete group (one which may or may not be *explicitly* listed in the Genocide Convention). In any case, such a categorical distinction arguably should be maintained only if it contributes to better accountability of perpetrators and provides a useful framework for the description of objective and perceived facts on the ground surrounding the atrocities in question.

---

104 UN Commission of Inquiry on Darfur (2005, p. 160, para 638, emphasis added).

105 UN Commission of Inquiry on Darfur (2005, p. 160, para 640, emphasis added).

106 Prosecutor v Al Bashir (Second Warrant of Arrest, 12 July, 2010, ICC Pre-Trial Chamber I).

107 Genocide Convention (1951).

108 Genocide Convention (1951).

1.5 'Restrictive Interpretation' of Genocide Provisions: Implications for the Notion of Children as Persons

The current commonly held view is that genocide must be a targeted attack against one or more of the protected groups explicitly listed in the Genocide Convention (GC)[109] by one or more of the means specified in the GC with the intent to destroy the group in whole or in part. It is here argued that the latter view greatly diminishes the personhood and perceived status of children under international law as a special protected group *in their own right* regardless their ethnic, religious, national or so-called racial group membership all of which are a function, directly or indirectly, of the children's parentage. Thus, children who do *not* belong to a targeted perceived ethnic, religious, racial or national group (the four "protected groups" explicitly listed in the Genocide Convention[110]) would *not* be considered as potential victims of the genocidal forcible transfer of children of the group to another group. Thus, perpetrators could not be charged with this specific category of international crime as regards these aforementioned particular children (child groups). The contention here is that, for the reasons previously discussed, this result is unjust, unreasonable and legally insupportable and stems from an erroneous *under-inclusive* interpretation of 'protected group' in Article 2 of the Genocide Convention[111] which finds a re-iteration at Article 6 of the Rome Statute.[112]

It is a legal fiction that *any* children can be legitimately excluded from protection under the Genocide Convention[113] from genocidal forcible transfer to a perpetrator group though there was genocidal intent to destroy the children's group of origin, *however defined*, by transferring a segment of the group's children to the perpetrator group. To suggest otherwise is to give privileged treatment under international law to some child groups and not others. It is then an inconsistent application of the international humanitarian and human rights law principle that provides for children receiving special protection to maintain the fallacious proposition that only children belonging to the four explicitly listed protected groups in the Genocide Convention[114] can be the victims of the genocidal forcible transfer of children from their group to a genocidal perpetrator group.

Consider also (in regard to the notion that the Genocide Convention[115] and Rome Statute[116] provision on genocide contemplate but a limited set of protected groups) the following admonition regarding treaty interpretation:

---

[109] Genocide Convention (1951).

[110] Genocide Convention (1951).

[111] Genocide Convention (1951).

[112] Rome Statute (2002).

[113] Genocide Convention (1951).

[114] Genocide Convention (1951).

[115] Genocide Convention (1951).

[116] Rome Statute (2002).

> *The definition of protected groups.* While they specify the classes of prohibited conduct, *international rules on genocide use a broad and loose terminology when indicating the various groups against which one can engage in acts of genocide, including references to notions that may overlap (for instance, "national" and "ethnical").* This terminology is criticised for referring to notions such as 'race', which are now universally regarded as outmoded or even fallacious. Nevertheless, the principle of interpretation of international rules whereby one should give such rules their maximum effect (principle of effectiveness, also expressed by the Latin maxim *ut res magis valeat quam pereat*) suggests that *the rules on genocide should be construed in such a manner as to give them their maximum legal effects.*[117]

The previous discussion here regarding the special protected status of children under international law highlights the fact that limiting the interpretation of 'protected group' to the four socially constructed groups explicitly stipulated at Article 6 of the Rome Statute[118] does *not* in fact give the rules of treaty interpretation (here the rules on genocide) their maximum effect. Rather, such an interpretation of the Statute leaves things as unclear as ever given the ambiguity of the four group categories explicitly listed at Article 6 of the Rome Statute.[119] Furthermore, there is no logical or legal basis to suppose that the drafters of, for instance, Genocide Convention, Article 2(e)[120] (duplicated at Rome Statute, Article 6(e)) [121] intended that the aforementioned provision would afford only *some* children protection from the grave crime of *specifically targeting children* of the group for forcible transfer to another group (in an effort to destroy in whole or in part the targeted group to which the children belong). This lack of foundation for excluding any child group as a protected group arises, as discussed, in that all children are a special protected group under international law. Thus, on the analysis here, giving maximum effect to the rules of interpretation for the genocide provision of the Rome Statute[122] in actual fact requires: (1) an expansive liberal interpretation of what constitutes the four protected groups specifically set out at Article 6 of the Rome Statute[123] considering the ambiguity of all the terms and, in particular, the terms "ethnical" and "racial" and (2) an interpretation that contemplates children belonging to other perceived identifiable groups than those explicitly listed at Article 6 of the Rome Statute[124] (namely groups other than ethnic, 'racial', religious or national groups) also being considered as members of 'protected groups.' Thus, for instance, children victimized because their parents belong to the political opposition would be considered the target of genocide if they were subjected to any of the genocidal

[117] UN Commission of Inquiry on Darfur (2011, p. 125, para 494, emphasis added).

[118] Rome Statute (2002).

[119] Rome Statute (2002).

[120] Genocide Convention (1951).

[121] Rome Statute (2002).

[122] Rome Statute (2002).

[123] Rome Statute (2002).

[124] Rome Statute (2002).

acts detailed at Article 6 of the Rome Statute[125] as a means of destroying the child group and, in the process, in whole or in part, also the targeted political group with which the children's parents are affiliated.[126]

1.5.1 Restrictive Interpretation That Favours the Intention of the Parties Versus What Is Expressed in Text

The objection may be raised that the suggested approach to interpreting Article 6(e) of the Rome Statute[127] (regarding the genocidal forcible transfer of children) violates the rule regarding restrictive interpretation that seems to be incorporated into the Rome Statute itself at Article 22(2) as follows:

> The definition of a crime shall be strictly construed and shall not be extended by analogy. In case of ambiguity, the definition shall be interpreted in favour of the person being investigated, prosecuted or convicted.[128]

Crema points out, however, that:

> "'restrictive interpretation' is the interpretative choice which restricts the meaning of a text" and ... "In an original sense, ***it is restrictive in favour of the real intentions of the parties as opposed to what is expressed in a text.***"[129]

The point made by Crema that in fact "restrictive interpretation" is interpretation "*in favour of the real intentions of the parties* as opposed to what is expressed in a text"[130] is especially relevant in regards to the genocide provision of the Rome Statute[131] where we are dealing with ambiguous terminology in regards to the specifically listed categories of protected groups. The current author has suggested in the foregoing discussion that the intent of the drafters of the Genocide Convention[132] could *not* have been to leave unprotected any group of children from forcible transfer to another group where the intent of the perpetrators is to destroy in whole or in part the children's original group through full appropriation of some or all of their children. This in that international treaty and customary law does not

[125] Rome Statute (2002).

[126] Note that certain scholars of international law have argued that where there is a non-exhaustive list for one requirement (a gap) in the definition of the crime there is no bar to filling in the gap. (See Triffterer 2008) The argument here is that the list of protected groups in the Genocide Convention (1951) [duplicated in the Rome Statute (2002)] is in fact a *non-exhaustive* one given (1) the lack of clarity in the terms used to describe the protected groups and (2) the gaps in protection that arise if the list is considered exhaustive.

[127] Rome Statute (2002).

[128] Rome Statute (2002).

[129] Crema (2010, pp. 682–683, emphasis added).

[130] Crema (2010, pp. 682–683, emphasis added).

[131] Rome Statute (2002).

[132] Genocide Convention (1951).

contemplate that the special protected or privileged status of children, especially during armed conflict, should be moderated by a limited set of group identifications in terms of ethnicity, nationality, religion and 'race' such that (1) children who belong to a group of origin not targeted in these terms cannot be considered to be the victims of the genocidal forcible transfer of children and (2) the perpetrators of these children's forcible transfer to another group with the intent of destroying the children's group of origin thus enjoy impunity.

Consistent with the view that the drafters of the Genocide Convention (GC)[133] intended to protect all children and viewed children as a protected group *per se*[134] is the inclusion of a child specific provision at GC Article 2(e)[135] (duplicated at Article 6(e) of the Rome Statute).[136] That provision specifies not only a particular mechanism (course of conduct) for carrying out genocide but is also an acknowledgment that children are a special group in and of themselves that may be targeted with genocidal intent (a protected group defined in terms of age that exists independent of all other group identifications). It is incorrect, it is here suggested, to maintain that Genocide Convention, Article 2(e)[137] (or Rome Statute, Article 6(e))[138] is directed only to protecting the groups of origin of the children as opposed to also the children themselves (as a protected group *as such*) separate and apart from the group of origin to which they belong. To this point; note that no mention is made of the genocidal forcible transfer of women of the group to another group, for instance, even though this too, for instance, would reduce the reproductive capacity of the targeted group of origin.[139] Indeed, there is no explicit mention of the targeting of any gender group; male or female specifically. Genocidal acts such as separating men and women of the group through the forcible deportation or expulsion of men and boys or the murder of men and boys (as has occurred typically in many instances of ethnic cleansing) with the intent to reduce the reproductive capacity of the group of origin can be considered under Article 6(d)

---

[133] Genocide Convention (1951).

[134] The notion of children as a protected group is reflected in, for instance, Geneva Convention IV (1949) at Articles 50 and 68 which codify what may arguably be considered various customary law protections for children caught up in armed conflict.

[135] Genocide Convention (1951).

[136] Rome Statute (2002).

[137] Genocide Convention (1951).

[138] Rome Statute (2002).

[139] This is *not* to imply that other distinct groups such as women, for instance, should not be considered a protected group when analyzing a particular genocidal situation in which women were, for instance, targeted for mass rape in an effort to destroy not only the women but the larger identifiable group to which they belong. The points being made here are rather that: (1) the drafters of Genocide Convention (1951) Article 2(e) emphasized the fact that children are a protected group *per se* by *explicitly* including a child-specific provision and (2) the notion of children as a protected group in times of armed conflict was already well established in customary international law at the time of the drafting of the Genocide Convention adopted by the U.N. General Assembly 9 December, 1948 (entry into force 1951).

of the Rome Statute[140] and, depending on the particular facts, certain other Rome Statute[141] provisions at Article 6 [i.e. killing members of the group (Article 6(a)); and/or causing serious mental or physical harm (Article 6(b)); and, in some instances, Article 6(c): Deliberately inflicting on the group conditions of life calculated to bring about its physical destruction in whole or in part i.e. where members of the group are expelled and have no means of obtaining life's necessities can also be considered in part as a vehicle for interfering with the reproductive capacity/viability of the targeted group].[142]

It is here contended that Genocide Convention, Article 2(e)[143] (unlike Genocide Convention,[144] Article 2(d) "Imposing measures intended to prevent births within the group") (the latter also duplicated in the Rome Statute[145]) was *not* primarily or exclusively included in the GC in respect of the issue of loss of reproductive capacity of the group of origin. This is evidenced by the fact that the transfer of some or all of the women for instance, as discussed, was not specifically listed but goes to the same issue; namely loss of reproductive capacity of the group. Rather, Article 2(e) of the Genocide Convention[146] (duplicated in the Rome Statute[147] at Article 6(e)) concerning the genocidal forcible transfer of children was included; it is here contended, to highlight the group of origin's inviolable right to its children and the necessity of children to the emotional, spiritual and cultural viability of the group as well as its longevity and reproductive capacity.

Consider in respect of Article 2(e) of the Genocide Convention[148] the example of the Nazi Lebensborn program. That effort involving, in part, the genocidal forcible transfer of children born to Nazi fathers and Nordic women was directed to appropriating persons whom the perpetrators hoped would be future leaders of Nazism. In addition, the Lebensborn program expanded from 'recruiting' Nordic women to bear the children of Nazi officers (the children to be raised in Germany)

---

[140] Rome Statute (2002).

[141] Rome Statute (2002).

[142] The current author does consider certain categories of ethnic cleansing such as that involving the forcible permanent separation of males and females of the group through, for instance, the forcible transfer of men and boys away from the group and/or the killing of men and boys as possible mechanisms of genocide. This being the case where the intent is to destroy the group targeted in whole or in part through these acts (i.e. by reducing the reproductive capacity of the targeted group, causing severe mental suffering etc.).

[143] Genocide Convention (1951).

[144] Genocide Convention (1951).

[145] Rome Statute (2002).

[146] Genocide Convention (1951).

[147] Rome Statute (2002).

[148] Genocide Convention (1951).

to include the kidnapping of so-called racially pure children[149] who were deemed to look Aryan and hence possess so-called Aryan qualities. The latter group of children who were the victims of this abduction and genocidal forcible transfer away from their families and communities were considered prized Aryan specimens. It is the Nazi Lebensborn program that no doubt inspired, at least in part, the Genocide Convention,[150] Article 2(e) prohibition later duplicated in the Rome Statute,[151] Article 6(e). In the post-conflict period, both the women who were 'recruited' to be part of the Nazi Lebensborn program as birth mothers and their offspring were generally shunned by their groups of origin and viewed as part of the perpetrator group.

In the final analysis then Article 2(e) of the Genocide Convention[152] and Article 6(e) of the Rome Statute[153] are as much about the rights of children as a protected group *as such* (in their own right) (i.e. their right to the family unit as constituted before the genocidal forcible transfer) as about the rights of the children's group of origin (i.e. the group's right to retain its reproductive capacity by holding on to its children who later will bear their own children etc.).

This author would thus contest the notion that a restrictive interpretation (as set out at Article 22(2) of the Rome Statute[154]) requires interpreting Article 6(e) of the Rome Statute concerning the genocidal forcible transfer of children of the group to another group such that there are *gaps* in protection for some children: (1) namely in respect of children who are not members of a targeted 'racial', ethnic, religious or national group (that is, not members of the alleged exhaustive list of protected groups listed under the genocide provision at Article 6 of the Rome Statute and stipulated in the introduction to the Article) and (2) with regards to lack of accountability of perpetrators of the forcible transfer of some children to another group carried out with genocidal intent. Rather, it is here argued that Article 6(e) of the Rome Statute[155] (the duplicate of Article 2(e) of the Genocide Convention[156]) goes to the issue of: (1) protecting children as a group *as such* (in their own right) *regardless of their other group affiliations* as well as protecting their group of origin however defined or perceived (that group of origin

[149] The intent was thus not to eliminate the children's Nordic group of origin as that group of origin was considered a useful ongoing pool of Aryan-looking children to be forcibly transferred to the Nazi perpetrator group; and a source for the hoped for potential future Nazi leaders. Thus, the genocidal forcible transfer of these children can be considered as in part a genocidal attack on the child group *per se* as a protected group. At the same time, the Nazis were well aware that abducting these children would cause the Nordic families and communities affected severe mental suffering and that they would be destroyed in part as originally constituted.

[150] Genocide Convention (1951).

[151] Rome Statute (2002).

[152] Genocide Convention (1951).

[153] Rome Statute (2002).

[154] Rome Statute (2002).

[155] Rome Statute (2002).

[156] Genocide Convention (1951).

then not necessarily being defined in so-called 'racial', ethnic, religious or national terms) and (2) protecting the integrity of the existing family unit and community.

1.6 Foreseeability, Perpetrator Accountability and Rome Statute Article 6(e)

It is here argued that it is evident to any group of perpetrators of mass atrocities and genocide that the forcible transfer of children of *any* identifiable distinct group to the perpetrator group is *manifestly unlawful* (where forcible transfer refers to all manner of coercion whether through a variety of direct or indirect means and circumstances and is not limited to the use of physical force). This is the case since the integrity of the family (however family is conceived[157]) and of the home community is a universal value of humanity. The dissolution in large part of families due to the forcible transfer of the children away from the family and the group to another group entirely causes severe mental suffering to both the children transferred and the families and communities affected. Perpetrators of the forcible transfer of children of any distinct group away from their families and group thus have *pre-existing knowledge* (there is foreseeability) that the forcible transfer of these children (a special protected group as children under international law) away from their families and home communities is a violation of international customary law.

The perpetrators referred to here have a genocidal intent. This is the case in that they know that by transferring the children away from their families and their original group to the perpetrator group; the children's group of origin will be destroyed in part.[158] Indeed the *prohibition* on such conduct (namely causing the disintegration of families and local communities by ripping the children from them) which conduct, on the analysis here, involves a genocidal intent irrespective of to

[157] In some cultural situations the children may be raised by the community and viewed as children of the community as opposed to being exclusively the children of any particular family. The existing immediate family in various cases at the time of the genocidal forcible transfer of the children of the group to another group may include the children's biological parents and/or kinship primary caretakers or others authorized by the community to be the primary caretakers for the children (this would include, but is not limited to, for instance, persons designated as the children's legal guardians or adoptive parents depending on the cultural context).

[158] The perpetrators (such as an armed force committing mass atrocities or genocide) may forcibly transfer children to be child soldiers and ensure that the children are permanently alienated from their families and communities by having the children commit atrocities often against their own family and/or community. This author has argued that such appropriation of children constitutes an instance of the genocidal forcible transfer of children (See Grover 2012).

which group of origin the children "belong,"[159] can be considered a *jus cogens* norm that is reflected in customary law. For example, Additional Protocols I and II to the 1949 Geneva Conventions[160] (which are arguably part of customary law) stress the importance in times of armed conflict of: (1) keeping families together if practicable and safe or (2) alternatively; reuniting the children with their families as soon as feasible if, for instance, the children had to be evacuated from their home territory for their own safety or became separated from family in some other fashion. The right of children to their parents in the normal course is also recognized in the Convention on the Rights of the Child at Article 9:

Convention on the Rights of the Child

Article 9

States Parties shall ensure that a child shall not be separated from his or her parents against their will, except when competent authorities subject to judicial review determine, in accordance with applicable law and procedures, that such separation is necessary for the best interests of the child. . . .[161]

So too children have a right to preserve their personal identity which is bound up with their family relationships and the children's integration in the home community as well as with their larger group affiliations. This notion is articulated at Article 8 of the Convention on the Rights of the Child:

Convention on the Rights of the Child

Article 8

1. *States Parties undertake to respect the right of the child to preserve his or her identity, including nationality, name and family relations as recognized by law without unlawful interference.*
2. Where a child is illegally deprived of some or all of the elements of his or her identity, States Parties shall provide appropriate assistance and protection, with a view to re-establishing speedily his or her identity.[162]

Maintaining the integrity of the family and community (thus preserving the personal identity of the child) is thus considered a high priority value that is, in the normal course, in the best interests of children and humanity generally and is a principle that is well established in international law. It can be considered self-evident then that the 'genocidal forcible transfer of children' to an armed group or force committing mass atrocities and/or genocide is 'manifestly unlawful'.

[159] The listed protected groups in the genocide provision at Article 6 of the Rome Statute (2002) ('racial', religious, national and ethnic) are ambiguous and ill-defined categories and it is a highly contentious matter whether the list is in fact to be interpreted as exhaustive.

[160] Additional Protocols I and II to the Geneva Conventions (1977).

[161] Convention on the Rights of the Child (1990, emphasis added).

[162] Convention on the Rights of the Child (1990, emphasis added).

1.6.1 The Nullum Crimen Principle and the Genocidal Forcible Transfer of Children to an Armed Group or Force

Article 11(2) of the 1948 Universal Declaration of Human Rights states that "international law may be a source of legality for the purpose of applying the *nullum crimen* principle" ...[163] Existing international law, apart from the Rome Statute,[164] as previously discussed, in fact points clearly to the foreseeability that the forcible transfer of children away from their families and communities (i.e. away from their group of origin however defined) [165] to an armed group or force committing mass atrocities and/ or genocide[166] would be considered manifestly unlawful; a form of genocide intended to destroy in whole or in part the targeted families; communities and larger group.[167] Thus, the legality principle *nullum crimen sine lege* (here States and their agents being aware of what constitutes the crime of genocidal forcible transfer of children) is in no way compromised by regarding all children from any identifiable distinct group of origin as being protected under Article 6 (e) of the Rome Statute[168] (including being protected against transfer to an armed group or force (State or non-State) that is perpetrating mass atrocities and/or genocide.[169] On the analysis here; the children, regardless of their group affiliation, are of course also protected against the other forms of genocidal conduct listed at Article 6 of the Rome Statute).[170] Put somewhat differently:

> ...the principle of strict construction is satisfied when a judicial interpretation, while not strictly in conformity with the wording of a criminal prohibition or relevant case law, [at least according to some legal scholars], is nonetheless *reasonably foreseeable* ...and is

[163] Universal Declaration of Human Rights (1948).

[164] Rome Statute (2002).

[165] The targeted group of origin to which the children transferred belong might be described by the perpetrator in political terms, or in terms of ethnicity, religion, nationality or some other dimension.

[166] An armed force or group (State or non-State) perpetrating mass atrocities and/or genocide is a separable, distinct entity operating outside the margins of normal civil society and international humanitarian and human rights law.

[167] The requirement for genocidal intent here is met also since the perpetrator group has foreknowledge of the enormously destructive impact on the children's original group that will ensue due to the forcible transfer of the children from that group to the perpetrator group and perpetrates the children's forcible transfer in any case.

[168] Rome Statute (2002).

[169] There is no suggestion here that the recruitment and use of children for active participation in hostilities is in every instance a form of *genocide*. Genocidal forcible transfer of children for the purpose of child soldiering occurs, it is here contended, when: (1) the armed group or force is engaged in mass atrocities and/or genocide; (2) the armed group or force is intent on alienating the child recruits from their families and communities and alienating the families and communities from the children and (3) the armed group or force aims to permanently appropriate the children transferred away from their original group.

[170] Rome Statute (2002).

> *consistent with the essence of the offence*[171][such that there is no arbitrary investigation, prosecution or conviction].

It is here argued then that the principle of restrictive interpretation must itself not be misinterpreted to be a purported justification to deny legitimate interpretations of an international criminal law provision where: (1) the interpretation is entirely foreseeable, consistent with other international law (i.e. international humanitarian and human rights principles and values) and with the overriding purpose of the Statute which incorporates the provision being interpreted and (2) the perpetrator can be assumed to have knowledge of the illegality of the act as construed (for instance, the act is 'manifestly illegal' and held unlawful under customary and/or treaty law and *jus cogens* norms):

> In addition to the qualifications of foreseeability and constructive knowledge of the illegality of criminal conduct, it is often asserted [as it is by the current author] that strict construction cannot surreptitiously gut the concept of interpretation of all meaning...This interpretive exercise is not considered to undermine the notion of fair warning or separation of powers concerns as long as the Court's reasoning does not yield a new crime not contemplated by the states parties.[172]

It is here contended that *no* new crime is contemplated when the genocidal forcible transfer of children is interpreted to include conduct in which children (of an identifiable national or ethnic group *or other identifiable group*) are: (1) appropriated as child soldiers by a State or non-State armed group or force perpetrating mass atrocities and /or genocide and/or are (2) appropriated through their sexual victimization by such an armed group or force as part of a systematic and widespread campaign of sexual violation of children and other mass atrocities (where the children may or may not serve as sexual slaves to the armed force or group and/or also as child soldiers carrying out direct or indirect combat related functions). Such an interpretation is, as explained, an entirely foreseeable one in respect of Article 6(e) of the Rome Statute. The perpetrators can be held to have knowledge of the fact that such conduct constitutes a violation of the international *jus cogens* and treaty norm against the genocidal forcible transfer of children. This interpretation is further consistent with a good faith reading of the genocide provision at Article 6(e) of the Rome Statute[173] and consistent with the purpose and context of that provision and the overall purpose of the Rome Statute.[174] For instance: (1) the Preamble to the Rome Statute places an emphasis on the preservation of common bonds within and across identifiable groups[175] and on ending mass atrocities including those perpetrated against children while (2) Article 6 of the Statute[176] speaks to the issue of preserving identifiable groups which entails, in part,

---

[171] European Court of Human Rights *SW and CR v United Kingdom* Cited in Grover (2010, p. 555, emphasis added).

[172] Grover (2010, p. 555).

[173] Rome Statute (2002).

[174] Rome Statute (2002).

[175] The Preamble makes reference to cultural groups however that term is contentious and open to broad interpretation as are the terms ethnic, racial and religious at Article 6 of the Rome Statute (2002).

[176] Rome Statute (2002).

the group being able to have custody of its children. It has already been explained here that substantive justice considerations and existing international human rights and humanitarian law supports the interpretation that: (1) children of *any* identifiable group have a right to maintain their bonds with their existing families, communities and original larger group (however defined) in the normal course and that (2) children are a special protected group during wartime and peacetime.[177]

This author would also argue that the above interpretation of the genocidal forcible transfer of children is *not* arguing by analogy any more than is interpreting what has been termed by Grover (2010) "the residual category of 'other inhumane acts of a similar character' as a crime against humanity."[178] No new crimes are contemplated in either case for the reasons explained (considering the perpetrators' purpose in committing the genocidal forcible transfer of the children away from the children's original group, the foreseeability that the conduct will destroy the children's original group; at least in part, and the legal supportability of holding that the perpetrators had knowledge of the *manifest unlawfulness* of the act according to existing customary law as well as *jus cogens* and relevant treaty norms). Just as "states parties may have left the door open for substantive justice considerations when interpreting the residual category of 'other inhumane acts of a similar character' as a crime against humanity"[179] so, too, it is here argued, they have left the door open for the same in regards to the interpretation of the notion of the genocidal forcible transfer of children. Leaving that door open to substantive justice considerations in the proper circumstances, it is here contended, in regards to the "crime of crimes" (for instance the genocidal forcible transfer of children) is consistent with the purpose of the treaty itself and the proper application of the Rome Statute.[180] This is apparent also from a good faith reading of Article 21(3) of the Rome Statute dealing with applicable law which includes the following:

> **Rome Statute**
>
> **Article 21(3)**
> *The application and interpretation of law pursuant to this article must be consistent with internationally recognized human rights, and be without any adverse distinction founded on grounds such as...* gender... age, race, colour, language, religion or belief, political or other opinion, national, ethnic or social origin, wealth, birth or other status.[181]

---

[177] A discussion of issues of cross-national or cross-ethnic adoption and the like, in accord with international law, where in the best interests of the children is beyond the scope of this book.

[178] Grover (2010, p. 557).

[179] Grover (2010, p. 557).

[180] Where no new crime is postulated per a nonetheless unjustifiably contested interpretation (that is in fact consistent with treaty and customary international human rights law and *jus cogens* norms) that contested interpretation is *not* inconsistent with restrictive interpretation of the treaty provision in any meaningful way.

[181] Rome Statute (2002, emphasis added).

Hence, the interpretation of the notion of 'genocidal forcible transfer of children' must be consistent with international law provisions in other international treaties that affirm certain universal fundamental human rights in respect of children. This would include, for instance, the Additional Protocols to the Geneva Conventions,[182] the Convention on the Rights of the Child[183] and its first two protocols among others that: (1) recognize that all children without discrimination or restriction belong to a special protected group during armed conflict and in peacetime and that (2) all children in the normal course have a right to their existing family, community and original larger group however identified (such that children belonging to a group targeted on a political basis, for instance, would receive the same protection from unlawful forcible transfer[184] to another group as would children belonging to a group targeted based on so-called race, ethnicity, religion or nationality).

Substantive justice considerations in the interpretation of the Rome Statute[185] definition of crimes under ICC jurisdiction cannot be excluded simply by reference to Latin maxims and an ill-informed interpretation of Article 22(2).[186] The justification for what is held to constitute the proper interpretation of a provision of the Rome Statute[187] must not be reduced to empty semantic rhetoric and the use of Latin maxims:

> As in the past ...value-oriented interpretations ...are also obtained by means of Latin maxims. The "advantage" of this technique is to lead to an interpretive result presenting it as a necessary one, and without giving reasons for its basis.[188]

The Latin maxims, as Crema explains, do not in fact describe *why* one should reach a certain interpretive result[189] in assigning the meaning to a provision with ambiguities or certain gaps in the text.[190] Rather, the maxims are a tautological

---

[182] Additional Protocols I and II to the Geneva Conventions (1977).

[183] Convention on the Rights of the Child (1990).

[184] The forcible transfer of children from their group to the perpetrator group is unlawful notwithstanding any laws that may be in place that endorse such a transfer such as laws passed by the Nazis that violate international human rights norms.

[185] Rome Statute (2002).

[186] The interpretation must, in accord with the thrust of the Vienna Convention on the Law of Treaties (1969), respect both the rights of the perpetrator to due process at all stages of the ICC process and those of the victims consistent with consideration of well-established international human rights law, other sources of law (including developing ICC case law) and the purpose of the Rome Statute (2002).

[187] Rome Statute (2002).

[188] Crema (2010, p. 691).

[189] Crema (2010, p. 694).

[190] Gaps and ambiguities exist in the *precise text* of Article 6 of the Rome Statute (2002) provision on genocide regarding respectively: (1) the precise meaning of the terms religious, ethnical, 'racial' or national group; (2) the precise meaning of the term genocidal forcible transfer of children of the group to another and in terms of (3) the scope of coverage regarding children as a protected group as such (in their own right) regardless of their other group affiliations given substantive law and justice considerations and existing relevant international human rights and humanitarian law and jus cogens norms.

method of justifying the particular interpretive result and attributing it automatically to *alleged* strict textual construction:

Note also that Article 22(1) of the Rome Statute refers to 'crimes under the jurisdiction' of the Court and Article 22(2) to strict construction but *without* making reference to the Statute text *per se* [the word 'statute' does not appear at 22(2)].

Rome Statute: Article 22

Nullum crimen sine lege

(1) A person shall not be criminally responsible under this Statute unless the conduct in question constitutes, at the time it takes place, *a crime within the jurisdiction of the Court.*

(2) The definition of a crime shall be strictly construed and shall not be extended by analogy. In case of ambiguity, the definition shall be interpreted in favour of the person being investigated, prosecuted or convicted.[191]

[...]

Hence it is reasonable to hold, it is here argued, that: (1) substantive justice considerations properly must inform a so-called 'restrictive interpretation' of the law (i.e. Article 6 of the Rome Statute[192]) and that (2) such an approach is *not* inconsistent with the drafter's intent. The textual formulation or crafting of Article 22 of the Rome Statute[193] thus suggests that: (1) substantive justice considerations and (2) reference to other sources of international law in regards to proper interpretation of the Rome Statute[194] and resolving any ambiguities or gaps in the text were in fact contemplated by the drafters.[195]

1.6.2 Evolving Conceptions of What Constitutes a Protected Group

To interpret Article 6(e) of the Rome Statute[196] as prohibiting persons from participating in or facilitating in any way the forcible transfer of children from *any* distinct group of origin to an armed group or force (State or non-State) that is perpetrating mass atrocities and/or genocide is *no*t to invent a new crime. This is the case given: (1) the right of all children (as a special privileged group under international humanitarian and customary law) to maximum and equal protection from all forms of grave international crimes in times of armed conflict and in peace

[191] Rome Statute (2002).

[192] Rome Statute (2002).

[193] Rome Statute (2002).

[194] Rome Statute (2002).

[195] See Triffterer (2008) for a discussion of the specific wording of Article 22 (1).

[196] Rome Statute (2002).

and (2) the fact that restrictive interpretation cannot be taken to mean an interpretation that in actuality leaves gaps in terms of which children (a special protected group under international law) are in fact protected from forcible transfer to an armed group or force (State or non-State) perpetrating mass atrocities and/or genocide. Consider in this regard the following particularly pertinent and succinct statement from Leena Grover [197]on the question of restrictive interpretation of international criminal law treaties:

> . . .international criminal law cannot adhere to the strict legality doctrine absolutely. Some crimes are inherently vague, some vagueness[198] is inevitable to avoid 'excessive rigidity and to keep pace with changing circumstances.'[199]

In fact, the protected groups listed at Article 6 of the Rome Statute[200] introduce great vagueness into that provision. Consider in this regard the following commentary from the UN Commission of Inquiry on Darfur regarding the proper interpretation regarding what constitutes a protected group under the Rome Statute:

> The Darfur Commission also noted that *'the approach taken to determine whether a group is a (fully) protected one* ***has evolved*** from an objective to a subjective standard to take into account that "collective identities", and in particular ethnicity, are by their very nature social constructs, ***'imagined' identities*** entirely dependent on variable and contingent perceptions, and not social facts, which are verifiable . . .'[201]

Thus to decline, for instance, to consider as victims of the genocidal forcible transfer of children those children forcibly transferred to another group by perpetrators targeting the children of parents belonging to certain *political groups*, would be to: (1) negate the possibility of the genocidal forcible transfer of children whose parents belong to a targeted *objectively defined group* characterized in terms of its political credo and program of action that sets it apart from other political groups while (2) accepting as a protected group children belonging, for instance, to an *imaginary group* i.e. an invented ethnic group that has no objective existence in terms of distinct language, religion or cultural tradition that sets it apart from other groups in the region. (Such a supposed 'ethnic' group might be one defined in terms of colonially inspired social categories objectified via identity cards held by members labelling them as belonging to that group. Such was the case in regard to the Tutsi and Hutu where ethnic distinctions between them were socially constructed by Belgian colonialists based on extraneous factors such as each

---

[197] Grover (2010).

[198] For instance, at Article 7(1) (k) of the Rome Statute: "other inhumane acts of a similar character."

[199] Such changing circumstances relevant to the current discussion include developments in international humanitarian and human rights law in terms of better acknowledging the scope of fundamental human rights of children during armed conflict and the extent of obligations of the State in protecting those rights and interests of children.

[200] Rome Statute (2002).

[201] Schabas (2010, p. 130, emphasis added).

group's major means of livelihood; a factor not normally considered by social scientists to be a basis for making ethnic distinctions in the first instance).

The suggestion here is that the notion of 'protected group' must evolve yet again to ensure that its interpretation provides for all children being considered protected in respect, for instance, of Article 6 (e) of the Rome Statute[202] dealing with the genocidal forcible transfer of children. That is, the children would be protected whether they are targeted as being members of a particular 'racial', ethnic, religious, or national group or based on their perceived membership in some other targeted identifiable group. This would be the correct interpretive result regarding Article 6 of the Rome Statute[203] given that there is no distinction between children (i.e. based on their membership in a certain identifiable distinct group of origin or on any other basis) in terms of their right to be considered as members of a privileged group under international law entitled to certain special protections.

Consider also in regard to evolving conceptions of 'protected group' that in fact the Rome Statute[204] is to be interpreted with reference to the overall purpose of the treaty and the context of the provision under consideration as are all treaties according to the dictates of the Vienna Convention on the Law of Treaties[205]:

> As a general rule, the *[Rome] Statute* has been construed with regard to the provisions of the Vienna Convention on the Law of Treaties. These prescribe contextual and teleological interpretations; with no special rule applicable to penal law treaties... *.One tautological result is that* ***article 22(2) itself is not to be interpreted strictly, but rather in a contextual and purposive manner, like other provisions of the Statute***.[206]

Relevant then in respect of the need not to interpret Rome Statute Article 22 (2)[207] in such a manner as to defeat the purpose of the genocide provision[208] is Article 31 of the Vienna Convention on the Law of Treaties which reads in part:

> **SECTION 3. INTERPRETATION OF TREATIES**
>
> **Article 31**
> **General rule of interpretation**
> 1. A treaty shall be interpreted in good faith in accordance with the ordinary meaning to be given to the terms of the treaty *in their context and in the light of its object and purpose.*

---

202 Rome Statute (2002).

203 Rome Statute (2002).

204 Rome Statute (2002).

205 Vienna Convention on the Law of Treaties (1969, emphais added).

206 Schabas (2010, p. 410, emphasis added).

207 Recall that Article 22 of the Rome Statute (2002) concerns the principle of *nullum crimen sine lege*.

208 With regard to Rome Statute (2002) Article 6 (e); this author has argued that the purpose is to protect all children from forcible transfer to a perpetrator group regardless of the children's perceived or actual group of origin.

2. *The context for the purpose of the interpretation of a treaty shall comprise, in addition to the text, including its preamble and annexes*:
   [. . ..]
3. There shall be taken into account, together with the context. . .[209]

This author has here previously described the importance of considering context and substantive justice matters in order to achieve a correct interpretive result (i.e. such matters as the purpose of the Rome Statute,[210] the values expressed in the Statute preamble regarding the right to maintain the integrity of one's group and, by implication, one's original personal identity, the affirmation in certain existing international human rights and humanitarian law of children as a special protected group *as such* with their own inherent rights to family and personal identity etc.).

1.7 The Rome Statute Article 6 Protected Group "As Such" Terminology

It is here contended that the enigmatic and, on its face, redundant expression "as such" which appears in the genocide provision of the Rome Statute at Article 6[211] (and over which so much confusion still persists) in all likelihood is properly construed as an indirect reference to groups analogous to those explicitly listed. It is the perpetrator's perception of the group in comparable terms that makes the group analogous to an ethnic, so-called 'racial', national or religious group. This approach likely was the compromise instead of explicitly listing political groups, for instance, given the objections from some States to listing political groups as a protected group. Instead, where political groups were characterized by the perpetrator group in 'racial' terms, for instance, these targeted groups too would then presumably also meet the definition of 'protected group'.[212] Consider then the following re-interpretation of 'protected group.'

> **Article 6 Rome Statute**: For the purpose of this Statute, "genocide" means any of the following acts committed with intent to destroy, in whole or in part, a national, ethnical, racial or religious group, *as such*. . .[213]

> **Current Author's Translation**: For the purpose of this Statute, "genocide" means any of the following acts committed with intent to destroy, in whole or in part, a national, ethnical, racial or religious group, [or any other group (i.e. political or other group such homosexuals etc.) which has been subjectively defined by the perpetrator group as a national, ethnical, racial or religious group to be targeted as a matter of alleged self-preservation of the purportedly superior and righteous perpetrator group].

---

209 Vienna Convention on the Law of Treaties (1969, emphasis added).

210 Rome Statute (2002).

211 Rome Statute (2002).

212 Consider also that certain political groups often overlap in terms of membership with particular ethnic groups or groups defined along other dimensions.

213 Rome Statue (2002, Article 6, emphasis added).

Consider in this regard, for instance, that maniacal Nazi theories regarding homosexuals, Jews, Roma peoples, disabled people, and people of mixed ethnic heritage can be considered fundamentally racist. That is, all these groups were persecuted based on their presumed exclusion from the purported Master race; and, in that sense, the groups targeted were all defined in *perpetrator conceived* 'racial' terms.[214] So too in the situation in Darfur, Al Bashir and his cohorts target(ed) the victim groups that posed a perceived political threat by characterizing these groups in invented racial terms. *Genocidaires* do not as a rule typically define the group targeted for annihilation in whole or in part (by whatever means) in political terms nor in accurate scientific terms that would make manifest their true motives in attempting to annihilate the targeted group in whole or in part or the inhumanity of the genocidal act. If this analysis of the term "as such" is correct then the term "as such" (which appears in the Genocide Convention[215] at Article 2 and is duplicated at Article 6 of the Rome Statute[216]) in fact allows for inclusion of perpetrator perceived/constructed *analogous* groups as protected groups (that is, groups *analogous* to those explicitly listed which the perpetrator intentionally targets for destruction in whole or in part as perceived distinct groups).[217]

1.7.1 *'Forcible Displacement'* vs. *'Genocidal Forcible Transfer of Children'*

Currently, the crime of forcibly transferring children from their group to a perpetrator group as part of a widespread attack on civilians would likely be labeled exclusively as a 'crime against humanity' [i.e. "forcible displacement" as a 'crime against humanity' per Rome Statute Article 7(1)(d)][218] (rather than also as the 'genocidal forcible transfer of children' to another group) where these children are *not* targeted based on their membership in one or more of the protected groups *explicitly* listed at Rome Statute Article 6[219] [duplicating Genocide Convention (Article 2)].[220] This then would be the case even where the intent was to destroy the children's original group in whole or in part (i.e. it was known by the perpetrators that such forcible transfer of the children of the group to another group would destroy the children's group of origin in part or in whole). These children would then wrongly *not* benefit from the fact that the Genocide Convention[221] was intended to provide prevention against and punishment of

[214] This author has noted here previously that the concept of race in fact has no scientific basis.

[215] Genocide Convention (1951).

[216] Rome Statute (2002).

[217] The motives for such targeting being left undefined.

[218] Rome Statute (2002).

[219] Rome Statute (2002).

[220] Genocide Convention (1951).

[221] Genocide Convention (1951).

genocide (as is reflected in the Convention's title itself) by for instance: (1) placing obligations on States Parties in regards to their domestic law to prevent and punish genocide; and (2) by stipulating the State Parties' obligation to extradite persons charged with genocide where required in order to bring the alleged perpetrators to justice before an international tribunal. (There is to date no separate Convention specifically dealing with the prevention and punishment of 'crimes against humanity' though efforts are being made in this regard).[222] Likewise, these children would unjustifiably not benefit from the protections against genocide flowing from Article 6 of the Rome Statute[223] on an interpretation where they must be members of a 'racial', ethnic, religious or national group targeted for destruction in whole or in part as a group. However, to exclude these children from protection under Article 6 of the Rome Statute[224] (or Article 2 of the Genocide Convention)[225] is not legitimately possible. This is the case in that international law does not contemplate qualifying or limiting for some children (based on their perceived certain group affiliation or lack thereof) the special protection to be accorded to *all* children as children. It is not legally supportable then to hold that children *not* targeted for transfer from their group to another group based on their membership in one or more of the protected groups *explicitly* listed in the Genocide Convention[226] (or Rome Statute Article 6),[227] for instance, have no recognized protection against genocidal forcible transfer as accorded under international law (i.e. that they are not contemplated as a child victim group under the definition of the 'genocidal forcible transfer of children'). Put somewhat differently, it is not legally permissible (given *all* children's special protection rights under international humanitarian and human rights law) to interpret the crime of 'genocidal forcible transfer of children' as excluding certain child groups from protection under i.e. the Rome Statute Article 6(e) or under the Genocide Convention Article 2(e) (i.e. a child group defined by and targeted due to their parent's perceived political affiliation). To exclude any child group from protection under Article 6 of the Rome Statute[228] (or Article 2 of the Genocide Convention[229]) for the reason that the children are not members of a targeted ethnic, 'racial', religious or national group is a legally insupportable and inconsistent result based on an erroneous but common interpretation of the list of protected groups as being constrained and limited to just those expressly stipulated in the genocide provisions of the aforementioned legal instruments.

---

[222] Sadat (2011).

[223] Rome Statute (2002).

[224] Rome Statute (2002).

[225] Genocide Convention (1951).

[226] Genocide Convention (1951).

[227] Rome Statute (2002).

[228] Rome Statute (2002).

[229] Genocide Convention (1951).

This author, furthermore, respectfully disputes the contention of W.A. Schabas[230] that the article dealing with forcible transfer of children of the group to another group as a form of genocide (Article 2(e) of the Genocide Convention)[231] was simply an "afterthought" for the drafters of the Convention[232] and but an indirect substitute for incorporation of the contentious notion of 'cultural genocide.' As Mundorff notes:

> ...Article 2(e)...was formulated in the direct aftermath of World War II, when the awareness of the importance of groups remained high and memories of Himmler's campaign to steal children for the Reich[233] had not yet faded.[234]

In fact, children are, under international law, considered much more than simply conduits for the preservation of culture. Rather, they are viewed as persons in their own right with fundamental inherent protection and now participation and various civil rights.[235] Certainly, Rome Statute Article 6[236] must be interpreted in the context of other international law as well such as the Convention on the Rights of the Child[237] when considering, for instance, the proper interpretation of Rome Statute Article 6(e)[238] concerning the forcible transfer of children as an act of genocide. In addition, note that the 'genocidal forcible transfer of children' can and does frequently also occur in respect of children who are completely marginalized from mainstream society such that the issue of protecting these children is not necessarily one of preserving culture through these marginalized child groups. For instance, where abandoned children who are a group *as such* (in their own right) living on the street, very young children living on their own and functioning as the head of households (as their parents have died of AIDS or due to armed conflict etc.), and other such marginalized child groups are forcibly transferred to an armed group or force perpetrating mass atrocities or genocide; this too constitutes the 'genocidal forcible transfer of children'. That is, the children's original group is yet destroyed to a greater or lesser extent[239] due to the loss of this generation in whole or in part as is well understood by the perpetrators. Furthermore, the child group has intrinsic value that must be protected regardless whether or not the particular child group is comprised of marginalized children. These children too then under

[230] Schabas (2000, p. 175). Cited in Mundorff (2007, p. 30, FN 117).

[231] Genocide Convention (1951).

[232] Genocide Convention (1951).

[233] Schabas wrongly asserted, as Mundorff explains, that Himmler's vows to steal children for the Reich amounted only to threats (Schabas 2000, p, 178, Cited at Mundorff (2007, p. 30, FN 117).

[234] Mundorff (2007, p. 30).

[235] See the Convention on the Rights of the Child (1990).

[236] Rome Statute (2002).

[237] Convention on the Rights of the Child (1990).

[238] Rome Statute (2002).

[239] That destruction is in terms of reproductive capacity of the group of origin as well as in other terms such as the loss in vitality and morale of the group of origin.

international law have a fundamental legal entitlement to be protected from 'genocidal forcible transfer' to a perpetrator group and from other grave international crimes.

1.7.2 Genocide's Special Targets and the Destruction of Future Generations

"The intent to destroy, in whole or in part, a national, ethnical, racial or religious group, as such"[240] must of necessity involve methods that include one or more of the following directed to destroying future generations: (a) the destruction of adult caretakers of children through murder such that the children are at high risk of being unable to survive, (b) the destruction of children directly through murder, (c) incapacitating adult caretakers or significantly adversely impacting their child rearing capabilities by inflicting grave psychological and physical harms upon them (i.e. resulting, for instance, in inter-generational psychological trauma effects that impact on effective child rearing and psychological and physical adverse health consequences across generations) and/or (d) assimilating the children to the perpetrator group thus reducing the reproductive capacity of their group of origin, alienating the children from their group of origin and destroying the children's personal and original group identity. Article 6 of the Rome Statute[241] [as with Article 2 of the Genocide Convention (GC)[242]] is thus fundamentally: (1) a provision which addresses genocidal intent in terms of the destruction of future generations and therefore (2) directly or indirectly concerns the impact on children and the as yet unborn of mass atrocity driven by genocidal intent. Consider then from this perspective Article 2 of the Genocide Convention which follows:

Genocide Convention Article 2:

In the present Convention, genocide means any of the following acts committed with intent to destroy, in whole or in part, a national, ethnical, racial or religious group, as such:

(a) Killing members of the group;
(b) Causing serious bodily or mental harm to members of the group;
(c) Deliberately inflicting on the group conditions of life calculated to bring about its physical destruction in whole or in part;
(d) Imposing measures intended to prevent births within the group;
(e) Forcibly transferring children of the group to another group.[243]

Where children, and women (especially pregnant women) become special targets in the systematic widespread attack on civilians and where sexual violence

[240] Rome Statute (2002, Article 6).

[241] Rome Statute (2002).

[242] Genocide Convention (1951).

[243] Genocide Convention (1951, Article 2).

is prevalent (i.e. gang rapes of women and girls, mutilation of the sex organs of males and females etc.); this is a marker for genocide. The destruction of the children might be physical (as in torturing and/or murdering children or ensuring that their caretakers are incapacitated or eliminated such that the children's survival is put at grave risk) or it can be in terms of destroying the children's personhood by quashing the expression of the children's inherent potentialities and instead molding the children in the image of the perpetrator and with the world view of the particular *genocidaire* involved (i.e. as an aspect of the genocidal forcible transfer of the children to the perpetrator group).

The current author, in accord with Goldhagen, holds then that the special targeting of children as direct victims of atrocity and the most extreme cruelty is a key marker for genocide:

> Mass murder and elimination's perpetrators' comparative treatment of children is significant in multiple ways...First, and most significant, is the perpetrators' disposition of the children themselves... [For example] [T]hey [the Nazis]stole and reared as Germans victim peoples' children conforming in their personal physiognomy to the ideal of the master race according to the Germans' crackpot racial-biological ideological and political accounting system [an example of genocidal forcible transfer of children to a genocidal perpetrator group]... Second, *...all those said to be killing or expelling the victims against their will, or merely out of obedience [i.e. to a command order]...would not possibly descend on victims' children with the [genocidal] perpetrators' fury, willful excess brutality and glee.* Third, the perpetrators' enormously widespread cruelty towards children tells us some further specific things about perpetrators' cruelty in general...*Only to mindsets such as those of the German [Nazi] perpetrators [genocidal mindsets] would it make sense for perpetrators to feel such vengeful fury at the targeted group's children...Finally, the perpetrators' slaughter of and cruelty toward children [children not offering any resistance; including very young children and babies] thoroughly belie their [the perpetrators'] hollow self-exculpatory claims that they merely carry out a necessary task [i.e. relating to 'military necessity'], or did not know they were acting wrongly or criminally, or had no choice...[the acts are so cruel to the children as to be manifestly unlawful and committed with an intent rendering the acts genocidal in nature].*[244]

Keeping in mind Goldhagen's[245] perspective on the significance of the targeting of and extreme cruelty toward children during armed conflict, consider the following excerpt from the UN Commission of Inquiry on Darfur reporting examples of extreme cruelty to and specific targeting of children which evidence undercuts the notion that the Al Bashir forces and allied militia (Janjaweed) were simply engaged in counter-insurgency in Darfur with no genocidal intent:

> The Commission also notes that Janjaweed have, on a number of occasions, *specifically targeted and killed children* ...The Commission received many reports of *random and/or targeted killing of children, sometimes in horrific circumstances such as by burning or mutilation.* Several incidents of this nature were verified by the Commission... [246]

[244] Goldhagen (2009, pp. 474–476, emphasis added).

[245] Goldhagen (2009, pp. 474–476).

[246] UN Commission of Inquiry on Darfur (2005, p.76, para 278–279, emphasis added).

Thus, child civilians and, in particular, also infants and young children (all of whom, of course, have no political power) are often targeted for extreme cruelty in the context of mass atrocities typically categorized only as 'crimes against humanity' and/or 'war crimes'. The facts regarding the targeting of children and the nature of the attacks upon them in the context of mass atrocities, however, demonstrates that such widespread attacks on the civilian population also, in many instances, have genocidal qualities (i.e. the attacks are geared to destroying future generations rather than simply quelling resistance if in fact there was significant political resistance at all).

The current author differs somewhat on a certain point from Goldhagen in his assessment that certain perpetrators of mass atrocity have 'spared children' when they allowed children to live with surviving relatives rather than eliminating the children for instance.[247] The surviving children, as has been here noted previously, are often destroyed to some degree through their trauma[248] and though some may cope reasonably well eventually; many more pass on the legacy of genocidal trauma to the next generation (i.e. through inadequate parenting, communicating to that next generation, intentionally or unintentionally; but without malice, a sense of profound insecurity etc.) such that the suffering in the family is perpetuated across generations. Thus, though these surviving children were spared the fate of death; they were not spared a legacy of personal suffering that they will, to some extent, generally then pass on to their own children to some degree in some form or fashion.

On the foregoing analysis, for instance, the high ranking leaders of the LRA (the Lord's Resistance Army) have and are committing genocide and not just crimes against humanity and/or war crimes. This is the case in that the LRA is notorious for targeting infants, children and pregnant women for especially gruesome deaths where the adults of a village offer up any resistance or the LRA's abducted child soldiers originating from a particular village attempt to escape back to that village. The abduction and conscription or alleged 'enlistment' of children and their appropriation into the murderous LRA, on the analysis here, constitutes the genocidal forcible transfer of children[249] whether or not the children are targeted based on membership in any particular ethnic, religious, 'racial' or national group. This is the case in that the LRA attempts through various inhumane means to alienate the child recruits from their families and communities and to appropriate them permanently as LRA both in a physical and psychological sense (the latter in part through

[247] Goldhagen (2009, p. 468).

[248] The trauma suffered by the surviving children relates to their perhaps having lost their parent(s) and/or other loved ones to the mass atrocities; having witnessed the atrocities if they were old enough to comprehend at some level etc.

[249] Grover (2012).

indoctrination and fear). Yet, the LRA high ranking perpetrators (such as the Commander-in-Chief Kony) are charged by the International Criminal Court (ICC) *not* with genocide (along with other crimes) but instead exclusively with crimes against humanity and war crimes.[250] This, it is here respectfully argued, is a gross error as will be discussed in Part II of this book which addresses various ICC cases which are highly instructive on this point.

As the *genocidaire's* objective is to eliminate and/or appropriate, in part or in whole, future generations,[251] of the targeted group; women generally, and most particularly pregnant women and, in addition, children become prized victims for their symbolic significance (i.e. infants and children as the flesh and blood embodiment of the next generation and all its potential in adding to the vitality of a targeted group; and women as those giving birth to this next generation). Genocide is fundamentally then (as an attack on future generations) both literally and symbolically an attack on humanity generally and *not* simply an attack on one or more identifiable groups (such as those listed in the Genocide Convention[252]) or on the direct individual victims. Every distinct child population then, as part of humanity's children, is entitled to the full protection of international humanitarian, human rights and criminal law regardless the children's targeted group of origin and notwithstanding how that group of origin is defined by the perpetrator and/or the targeted group's members (i.e. in ethnic, religious, national or so-called racial *or other terms*). A civilized international community can do no less than to provide all children the full range of protection under international law. Thus, the concept of 'protected group' as such (as incorporated in the Genocide Convention Article 2[253] and the Rome Statute Article 6[254]), correctly interpreted, must include children as a protected group in and of itself (children as protected in their own right). The argument for the same is especially compelling when one acknowledges that: (1) children (persons under 18) are most often prized victims for the genocidal perpetrator bent on sending symbolic propaganda messages by virtue of the victims chosen for special cruelties; especially the most defenseless while at the same time (2) children, regardless their group of origin, are recognized as a special protected group in customary law, and various international human rights and humanitarian law instruments as previously discussed.

It is to be understood, as previously here alluded to, that children are *not* to be valued most importantly as simply vehicles for: (1) the perpetuation of the protected

[250] Prosecutor v Joseph Kony, Warrant of Arrest (2005).

[251] The genocidal forcible transfer of children involves such an appropriation of children.

[252] Note that in the view of many genocide scholars the Genocide Convention (1951) does *not* preclude the possibility of 'autogenocide' such that not every instance of genocide need necessarily involve a minority group (i.e. See Forster 2011).

[253] Genocide Convention (1951).

[254] Rome Statute (2002).

groups explicitly articulated in the Genocide Convention[255] at Article 2[256] and (2) the preservation of the richness these peoples bring to the mosaic that is humanity. Instead, children are to be regarded as having intrinsic value in and of themselves as 'humanity's children.' Children are, of course, the realization of the continuation of and hope for humanity generally and not just for any particular identifiable protected group (however defined). Thus, on the analysis here wherein children are considered a protected group *per se* (in their own right); any widespread attack on a civilian population that includes the special targeting of pregnant women[257] and of children (persons under 18), constitutes genocide (as well as 'crimes against humanity' and, depending on the context, perhaps also 'war crimes').

The view articulated here of children as having intrinsic value rather than just being: (1) purveyors of the culture, language, religion, history etc. of protected groups and (2) representatives of the group who will perpetuate the group as such is implicitly reflected in Article 6 of the Convention on the Rights of the Child (CRC).[258] This is the case in that the CRC values children's right to life, survival and development as *inherent* and not dependent on the children's group affiliation; however that group is defined:

Convention on the Rights of the Child

Article 6

1. States Parties recognize that every child has the *inherent* right to life.
2. States Parties shall ensure to the maximum extent possible the survival and development of the child. [259]

Clearly, many hundreds of thousands of children in conflicts globally have had their Article 6 CRC[260] rights violated in part through being the victims of the genocidal forcible transfer to State or non-State armed forces or groups committing mass atrocities and/or genocide.

Note that under the Convention on the Rights of the Child[261] children[262] are not obligated to be bound to their so-called 'protected group' (i.e. ethnic, religious or

---

[255] Nor are children to be valued, for that matter, simply as vehicles for the perpetuation of *any* particular socially constructed or otherwise identifiable or perceived group whether classified on some social, political, economic, national, ethnic, biologic, religious or other dimension or combination of these (real or imagined characteristics).

[256] Genocide Convention (1951).

[257] This is not at all to suggest that other identifiable groups such as women are not also to be considered protected groups when under siege by a genocidal perpetrator group.

[258] Convention on the Rights of the Child (1990).

[259] Convention on the Rights of the Child (1990, emphasis added).

[260] Convention on the Rights of the Child (1990).

[261] Convention on the Rights of the Child (1990).

[262] The notion of 'child' is stipulated in the Convention on the Rights of the Child (1990) as including persons under age 18 unless otherwise specified in domestic law with respect to a particular legal domain.

national group[263] etc.) in order to perpetuate the culture (language and religion etc.) and ethnic character of that group. Children under the CRC thus are considered to have the inherent civil rights of freedom of association and freedom of religion (that effectively emancipate them to a degree from the protected group) to the extent that exercise of these freedoms is consistent with: (1) the values and needs of a democratic society; (2) the best interests of the particular children involved and where (3) due consideration is given to the children's inherent fundamental rights and maturity level at the time they exercise these rights.[264] In this regard consider Article 15 of the CRC:

Convention on the Rights of the Child

Article 15

1. States Parties recognize the rights of the child to freedom of association...
2. No restrictions may be placed on the exercise of these rights other than those imposed in conformity with the law and which are necessary in a democratic society in the interests of national security or public safety, public order (ordre public), the protection of public health or morals or the protection of the rights and freedoms of others.[265]

The inherent civil rights of children affirmed in the Convention on the Rights of the Child[266] (CRC), while not unlimited or unqualified rights, suggest that children who may wish to identify with an alternate ethnic, religious or national group may under the right circumstances seek emancipation from their 'own' protected group (such instances might include, for instance, unaccompanied children who seek asylum in another country for any variety of reasons such as fear of persecution and who wish to assume a new nationality; children who wish to convert to another religion, children who wish to leave the confines of their particular ethnic group such as children who have decided to permanently leave the cloistered environs of a particular ethnic/religious group; children (persons over the domestic legal age of consent regarding marriage but under age 18) who may wish to marry persons of another color who are perceived by some in terms of the unscientific concept of 'race' as being of a different 'race' etc.). Recognition of: (1) *children's civil rights* (Article 13: freedom of expression, Article 14: freedom of thought, conscience and religion, Article 15: freedom of association, and Article 17: right to access information via various sources and mass media including international sources) and (2) *children's participation rights* (Article 12) under the Convention on the Rights of the Child[267] is a key innovative aspect of the Convention. Consistent then with one

---

[263] For instance, the Convention on the Rights of the Child (1990) contemplates the right of a child to abandon his or her national group and seek asylum where in the child's best interest.

[264] The Convention on the Rights of the Child (1990) Articles 5 and 18 also recognizes the parents' right to raise their child in accord with the parents' cultural traditions and values with due regard to the child's evolving capacities for independent decision-making.

[265] Convention on the Rights of the Child (1990).

[266] Convention on the Rights of the Child (1990).

[267] Convention on the Rights of the Child (1990).

of the preeminent pieces of international human rights law concerning children (the Convention on the Rights of the Child[268]); children are *not* to be regarded under Rome Statute Article 6(e)[269] simply as vehicles for the perpetuation of the "protected groups" (i.e. 'racial', ethnic, religious or national) explicitly listed in that Article (or the duplicate found at Article 2(e) of the Genocide Convention[270]); or of any other group of origin, however defined, for that matter. This being the case in that the child group itself (*as such*) has intrinsic value separate and apart from the children's group of origin.[271] An appreciation of: (1) the intrinsic value of children in and of themselves and, hence, (2) children as a protected group *per se* (in their own right) under the Genocide Convention Article 2[272] (and Rome Statute Article 6[273]) inevitably leads to the conclusion that the appropriation (forcible transfer)[274] of children from *any* identifiable group to a group perpetrating mass atrocities and/or genocide constitutes the 'genocidal forcible transfer of children'.

Literature, Materials and Situations/Cases

Literature

Crema L (2010) Disappearance and new sightings of restrictive interpretations. Eur J Int Law 21(3):681–700

Eastwood M (2011) Lessons in hatred: the indoctrination and education of Germany's youth. Int J Hum Rights 15(8):1291–1314

Forster TK (2011) The Khmer Rouge and the crime of genocide: issues of genocidal intent with regard to the Khmer Rouge mass atrocities. http://www.cambodiatribunal.org/sites/default/files/reports/KHMER%20ROUGE%20AND%20THE%20CRIMES%20OF%20GENOCIDE.pdf. Accessed 18 Jun 2012

Goldhagen DJ (2009) Worse than war: genocide, eliminationism, and the ongoing assault on humanity. Public Affairs/Perseus Book Group, New York

Grover L (2010) A call to arms: fundamental dilemmas confronting the interpretation of crimes in the Rome Statute of the International Criminal Court European. J Int Law 21(3):543–583

---

[268] Convention on the Rights of the Child (1990).

[269] Rome Statute (2002).

[270] Genocide Convention (1951).

[271] Recall that under Article 21(3) of the Rome Statute (2002): "The application and interpretation of law [the Rome Statute (2002)] pursuant to [that] article must be consistent with internationally recognized human rights…"[i.e. such as those recognized universal children's human rights articulated in the Convention on the Rights of the Child (1990)].

[272] Genocide Convention (1951).

[273] Rome Statute (2002).

[274] Children in fact cannot consent to their own genocidal forcible transfer thus, for instance, children who are alleged to have 'volunteered' for participation in an armed group or force perpetrating mass atrocities and/or genocide are also victims of a violation of Rome Statute Article 6 (e).

Grover S (2012) Child soldier victims of genocidal forcible transfer: exonerating child soldiers charged with grave conflict-related international crimes. Springer, Berlin
Grover S (2011a) The Lebensborn children of Norway (children born of Nazi fathers during WWII) and the silencing of their voices by an international human rights court: an analysis of the 2007 European Court of Human Rights decision in Werner Hermann Thiermann and others v. Norway. Int J Interdiscipl Soc Sci 5(8):25–36
Grover S (2011b) Schoolchildren as propaganda tools in the war on terror: violating the rights of Afghani children under international law. Springer, Berlin
Mundorff K (2007) Taking 2(e) seriously: forcible child transfers and the Convention on the Prevention and Punishment of the Crime of Genocide. Master of Laws Thesis, University of British Columbia. https://circle.ubc.ca/bitstream/handle/2429/31682/ubc_2007-0524.pdf?sequence=1. Accessed 19 May 2012
Sadat LN (ed) (2011) Forging a convention for crimes against humanity. Cambridge University Press, Cambridge
Schabas WA (2010) The International Criminal Court: a commentary on the Rome Statute (Oxford commentaries on international law). Oxford University Press, New York
Schabas WA (2000) Genocide in international law. University of Cambridge Press, Cambridge
Sobsey R (2007) Implementing the rights of children with disabilities. In: Covell K, Howe RB (eds) Children's rights in Canada: a question of commitment. Wilfred Laurier Press, Waterloo, pp 373–394
Triffterer O (2008) Commentary on the Rome Statute of the International Criminal Court. C.H. Beck/Hart Publishers, Baden-Baden

Materials

Cimpric A (2010) Children accused of witchcraft: an anthropological study of contemporary practices in Africa (A report prepared for UNICEF). http://www.unicef.org/wcaro/wcaro_children-accused-of-witchcraft-in-Africa.pdf. Accessed 13 May 2012
Convention on the Rights of the Child (CRC) (1990) Entered into force 2 September 1990. http://www2.ohchr.org/english/law/pdf/crc.pdf. Accessed 27 Oct 2011
Geneva Convention IV Relative to the Protection of Civilian Persons in Times of War, 12 August, 1949. http://www.icrc.org/ihl.nsf/WebList?ReadForm&id=380&t=art. Accessed 16 May 2012
Genocide Convention (Convention on the Prevention and Punishment of the Crime of Genocide). Entry into force 1951. http://www.preventgenocide.org/law/convention/text.htm. Accessed 3 Feb 2012
Nuremberg Charter (1945) Agreement for the Prosecution and Punishment of the Major War Criminals of the European Axis, and Charter of the International Military Tribunal. London, 8 August 1945. http://www.icrc.org/ihl.nsf/INTRO/350?OpenDocument. Accessed 7 May 2012
Optional Protocol to the Convention on the Rights of the Child on the involvement of children in armed conflict (2002) Entered into force 12 February, 2002. http://www2.ohchr.org/english/law/crc-conflict.htm. Accessed 26 Feb 2012
Optional Protocol to the Convention on the Rights of the Child on the sale of children, child prostitution and child pornography (2002) Entered into force 18 January, 2002. http://www2.ohchr.org/english/law/crc-sale.htm. Accessed 26 Feb 2012
Protocol Additional to the 1949 Geneva Conventions relating to the Protection of victims of international armed conflicts (Protocol I) (8 June, 1977) http://www.icrc.org/ihl.nsf/FULL/470?OpenDocument. Accessed 18 Jan 2012

Protocol Additional to the 1949 Geneva Conventions Relating to the Protection of victims of non-international armed conflicts (Protocol II) (8 June, 1977) http://www.icrc.org/ihl.nsf/INTRO/475. Accessed 18 Jan 2012
Rome Statute (2002) Entered into force 7 January, 2002 http://untreaty.un.org/cod/icc/statute/romefra.htm. Accessed 17 Jan 2011
Security Council Working Group on Children and Armed Conflict (2005) http://www.un.org/children/conflict/english/securitycouncilwg.html. Accessed 8 May 2012
UN Commission of Inquiry on Darfur (2005). http://www.un.org/news/dh/sudan/com_inq_darfur.pdf. Accessed 25 Feb 2012
Universal Declaration of Human Rights, adopted by the UN General Assembly on 10 December 1948 http://www.un.org/en/documents/udhr/. Accessed 16 Apr 2012
Vienna Convention on the Law of Treaties (1969) Entered into force on 27 January 1980. http://untreaty.un.org/ilc/texts/instruments/english/conventions/1_1_1969.pdf. Accessed 16 Apr 2012

Situations and Cases

International Military Tribunal Trial of the Major War Criminals, Vol. 19 (29 July, 1946, p. 616) http://avalon.law.yale.edu/imt/07-29-46.asp. Accessed 8 May 2012
Prosecutor v. Omar Hassan Ahmad Al Bashir, Second Warrant for Arrest for Omar Hassan Ahmad Al Bashir (Pre-Trial Chamber I, 12 July, 2010) http://www.icc-cpi.int/iccdocs/doc/doc907140.pdf. Accessed 14 May 2012
Prosecutor v Joseph Kony. Warrant for Arrest for Joseph Kony Issued on 8 July, 2005 as amended on 27 September, 2005 http://www.icc-cpi.int/iccdocs/doc/doc97185.PDF. Accessed 1 Mar 2012

Part II
ICC Prosecutor Case Selection and Charging Decisions

Chapter 2
Gravity and Interests of Justice Considerations

2.1 Ambiguity of the Test for 'Sufficient Gravity' Regarding Admissibility of the Case

It has been said that the concept of gravity "resides at the epicenter of the legal regime of the International Criminal Court."[1] Indeed, as deGuzman reminds us; the Rome Statute stipulates that the function of the ICC is to end impunity for "the most serious crimes of concern to the international community as a whole."[2] Hence, gravity "is at the heart of . . .ICC determinations" [regarding] "which situations and cases merit international adjudication."[3] Notwithstanding the latter, however, it is to be emphasized that a pre-determination by an ICC Pre-Trial Chamber that a case is admissible (a gravity assessment being part of that determination) is *not* a prerequisite for issuance of an arrest warrant pursuant to Article 58(1) of the Rome Statute.[4] An arrest warrant is to be issued based only on whether: (1) there are reasonable grounds to believe the person committed a crime within the jurisdiction of the ICC and (2) the arrest of the person appears necessary:

Rome Statute

Article 58(1)
Issuance by the Pre-Trial Chamber of a warrant of arrest or a summons to appear

1. At any time after the initiation of an investigation, the Pre-Trial Chamber shall, on the application of the Prosecutor, issue a warrant of arrest of a person if, having examined the application and the evidence or other information submitted by the Prosecutor, it is satisfied that:

---

[1] DeGuzman (2009, p. 1400).

[2] DeGuzman (2009, p. 1400).

[3] DeGuzman (2009, p. 1402).

[4] See Situation in the Democratic Republic of the Congo, Ex Parte, Prosecutor Only (2006, p. 2, para 1 under "Reasons").

S.C. Grover, *Humanity's Children*, DOI 10.1007/978-3-642-32501-4_2,

(a) . . .
(b) The arrest of the person appears necessary:
(i) To ensure the person's appearance at trial,
(ii) To ensure that the person does not obstruct or endanger the investigation or the court proceedings, or
(iii) Where applicable, to prevent the person from continuing with the commission of that crime or a related crime which is within the jurisdiction of the Court and which arises out of the same circumstances. . ..[5]

The current author concurs that "the concept of gravity is central to the ICC's purpose and its application will be an integral part of the Court's work."[6] With respect, it is contended here however that to date, unjustifiably, neither the ICC Prosecutor nor the various Chambers of the ICC have addressed the evidence for the occurrence, in various cases, of the grave crime of 'genocidal forcible transfer of children' (an international crime falling under the jurisdiction of the ICC) as will be illustrated through selected cases in Part III of this book.

Gravity assessments affect the ICC Prosecutor's selection of situations and cases to investigate *proprio motu*[7] and potentially prosecute, as well as the nature of the charges brought, if any, in any particular case. (In this instance, the Prosecutor must also receive ICC authorization for the thorough investigation he or she plans to undertake). Hence, as deGuzman's points out; gravity [assessments] serve to "legitimize the Court [the ICC]. . ." in terms of the selection of cases ultimately prosecuted from amongst the myriad of potentially admissible cases.[8] To the extent then that the gravity threshold is not properly determined and factual evidence of the occurrence of, for instance, the 'genocidal forcible transfer of children' is ignored by the Prosecutor and the Court, the moral legitimacy of the ICC is undermined to some extent. Consider in this regard that Article 5 of the Rome Statute[9] specifies that genocide is "one of the most serious crimes of concern to the international community as a whole" and that Article 6(e) of the Rome Statute lists "forcibly transferring children of the group to another group" as a form of genocide.

Let us consider then the position that the ICC has taken in terms of the interpretation of what constitutes "sufficient gravity" of a case to render it admissible (assuming all other admissibility requirements are also met). That is, we will review next what, if anything, the ICC has fashioned as the test regarding Article 17(d) of the Rome Statute[10] regarding admissibility and how the Court addresses then the question of gravity of the case. Article 17(d) states:

---

[5] Rome Statute (2002, Article 58(1)).

[6] DeGuzman (2009, p. 1400).

[7] Also when a 'situation' is *referred* to the Prosecutor by the UN Security Council or through some other source such an individual or NGO: (1) the Prosecutor *must* decide if there is a reasonable basis to investigate taking into consideration gravity amongst other factors and (2) If he or she decides that there is such a basis; the Prosecutor then must initiate the investigation.

[8] DeGuzman (2009, p. 1404).

[9] Rome Statute (2002).

[10] Rome Statute (2002).

Rome Statute

Article 17(d)

"Having regard to paragraph 10 of the Preamble and article 1, the Court shall determine that a case is inadmissible where: . . .d) *the case is not of sufficient gravity to justify further action by the Court.*[11]

The issue of the meaning of Article 17(d) of the Rome Statute[12] (pertaining to the gravity test) arose in the context of the situation in the Democratic Republic of Congo (DRC) and the Prosecutor's desire to issue warrants of arrest for certain individuals involved in that situation.[13] With respect to the situation in the DRC and the Prosecutor's 2006 *ex parte* application regarding arrest warrants,[14] the Pre-Trial Chamber issued its opinion on what constitutes the basis for an arrest warrant and also discussed the gravity test. However, that opinion was overturned by the ICC Appeal Chamber. We will here then focus on the review of the Pre-Trial Chamber's decision by the Appeal Chamber and the latter's legal conclusions regarding in what ways the Pre-Trial Chamber's test of gravity and its application were allegedly flawed. We will consider what the Appeal Chamber postulated is the correct test and application of the law regarding gravity and pertaining to the admissibility of a case. Thereafter, the current author will offer a somewhat different position regarding the proper test for gravity as set out in Article 17(d) of the Rome Statute.[15]

2.2 The Situation in the DRC: Case Selection and Gravity

The ICC Pre-Trial Chamber considering the situation in the Democratic Republic of Congo (DRC) held that the gravity test is met as set out in Article 17(d) of the Rome Statute[16] if:

1. . . .the conduct which is the object of a case [is] ***systematic or large-scale*** due consideration . . .also [being] given to the ***social alarm*** caused to the international community by the . . .conduct;
2. The [perpetrator's] position in the State entity, organization or armed group. . .falls within the category of most senior leaders of the situation under investigation;
3. . . .the relevant person. . .[being amongst] the most senior leaders [is] suspected of being most responsible considering (i) the role played by the relevant person through acts or omissions when the States entities , organizations or armed groups to which he belongs

[11] Rome Statute (2002, emphasis added).

[12] Rome Statute (2002).

[13] Situation in the Democratic Republic of the Congo, Ex Parte, Prosecutor Only (2006).

[14] Situation in the Democratic Republic of the Congo, Ex Parte, Prosecutor Only (2006).

[15] Rome Statute (2002).

[16] Rome Statute (2002).

> commit systematic or large-scale crimes within the jurisdiction of the Court [the ICC], and (ii) the role played by such States entities , organizations or armed groups in the overall commission of crimes within the jurisdiction of the Court [the ICC] in the relevant situation.[17]

The ICC Appeal Court found the above test for gravity flawed in a number of respects. The Appeals Court held that crimes need *not* necessarily be systematic or widespread in order for a case to be admissible to the ICC. The Appeal Chamber pointed out that war crimes need to be part of a plan/policy ***or*** be widespread/ systematic (***or*** both) to generate admissible ICC cases. To suggest that war crimes need to be widespread and/or systematic to generate admissible ICC cases, the Appeal Chamber explained, is to confound the contextual criteria for 'war crimes' with that for 'crimes against humanity'. In addition, the ICC Appeal Chamber rejected the Pre-Trial Chamber's assumption that the deterrent effect of prosecution would be greatest if the most senior leaders were prosecuted. The Appeal Chamber found instead that the deterrent effect would be highest if *no category* of perpetrators were automatically excluded from prosecution.[18] The ICC Appeal Chamber judgment regarding the situation in the DRC thus set out what, in the Appeal Chamber's opinion, were flaws in the gravity test as construed by the Pre-Trial Chamber in addressing potential admissible cases pertaining to the situation in the DRC.[19] However, the Appeal Chamber in that instance did not specify in positive terms what criteria do have to be met to satisfy the gravity test for admissibility of a case for adjudication by the ICC (as opposed to establishing the grounds for issuing an arrest warrant).[20]

The point is highlighted here that, in any case, the 'genocidal forcible transfer of children'[21] typically involves: (1) systematic and widespread criminal conduct involving multiple commissions of the crime (i.e. the widespread and systematic forcible transfer of children to another group) and other atrocities (2) generally involves a plan or policy utilizing various means of transferring the children and alienating the children from their families and home communities (i.e. using the children as child soldiers to commit atrocities against their own families and communities, raping the children and/or sexually enslaving the children en masse etc. such that the community comes to perceive the children as 'of' the perpetrator

[17] Situation in the Democratic Republic of the Congo, Ex Parte, Prosecutor Only (2006, pp. 13–14, para 56, emphasis added).

[18] Situation in the Democratic Republic of the Congo, Ex Parte, Prosecutor Only (2006, pp. 18–22, para 73).

[19] The Appeal Chamber also, as mentioned, found that cases need not be found admissible before a warrant for arrest can be issued.

[20] Situation in the Democratic Republic of the Congo, Ex Parte, Prosecutor Only (2006, pp. 18–22, para 68–82).

[21] Thus, for instance, in regards to the appropriation of children as child soldiers by an armed group or force perpetrating mass atrocities and/or genocide; this genocidal forcible transfer of children is typically widespread and systematic with thousands of children often affected in any particular armed conflict situation.

group as do the children themselves). Further, those in high commander-in-chief positions and other military and political leaders such as Lubanga and Al Bashir are generally in a position to at least attempt to put a stop to implementation of the common plan for the genocidal forcible transfer of children. That the genocidal forcible transfer of children as a phenomenon creates "social alarm" in the international community, at least in principle or theory, is evidenced by a number of facts: (1) there is *separate* recognition under the Rome Statute, Article 6(e)[22] of the forcible transfer of children from the group to another group with genocidal intent as itself a form of genocide; and (2) all forms of genocide are considered under the Rome Statute as "manifestly unlawful" such that the social alarm aspect is implicit in this aspect. Hence, even superior orders and alleged lack of knowledge that the orders were unlawful cannot provide a defence for the commission of genocidal acts:

Rome Statute

Article 33
Superior orders and prescription of law

1. The fact that a crime within the jurisdiction of the Court has been committed by a person pursuant to an order of a Government or of a superior, whether military or civilian, shall not relieve that person of criminal responsibility ***unless*:**

   (a) The person was under a legal obligation to obey orders of the Government or the superior in question;
   (b) The person did not know that the order was unlawful; ***and***
   (c) ***The order was not manifestly unlawful.***

2. **For the purposes of this article, orders to commit genocide or crimes against humanity *are* manifestly unlawful.**[23]

Hence, cases involving the 'genocidal forcible transfer of children' meet the high bar set by the ICC Pre-Trial Chamber (in the DRC situation Pre-Trial Chamber judgment mentioned previously) for the gravity test regarding admissibility; at least insofar as the crime itself is concerned[24] (notwithstanding the fact that the test is, according to the ICC Appeals Chamber ruling on the matter, too restrictive).[25]

Note that despite evidence for "social alarm" in the international community regarding the 'genocidal forcible transfer of children'[26]; *in practice* incidences of

---

[22] Rome Statute (2002).

[23] Rome Statute (2002, Article 33, emphasis added).

[24] See Situation in the Democratic Republic of the Congo, Ex Parte, Prosecutor Only (2006, pp. 13–14, para 56).

[25] Situation in the Democratic Republic of the Congo, Ex Parte, Prosecutor Only (2006, pp. 18–22, para 68–82).

[26] For example, as reflected in the fact that the crime of genocidal forcible transfer of children falls under the Rome Statute (2002) at Article 6(e) thus, in principle, allowing, in certain circumstances, for prosecution by the ICC of some or all of the individuals most responsible for this crime in a particular situation.

this crime post the entry into force of the Rome Statute,[27] to date, have *not* been acknowledged by the ICC or by international criminal tribunals to have occurred. This is the case though, on the analysis here, the grave international crime of 'genocidal forcible transfer of children' has in fact been perpetrated since the entry into force of the Rome Statute,[28] even on a massive scale, as will be discussed here in the context of specific cases in Part III of this book. Let us examine then further the ICC Prosecutor's reasoning regarding gravity assessments.

2.3 The Situation in Darfur: Case Selection and Gravity

Consider the discussion of gravity (as a criterion for admissibility of an ICC case) included in the Prosecution's application of 20 November, 2008 to the Pre-Trial Chamber requesting arrest warrants for certain rebel leaders who, during the conflict in Darfur, commanded an attack 29 September, 2007 directed against UN peacekeepers. That attack killed 12 and severely injured eight peacekeepers belonging to the African Union Mission in Sudan (AMIS)[29]:

> AMIS was a peacekeeping mission authorized in accordance with the United Nations Charter, first through UN Security Council Resolution ("UNSCR") 1556 of 30 July 2004 and then through subsequent resolutions. . . AMIS personnel were not taking any active part in hostilities before, or at the time of the attack.[30]

While acknowledging that the ICC Appeal Chamber had previously ruled that "an initial determination on the admissibility of a case cannot be made an integral part of the decision on an application for a warrant of arrest for the reason that article 58 (1) of the Statute lists the substantive prerequisites for the issuance of a warrant of arrest exhaustively. . ."; the Prosecutor presented observations on what, in the view of the Office of the Prosecutor, constitutes the threshold for gravity.[31] The Prosecutor in his 20 November, 2008 application to the Pre-Trial Chamber for warrants relating to the international crimes perpetrated by virtue of the rebel attack on the AMIS peacekeepers in Darfur stated, in part, the following in regards to gravity of the crime:

> In assessing the gravity of the crimes charged in this Application, and consistent with the Appeals Chamber ruling that [the] Article 8 Chapeau requirement "in particular when committed as part of a plan or policy or as part of a large-scale commission of such crimes"

---

[27] Rome Statute (2002).

[28] Rome Statute (2002).

[29] Situation in Darfur, the Sudan: Summary of the Prosecutor's Application under Article 58 (Pre-Trial Chamber 1) ICC-02/05-162, 20 November, 2008.

[30] Situation in Darfur, the Sudan: Summary of the Prosecutor's Application under Article 58 (Pre-Trial Chamber 1) ICC-02/05-162, 20 November, 2008, p. 4, para 5.

[31] Situation in Darfur, the Sudan: Summary of the Prosecutor's Application under Article 58 (Pre-Trial Chamber 1) ICC-02/05-162, 20 November, 2008, p. 4, para 6.

> *should not be construed narrowly, the issues of the nature, manner and impact of the attack are critical.* In the present case, an attack was intentionally directed at international peacekeepers, 12 of whom were killed, 8 of whom were severely wounded. AMIS facilities were completely destroyed and properties that were needed for effective discharge of its mandate pillaged. AMIS operations were severely disrupted, thus affecting its protective mandated roles with respect to millions of Darfurian civilians in need of humanitarian aid and security.... Peacekeepers are mandated to protect and attacking them jeopardizes their mandate and puts at risk the very viability and continuation of their operations. ... Moreover, as the International Law Commission commented in relation to such attacks in the context of the 1996 Draft Code of Crimes, *such attacks "constitute violent crimes of exceptionally serious gravity which have serious consequences not only for the victims, but also for the international community."*[32]

It is suggested here, consistent with the Prosecutor's observations regarding the gravity threshold, that "the nature, manner and impact of the attack are critical"[33] in assessing gravity of the international crimes committed (not just in respect of war crimes but also in regards to other crimes under ICC jurisdiction). While establishing that the crime of genocide has occurred does *not* require proving the existence of widespread or systematic genocidal acts[34]; the nature, manner and impact of the genocidal attacks reflect both the inherent gravity of the crime and the scope of its expression in a particular situation. As was discussed previously, genocidal attacks on children (including the forcible transfer of the children to another group through mass rape,[35] recruitment and use of children for active participation in hostilities by armed groups or forces perpetrating mass atrocities and/or genocide etc.) inflict great mental suffering on the children and their families and often involve grave physical harms to the children transferred as well.

In considering the aforementioned rebel attack on U.N. peacekeepers in Darfur, note that there are in fact distinct parallels between the situation of peacekeepers and children as victims of international crimes perpetrated in the context of armed conflict. Those parallel dimensions speak to the issue of the severe gravity of the international crimes involved when either of these protected groups fall victim to one of the international crimes under ICC jurisdiction:

---

[32] Situation in Darfur, the Sudan: Summary of the Prosecutor's Application under Article 58 (Pre-Trial Chamber 1) ICC-02/05-162, 20 November, 2008, p. 5, para 7, emphasis added.

[33] Situation in Darfur, the Sudan: Summary of the Prosecutor's Application under Article 58 (Pre-Trial Chamber 1) ICC-02/05-162, 20 November, 2008, p. 5, para 7.

[34] Notwithstanding this fact; genocide in its various forms generally involves a plan for achieving the genocidal objective and implementation of that 'common plan' usually results in widespread and systematic atrocity involving large numbers of victims. Thus, it is unlikely that cases of genocide would on any aspect of gravity of the crime be ruled by the ICC as inadmissible.

[35] Note that children sexually enslaved as 'bush wives' (as occurs not infrequently where armed groups or forces are perpetrating mass atrocities and/or genocide) are the victims also of repeated rape in this context. This for a variety of reasons including the duress inherent in the situation; the children's legal incompetence to provide lawful consent given the duress and often also the children's age thus rendering the situation one of sexual enslavement as opposed to a mutually consensual marriage arrangement recognized in law. (It should be recalled also, however, that rape can occur even in the context of a lawful marriage; see Palmer (1997) on the latter point).

2.3.1 *Parallels Between U.N. Peacekeepers and Children as 'Protected Groups'*

1. Like U.N. peacekeepers; children are a special protected group under international humanitarian law which has arguably attained the status of customary law[36] [as well as under international human rights law[37] (where 'children' refers to persons up to age 18)];
2. The State and the international community as a whole owe children a high fiduciary duty just as they do in regards to U.N. peacekeepers and other representatives of the international legal system. Part of that fiduciary duty, it is here argued, is to prosecute those who have perpetrated or contributed to; or attempted to perpetrate international crimes against these specially protected persons/groups[38];
3. Children, just as is the case with U.N. peacekeepers, have personally nothing to gain politically if one side or the other in an armed conflict gains power (the U.N. peacekeepers are mandated to keep the peace and security and provide humanitarian assistance).[39] That is, children *as children* will remain personally politically and economically disempowered regardless who has the political and/or military upper hand in any particular armed conflict situation (regardless any propaganda by perpetrators to the contrary);
4. Attacks on children (i.e. such as those constituting the 'genocidal forcible transfer of children') are attacks not just on the direct victims but on the international community as a whole (as is the situation also with attacks on U.N. peacekeepers). This is the case since the genocidal forcible transfer of children to an armed group or force perpetrating mass atrocities undermines the viability of the children's home communities and groups of origin and seriously undermines both the short and long-term potential for peace and security in the region (many of the child victims of genocidal forcible transfer are moreover child soldiers recruited to contribute to prolonging the armed conflict).

[36] Protocol I and II Additional to the Geneva Conventions (1977).

[37] Convention on then Rights of the Child (1990).

[38] As noted in the Preparatory work to the Establishment of an International Criminal Court "attacks [were] committed against persons who represented the international community and protected its interests; [the] attacks [were] in effect directed or committed against the international community....and the international community had a special responsibility to ensure the prosecution and punishment of these crimes." (Summary of the Proceedings of the Preparatory Committee, A/AC.249/1, 7 May 1996, Cited in Situation in Darfur, the Sudan: Summary of the Prosecutor's Application under Article 58 (Pre-Trial Chamber 1) ICC-02/05-162, 20 November, 2008, p. 5 para 7).

[39] The stated AMIS mission was one of providing humanitarian assistance to the people of Darfur and ensuring peace and security in the region. The peacekeepers were not engaged in the hostilities on one side or the other.

Despite children's status as a special protected group and the gravity of the international crimes perpetrated against children in Darfur; no charges were filed by the ICC Prosecutor relating to the situation in Darfur pertaining specifically to the child victims. (The ICC case against Al Bashir is discussed in detail in Part III of this book). Thus, for instance, to date *no ICC charges* have been brought against: (1) Al Bashir or his co-perpetrators in regards to the Al Bashir government and allied militia's recruitment and use of child soldiers to participate in the government's genocidal campaign nor against: (2) rebel leaders who used child soldiers, some under age 15, in contravention of international law.[40] In contrast, charges *were* filed by the Prosecutor against three rebel commanders accused of senior responsibility for the 29 September, 2007 attack on the African Mission in Sudan (AMIS) peacekeepers.[41] Thus, though children are no less a special protected group under international law than is an internationally sanctioned peacekeeper group; [and notwithstanding the fact that: (1) the number of child victims of grave international crimes perpetrated in Darfur dwarfs the number of victims in the attacked AMIS peacekeeper group and that (2) the harms done to children in Darfur were/are grave and will have an inter-generational longstanding adverse impact on the population]; the ICC prosecution strategy regarding cases relating to the situation in Darfur does *not* reflect regard for children as a 'special protected group' in their own right.[42]

2.4 Legal Characterization of the Facts and the Assessment of Gravity

It is here argued that the perceived gravity of the crimes committed against children are undermined when the factual evidence supporting charges regarding the 'genocidal forcible transfer of children' is wrongly characterized *exclusively* instead as evidence for 'war crimes' (i.e. "*serious violations* of the laws and customs applicable in international [or internal] armed conflict, within the established framework of international law...").[43] Such serious violations include, but are not limited to,

[40] The crimes committed against children in Darfur were not limited to using children in the hostilities to perpetrate mass atrocity. Other grave international crimes included, for instance, the Al Bashir government blocking critical humanitarian aid to the civilian population, including children, thus significantly compromising the chances for survival of the people in desperate need of that aid.

[41] See The Prosecutor v. Abdallah Banda Abakaer Nourain and Saleh Mohammed Jerbo Jamus and the Prosecutor v Bahar Idriss Abu Grada (Summons to Appear before the ICC issued in 2009 in each case).

[42] This is not at all to diminish the need for ICC prosecution of the perpetrators of the 2007 attack in Darfur on the AMIS peacekeepers and subsequent attacks on the new joint UN-African Union peacekeeping force in Sudan.

[43] See Rome Statute [2002, Article 8(2)(b) xxvi, xxii and Article 8(2)(e) (vi)(vii)].

rape, sexual slavery, and the conscription and/or enlistment and use of children by State forces or non-State armed groups for active participation in armed hostilities. It is argued here that rape, and sexual slavery of children as well as the recruitment and use of children (persons under age 18) in armed hostilities by an armed force or group committing mass atrocity and/or genocide *also* meets the criteria for the 'genocidal forcible transfer of children'.[44]

The ICC is mandated to exercise jurisdiction over war crimes "in particular" when there is established a perpetrator common plan in regards to the war crimes committed and/or there is a large scale and systematic commission of such crimes. It is noteworthy that it is precisely in the context of the widespread and systematic commission of war crimes that children often become particular prized targets for: (1) sexual violence (i.e. rape, sexual slavery etc.); and (2) recruitment and use for active participation in the armed hostilities and for use in the commission of atrocities or even genocide. Victimizing children in this way destroys future generations psychologically and, to some degree, physically while simultaneously rendering the children's group of origin, however defined, less viable.

It is here contended then that the rape and sexual enslavement of children during armed conflict and their recruitment and use by armed groups or forces committing mass atrocity and/or genocide constitute, for the reasons previously explained, the crime of genocidal forcible transfer of children as well as war crimes.[45] The Rome Statute war crimes charges, when based largely on the same facts that support a charge of the genocidal forcible transfer[46] of children, must also be considered then to meet not just the threshold for "serious violations of the laws and customs applicable in international armed conflicts"[47] but also that for "grave breaches of the Geneva Conventions" if related to an international armed conflict[48] [in terms of, for instance, "inhuman treatment"; "willfully causing great suffering, or serious injury to body or health" and "unlawful transfer"[49] i.e. transfer to the custody and control of an armed group or force perpetrating mass atrocity and/or genocide (a force which will most often have an operating conflict theatre which extends far from the child soldiers' home communities such that the children are participating in the armed conflict in unfamiliar territory making escape all the more difficult)].

---

[44] The elements of the crime for the genocidal forcible transfer of children defines 'children' as persons under 18.

[45] The Rome Statute sets out recruitment and use of child soldiers for active participation in the hostilities as a war crime only in regards to child victims under 15.

[46] A charge of genocide involves a specific intent element (that is, the intent to commit genocide in addition to the intent to commit the specific acts alleged).

[47] Rome Statute (2002, Article 8(2)(b) and Article 8(2)(e)).

[48] Grave breaches of the 1949 Geneva Conventions can also occur in the context of a war of national liberation as the latter has been incorporated into the notion of an international armed conflict (Oberg 2009, p. 170).

[49] Rome Statute [2002, Article 8(2)(a)(ii)(iii)(vii)]

2.4.1 'Relative Gravity' and the 'Genocidal Forcible Transfer of Children'

It is here argued that any case of the 'genocidal forcible transfer of children' would meet the test for 'relative gravity'[50] (that is, any such instance of genocide would meet the test for sufficient gravity regarding ICC case admissibility in comparison to other crimes characterizing other cases). Thus, it is here contended that the ICC Prosecutor does not have the discretion *in practice* to: (1) ignore evidence indicating that the genocidal forcible transfer of children has occurred and/or to (2) decline to charge those most responsible in relation to any case of the genocidal forcible transfer of children given the gravity of the crime. To decline to prosecute cases of the genocidal forcible transfer of children is neither in the interests of justice generally nor, more specifically, consistent with the right to justice of the direct and indirect victims of this grave international crime (i.e. respectively the children and their immediate families/group of origin/home communities). The failure to prosecute such cases serves to: (1) further devalue the human dignity of the child victims of genocidal forcible transfer as persons in their own right; and (2) deny these children equal access to international justice in respect to holding to account those who rendered them victims of genocide (i.e. by means of their genocidal forcible transfer to another group).[51] Note that child victims of international human rights violations during armed conflict when interviewed have generally expressed the view that they wish the perpetrators to be brought to justice.[52] It is important to consider also that the failure of the ICC Prosecutor to prosecute (1) the grave international crime of 'genocidal forcible transfer of children' (where the case clearly falls under ICC jurisdiction and all admissibility requirements are fulfilled) or (2) other crimes targeting children *in particular* (i.e. recruitment and use of under 15s for active participation in hostilities) in Darfur or elsewhere may decrease the probability that child victims will receive reparations (monetary and/or otherwise) on order of the Court from either the perpetrators and/or through the ICC Victim Trust Fund set up by the Assembly of States Parties to the Rome Statute[53] in 2002.

---

[50] The 'genocidal forcible transfer of children' meets the test for grave international crime worthy of prosecution based on many factors including but not limited to: (a) *genocidal intent*; (b) *extent of harm* done to the child victims, their group of origin and society generally domestically and internationally; (c) *nature of the harm caused to the direct and indirect victims* in terms of severe mental suffering, alienation of the children from their own communities and families as well as other severe harms such as the loss of vitality and reproductive capacity in the children's group of origin and (d) *undermining of the peace and security in the region* especially where the children have been appropriated as child soldiers by an armed group or force perpetrating mass atrocities and/or genocide.

[51] It is a concern to the current author that to date several ICC defendants known to have been perpetrators of widespread child soldiering and the use of child soldiers to perpetrate atrocities and/or genocidal acts (i.e. Al Bashir) have not been charged with war crimes in regards to the recruitment and use of child soldiers or the 'genocidal forcible transfer of children' thus undermining children's right to international justice.

[52] Office of the Secretary-General for Children and Armed Conflict, Working Paper No. 3 (2011, p. 12).

[53] Rome Statute (2002).

2.5 Children's Right to Justice and Legal Empowerment

In regards to children's right to justice; recall the 'UN Common Approach to Justice for Children' definition of what constitutes children's access to justice:

> Access to justice can be defined as the ability to obtain a just and timely remedy for violations of rights as put forth in national and international norms and standards [. . .].
>
> Proper access to justice requires legal empowerment of all children; all should be enabled to claim their rights, through legal and other services such as child rights education or advice and support from knowledgeable adults.[54]

Denying the occurrence of the 'genocidal forcible transfer of children' (or any other grave international crime under ICC jurisdiction) where the facts belie the denial; and failing to prosecute those most responsible is of course inconsistent with the 'UN Common Approach to Justice for Children'. The latter stipulates: (1) the need to provide children with a timely and just remedy for the grave violation of their fundamental human rights[55] and emphasizes (2) the children's independent right to legal empowerment.[56] That legal empowerment might include acting as a 'victim participant' and/or 'witness' before the ICC where, for instance, a case involving the genocidal forcible transfer of children is being prosecuted. Being able to act as a 'victim participant' at the ICC is a form of self-advocacy that likely has psychological therapeutic benefits for the children that, in many instances, supersede, in some ways, the benefits of being 'witnesses' before the Court (the latter being a somewhat passive role in that the 'witness' is *not* a party to the proceedings with all that the latter entails).[57] Regardless of whether the child is 'victim participant' or 'witness', however, he or she must be effectively protected by the ICC (i.e. from retaliation from perpetrators etc.) at all stages from preliminary to post-trial where necessary (i.e. to whit; the ICC's 'Protection Program' which can provide, when needed, various short or long-term protective measures; even relocation of the witness outside their home country for security purposes etc.). The ICC has a 'Victim and Witnesses Unit' dedicated in part to the protection of witnesses and victim participants; including *children* falling into one or both of these ICC status categories. In addition, the Unit provides psychological and other tangible forms of support.[58]

---

[54] UN Common Approach to Justice for Children (2008, p. 4). See also Grover (2008a) for an examination of children's access to legal standing as a basic human right).

[55] Compare UN Common Approach to Justice for Children (2008, p. 4).

[56] Compare UN Common Approach to Justice for Children (2008, p. 4).

[57] This is not to undermine the importance of child witnesses in international criminal cases or the benefit that may be derived for some children by testifying depending on the particular circumstances.

[58] Office of the Secretary-General for Children and Armed Conflict, Working Paper No. 3 (2011, p. 16).

Note that the ICC 'victim participant' does *not* have to personally testify before the court (unlike the situation for a child holding the status of 'witness'). The children granted 'victim participant' status by the ICC are independent parties to the proceedings through their legal representatives who are acting on behalf of these child victim participants *as a group* which group may or may not be sizable (in contrast there is a possibility for only a comparatively small number of child witnesses to participate in any case for a number of logistical and other reasons).[59]

Some experts maintain that a child having ICC 'victim participant' status "may be less stressful for a child and is less likely to cause re-traumatisation" than the child fulfilling the role of ICC 'witness' who must personally testify if competent to do so (presumably that re-traumatisation, in some instances, may occur even where the child witness testifies anonymously (with the Court's permission); the child's face hidden and voice distorted).[60] Children holding 'victim participant status' before the ICC means that:

> Child victims can participate either directly or through their legal representatives in a number of ways, though they may need to apply for permission to do so from the Court.
>
> Children may:
>
> 1. Give observations to the judges while the Court is still deciding whether or not to proceed with an investigation or case;
> 2. Present their views to the judges when the Court is considering what charges will be brought against the accused person;
> 3. Attend and participate in hearings before the Court;
> 4. Ask questions to a witness or expert who is giving evidence before the Court, or to the accused;
> 5. Make statements before the Court at the beginning and end of a stage of proceedings.[61]

Many child victims of international crimes under the jurisdiction of the ICC, perhaps most, have no person or group to advocate on their behalf to access international justice in the first instance. There may be no outreach from the ICC or NGOs or from other groups or persons to these particular children to assist them to become either part of a 'victim participant' group before the ICC or ICC witnesses. This despite the fact that assuming one of these roles may be in the particular children's best interest and the children may have key first hand information to proffer relevant to the case. It is, in any case, important that key victim groups, including child victims, also have their voices heard during the proceedings if justice is to be done and victims to be fully respected.

Note that in the Lubanga case involving the war crime of recruiting and using children under age 15 for active participation in hostilities; only nine child witnesses were called by the Prosecution to testify as former child soldiers.[62] This limited number of child witnesses created some difficulties during the trial in respect of

---

[59] Office of the Secretary-General for Children and Armed Conflict, Working Paper No. 3 (2011, p. 18).

[60] Office of the Secretary-General for Children and Armed Conflict, Working Paper No. 3 (2011, p. 18).

[61] Office of the Secretary-General for Children and Armed Conflict, Working Paper No. 3 (2011, p. 15).

[62] Office of the Secretary-General for Children and Armed Conflict, Working Paper No. 3 (2011, p. 18).

establishing various facts. However, the credibility of certain of the child witnesses and the totality of the evidence from diverse sources including NGO representatives in the field at the relevant time was compelling enough for a conviction on the aforementioned war crime. (There were, in addition, 103 'victim participants' in the Lubanga case participating through their group's legal representatives).

As mentioned, there are marginalized child victims who are not heard at ICC proceedings despite their potential willingness and the critical importance of their particular evidence and insights regarding the facts of the case given their relevant personal experience. For instance, in respect of 'child soldiers':

> ...most children who have been recruited into armed forces have been separated from their parents and families at a young age, have not yet been reunited with their families and have no legal guardians.[63]

Unless a teacher; or some other adult; an NGO or ICC representative etc. assists such an ex child soldier to access justice and advocates for that child,[64] the child is unable to assume the role of 'victim participant' and/or witness before the ICC or readily access reparations for the harms caused to him or her as a direct victim. To become a 'victim participant' the child must make a formal application either directly or through a representative acting on the child's behalf[65] and most children do not have the skills to be able to do so on their own. Furthermore, anyone acting on behalf of the child must have the child's prior informed consent to do so in pursuing ICC victim participant status for the child and be able to prove the child's identity.[66] It may in fact be difficult to prove the child's identity and even their age given the lack of birth registration and difficulty or impossibility of obtaining other necessary and accurate documents in many countries; especially those that have experienced long periods of armed conflict. It may also be difficult to obtain the children's informed consent to act as 'victim participants' (i.e. the children in question may have been intimidated by the perpetrator group, the children may be too young to give informed consent and have no legal guardians or other acceptable representatives who can do so etc.). The ICC has, in some instances, however, accepted teachers and certain other adults as representatives of the child 'victim participants' where there are no legal guardians available so as not to deny these children the opportunity to access their legal entitlement to become ICC 'victim participants' and have their voice heard in the case.[67]

---

[63] Office of the Secretary-General for Children and Armed Conflict, Working Paper No. 3 (2011, p. 18).

[64] Office of the Secretary-General for Children and Armed Conflict, Working Paper No. 3 (2011, p. 18): "The number of children who may apply for victim status...is unlimited. Lawyers can act for groups of children, thus reducing legal costs for the Court and making it more likely that the child is able to access legal assistance."

[65] Office of the Secretary-General for Children and Armed Conflict, Working Paper No. 3 (2011, p. 18).

[66] Office of the Secretary-General for Children and Armed Conflict, Working Paper No. 3 (2011, p. 18).

[67] Office of the Secretary-General for Children and Armed Conflict, Working Paper No. 3 (2011, p. 18).

2.6 Truth and Reconciliation Mechanisms and Child Victims

To address the accountability of perpetrators of international crimes committed against children (i.e. 'genocidal forcible transfer of children' by means of the mass rape of children, sexual enslavement of children, the recruitment and use of children as child soldiers by armed groups or forces perpetrating mass atrocities and/or genocide) *exclusively* through Truth and Reconciliation processes (rather also through criminal prosecutions) would, on the analysis here, be to introduce an impermissible element of systemic discrimination based on age of the victims (in terms of ability to access the international criminal justice system). Sadly; it appears that many children participate in Truth and Reconciliation processes with false hopes of meaningful reparations[68] and a better life that never materialize:

> For most children, reparations which focused on providing access to education, health care, and accommodation were more important than a cash payment.[69]
>
> Children have high expectations of non-judicial justice processes, and especially of TRCs. Follow-up research with children who participated in such commissions revealed that they had expected that this form of justice would support them to find their families, help them return to education, assist them to learn a trade so that they could find employment, and live independently. *Those expectations, inevitably, could not all be met, leaving many children disappointed and disillusioned.*[70]

It is an open question as to whether in some, many or most instances; the children's cooperation with Truth and Reconciliation processes were obtained by raising false hopes for the children and/or their parents regarding what the children's participation would garner the children and/or their families in terms of assistance and access to a better quality of life. Note also that though child victims of international humanitarian and human rights law violations often prefer approaches to accountability in terms of traditional justice (justice according to local custom in their home territory), this approach was often not in the children's best interest:

> Research in Uganda has shown that although children favoured traditional justice, in practice, they had little understanding of it, and as a result derived little relief from it.[71]

The position advanced here is that: (1) respect for children as persons with human dignity and (2) upholding international humanitarian and human rights norms requires that access to justice for child victims of genocidal forcible transfer not be subverted by the failure to address the aforementioned grave international crime and to criminally prosecute those perpetrators most responsible for its

---

[68] Office of the Secretary-General for Children and Armed Conflict, Working Paper No. 3 (2011, p. 24): "In reality, reparations for children have been very limited. Even where the possibility of providing reparations exists in a country which has been engaged in armed conflict, funding for reparations has been an issue of concern."

[69] Office of the Secretary-General for Children and Armed Conflict, Working Paper No. 3 (2011, p. 24).

[70] Office of the Secretary-General for Children and Armed Conflict, Working Paper No. 3 (2011, p. 12, emphasis added).

[71] Office of the Secretary-General for Children and Armed Conflict, Working Paper No. 3 (2011, p. 23).

occurrence (the same applies of course in regards to other international crimes perpetrated against children). Child victims should have an opportunity to participate in such criminal prosecution processes as witnesses and/or victim participants. The perspective taken here is contrary to that of the Special Representative of the Secretary-General for Children and Armed Conflict who takes the position that access to justice for children can be "maximized"[72] by allowing children to participate in alternative accountability mechanisms such as 'Truth and Reconciliation Commissions'(TRC). The position taken by the current author is, in contrast, that simply "allow[ing] a wider number of children's voices to be heard"[73] at *non-judicial forums* has not, in practice, to date generally translated into much more than children reliving their suffering with no tangible benefit to the children; sense of vindication or judicial or other remedy for these child victims. Such non-judicial mechanisms then, on the analysis here, do *not* maximize justice (in theory or in practice) for children where perpetrators of international crimes under the jurisdiction of the ICC (crimes often involving masses of child victims) are not vigorously prosecuted by that august Court. Rather, on the view here, the failure to hold to account those most responsible through the mechanism of the ICC (where the domestic system has failed to do so) and/or relegating children to participation only in TRC forums results, in many instances, in a two tier system of international justice. That two tier system of international justice is one in which child victims are denied (ostensibly based on an alleged 'best interests of the child' rationale)[74] access to international criminal justice as victims in their own right (i.e. they are denied then the opportunity to hold the ICC status of witnesses and/or victim participants playing a direct role in the ICC proceedings and potentially also the opportunity for deserved reparations through the ICC depending on the situation).

Note that reparations can be ordered by the ICC to be made via the 'Trust Fund for Victims' (set up by the Assembly of States Parties in September 2002) and/or by the perpetrator(s) as provided for under Article 75 of the Rome Statute which follows:

Article 75

Reparations to victims

1. The Court shall establish principles relating to reparations to, or in respect of, victims, including restitution, compensation and rehabilitation. On this basis, in its decision the Court may, either upon request or on its own motion in exceptional circumstances, determine the scope and extent of any damage, loss and injury to, or in respect of, victims and will state the principles on which it is acting.

[72] Office of the Secretary-General for Children and Armed Conflict, Working Paper No. 3 (2011, p. 12).

[73] Office of the Secretary-General for Children and Armed Conflict, Working Paper No. 3 (2011, p. 12).

[74] Even very young children and highly traumatized children could be represented as victim participants before the ICC such that they need not personally testify. In some instances, this would likely be less stressful than such children testifying before a Truth and Reconciliation forum.

2. The Court may make an order directly against a convicted person specifying appropriate reparations to, or in respect of, victims, including restitution, compensation and rehabilitation.

 Where appropriate, the Court may order that the award for reparations be made through the Trust Fund provided for in article 79…[75]

Maximizing for children the quality of international criminal justice received and their access to justice under international criminal law (such as under the Rome Statute[76]) then, on the view here, requires, as a precondition, *parity* in terms of: (1) vigorous prosecution also of the perpetrators most responsible for grave violations of international criminal law in respect of the child victim group *in particular* as compared to victim groups of mixed ages or groups comprised exclusively of persons aged 18 years and over; (2) equal access to justice in terms of a representative sample of the range of child victims playing a role in the international criminal proceedings as 'witnesses' and/or 'victim participants'; and (3) equal access to reparations compared to adult victims in consideration of the severity of the harms done to the child victims (due to the crimes perpetrated against them as defined under international criminal law statutes) and such other relevant factors as can be established.

2.7 An Additional Note Regarding Child Soldier Victims of the 'Genocidal Forcible Transfer of Children'

This author has argued that it is consistent with: (1) the interests of justice and (2) a legally supportable analysis of the Rome Statute[77] provision on genocide that children recruited into armed forces or groups perpetrating mass atrocity and/or genocide be regarded as victims of the genocidal forcible transfer of children and hence non-culpable for any international crimes they commit while so victimized. Others have argued, in contrast, that child soldier members of State or non-State armed forces or groups perpetrating conflict-related international crimes who themselves commit atrocities are 'war criminals' (even if also victims) who need to be held to account; preferably through non-judicial accountability mechanisms such as Truth and Reconciliation or customary local accountability mechanisms.[78]

The current author maintains instead that:

> …individual criminal culpability does not attach to child soldiers (persons under age 18 at the time of the [perpetrating of the] alleged international crimes)…operating… as victims of genocidal forcible transfer to another group [the armed State or non-State group or force perpetrating the mass atrocities and/or genocide].[79]

[75] Rome Statute (2002).

[76] Rome Statute (2002).

[77] Rome Statute (2002).

[78] Drumbl (2012).

[79] Grover (2012, p. 31).

This author has argued that children who have been what is euphemistically referred to as 'recruited' to State or non-State armed forces or groups committing mass atrocities and/or genocide are in fact: (1) non-combatant civilians who have no unqualified right under international humanitarian law to be soldiers in any case unlike the situation for adults (were the latter recruited into a lawful force)[80] and (2) victims of the grave international crime of the genocidal forcible transfer of children to another group (here that other group being the State or non-State armed force or group operating outside the margins of civilized society and committing heinous international crimes).[81] Children's participation in armed hostilities is considered in principle to be an anomaly under international humanitarian law and no more so than when these children are actively participating with armed forces or groups perpetrating grave international crimes. The latter customary humanitarian law perspective has been even more clearly affirmed under newly evolved international human rights law, at least in respect of the direct involvement of children in hostilities generally. That is to say, for instance, that Article 1 of the Optional Protocol to the Convention on the Rights of the Child on the involvement of children in armed conflict (OP-CRC-AC) requires that: "Sates Parties shall take all feasible measures to ensure that members of their armed forces who have not attained the age of 18 years do not take a direct part in hostilities" while Article 4(1) of the same Protocol stipulates that: "Armed groups that are distinct from the armed forces of a State should not, under any circumstances, recruit or use in hostilities persons under the age of 18 years."[82]

Thus, on the analysis here, child soldiers as victims of 'genocidal forcible transfer' to State or non-State armed forces or groups *committing mass atrocities and/or genocide* are in a situation that, by definition, involves duress (i.e. the children are not free to leave these murderous armed groups or forces or to decline orders to commit atrocities and any attempt to do so is at the risk of their lives etc.). The status of these children as victims of genocidal forcible transfer thus renders inapplicable the question of the children's *mens rea* to commit war crimes and other conflict-related international crimes and the issue of accountability on the part of these children as alleged perpetrators.

The contention here is, further, that these child soldier victims of the 'genocidal forcible transfer of children' retain their status as child civilians entitled under international humanitarian law to special protection by the State and international community in times of armed conflict[83] (special protection that the State and international community failed abysmally to deliver). This is not at all to say (contrary to the implication that Drumbl has erroneously taken away from this author's comments in a previous work)[84] that in general civilians caught up in internal armed conflict are not bound by the rules of war and cannot be held culpable for war crimes or other

---

[80] Grover (2008b).

[81] Grover (2012).

[82] OP-CRC-AC (2002).

[83] Note that the children retain their civilian status even after 'recruitment' as so-called 'child soldiers' to armed groups or forces committing international crimes.

[84] Drumbl (2012, p. 106).

conflict-related international crimes. The latter cases, however, can be distinguished from the situation of child soldier victims of genocidal forcible transfer to State or non-State armed forces or groups committing mass atrocities and/or genocide. This is best illustrated by way of a couple of case examples in which civilians have been charged with war crimes. We will consider then the Essen Lynching case, *Hadamar* and the Zyklon B cases[85] simply because these are the cases referred to by name in Drumbl's aforementioned comments regarding civilians charged with war crimes and his contention that child soldiers are justifiably equally liable under international criminal law for conflict-related atrocity (although he suggests that it is best to hold such children to account via non-judicial mechanisms).

The Essen Lynching case was tried before the British Military Court for the trial of war criminals, Essen, 1945. The case dealt, in part, with German *civilians* who had killed three unarmed British prisoners of war while the POWs were in the custody of a German private who had been entrusted with their safety and they were being marched through the streets of Essen on the way to a Luftwaffe unit for interrogation. The civilians who had committed these killings did so on their own volition rather than under duress. One civilian was sentenced to death, two to imprisonment and two were acquitted by the military tribunal.

The Hadamar case (tried before the United States Military Commission, Wiesbaden, Germany, 1945) involved civilians who were staff at a sanatorium in Hadamar, Germany who killed 400 allied nationals (Poles and Soviets) by means of lethal poisonous injections:

> It was clearly established that between 5th or 6th June, 1944, and 13th March, 1945, there took place numerous shipments of Polish and Russian men, women and children to Hadamar from various other institutions and camps in Germany or German-occupied territory. Their number totalled 476 and all were killed within one or two days after their arrival at the institution, either by hypodermic injections of morphine or scopolamine, or derivatives thereof, or by doses of veronal or chloral. It was repeatedly testified that all were killed and that there was no evidence that any who arrived avoided death, except for one woman who escaped from the institution.[86]

Amongst other pleas, the civilians accused in *Hadamar*, argued duress:

> The accused also pleaded coercion or necessity but the Military Commission considered this defence to be established neither in fact nor in law.[87]

The Zylon B case (tried by British Military Court, Hamburg, Germany, 1946) involved the complicity of civilians in the murder by means of poisonous gas (Zylon B) of allied nationals interned in Nazi concentration camps. The civilians charged were the owner and technicians of a firm that supplied poisonous gas to the SS and held the monopoly in this regard:

> The activities with which the accused in the ...case were charged were commercial transactions conducted by civilians.[88]

---

85 UN War Crimes Commission, Law Reports of Trials of War Criminals, Vol. 1 (1947).

86 UN War Crimes Commission, Law Reports of Trials of War Criminals, Vol. 1 (1947, p. 47).

87 UN War Crimes Commission, Law Reports of Trials of War Criminals, Vol. 1 (1947, p. 47).

88 UN War Crimes Commission, Law Reports of Trials of War Criminals, Vol. 1 (1947, p. 103).

The Court rejected the notion that the two civilians ultimately found guilty had no knowledge of the use to which the Zylon B was being put by the SS in the concentration camps or that these civilians had no power to interfere with its shipment in furtherance of the Nazi objective. Two of the three civilians in the Zylon B case were found guilty and executed, the third accused was acquitted.

In each of the above cases the civilians criminally charged were not directly in the custody and control of commanders ordering that they commit violations of international humanitarian law. Furthermore, duress was not factually or legally established. Whether one agrees with the military court rulings in the aforementioned cases regarding duress in every instance or not; this aspect of the case analysis was clearly central to the case outcomes.[89] In contrast then child soldier members of armed groups or forces perpetrating mass atrocities or genocide are: (1) civilians who are directly in the custody and control of commanders ordering that they commit grave violations of international humanitarian law (they are victims of genocidal forcible transfer of children where 'child', according to the elements of the crime as set out in Rome Statute Article 6(e), refers to a person under age 18)[90] and are (2) under extreme duress as the factual evidence in cases such as Lubanga[91] and Joseph Kony[92] demonstrate (i.e. the children receive brutal military training and as part of the training are ordered to commit atrocities (often against their own family or communities), children face beatings and even possible execution if they try to escape the custody of the armed group or force and child soldiers are directly ordered to participate in mass atrocities and even, in some instances, genocide).

There have been cases where children too have been tried by military tribunals by the very States that failed to fulfill their *jus cogens* obligation[93] to protect the children to the extent feasible from participation with armed groups or forces committing mass atrocities and/or genocide:

> In . . .The Democratic Republic of the Congo (DRC), child soldiers who have escaped the armed forces have been charged with desertion, tried before a military tribunal, and sentenced to imprisonment. In the DRC, child soldiers who have been convicted by a military tribunal have, in some cases, even been executed. In 2000, a 14-year-old child soldier was tried by a military court for murder and executed 30 minutes later.[94]

---

[89] There may be borderline cases involving civilians charged with war crimes where the ruling on duress is difficult to make in certain instances. The point here, however, is rather that the existence of duress for child soldier members of armed groups or forces committing mass atrocities and/or genocide is an inherent feature of such a situation (i.e. the children have been forcibly transferred to the group or force such that they have been completely appropriated by the group or force whether initially recruited through alleged voluntary enlistment or not).

[90] Rome Statute Elements of the Crime (2002).

[91] Prosecutor v Lubanga (2012).

[92] Prosecutor v Joseph Kony (2005).

[93] Grover (2012, pp. 28–50).

[94] Office of the Secretary-General for Children and Armed Conflict, Working Paper No. 3 (2011, p.40).

It should be noted also that children's fundamental rights in such military tribunal prosecutions have most often been severely compromised, if respected at all, such that these child defendants have been denied justice and due process:

> Children are frequently tried without any legal representation or assistance, are not accompanied by their parents or legal guardian, and often do not have access to the charges brought against them.[95] Military tribunals are not required to treat children's best interests as their primary concern, and, therefore, are not an appropriate forum for hearing cases against children. Not surprisingly, the CRC Committee has recommended that children should not be tried before military tribunals.[96]

It appears that States are often intent on creating *the illusion* of pursuing justice through holding 'child soldier' victims of genocidal forcible transfer to account through military or non-military judicial process or via alternative accountability mechanisms (i.e. the TRC forum). This attempt to hold accountable child victims of genocidal forcible transfer is legally insupportable given the entirely foreseeable consequences of the *State's failure to protect* these children during armed conflict (i.e. from 'recruitment' into armed groups or forces perpetrating mass atrocities and/or genocide). For instance:

> Rwanda was the first country to hold individuals accountable for crimes of genocide committed as "minors," defined under the Rwandan Penal Code as individuals aged 14–18 when the crime was committed. Of the 120,000 people arrested and detained following the adoption of the Genocide Law in 1996, more than 4,000 were children.
>
> Up until 2007, when a separate provision for "mitigating circumstances for children" was introduced, those who were found to have committed genocide when they were still a child received the same punishment as adults. Despite the late recognition of the status of children and reduced sentences, no specific procedures were put in place for an accused or witness who was a minor during the genocide.[97]

It should be noted also that children captured and held in detention during armed conflict as alleged security threats or due to their involvement with armed groups or forces committing international crimes are often held under conditions that violate international human rights and humanitarian law.[98]

In contrast to military tribunals or State non-military court prosecutions of child soldiers, international criminal tribunals such as the ICTY and ICTR that incorporated *no* minimum age of criminal responsibility chose *not* to prosecute child soldiers (persons under 18 at the time of committing the crime)[99] as was also the case for the SCSL which in fact had jurisdiction over children aged 15 and over who had committed crimes falling under the court's purview.[100]

---

[95] On the point of military tribunals denying children's fundamental legal rights see also the following regarding the U.S. case of Omar Khadr: Grover (2009, 2011).

[96] Office of the Secretary-General for Children and Armed Conflict, Working Paper No. 3 (2011, p.40).

[97] Office of the Secretary-General for Children and Armed Conflict, Working Paper No. 3 (2011, p. 40).

[98] Office of the Secretary-General for Children and Armed Conflict, Working Paper No. 3 (2011, p. 41).

[99] Office of the Secretary-General for Children and Armed Conflict, Working Paper No. 3 (2011, p. 37).

[100] Office of the Secretary-General for Children and Armed Conflict, Working Paper No. 3 (2011, p. 37).

2.8 Child Soldiers and the Question of Potential State Criminal Liability

While this book concerns ICC jurisprudence which deals exclusively with the criminal liability of *individual perpetrators* of the crimes under the jurisdiction of the Court, it is relevant to raise the question of potential State criminal liability for: (1) failure of the State to protect children from genocidal forcible transfer to another group (such as armed groups or forces perpetrating mass atrocities and/or genocide) and from other international crimes and for (2) possible complicity in the commission of grave international crimes which victimize children also or children in particular. To date no State has been held *criminally liable* for genocide or other grave international crimes nor has the notion of State criminal liability as of yet been generally considered practicable under international law.

The current author contends that where the State intentionally and knowingly: (1) refrains from doing what is feasible and necessary for that State, given its resources and the circumstances, to prevent individuals or organized networks of *genocidaires* from carrying out their genocidal intentions within its territory or in neighboring territories and/or (2) declines to punish these perpetrators of genocide most responsible even where feasible in the circumstance, this amounts to the State *committing* or facilitating genocide and triggers State criminal liability.[101] That is, the aforementioned facts can, on the current analysis, be taken to prove *State* genocidal intent which, along with the occurrence of genocidal acts perpetrated by agents of the State or rebels, supports the notion of State criminal liability. In this regard, however, recall that the International Court of Justice in *Bosnian Genocide* held that the Genocide Convention[102] does not *expressly* prohibit *States* from committing genocide[103]; a point we will return to momentarily. It is in part perhaps for the reason that the Genocide Convention[104] contains no such *express* prohibition on States that perhaps most legal scholars contend (erroneously on the respectful view here) that the Genocide Convention[105] only stipulates that individuals (but not States) can be held criminally liable for genocide.

State political considerations and concerns with State sovereignty and how to avoid unwanted interventions by the international community seem key to the resistance by States to the notion of State criminal liability for genocide (as opposed

[101] It may be necessary, in some instances, consistent with the ICC complementarity principle; and in order to meet State legal obligations under international law, for the State Party to self-refer the matter to the ICC. Even if a non-State party to the Rome Statute (2002); it may be necessary in the interests of respecting international legal norms for the State to accept the jurisdiction of the ICC in regards to situations involving genocide and other international crimes under ICC jurisdiction (i.e. where the State is unwilling or unable to properly investigate and prosecute perpetrators).

[102] Genocide Convention (1951).

[103] Bosnia and Herzegovina v. Serbia and Montenegro (2007, p. 74, para 166).

[104] Genocide Convention (1951).

[105] Genocide Convention (1951).

to that approach being based on sound and just legal principles). The failure to attribute criminal liability to States in respect of genocide, on the view here, contradicts the spirit of international criminal law such as the genocide provision in the Rome Statute[106] and the Genocide Convention[107] since:

> ...an exclusive individualistic approach ...completely fails to capture the involvement of the State in the perpetration of the crime. As States must have been aware just a few years after the Holocaust, *genocide is hardly conceivable without the availability of a State apparatus. Its systematic nature requires active participation of the State, or at the very least its acquiescence.*[108]

Indeed, the International Court of Justice in *Bosnian Genocide* held that despite there being in the Genocide Convention no *express* prohibition on States not to commit genocide; this prohibition was yet implied:

> ...in the view of the Court, taking into account the established purpose of the Convention, the *effect of Article I is to prohibit States from themselves committing genocide*. Such a prohibition follows, first, from the fact that the Article categorizes genocide as "a crime under international law": by agreeing to such a categorization, the States parties must logically be undertaking not to commit the act so described. Secondly, it follows from the expressly stated obligation to prevent the commission of acts of genocide.[109]

Certain judges on the *Bosnian Genocide* International Court of Justice panel contended that to hold that a State can *commit* genocide was at the same time to affirm that the notion of State criminal liability was, by implication, contemplated in theory (though the majority in *Bosnian Genocide* explicitly rejected that inference as being a necessary one)[110]:

> At least five Judges within the majority argued in declarations and separate opinions that the acceptance by the Court that a State can *commit* the crime of genocide necessarily implies accepting that *a State can incur criminal responsibility*.[111]

It is here contended that it is legally justifiable that criminal liability attach to the State in cases of genocide (and in cases of crimes against humanity or widespread or planned war crimes) where: (1) the State apparatus was vital to perpetrating the crime and/or (2) no efforts were made by State officials in a position to affect the course of events to any material degree to stop or at least hinder the commission of these systematic and widespread international crimes. At present, only civil liability potentially attaches to the State in such instances as per Article IX of the

---

[106] Rome Statute (2002).

[107] Genocide Convention (1951).

[108] Breuker (2007, p.46, emphasis added).

[109] Bosnia and Herzegovina v. Serbia and Montenegro (2007, p. 74, para 166, emphasis added).

[110] Bosnia and Herzegovina v. Serbia and Montenegro (2007, p. 74, para 167): "... the international responsibility of a State — even though quite different in nature from criminal responsibility...".

[111] Breuker (2007, p.44, emphasis added).

Genocide Convention.[112] The current author would argue that just as the potential civil liability attaching to a State in cases such as genocide does not imply 'collective responsibility' so too is this the case should criminal liability also attach to the State in the same circumstance. Rather, the State criminal liability affirmed by the international community would be an acknowledgement simply that the State apparatus was used to inflict enormous harms arising out of systematic and/or widespread grave international crimes (the latter occurring with or without the acquiescence and endorsement of the general civilian population and/or domestic military for instance depending on the situation/case) and/or the State was non-resistant.

The current author has alluded elsewhere to the need to hold States also criminally liable (and not just individual perpetrators) for the recruitment and use of child soldiers to participate in armed hostilities with armed groups or forces perpetrating mass atrocities and/or genocide[113] (such recruitment and use of children amounting to the 'genocidal forcible transfer of children').[114] In this regard, however, Drumbl asks:

> Many child soldiers are used by armed groups that fight against the state. How can the state realistically be held criminally responsible for the unlawful use of children by such armed groups?[115]

It is here contended that the criminal liability of the State derives from: (1) the failure of the State to prevent; or at least make all necessary and feasible efforts to prevent or hinder the genocidal forcible transfer of children (i.e. as when children under the State's jurisdiction and control are recruited and used by armed groups or forces to perpetrate mass atrocities and/or genocide in the context of an international or internal armed conflict) and/or (2) the unjustified failure of the State to punish the perpetrators most responsible for this form of the genocidal forcible transfer of children (using the principle of universal jurisdiction if need be)[116] and for other international crimes (i.e. 'war crimes' and 'crimes against humanity') and/or (3) the State's failure to protect; or attempt to take all feasible and necessary measures to protect children affected by armed conflict as a special protected group under international humanitarian law (i.e. as per Protocols I or II Additional the Geneva Convention; whichever is applicable in the situation).[117] The criminal

[112] Article IX Genocide Convention (1951): Disputes between the Contracting Parties relating to the interpretation, application or fulfilment of the present Convention, including those relating to the *responsibility of a State for genocide or for any of the other acts enumerated in article III*, shall be submitted to the International Court of Justice at the request of any of the parties to the dispute (emphasis added).

[113] Grover (2008b, pp. 61–62).

[114] Grover (2012).

[115] Drumbl (2012, p. 107).

[116] The obligation to prevent genocide and punish perpetrators attaches to the State parties to the Genocide Convention and under the Rome Statute even to States that are not a party to the Rome Statute (where situations are referred to the ICC).

[117] Protocols I and II Additional to the Geneva Conventions (1977).

liability, for instance, of the State in respect of the recruitment and use of children (persons under 18) by armed groups or forces perpetrating grave international crimes thus, in large part, derives from the *failure to protect* these children from State and/or rebel perpetrators to the extent feasible and necessary. Thus, on the perspective here, State criminal liability derives from the 'failure to protect' and/or from direct complicity of the State in perpetrating international crimes and/or failure to prosecute perpetrators to the extent feasible.[118] This author is in accord then with those judges in *Bosnian Genocide*[119] who held that to accede to the notion that the State can "commit" genocide (as did the ICJ majority in *Bosnian Genocide*[120]) is to conclude that the State can potentially be held criminally liable for genocide.

2.9 'The Interests of Justice' and ICC Case Admissibility

Where the State is or has been unwilling or unable to adequately protect children from genocidal forcible transfer (or from other international crimes under ICC jurisdiction for that matter) and provide the child victims reparations for past such violations; it is, on the view here, obviously *not* in the interests of justice for the ICC prosecutor to: (1) decline to initiate an investigation or (2) refrain from prosecuting the crime of 'genocidal forcible transfer of children' despite the gravity of the crime where, in a particular case, there is a reasonable basis for prosecution by the ICC. The current author holds, further, that in any case where the grave crime of genocidal forcible transfer of children is not investigated and vigorously prosecuted by the ICC Prosecutor (assuming all jurisdictional and admissibility requirements are met): (1) children's best interests and fundamental rights as human beings and legal persons are grossly devalued if not negated; (2) the international community has failed in meeting its general fiduciary duty as stipulated under international human rights and humanitarian law to this special protected group (children) and (3) the integrity and credibility of the international legal system itself is damaged as: (a) the gravity of certain international crimes committed against some of the most vulnerable among us (children) are then in practice *in effect* not adequately acknowledged and (b) the perpetrators most responsible for committing these atrocities enjoy impunity and are thereby encouraged in some instances to persist with such crimes. Thus, on the analysis here, the failure to investigate and to prosecute the crime of the genocidal forcible transfer of children is never in the interests of justice nor that of the international

[118] The discussion here has focused on the State duty to protect children (persons under age 18) against becoming child soldier victims of genocidal forcible transfer but there is also a State duty under international humanitarian law [and for State Parties to the Rome Statute (2002)] to protect children under age 15 from recruitment as child soldiers and/or participation in armed conflict regardless whether the armed group or force involved follows international law in other respects.

[119] Bosnia and Herzegovina v. Serbia and Montenegro (2007).

[120] Bosnia and Herzegovina v. Serbia and Montenegro (2007).

legal regime. Let us consider then in more detail what constitutes "the interests of justice" in the ICC legal regime as that notion is set out in Article 53 of the Rome Statute:

> **Rome Statute**
> PART 5. INVESTIGATION AND PROSECUTION
> Article 53
> **Initiation of an investigation**
>
> The Prosecutor shall, having evaluated the information made available to him or her, initiate an investigation unless he or she determines that there is no reasonable basis to proceed under this Statute. In deciding whether to initiate an investigation, the Prosecutor shall consider whether:
>
> (a) The information available to the Prosecutor provides a reasonable basis to believe that a crime within the jurisdiction of the Court has been or is being committed;
>
> (b) The case is or would be admissible under article 17; and
>
> (c) ***Taking into account the gravity of the crime and the interests of victims, there are nonetheless substantial reasons to believe that an investigation would not serve the interests of justice.***
>
> If the Prosecutor determines that there is no reasonable basis to proceed and his or her determination is based solely on subparagraph (c) above, he or she shall inform the Pre-Trial Chamber.
>
> 2. If, upon investigation, the Prosecutor concludes that there is not a sufficient basis for a prosecution because:
>
> (a) There is not a sufficient legal or factual basis to seek a warrant or summons under article 58;
>
> (b) The case is inadmissible under article 17; or
>
> (c) ***A prosecution is not in the interests of justice, taking into account all the circumstances, including the gravity of the crime, the interests of victims and the age or infirmity of the alleged perpetrator, and his or her role in the alleged crime;***
>
> *the Prosecutor shall inform the Pre-Trial Chamber and the State making a referral under article 14 or the Security Council in a case under article 13, paragraph (b), of his or her conclusion and the reasons for the conclusion.*
>
> 3. (a) At the request of the State making a referral under article 14 or the Security Council under article 13, paragraph (b), the Pre-Trial Chamber may review a decision of the Prosecutor under paragraph 1 or 2 not to proceed and may request the Prosecutor to reconsider that decision.
>
> (b) In addition, the Pre-Trial Chamber may, on its own initiative, review a decision of the Prosecutor not to proceed if it is based solely on paragraph 1 (c) or 2 (c). In such a case, the decision of the Prosecutor shall be effective only if confirmed by the Pre-Trial Chamber.
>
> 4. The Prosecutor may, at any time, reconsider a decision whether to initiate an investigation or prosecution based on new facts or information.[121]

The ICC Prosecutor has expressed the view that "the issue of the interests of justice, as it appears in Article 53 of the Rome Statute, represents one of the most complex aspects of the Treaty" and has pointed out that "there is no clear guidance on what the content of the idea [interests of justice] is... [and] it is never defined [in the ICC Statute or Rules of Procedure and Evidence]"[122] though it is clear that the

[121] Rome Statute, Article 53 (2002, emphasis added).

[122] ICC Office of the Prosecutor (2007). Policy Paper on the Interests of Justice (2007, p. 2).

concept is *not* equivalent to the notion of "the interests of peace."[123] The ICC Prosecutor has also held that:

> ...the exercise of the Prosecutor's discretion under Article 53(1)(c) and 53 (2)(c) is exceptional in its nature ... ***there is a presumption in favour of investigation or prosecution wherever the criteria established in Article 53(1) (a) and (b) or Article 53(2)(a) and (b) have been met.***[124]

The ICC Prosecutor has clarified the point that the OTP need *not* establish that an investigation is in the interests of justice in order to be able to proceed (assuming admissibility and jurisdictional criteria have been met). Rather, 'interests of justice' considerations may act as a *countervailing* factor to block an investigation or prosecution notwithstanding the fact that all other tests are met·[125] In his 2007 policy paper, the ICC Prosecutor claimed that: "The Prosecutor has not yet made a decision not to investigate or not to proceed with a prosecution because it would not serve the interests of justice."[126] Yet, arguably by failing to acknowledge the rampant occurrence of the grave international crime of the 'genocidal forcible transfer of children'[127] as will be discussed here in Part III to follow, the *de facto* erroneous implication is that it is not in the 'interests of justice' to investigate, charge and prosecute the crime of 'genocidal forcible transfer of children'.

Note also that the ICC Prosecutor states that:

> It is possible ...that even an individual deemed by the OTP to be among the "most responsible" would not be prosecuted in the "interests of justice." If the Court is to achieve the lasting respect for the enforcement of international justice, it is essential that it considers also the interests of the accused. It is common in many legal systems to require consideration of the circumstances of the accused before determining whether to proceed to a prosecution. For example, international justice may not be served by the prosecution of a ...defendant or a suspect who has been the subject of abuse amounting to serious human rights violations.[128]

In regards to the quote immediately above then it is relevant to note that the OTP chose to investigate and prosecute Dominic Ongwen; a commander in the LRA despite the fact that Ongwen was abducted at age 10 and transferred to the LRA to participate in the commission of mass atrocities as a child soldier. It is indisputable that as a child soldier with the LRA, Ongwen had been subjected to grave human rights violations for decades before it came to pass that he himself committed

---

[123] ICC Office of the Prosecutor (2007). Policy Paper on the Interests of Justice (2007, p. 4).

[124] ICC Office of the Prosecutor (2007). Policy Paper on the Interests of Justice (2007, p. 1, emphasis added).

[125] ICC Office of the Prosecutor (2007). Policy Paper on the Interests of Justice (2007, p. 2).

[126] ICC Office of the Prosecutor (2007). Policy Paper on the Interests of Justice (2007, p. 4).

[127] The reference here is to genocidal forcible transfer of children by means of the recruitment and use of children for participation as child soldiers with armed groups or forces committing mass atrocities and/or genocide, and the mass rape and sexual enslavement of children by such perpetrators (where 'children' refers to persons under age 18) such that the children are considered 'children of the enemy' (or children of the perpetrator group).

[128] ICC Office of the Prosecutor (2007). Policy Paper on the Interests of Justice (2007, p. 7).

international crimes as an adult (a person aged 18 or over) such that the Court jurisdiction was not barred on account of the age of the perpetrator at the time of the crime (this author has argued in fact that Ongwen was a child victim of genocidal forcible transfer to the LRA).[129] Yet, despite, on the view here, Ongwen being the victim of genocidal forcible transfer to the LRA, this was not an apparent consideration under the 'interests of justice' criterion in the ICC Prosecutor's assessment of that particular case.

The ICC Prosecutor has stated that: "The best guidance on the Office's [ICC OTP] approach to these issues [i.e. 'interests of justice' issues in considering whether to investigate and/or prosecute] can be gathered *from the way it has dealt with real situations*."[130] On that basis then one may rightfully be deeply concerned by the failure of ICC jurisprudence to address the issue of the 'genocidal forcible transfer of children' in a host of situations and cases dealt with by the Court but framed so as to exclude any consideration of the aforementioned crime. Let us turn then to Part III of this book to: (1) examine selected ICC cases and situations in the context of which, according to the analysis here, the genocidal forcible transfer of children did occur and (2) the ICC failure to: (a) address the phenomenon of genocidal forcible transfer of children in its various forms and (b) to hold to account the perpetrators most responsible for this grave international crime perpetrated against children.

Literature, Materials and Situations/Cases

Literature

Breuker L (2007) The nature of the genocide case. Hague Justice J 2:44–54

DeGuzman MM (2009) Gravity and the legitimacy of the International Criminal Court. Fordham Int Law J 32(5):1400–1465

Drumbl MA (2012) Reimagining child soldiers in international law and policy. Oxford University Press, New York

Grover S (2012) Child soldier victims of genocidal forcible transfer: exonerating child soldiers charged with grave conflict-related international crimes. Springer, Berlin

Grover S (2011) The Supreme Court of Canada's declining of its jurisdiction in not ordering the repatriation of a Canadian Guantanamo detainee: implications of the case for our understanding of international humanitarian law. Int J Hum Rights 15(3):481–508

Grover S (2009) Canada's refusal to repatriate a Canadian citizen from Guantanamo Bay as a violation of the humanitarian values underlying the principle of non-refoulement: a reanalysis of the reasoning in Omar Ahmed Khadr v The Prime Minister of Canada et al. High Court Q Rev 5(2):42–48

Grover S (2008a) The child's right to legal standing. LexisNexis, Markham

[129] Grover (2012, pp. 248–255).

[130] ICC Office of the Prosecutor (2007). Policy Paper on the Interests of Justice (2007, p. 9, emphasis added).

Grover S (2008b) Child soldiers as non-combatants: the inapplicability of the Refugee Convention exclusion clause. Int J Hum Right 12(1):53–65

Oberg MD (2009) The absorption of grave breaches into war crimes law. Int Rev Red Cross 91(873). http://www.icrc.org/eng/assets/files/other/irrc-873-divac-oberg.pdf. Accessed 10 Jun 2012

Palmer S (1997) Case note: rape in marriage and the European Convention on Human Rights (*SW v United Kingdom and CR v United Kingdom*). Feminist Legal Stud 5(I):91–97

Materials

Convention on the Rights of the Child (CRC) (1990) Entered into force 2 September 1990. http://www2.ohchr.org/english/law/pdf/crc.pdf. Accessed 27 Oct 2011

Genocide Convention (1951) (Convention on the Prevention and Punishment of the Crime of Genocide) Entry into force 1951. http://www.preventgenocide.org/law/convention/text.htm. Accessed 3 Feb 2012

ICC Office of the Prosecutor (2007) Policy paper on the interests of justice. http://www.icc-cpi.int/NR/rdonlyres/772C95C9-F54D-4321-BF09-73422BB23528/143640/ICCOTPInterestsOfJustice.pdf. Accessed 13 Mar 2012

Office of the Secretary-General for Children and Armed Conflict (2011) Working Paper No. 3: Children and justice during and in the aftermath of armed conflict. http://reliefweb.int/sites/reliefweb.int/files/resources/Full_Report_1957.pdf. Accessed 7 Mar 2012

Optional Protocol to the Convention on the Rights of the Child on the involvement of children in armed conflict (2002) Entered into force 12 February, 2002. http://www2.ohchr.org/english/law/crc-conflict.htm. Accessed 26 Feb 2012

Protocol Additional to the 1949 Geneva Conventions relating to the Protection of victims of international armed conflicts (Protocol I) (8 June, 1977) http://www.icrc.org/ihl.nsf/FULL/470?OpenDocument. Accessed 18 Jan 2012

Protocol Additional to the 1949 Geneva Conventions Relating to the Protection of victims of non-international armed conflicts (Protocol II) (8 June, 1977) http://www.icrc.org/ihl.nsf/INTRO/475. Accessed 18 Jan 2012

Rome Statute (2002) Entered into force 7 January, 2002. http://untreaty.un.org/cod/icc/statute/romefra.htm. Accessed 17 Jan 2011

UN Common Approach to Justice for Children (2008) http://www.unrol.org/doc.aspx?n=UNCommonApproachJfCFinal.doc. Accessed 7 Mar 2012

Situations and Cases

Bosnia and Herzegovina v. Serbia and Montenegro (International Court of Justice) (Judgment of 26 February, 2007) http://www.icj-cij.org/docket/files/91/13685.pdf. Accessed 13 Mar 2012

Prosecutor v. Abdallah Banda Abakaer Nourain and Saleh Mohammed Jerbo Jamus (Summons to Appear 27 August, 2009) http://www.icc-cpi.int/menus/icc/situations%20and%20cases/situations/situation%20icc%200205/related%20cases/icc02050309/icc02050309. Accessed 12 Mar 2012

Prosecutor v. Omar Hassan Ahmad Al Bashir, Second Warrant for Arrest for Omar Hassan Ahmad Al Bashir (Pre-Trial Chamber I, 12 July, 2010) http://www.icc-cpi.int/iccdocs/doc/doc907140.pdf. Accessed 14 May 2012

Prosecutor v Bahar Idriss Abu Grada (Summons to Appear 7 May, 2009) http://www.icc-cpi.int/Menus/ICC/Situations+and+Cases/Situations/Situation+ICC+0205/. Accessed 12 Mar 2012

Prosecutor v Joseph Kony. Warrant for Arrest for Joseph Kony Issued on 8 July, 2005 as amended on 27 September, 2005 http://www.icc-cpi.int/iccdocs/doc/doc97185.PDF. Accessed 1 Mar 2012

Prosecutor v Thomas Lubanga Dyilo, Final Trial Judgement Pursuant to Article 74 of the Rome Statute (14 March, 2012) http://www.icc-cpi.int/iccdocs/doc/doc1379838.pdf. Accessed 20 Mar 2012

Situation in Darfur, Sudan, Pre-Trial Chamber I Summary of the Prosecutor's Application under Article 58, 20 November, 2008 (ICC-02/05-162) http://www.haguejusticeportal.net/Docs/Court%20Documents/ICC/Bahar-Idriss-Abu-Garda-Summary-of-Prosecutor-Application-under-Article-58.pdf. Accessed 11 Mar 2012

Situation in the Democratic Republic of the Congo, Ex Parte, Prosecutor Only, ICC Appeals Chamber, Judgment on the Prosecutor's Appeal Against the Decision of Pre-Trial Chamber I entitled "Decision on the Prosecutor's Application for Warrants of Arrest, Article 58"(13 July, 2006) http://www.icc-cpi.int/NR/exeres/A9D9C589-BE55-45F9-9F33-AD682A506531.htm. Accessed 9 Mar 2012

UN War Crimes Commission, Law Reports of Trials of War Criminals, Vol. 1 (1947) pp 46–54, 88–92, 93–103. www.loc.gov/rr/frd/Military_Law/pdf/Law-Reports_Vol-1.pdf. Accessed 10 Mar 2012

Part III
Selected ICC Cases Illustrating the Failure to Address the Genocidal Forcible Transfer of Children

Chapter 3
Case 1: Prosecutor v. Thomas Lubanga Dyilo (Hereafter Also Referred to as *Lubanga*)

3.1 The War Crimes Charges: On Why They Were Insufficient

3.1.1 The Confirmed Charges[1]

(1) Thomas Lubanga Dyilo was charged as co-perpetrator under Rome Statute Article 8(2)(b)(xxvi) ("Other serious violations of the laws and customs applicable in *international* armed conflict, within the established framework of international law") with conscripting and enlisting children under the age of 15 years into the FPLC (Patriotic Forces for the Liberation of Congo) and using them to participate actively in hostilities from early September 2002 to 2 June, 2003[2] and (2) as co-perpetrator under Rome Statute Article 8(2)(e)(vii) ("Other serious violations of the laws and customs applicable in armed conflicts *not* of an international character, within the established framework of international law") with conscripting and enlisting children under the age of 15 years into the FPLC and using them to participate actively in hostilities from 2 June to 13 August, 2003.[3] As co-perpetrator Lubanga is held to have made, at a minimum, a 'substantial' (though not necessarily 'essential') contribution to the common plan which involved the commission of the crimes charged (that is, the crimes charged could have occurred without his contribution but not without great difficulty).[4] Note that the Trial Chamber in

[1] *Prosecutor v. Thomas Lubanga Dyilo,* Decision on Confirmation of Charges (29 January, 2007).

[2] Note that the Pre-Trial Chamber considered that the FPLC was a national armed force even though non-State and that hence the elements of the war crime articulated at Rome Statute Article 8(2)(b)(xxvi) were met in regards to recruitment and use by a national armed force. (See *Prosecutor v. Thomas Lubanga Dyilo* Decision on Confirmation of Charges (29 January, 2007, p. 98, para 285)

[3] Rome Statute (2002).

[4] *Prosecutor v. Thomas Lubanga Dyilo*, Prosecution closing brief (2011, pp. 36–37, para 65).

S.C. Grover, *Humanity's Children*, DOI 10.1007/978-3-642-32501-4_3,

Lubanga as a result of a legal re-characterization of the facts found that the UPC/FPLC was engaged in an internal conflict from early September 2002 to 13 August, 2003.[5]

3.1.2 The Prosecution's Closing: Selected Issues Arising

3.1.2.1 Genocidal Forcible Transfer of 'Child Soldiers'

Thomas Lubanga Dyilo was commander-in chief of the FPLC (the *Force Patriotique pour la Liberation du Congo*) which was the armed fighting wing of the UPC and he was the former President of the UPC (the *Union des Patriotes Congolais*). Thomas Lubanga was, as described above, charged with war crimes perpetrated against children under the age of 15 stemming from their recruitment to the FPLC and their use for active participation in armed hostilities.

The Prosecution, on the view here, *erroneously* framed the situation as one in which the children were being used as 'child soldiers':

> MS. BENSOUDA: Mr. President, your Honours, at the beginning of this trial, the Office of the Prosecutor submitted that the evidence we will present will prove beyond any reasonable doubt that *between the 1st of September, 2002, and the 13th of August, 2003, Mr. Thomas Lubanga, in a common plan with others, systematically recruited children under the age of 15 as soldiers in his political movement known as the UPC/FPLC and used them in hostilities.*[6]
>
> At the end of their training, they were given weapons and military uniforms. Then they were ready to serve the army as *soldiers*. They were ready to be used to participate actively in hostilities by the UPC/FPLC.[7]

The Prosecution in *Lubanga* thus fell into the trap of falsely framing the UPC/FPLC child 'recruits' activities as 'child soldiering' as did the commanders of the UPC/FPLC and the children themselves who had been indoctrinated in the UPC/FPLC 'military' camps to think of their conflict-related activities (committing atrocity) as normal soldiering:

> Witness 0016 explained it this way: "Once you leave the centre, you're no longer a recruit. *You're a soldier*. They had become *soldiers* regardless of their age, and they were deployed the same way as everyone else. There was no difference."[8]

---

[5] *Prosecutor v. Thomas Lubanga Dyilo* Summary of the "Judgment pursuant to Article 74 of the Statute (14 March, 2012, p. 9, para 22).

[6] *Prosecutor v. Thomas Lubanga Dyilo*, Prosecution Closing Statement (2011, p. 3, emphasis added).

[7] *Prosecutor v. Thomas Lubanga Dyilo*, Prosecution Closing Statement (2011, p. 14, emphasis added).

[8] *Prosecutor v. Thomas Lubanga Dyilo*, Prosecution Closing Statement (2011, p. 15, emphasis added).

However, it is here argued that since the UPC/FPLC engaged in a systematic and widespread campaign of mass atrocity; the conduct of its so-called 'military' wing (the FPLC) cannot be classed under international law as 'soldering' (i.e. forces comprised of 'soldiers' are distinguishable from unlawful armed forces or armed groups in large part by their compliance; generally speaking-though there may be, of course, some exceptions in respect of the conduct of particular individual soldiers-with the customary rules of war as codified in the Geneva Conventions).[9] Hence, children of Hema ethnicity 'recruited' into the UPC/FPLC to participate directly or indirectly in planned widespread atrocity against other ethnic groups in the Ituri region cannot be regarded as 'child soldiers' notwithstanding their wearing FPLC military uniforms. Rather, those children who participated in or contributed to the mass atrocity, whether forcibly 'recruited' or allegedly 'voluntarily' recruited, must be regarded as the victims of genocidal forcible transfer.[10] These children were victims of the forcible genocidal transfer of children from their groups of origin to a group perceived as outside normal Ituri society; namely the UPC/FPLC; an armed group that was an entity unto itself with its self-styled brutal and inhumane cultural practice and norms.

The objective of the UPC/FPLC was in part to rid Ituri of particular ethnic groups namely the Lendu and Ngiti (a genocidal intent)[11] and this armed group employed children in significant numbers to that end:

> Witness 0294, a former child soldier...fought in Songolo, in Bule, and in Kasenyi. ***He said he was fighting to kill the Lendu and the Ngiti.***[12]

However, the UPC/FPLC in appropriating Hema children en masse (*with the goal of 'recruiting' at least three-quarters of the Hema child population to FPLC ranks*)[13] was in fact also involved in an autogenocide. The latter in the form of the genocidal forcible transfer of Hema children to the FPLC for the purpose of committing atrocity against their own and other ethnic groups such that the children would forever be identified as FPLC and a level of mistrust and alienation between these transferred children and their communities would persist. This author is in accord then with those genocide scholars who contend that the definition of genocide must conceptually be understood to include autogenocide though the *customary* interpretation of the Genocide Convention[14] excludes that possibility:

> The U.N. Convention on Genocide confirmed that genocide was a crime under international law. It defined the crime to include the killing of members of any national, ethnic, racial or religious entity [and genocidal attacks on these distinct groups by various other defined

[9] Geneva Conventions (1949).

[10] Grover (2012).

[11] Human Rights Watch (2003, pp. 21–22).

[12] *Prosecutor v. Thomas Lubanga Dyilo*, Prosecution Closing Statement (2011, p. 15, emphasis added).

[13] *Prosecutor v. Thomas Lubanga Dyilo*, Prosecution's Reply to the Conclusions finales de la Défense (2011, p. 13, para 32).

[14] Convention on the Prevention and Punishment of the Crime of Genocide (1951).

> means intended to destroy the group in whole or in part]. Conspicuously omitted, as a result of political pressures at the time of the formulation of the Convention, are instances of killing political enemies, and there is also no coverage of the mass murder of a country's own nationals....The case of Pol Pot's regime in Cambodia [and its] murder of 1 to 3 million of its own nationals is an ...instance [of an exclusion as genocide under the Genocide Convention under the traditional interpretation]. *If only to mitigate the absurdity and injustice that such events do not qualify as genocide*, scholars seek nonetheless to prove that among the target population there were distinct national or religious entities earmarked for extermination because of their identity, hence some of these mass killings would also constitute genocide [under the traditional interpretation].[15]

The critical point has also been made by genocide scholars who call for a broader interpretation of the meaning of genocide that in many circumstances: "...it is impossible to disentangle the political component from the ethnic, racial or religious."[16] That certainly would appear to be the case in regards to the underlying causes for FPLC mass atrocities directed not only toward Lendu but also fellow Hema; especially in regards to the mass genocidal forcible transfer of Hema children to the FPLC.

It is here contended that the mass forcible transfer of Hema children to the FPLC constitutes the genocidal forcible transfer of children[17] intended to: (1) undermine the *national* allegiances of the Hema and (2) that group's recognition that the colonially constructed 'ethnic' divides in the DRC were in fact artificial:

> W-0055 elaborated that "Gegere wise men" such as Eloy Mafuta convinced people to "make youth available for the army so that they would contribute to the protection of their [perceived] ethnic group against the Lendu".[18]

The FPLC objective then, in part, was to ensure that nationalism and devotion to the best interest of the DRC and all its peoples be replaced by loyalty to the UPC/FPLC alone at all costs. Note that:

> Generally speaking, the Hema are associated with livestock rearing and business, and the Lendu with agriculture. A key Lendu grievance is a perception of unjust accumulation of land in Hema hands, inasmuch as Belgian colonial administrators favoured the Hema at independence with large land concessions. As the conflict has escalated, Hema leaders, on their side, have expressed fears of being targeted for "ethnic cleansing" or even genocide. In the ethnic ideology which has poisoned the Great Lakes region, the two are sometimes seen (however inaccurately) as representing two sides of a Bantu-Nilotic clash. A Human Rights Watch researcher has said that "the two groups are now identifying with the Hutu-Tutsi categories that figured in the Rwandan genocide. The Lendu are now thinking of themselves as kin to the Hutu, while the Hema are identifying with the Tutsi."[19]

---

[15] Charny (2009, pp. 36–37).

[16] Kuper (1981, p. 100).

[17] The facts regarding the transfer of children under 15 to the FPLC can, however, also be used to support Rome Statute (2002) Article 8 war crimes charges.

[18] *Prosecutor v. Thomas Lubanga Dyilo*, Prosecution Closing Statement (2011, p. 75, para 179).

[19] IRIN (The humanitarian news and analysis service of the UN Office for the Coordination of Humanitarian Affairs) (2002).

The situation in Ituri was similar (in terms of it qualifying in actuality as an 'autogenocide') to that in Rwanda between the Tutsi and the Hutu who in fact ethnically were one people notwithstanding colonially based *perceptions* of ethnic divides. In the Rwandan case as well masses of children (in that instance; Hutu children) were transferred as so-called child soldiers to an armed group with the prime objective of perpetrating mass atrocity on the perceived 'other'.

This author has furthermore argued here and elsewhere[20] that: (1) children are a protected group in their own right under international law and that (2) their right to be protected from genocidal forcible transfer is not simply derivative from the right of the children's group of origin to persist however that group of origin is characterized (i.e. as one of the protected groups explicitly listed in the Genocide Convention[21] distinguished on a so-called racial basis or in terms of one or more of the other defining group characteristics mentioned in the Genocide Convention[22] namely; nationality, ethnicity or religion; or along some other distinguishing dimension such as a political dimension). This author argues then that the Genocide Convention[23] protects the right of children to survive and be protected from all forms of genocide as an independent right belonging to children as children and not simply one linked to children as supposed conduits for the perpetuation of a particular so-called 'race', ethnicity, religion or nationality.[24] That is, children have an intrinsic value to humanity that cannot be reduced to their being living individual exemplars of other defined groups of which they are a member. Thus, the genocidal forcible transfer of children of the group to "another group" includes also children transferred from mainstream society to a fringe armed group or force (even if a national force) committing mass atrocity against, for instance, various perceived ethnic groups as well as their own (having an ethnicity shared by the children transferred). That the transfer of Hema children to the UPC/FPLC (which was essentially Hema) involved genocidal intent directed to destroying, in part, the Hema people themselves (as opposed to being simply reducible to building a strong 'army') is clear from the nature of the strategies employed for child recruitment to the FPLC. Not only did the recruitment of children en masse involve also under 15s; but there was no concern at the point of recruitment at least for the physical strength or health of the new recruits (unlike the situation for organized armed groups or forces internationally (i.e. armies) that routinely exclude from recruitment those with physical limitations; not necessarily for humane reasons but for practical reasons focused on what types of fighters are required to build a strong force). This disregard at the point of recruitment for the potential effectiveness of the new recruits as fighters was directly and indirectly testified to in the Prosecution case:

> [Prosecutor:W-0014 explained that he witnessed UPC/FPLC forced recruitment of youth without regard to their age:]

[20] Grover (2012).

[21] Genocide Convention (1951).

[22] Genocide Convention (1951).

[23] Genocide Convention (1951).

[24] Grover (2012).

> Well, in short what I can say is that as far as I know ***there was actually no age limit*** in the recruitment of children in the villages or anywhere else as far as I know. I can give you an example. [REDACTED] ***in our village, and I can confirm this to you, your Honour, amongst the children who were recruited they took just anybody, irrespective of age, irrespective of their health situation so on and so forth***.[25]

It is clear then that the purported objective of building a 'strong army' to suppress political opposition and resist the Lendu (as contended by Lubanga and his co-perpetrators) was not an intention clearly reflected in the actual child *recruitment strategies* adopted by the FPLC. On the other hand, the recruitment strategy (recruiting school age children both over and under age 15 and children with varying physical and health status) is clearly consistent with a program of the genocidal forcible transfer of Hema children to the FPLC. Clearly, there are other situations of the genocidal forcible transfer of children that do involve selecting for transfer to the genocidal group only those children who meet certain physical and health requirements (i.e. the Nazi Lebensborn program). In each case, however, the goal is the complete or partial destruction of the children's group of origin. The Lubanga and co-perpetrator 'common plan' to transfer fully *three quarters* of the child population of Hema communities to the FPLC is a clear indicia of the intent to perpetrate the genocidal forcible transfer of Hema children to the FPLC.[26]

Note that children cannot legally consent to their own genocidal transfer under international law since any form of genocide is unlawful and a violation of fundamental human rights which cannot be waived. Hence, the children's consent, where it is alleged by the UPC/FPLC or others to have occurred, is not a defence to the genocidal forcible transfer of children. The ICC Pre-Trial Chamber in the confirmation of charges decision in the Lubanga case acknowledged that a child's alleged consent is *not* a valid defence to unlawful forcible 'recruitment.'[27] However, rather than considering that the facts of the Lubanga case *prima facie* fit the charge also of genocidal forcible transfer of children, the Pre-Trial Chamber in *Lubanga* framed the transfer of the children to the UPC/FPLC only in the narrow terms of conscription or enlistment of under 15s which are war crimes under the Rome Statute[28] (see also the written submission in the Lubanga case of Radhika Coomaraswamy, United Nations Special Representative of the Secretary-General on Children and Armed Conflict on the illegitimacy of consent as a defence to recruitment of under 15s to armed forces or groups).[29]

Certainly children transferred to an armed group or force committing mass atrocity and/or genocide for the purpose of their active participation in, or contribution to, perpetrating mass atrocity are the victims of genocidal forcible transfer

---

[25] *Prosecutor v. Thomas Lubanga Dyilo*, Closing Brief (2011, p. 72, para 175, emphasis added).

[26] *Prosecutor v. Thomas Lubanga Dyilo*, Prosecution's Reply to the Conclusions finales de la Défense (2011, p. 13, para 32).

[27] *Prosecutor v. Thomas Lubanga Dyilo*, Decision on Confirmation of Charges (2007).

[28] Rome Statute (2002).

[29] *Prosecutor v. Thomas Lubanga Dyilo*, Amicus brief of Coomaraswamy, R. (United Nations Special Representative of the Secretary-General on Children and Armed Conflict) (2008).

(where 'child' refers to a person under age 18) as set out in the Rome Statute Elements of the Crime[30] (while arguably the facts *also* fit war crime charges under that statute insofar as the under 15s transferred by the UPC/FPLC are concerned).[31] Consider in regard to the issue of the 'genocidal forcible transfer of children' that the children 'recruited' by the UPC/FPLC were considered by the UPC/FPLC to forever belong to that armed group and not just for the duration of the armed conflict. The children, hence, were unlawfully *transferred* to the UPC/FPLC in every respect and cannot be considered to have been lawfully 'recruited' (through conscription or voluntary recruitment in the sense that the term 'recruitment' is normally understood) even in those cases where the children were 15 and over but under age 18 years. Alienating the children from their home communities by having them commit atrocities against the same; taking the children away from their home territory to fight in conflicts in distant parts of the Ituri region with which they were unfamiliar such that they could not find their way home even in the unlikely event that they escaped etc. were all ways to ensure the children's enduring affiliation with the UPC/FPLC and simultaneous alienation from their home communities even if they somehow returned there. It was hoped by the UPC/FPLC that the aforementioned measures would guarantee the children's lasting loyalty to the UPC/FPLC. Furthermore:

> The recruits were *not* allowed to leave the camp during the training. Deserters could be punished by execution. According to W-0299, Kisembo and Bosco ordered the execution of deserters. *Even for the children who initially enlisted* [allegedly] *of their own volition, they were thereafter not free to leave.*[32]

Once the children had actually participated in or contributed to the mass atrocity as members of the UPC/FPLC (as was the original intent of the UPC/FPLC in 'recruiting' the children in the first instance); or the children were perceived as perpetrators by the general populace by virtue of their simply being members of the UPC/FPLC; the children remained alienated from their group of origin to some degree. They had become 'children of the enemy' in the general societal view and also from the UPC/FPLC's perspective and thus forever stigmatized. This notwithstanding the re-integration efforts of NGOs which may have succeeded to varying degrees on the surface; at least for some children who survived the conflict and the brutal 'military' training of the UPC/FPLC and fortuitously became part of a child soldier NGO disarmament, demobilization and re-integration effort.

Since children are owed a high duty of care by the State and the international community to protect them against being the victims of genocide and other international crimes; the burden for their genocidal forcible transfer to the UPC/FPLC as

---

[30] Rome Statute (2002).

[31] The Rome Statute Elements of the Crime (2002) specifies that the term 'children', with respect to the crime of genocidal forcible transfer of children, refers to persons under the age of 18 whom the perpetrator knew or should have known were under the age of 18 years (Article 6(e)(5) and Article 6(e)(6)).

[32] *Prosecutor v. Thomas Lubanga Dyilo*, Prosecution Closing Brief (2011, p. 79, para 191, emphasis added).

'child soldiers' *cannot* legitimately be shifted to the children themselves[33] (i.e. using the purported rationale that the children allegedly consented to the forcible transfer to another group; namely the UPC/FPLC; an armed group committing mass atrocity and threatening anyone who stood in their way with brutalization and even death).

The Prosecution in *Lubanga* then on the one hand characterized the children's activities in the UPC/FPLC as 'soldiering' while on the other, and in contradictory fashion, acknowledged that the children's activities were; and were commanded to be; contrary to the customary and treaty rules of war (far removed from what is understood to constitute 'soldiering' under international humanitarian law):

Prosecution Closing Statement:

MS. BENSOUDA: Today we stand before this Chamber to submit that the evidence presented in this case has proved not just beyond a reasonable doubt but beyond any possible doubt that Mr. Thomas Lubanga is guilty of the *war crimes* charged against him, crimes that affected hundreds of children. *Those children were trained in about 20 camps around Ituri, a territory bigger than the Netherlands. They were used to fight in conflicts. They were used to kill, rape, and pillage throughout the 12-month period of these charges.*[34]

...

The Prosecution presented 25 witnesses... [including] nine *former child soldiers as witnesses*. They had to remember and relive yet again the details of the horrors that they were trying to forget, to leave behind. They had to tell this Court and, indeed, the whole world the miseries that they suffered. They are now on record, and we hope we can help them to understand that they are not alone, that *the failure to protect* them will not be repeated by this Court. The evidence is now on record in this case.[35]

That any particular child members of the UPC/FPLC managed to evade committing atrocity due to fortuitous circumstances in their situations is an unlikely scenario as: (1) the "children were routinely used to fight in conflicts [and to] kill, rape and pillage" and (2) the children were required from the start to commit atrocities as part of their 'military' initiation and training UPC/FPLC style:

Mr. Thomas Lubanga took these children and subjected them to the more – to the most cruel training. He forced them to stay in camps where boys and girls were beaten when they were sick or when they were tired. They were forced to beat and to abuse fellow child soldiers just to train them to obey orders. They lived in constant fear. They were taught to hate and to shoot and to kill unarmed civilians, the elderly, women, and children. These are the children, Mr. President, that the world has resolved to protect.[36]

That particular child 'recruits' had no knowledge of the widespread campaign of atrocity and terror carried out by the UPC/FPLC and therefore did not realize how their actions as members might be contributing to that campaign is also implausible.

---

[33] Grover (2012).

[34] *Prosecutor v. Thomas Lubanga Dyilo*, Closing Statement (2011, pp. 3–4, emphasis added).

[35] *Prosecutor v. Thomas Lubanga Dyilo*, Prosecution Closing Statement (2011, pp. 4–5, emphasis added).

[36] *Prosecutor v. Thomas Lubanga Dyilo*, Closing Statement (2011, p. 9).

This is the case given that the child soldiers generally participated in various conflicts and hence would have made observations of mass atrocity as the standard *modus operandi* of the UPC/FPLC. Further, former FPLC child soldiers who testified for the Prosecution told the Court that:

> During battles, they [the children] were incited to pillage and to steal money from the population and sometimes to rape. If they refused, they were killed or beaten.[37]

If too young to participate due to lack of physical strength and if lucky enough not to be murdered by their compatriots as a result, those children would still have observed the atrocities occurring within the FPLC 'military' training camps. Further, these children would have heard speeches by Lubanga and other commanders about killing and maiming their perceived opposition as their prime mission.

Thus, Lubanga and his co-perpetrators are guilty of war crimes under the Rome Statute[38] having contributed in a material and significant manner to the recruitment and use of children aged under 15 for active participation in hostilities (by ordering child recruitment without due regard to the age of the children and by requiring these children to participate in perpetrating atrocities). However, the children 'recruited' were *not*, as discussed in the previous commentary, 'child soldiers' recruited by whatever means. Rather, these were civilian children who, as the result of their 'genocidal forcible transfer' to the FPLC, ended up as members of that unlawful armed group of perpetrators engaged in committing international crimes on a systematic widespread basis as opposed to being members of a force engaged in 'soldiering'. Thus, on the analysis here (along with other charges relating to 'crimes against humanity' to be discussed in a later section); Lubanga should have been charged with various forms of genocide including but not necessarily limited to: (a) *the genocidal forcible transfer of children* (persons under 18); (b) *(With genocidal intent) causing serious bodily and mental harm to members of the group* that is; causing such harms to: (1) the children forcibly transferred to the FPLC to serve as child soldiers and/or sex slaves where the children are considered as a group in their own right and to (2) members of the transferred children's group of origin including their immediate families i.e. The parents suffered severe psychological harm at the loss of their children to the FPLC. This harm suffered by parents occurred whether their children were taken by overt force or consequent to other forms of coercion on the parents to 'voluntarily' surrender their children to the FPLC and (c) *(With genocidal intent) killing members of the group* [i.e. killing children transferred to the FPLC for sport and as a method of intimidating the other children into compliance as child soldiers, or as punishment for the children's attempted escape from the FPLC or for the children's other perceived infractions such as being ill or, for some other reason, unable to carry out the strenuous tasks assigned; killing members of the child's community of origin (often using children from that community to do so as an FPLC initiation rite and as a form of intimidation for the children recruited and any surviving community members)].

[37] *Prosecutor v. Thomas Lubanga Dyilo*, Closing Brief (2011, p, 87, para 211).

[38] Rome Statute (2002).

The Prosecution in *Lubanga* in its closing statement referred to FPLC 'conscription' of child soldiers:

> The UPC/FPLC also *forced* families to give up their children on pain of military punishments or fines. As Witness 0031 described it, *if parents didn't send their children, it was at the risk of their own life. This, your Honours, is conscription.*[39]

The current author argues that what the ICC Prosecution in *Lubanga* described in its submissions regarding the so-called 'recruitment' of children to the FPLC (i.e. threats to families and villages regarding their safety if they did not surrender their children to the FPLC, child abductions and transfer to the FPLC of masses of children regardless their age, forcing/inciting children to commit atrocities etc.) amounted not simply to 'conscription' (forced recruitment) but to the 'genocidal forcible transfer of children'. Lubanga and his co-perpetrators were well aware that their genocidal forcible transfer of large numbers of Hema children to the FPLC as 'child soldiers' to participate in the armed conflict and in perpetrating mass atrocities would result in: (1) destruction, in part, of this child group physically and/or psychologically as well as the (2) destruction, in part, of the families and communities from which the children originated thus greatly weakening the vitality and sustainability of the Hema general civilian population. Thus, it is here contended that the confirmed charges of war crimes in *Lubanga* (regarding so-called 'conscription' of under 15s and their use for active participation in the armed conflict) were not in themselves sufficient to take full account of the facts considered in the first instance by the ICC Pre-Trial Chamber.

3.1.3 The Context of Armed Conflict in Lubanga

It is here argued that the facts in *Lubanga* support both war crimes charges and the charge of the genocidal forcible transfer of children against Lubanga and his co-perpetrators. The latter crime does not have as an element a necessary nexus with an armed conflict as genocide can occur both in peacetime and in connection with an armed conflict of an international or non-international or a mixed nature. The Prosecution vigorously argued that the FPLC was a party to a *non-international* armed conflict.[40] The Prosecution was no doubt mindful that Additional Protocol I to the 1949 Geneva Conventions[41] (concerned with international conflicts) is not as strongly worded perhaps as to the prohibition on the recruitment of under 15s or their direct use in hostilities compared to Additional Protocol II to the 1949 Geneva Conventions (concerning non-international conflicts).[42] Protocol I at Article 77(2) states:

---

[39] *Prosecutor v. Thomas Lubanga Dyilo*, Closing Statement (2011, p. 13, emphasis added).

[40] *Prosecutor v. Thomas Lubanga Dyilo*, Prosecution closing brief (2011, pp. 17–18, para 31–32).

[41] Protocol Additional to the 1949 Geneva Conventions (Protocol I) (1977).

[42] Protocol Additional to the 1949 Geneva Conventions (Protocol II) (1977).

> The Parties to the conflict *shall take all* ***feasible measures*** in order that children who have not attained the age of fifteen years do not take a direct part in hostilities and, in particular, they *shall refrain from* ***recruiting*** *them into their armed forces*. In recruiting among those persons who have attained the age of fifteen years but who have not attained the age of eighteen years the Parties to the conflict shall endeavour to give priority to those who are oldest.[43]

Protocol II Article 4(3)(c) explicitly and absolutely prohibits the recruitment and use of children under 15 for active participation in hostilities: " children who have not attained the age of fifteen years *shall* neither be recruited in the armed forces or groups nor allowed to take part in hostilities".[44] Note, however, that: (1) neither Protocol I nor Protocol II Additional to the 1949 Geneva Conventions[45] specifies an age range for the term 'children' and that (2) Protocol I includes certain protections for children 15 and over as protected persons. This is consistent with the International Committee on the Red Cross perspective that the recruitment of children of any age for participation in armed conflict is an inhumane practice.

> Recent conflicts have all too often shown the harrowing spectacle of boys, who have barely left childhood behind them, brandishing rifles and machine-guns and ready to shoot indiscriminately at anything that moves. *Participation of children and adolescents in combat is an inhumane practice and the ICRC considered that it should come to an end.*[46]

Recall that the Rome Statute[47] prohibits in absolute terms the recruitment and use of children under 15 for active participation in hostilities in both non-international and international armed conflicts.

As mentioned, the Prosecution was anxious in *Lubanga* to establish (on the facts as it saw them) that the armed conflict in the DRC was exclusively non-international. This perhaps was the strategy in part also as the Prosecution had hoped to undermine any attempt by Lubanga to make out a potential 'mistake of law defence' (i.e. Lubanga arguing that the conflict was international and that he and his cohorts were unaware that recruiting under 15s and using them in an international armed conflict was unlawful as new developments in this legal area through the Rome Statute[48] were allegedly unfamiliar to the FPLC). In fact, the Defence in *Lubanga* ***did*** raise the defence of an alleged 'mistake of law' arguing that Lubanga did not know that his actions in regards to the recruitment and use of child soldiers were criminal under the Rome Statute.[49] More specifically, the Defence argued that: (1) the armed conflict in Ituri was purportedly international (a context in which recruitment and use of under

---

[43] Protocol Additional to the 1949 Geneva Conventions Relating to the Protection of victims of international armed conflicts (Protocol I, 1977, emphasis added).

[44] Protocol Additional to the 1949 Geneva Conventions Relating to the Protection of victims of non-international armed conflicts (Protocol II, 1977, emphasis added).

[45] Protocols Additional to the 1949 Geneva Conventions (Protocols I and II) (1977).

[46] International Committee on the Red Cross Commentary on Additional Protocol I to the 1949 Geneva Conventions (2005, emphasis added).

[47] Rome Statute (2002).

[48] Rome Statute (2002).

[49] Rome Statute (2002).

15s for active participation in hostilities is *allegedly* not explicitly prohibited under the 1949 Geneva Conventions[50] nor the accompanying additional protocols)[51] and that (2) "...neither Uganda nor the DRC brought to the knowledge of the inhabitants of Ituri the fact that the Rome Statute[52] had been ratified and that conscripting and enlisting child soldiers entailed individual criminal responsibility."[53]

> The Defence argues that, at the time, Thomas Lubanga Dyilo was unaware that voluntarily or forcibly recruiting children under the age of fifteen years and using them to participate actively in hostilities entailed his criminal responsibility under the [Rome] Statute.[54]

The Pre-Trial Chamber, however, pointed out that a 'mistake of law' defence cannot simply rely on the claim that the defendant was allegedly unaware that his conduct (i.e. both in conscripting or enlisting children under 15 and in using them in armed hostilities) constituted crimes under the jurisdiction of the ICC. The Chamber held that Lubanga did in fact know that his conduct in the aforementioned regard was criminal under the Rome Statute[55] as the "DRC ratified the Statute of the International Criminal Court on 11 April 2002, i.e. a few months before the period covered by the Prosecution charging document."[56] Further, the Pre-Trial Chamber noted that there was evidence that Lubanga had personal knowledge of the Rome Statute[57] and its implications regarding child protection matters:

> In her testimony before the Chamber, Kristine Peduto [UN child protection worker with the United Nations Mission in the DRC (MONUC)] explained that on 30 May, 2003 she discussed child protection issues and matters relating to the ratification of the Rome Statute by the DRC with Thomas Lubanga Dyilo.[58]

Pre-Trial Chamber I went on to conclude that, in any case, Lubanga did have the *mens rea* to commit the war crimes charged and that the subjective element of the crimes charged had *not* been negated by any 'mistake of law' on the defendant's part. The Pre-Trial Chamber held that children under 15 are 'protected persons' under international law[59] and that recruiting under 15s is a violation of international

---

[50] Geneva Conventions (1949).

[51] Protocols Additional to the 1949 Geneva Conventions (Protocols I and II) (1977).

[52] Rome Statute (2002).

[53] *Prosecutor v. Thomas Lubanga Dyilo*, Decision on Confirmation of Charges (2007, p. 102, para 296).

[54] *Prosecutor v. Thomas Lubanga Dyilo*, Decision on Confirmation of Charges (2007, p. 105, para 304).

[55] Rome Statute (2002).

[56] *Prosecutor v. Thomas Lubanga Dyilo*, Decision on Confirmation of Charges (2007, p. 105, para 307).

[57] Rome Statute (2002).

[58] *Prosecutor v. Thomas Lubanga Dyilo*, Decision on Confirmation of Charges (2007, p. 107, para 313).

[59] The current author has argued here (in the introduction section) that all children – persons under age 18-are a 'protected group' under international law. See also Grover (2012, Chapter 1) on this issue.

humanitarian law.[60] The Pre-Trial Chamber further held that "children under 15 must be considered as protected persons within the meaning of the Geneva Conventions and the two Protocols Additional of 1977."[61] The Pre-Trial Chamber found that Additional Protocols I and II to the 1949 Geneva Conventions prohibited *both* 'conscription' and 'enlistment' of under 15s or their use for active participation in hostilities.[62] The Pre-Trial Chamber also noted that the DRC had ratified the 1949 Geneva Conventions in 1961 and Protocol I Additional to the 1949 Geneva Conventions in 1981.[63] The Pre-Trial Chamber, in addition, endorsed the view of the Special Court of Sierra Leone that prior to 1996 the prohibition against recruiting under 15s had already "crystallized as a customary law norm" reflected in the fact that most countries banned such recruitment.[64]

It has been here argued in any case that, for the reasons previously explained, the child members of the FPLC were not 'recruited' child soldiers but rather child civilians who were the victims of the crime of 'genocidal forcible transfer of children'. As it is the case that the elements of the crime of genocidal forcible transfer of children substantiating individual culpability under the Rome Statute[65] are potentially met: (1) in either an international or non-international armed conflict situation or in peacetime, and (2) whether the children forcibly transferred with genocidal intent are under or over 15 or both (children referring to persons under age 18); the characterization of the armed conflict in relation to such a charge as well as the specific age range of the transferred children under 18 is irrelevant. Further, as any form of genocide is 'manifestly unlawful'; even an alleged 'mistake of law' defence cannot negate the mental element of the crime. Since Hema 'child soldier' members of the FPLC were the victims of the genocidal forcible transfer of children, it is here contended that Lubanga ought to have been charged with that crime as well in regards to his forcible transfer of children whether over or under age 15 years or a mixed group (that is, in respect of all 'children'; persons under age 18 so transferred) and regardless whether the armed conflict in the DRC for the relevant period was properly characterized as international, non-international or a mix of the two.

3.1.4 The Common Plan and Genocidal Intent

The Prosecution in *Lubanga* alleged a 'common plan' by the leaders of the UPC/FPLC (including most importantly Lubanga as head) which included the objective

---

[60] *Prosecutor v. Thomas Lubanga Dyilo*, Decision on Confirmation of Charges (2007, p. 105, para 308).

[61] *Prosecutor v. Thomas Lubanga Dyilo*, Decision on Confirmation of Charges (2007, p. 105, para 308).

[62] *Prosecutor v. Thomas Lubanga Dyilo*, Decision on Confirmation of Charges (2007, p. 105, para 308).

[63] *Prosecutor v. Thomas Lubanga Dyilo*, Decision on Confirmation of Charges (2007, p. 105, para 309).

[64] *Prosecutor v. Thomas Lubanga Dyilo*, Decision on Confirmation of Charges (2007, p. 106, para 311).

[65] Rome Statute (2002).

of appropriating children to the UPC/FPLC. This was to be accomplished by means of a systematic and widespread campaign of so-called 'recruitment' in order to use these children for active participation in the armed hostilities. It was alleged and proven at trial that Lubanga had a functional role in regards to that plan to commit the international crimes charged and made, at a minimum, a substantial contribution to the development of the common plan and its implementation through his role as head of the UPC/FPLC and his involvement with the orchestration of the plan (as is required to attribute criminal culpability under a theory of his being a co-perpetrator operating in concert). The Prosecution in its closing brief characterized the common plan in the following terms:

> There is direct evidence that the Accused and co-perpetrators agreed upon a plan and acted together since 2000, with greater intensity after April 2002, *to build an army of predominantly young persons*; to create a political movement; using the political and military elements, to take control of Bunia and to assume authority in Ituri with the Accused at the helm and the coperpetrators in key positions.[66]
>
> *Although the common plan did not directly target children under the age of 15*, the co-perpetrators *targeted young persons regardless of age* and did not verify the ages of the recruits.[67]
>
> The co-perpetrators orchestrated large-scale recruitment of youth, both voluntary and forcible, with particular intensity between September 2002 and 13 August 2003. There was even a special term for the under-age recruits – 'kadogos'.[68] [The Kadogo Unit was comprised mostly of children under age 15].

The Prosecution, furthermore, presented a video in evidence of Lubanga addressing his UPC/FPLC forces, including children, which included these words as follows:

> We come – we have come to see you and encourage you. Why give you courage? Because the work we are doing, we are doing with you. The work you know, being enlisted in the army ... trained, using weapons, is blessed.[69]

The major component of the common plan of 'recruiting' children has here been characterized as 'genocidal forcible transfer' of children for the purpose of: (1) their participation with/contribution to the UPC/FPLC overall plan of perpetrating mass atrocity; and of (2) creating greater stability for the UPC/FPLC in terms of the size of its force given the huge numbers of potential child 'recruits':

> The brigades needed to fill their ranks with soldiers in order to gain the military advantage in the battle for Ituri. As a result, along with his Chief of Staff and other top military commanders, the Accused put in place an efficient and effective campaign for military

---

[66] *Prosecutor v. Thomas Lubanga Dyilo*, Prosecution closing brief (2011, p. 40, para 74, emphasis added).

[67] *Prosecutor v. Thomas Lubanga Dyilo*, Prosecution closing brief (2011, p. 10, para 11, emphasis added).

[68] *Prosecutor v. Thomas Lubanga Dyilo*, Prosecution closing brief (2011, p. 65, para 151).

[69] Lubanga address. Cited in *Prosecutor v. Thomas Lubanga Dyilo*, Prosecution Closing Statement (2011, p. 8).

> *recruits of all ages, including children under the age of 15*, to be trained and then deployed to the front lines to fight for the UPC/FPLC in some of their strategic battles.[70]

The contention here is that: (1) the systematic and widespread nature of this so-called 'recruitment' of children to UPC/FPLC ranks regardless of the children's age, heath status, and physical strength was a constituent element of the crime of 'genocidal forcible transfer' of the children rather than exclusively an 'aggravating factor' relating to the war crimes of 'recruiting' and using children under age 15 years in armed hostilities. (Such aggravating factors, where they are present, render the war crimes an offence against 'the peace and security of mankind' and hence such war crimes are graver than are isolated instances of war crimes)[71] and that (2) the common plan to recruit children *regardless of age* and from all over the territory of Ituri is an indicia of genocidal intent (reflected also in the plan to forcibly transfer children on a permanent basis to the UPC/FPLC).[72]

Note that the Rome Statute[73] stipulates that a key element in the case analysis regarding the recruitment and use for active participation of child soldiers under age 15 in armed conflict is that the perpetrator either 'knew or should have known' that the children involved were under 15.[74] At the same time, the Rome Statute Elements of the Crime[75] of genocidal forcible transfer of children stipulates the age of potential victims of the latter crime as under 18 years and sets out that the perpetrator 'knew or should have known' that the victims were under 18 years. The current author, as has been emphasized, takes the position that the child members of the FPLC were in fact the victims of genocidal forcible transfer to that group; recruited not for 'soldiering' but for the purpose of perpetrating systematic atrocity against targeted civilians and any opposition groups.[76] In *Lubanga* the fact that children of *all ages* were targeted for recruitment and use in hostilities by the FPLC reveals that the UPC/FPLC 'knew or should have known' that under 15s would also be included as a result of this indiscriminate so-called recruiting strategy. The Prosecution in *Lubanga* in fact took the position that the UPC/FPLC leadership actually knew that: (1) under 15s and not just children 15 and over but under 18 were being recruited and used by the FPLC for active participation in the armed conflict and that (2) the number of under 15s involved was substantial:

---

[70] *Prosecutor v. Thomas Lubanga Dyilo*, Prosecution closing brief (2011, p. 10, para 14, emphasis added). Recall that the current author has noted that there was evidence presented at trial that even children with quite poor health status, and/or weak physical strength and/or of very young age under 15 were forcibly transferred to Lubanga's 'military' force such that the objective in forcibly transferring the children cannot be simply reduced to building the strength of the FPLC.

[71] Frulli (2001, p. 332).

[72] Under great pressure from the international community and NGOs in the field; Lubanga did release a small number of the FPLC child soldiers as a token gesture only as was revealed by credible testimony put on by the Prosecution at trial (i.e. See *Prosecutor v. Thomas Lubanga Dyilo*, Prosecution's Reply to the Conclusions finales de la Défense (2011, p. 19, para 53)).

[73] Rome Statute (2002).

[74] Rome Statute Elements of the Crime (2002), Article 8(2)(b)(xxvi) and Article 8 (2)(e)(vii)(3).

[75] Rome Statute Elements of the Crime (2002).

[76] Grover (2012).

> *Nearly every fact witness for the Prosecution testified to direct knowledge that children under the age of 15 had been recruited, trained or used by the UPC/FPLC.* These witnesses covered a broad range of actors in Ituri at the relevant time: UPC/FPLC insiders, UPC/FPLC child soldiers, parents of child soldiers, individuals working for or close to the UPC/FPLC in Bunia and persons who worked with NGOs that dealt with child soldiers in Ituri.[77]
>
> Inside the largest of Thomas Lubanga's 20 military training camps, we heard that around 35 per cent of the recruits from an estimated 2,500 to 5,000 were under the age of 15. This came from one of Mr. Lubanga's former commanders, Witness 0016.[78]

The Prosecution pointed out that in regards to the issue of knowledge that children under 15 were being recruited to the UPC/FPLC, that Prosecution witnesses testified that the officials of the political/military group and the commanders of the FPLC all used children as bodyguards; including under 15s.[79] It was alleged by the Prosecution and testified to by Prosecution witnesses further that Lubanga himself used under 15s (children aged 9 to 16)[80] in his personal bodyguard contingent:

> Witness 0031, an NGO worker who visited the accused regularly, testified and confirmed that children under the age of 15 were deployed at Thomas Lubanga's residence as bodyguards during the period of the charges.... all their testimonies are corroborated by the contemporaneous video records that were taken during the period of the crimes.[81]
>
> The evidence is that Thomas Lubanga made no effort to determine the age of his presidential guard. Even his own private secretary, Defence Witness 0011, did not know, could not recount whether there were any official UPC procedures to verify the ages of children. Of course, if there had been, then there would not be children aged 10 within Thomas Lubanga's protection unit.[82]

It appears that these child bodyguards under 15 were akin to mascots for the UPC/FPLC political leadership and 'military' commanders. The child bodyguards were a constant reminder of a stolen future generation over which the UPC/FPLC had complete control; symbolic, therefore, of the armed group's belief that it had control also of the political future and destiny of the Ituri region in all respects. This then may explain why all UPC/FPLC leaders and commanders apparently had included in their contingent of personal bodyguards those under 15 if the Prosecution witness testimony in this regard is accepted as factual as it was by the ICC Trial Chamber:

> W-0041, himself assigned a bodyguard who was under the age of 15, confirmed *that all UPC/FPLC military commanders had bodyguards* ***under the age of 15****, as did officials from the national secretaries to the President.*[83]
>
> He [W-0041] said... "We preferred to use young persons as body-guards."[84]

---

[77] *Prosecutor v. Thomas Lubanga Dyilo*, Prosecution closing brief (2011, p. 65, para 153, emphasis added).

[78] *Prosecutor v. Thomas Lubanga Dyilo*, Prosecution Closing Statement (2011, p. 11).

[79] *Prosecutor v. Thomas Lubanga Dyilo*, Prosecution closing brief (2011, p. 65, para 155).

[80] *Prosecutor v. Thomas Lubanga Dyilo*, Prosecution Closing Statement (2011, p. 33).

[81] *Prosecutor v. Thomas Lubanga Dyilo*, Prosecution Closing Statement (2011, p. 28).

[82] *Prosecutor v. Thomas Lubanga Dyilo*, Prosecution Closing Statement (2011, p. 29).

[83] *Prosecutor v. Thomas Lubanga Dyilo*, Prosecution closing brief (2011, p. 93, para 221, emphasis added).

[84] *Prosecutor v. Thomas Lubanga Dyilo*, Prosecution Closing Statement (2011, p. 12).

Since younger children are: (1) more easily open to manipulation by those who would wish to do harm to the UPC/FPLC leadership or commanders (and not just by those whom the children are charged with protecting) and (2) less likely to be as effective as bodyguards compared to those children 15 and over who have more years of strategic experience and combat training as well as greater physical acumen; it seems unlikely that UPC/FPLC 'military' commanders and officials had these children under 15 serve as their personal bodyguards due to the younger children's alleged superior competency as bodyguards compared to older children serving in that capacity. Rather, it would seem that having under 15s always as part of the bodyguard contingents sent an especially strong symbolic political message regarding: (1) the long-term viability of the UPC/FPLC (which allegedly would live on through this younger generation of recruits) and (2) the ruthlessness of the UPC/FPLC in transferring such young children from their group of origin (mainstream Hema society) to this murderous fringe group (the UPC/FPLC).

The UPC/FPLC leadership were targeting *children qua children*; persons under age 18 (a protected group under international humanitarian,[85] human rights[86] and customary law) for 'genocidal forcible transfer' not as 'soldiers'; but as children to be trained as perpetrators of mass atrocity. Hence, all members of the FPLC, including children of any age, were unlawfully recruited to that cause. Yet, the ICC Lubanga case pertained exclusively to the recruitment and use of children under age 15 for active participation in the hostilities which conduct was characterized only in terms of war crimes.

3.1.4.1 FPLC Appropriation of Children as 'Manifestly Unlawful'

It should be noted that the Rome Statute[87] classes the recruitment and use of children (persons under 18 years) by an armed group or force *perpetrating mass atrocities and/or genocide* as 'manifestly unlawful.' This is evidenced in part by the fact that neither a 'superior order' defence nor a 'mistake of law' defence is legitimately available to individual perpetrators such as FPLC commanders in this regard.

Knowledge and Genocidal Intent

The Rome Statute[88] prohibition (as a war crime) on recruitment and use of under 15s for active participation in hostilities is considered self-evident; it being part of customary law (as the Pre-Trial Chamber in *Lubanga* affirmed).[89] Thus, a 'mistake

[85] Protocols I and II Additional to the 1949 Geneva Convention (1977).

[86] Optional Protocol to the Convention on the Rights of the Child on the involvement of children in armed conflict (2002).

[87] Rome Statute (2002).

[88] Rome Statute (2002).

[89] *Prosecutor v. Thomas Lubanga Dyilo*, Decision on Confirmation of Charges (2007, p. 106, para 311).

of law' defence under the Rome Statute[90] in this regard would not be viable in any case on this account alone.[91] The requirement that needs to be proved in terms of knowledge respecting age of the recruits is only that the perpetrator 'knew *or should have known*' that under 15s were being recruited and/or used for active participation in hostilities as a result of the perpetrator's strategy.[92] The knowledge element can therefore be easily proven by the Prosecution wherever children are recruited and/or used for active participation in hostilities without effective or any age screening mechanisms in place as in *Lubanga*. Such an indiscriminate recruitment and use strategy with respect to age of the child (or health and physical status of the child) is also, as mentioned, a typical marker for the international crime of 'genocidal forcible transfer of the children' to the armed group or force usually occurring in a context of mass atrocities and/or genocide. Thus, for example, since: (1) the UPC/FPLC leadership and Lubanga as head intended to recruit and use children for active participation in the hostilities *without verifying ages* (a fact which the Defence did not deny; Lubanga denying only that he intended to recruit under 15s) and given that (2) such conduct could *foreseeably* lead to and did result in also recruiting and using under 15s; the knowledge element that under 15s were being recruited and used was held proven (i.e. that Lubanga 'should have known' that the FPLC recruitment and use of child soldiers without regard to age and no effort to determine age would result in his committing the war crimes charged was affirmed by the Trial Chamber). Note that this 'should have known' standard regarding the mental element of the crime (as pertains to knowledge of the victims' ages) is only found in relation to one other crime; namely that of the 'genocidal forcible transfer of children.' In respect of the latter crime; the Rome Statute Elements of the Crime[93] includes the stipulation that the perpetrator 'knew or *should have known*' that the persons forcibly transferred to the other group were under age 18 years.[94] The 'should have known' standard greatly increases the likelihood for accountability in regards to perpetrators who are tried for the commission of the war crimes of recruiting and using under 15s for active participation in hostilities and/or the genocidal forcible transfer of children (compared to a situation where actual knowledge is the test applied).

The intent and knowledge element in relation to the FPLC appropriation of children were thus met in *Lubanga* despite the fact that Article 30 of the Rome Statute[95] requires that the perpetrator actually 'knew' (was aware) that a particular unlawful circumstance existed or in fact 'knew' (was aware) that an unlawful consequence would in fact naturally flow from the actions taken not just that such a consequence might or likely would materialize:

---

[90] Rome Statute (2002).

[91] This was evidenced in *Lubanga* as the 'mistake of law' defence was raised and failed abysmally.

[92] Rome Statute, Elements of the Crime (2002) Article 8 (2)(e)(vii)(3) and Article 8(2)(b)xxvi(3).

[93] Rome Statute, Elements of the Crime (2002).

[94] Rome Statute, Elements of the Crime (2002)Article 6(e)(5).

[95] Rome Statute (2002).

Rome Statute

Article 30

Mental element

1. Unless otherwise provided, a person shall be criminally responsible and liable for punishment for a crime within the jurisdiction of the Court only if the material elements are committed with intent and knowledge.
2. For the purposes of this article, a person has intent where:

   (a) In relation to conduct, that person means to engage in the conduct;
   (b) *In relation to a consequence, that person means to cause that consequence or* ***is aware*** *that* ***it will occur*** *in the ordinary course of events.*

3. For the purposes of this article, *"knowledge" means* ***awareness*** *that a circumstance* ***exists*** *or a consequence* ***will occur*** *in the ordinary course of events.* "Know" and "knowingly" shall be construed accordingly.[96]

In *Lubanga* it was proven at trial that under 15s *were* recruited and used for active participation in hostilities given the policies and indiscriminate practices of the FPLC regarding 'child soldier' recruitment and use and that Lubanga therefore 'should have known' as much.

Thus, the test for determining perpetrator knowledge that children[97] were being victimized [i.e. in respect of the war crime of recruiting and using children under 15 for active participation in hostilities (whether intentionally or due to a disregard for age of the children) or with respect to the 'genocidal forcible transfer of children' (persons under age 18)] is not at all burdensome or stringent. By requiring only that, with respect to age of the victims, the Prosecutor show that the defendant 'should have known' that underage persons were being directly victimized; the Rome Statute[98] highlights that: (1) children are a special protected group in their own right and that (2) perpetrators that specifically target children for appropriation especially in a context of mass atrocities and/or genocide are at high risk of conviction once tried.

The 'manifest unlawfulness' of such appropriation of children (persons under age 18) to armed groups or forces committing mass atrocities and/or genocide is objectively self-evident based on the circumstances of that appropriation and the overall context in which it occurs (from which one can also infer genocidal intent). Recall at this point the explanation provided in the Rome Statute Elements of the Crime[99] with respect to the meaning of 'manifestly unlawful' and the mental element in respect of the crime of genocide (including then also 'genocidal forcible transfer of children'):

---

[96] Rome Statute (2002, Article 30, emphasis added).

[97] 'Children' refers here to under 15s in regards to the Rome Statute war crime of recruiting and/or using children for active participation in hostilities and to under 18s in respect of the Rome Statute crime of the genocidal forcible transfer of children.

[98] Rome Statute (2002).

[99] Rome Statute Elements of the Crime (2002).

Rome Statute: Article 6

Genocide

Introduction

[. . .]

-The term 'manifest' is an *objective qualification*;

– Notwithstanding the normal requirement for a mental element provided for in article 30, and recognizing that *knowledge of the circumstances will usually be addressed in proving genocidal intent, the appropriate requirement, if any, for a mental element regarding this circumstance will need to be decided by the Court on a case-by-case basis.*[100]

The contention made out here then is that: (1) the FPLC appropriation of children (persons under age 18) was 'manifestly unlawful'[101] as that concept is understood as articulated in the Rome Statute[102] and that (2) the knowledge of FPLC commanders, including Lubanga, of the circumstances of that recruitment and use of children by the FPLC and the overall context of mass atrocity allows for an attribution of genocidal intent (the intent to commit the crime of 'genocidal forcible transfer of children' to the FPLC).[103]

A 'superior orders' defence (i.e. for those lower in the chain of FPLC command) would also not be viable in regards to the indiscriminate recruitment and/or use of children for active participation in hostilities regardless the age, health or physical status of the children. This is the case given that it was entirely foreseeable that under 15s would be *unlawfully* recruited and/or used for active participation in the hostilities (one cannot use a superior order defence in respect of a clearly unlawful order). In addition, the fact that FPLC recruitment and use of children (persons under age 18; including under 15s) involved the intent and knowledge that: (1) these children were to participate in perpetrating mass atrocities and that (2) the children 'recruited' would never be returned to their families and villages also renders the superior orders defence unworkable.[104] In sum then neither a 'mistake

---

[100] Rome Statute, Elements of the Crime (2002)(Introduction: 'Genocide', emphasis added).

[101] The FPLC appropriation of children was accomplished through abductions and various other forms of direct and indirect coercion as well as exploitation of families' and children's desperate circumstances (the latter leading in instances to so-called 'voluntary recruitment'). The children were forced to commit atrocities often also against their own families and others close to them in order to alienate the children from their families and communities. The children were, furthermore, indoctrinated using brutal techniques and treated inhumanely by the FPLC. These factors and many others underscore the objectively evident 'manifest unlawfulness' of the FPLC appropriation of children.

[102] Rome Statute (2002).

[103] The UPC/FPLC intended to appropriate a huge segment of the Hema child population permanently to its ranks with full knowledge that the loss of the children would be devastating to the general Hema population and destroy that group at least in part. The latter thus constitutes the 'genocidal forcible transfer of children'.

[104] The child soldier victims of the FPLC genocidal forcible transfer were, as part of their assigned FPLC child soldier role, tasked to recruit other children into FPLC ranks, including under 15s, through abduction, other forms of coercion, lures etc. However, as themselves victims of genocide acting under extreme duress given their personal situation these 'child soldiers' cannot legitimately be held accountable for this conduct.

of law' defence nor a 'superior order' defence is available for the 'manifestly unlawful' appropriation of children (both those under and over 15) as FPLC 'child soldiers' for the purpose of their participating in the armed hostilities and in the commission of mass atrocities.

3.1.4.2 An Additional Note on Under 15s as 'Child Soldiers'

There may be particular individual instances where in fact the perpetrator could not have known that the child in question was under age 15 (the child looked older, had no documents pertaining to age on record such as birth certificate or school registration (these were destroyed in circumstances unrelated to the UPC/FPLC or never created and/or filed) and no family members nor others were available to verify age, or the child presented false identity documents etc.). Indeed, the Prosecution in *Lubanga* conceded the difficulty *in certain cases* of determining the age of children in Ituri *based on records*[105]:

> There's no doubt that obtaining reliable birth records in Ituri is difficult. The Court-appointed expert explained that the war in Ituri had a detrimental effect on rural civil registries, many of which disappeared during the war. . .Records were lost. Witness 0299 told the Court that his son's birth certificate was burned during the war. As for school records, even Defence Witness 0029 confirmed that school records in Ituri contain serious mistakes and major errors, even on dates of birth.[106]

Notwithstanding such difficulties in certain instances, there remains an obligation to determine the age of the individual recruited; something which the FPLC made no effort whatsoever to do. This was the case despite the fact that children were being recruited by the FPLC on a systematic and widespread basis.

That the Rome Statute[107] sets out that the perpetrator in all cases can either be assumed to know or be responsible criminally for not knowing the age (or approximate age) of child soldier recruits *where the latter was feasible to know* has profound implications. The only way practically to avoid the use of ineligible 'child soldiers' (under 15s)[108] in every case then is not to recruit children (persons under 18) at all. It is in this regard relevant to understand that though there is in the Rome Statute[109] no explicit prohibition on the recruitment and use in armed hostilities of children 15 and over[110]; there is, at the same time, no endorsement

[105] The Prosecution in *Lubanga* relied in part on scientific evidence in determining the age of former child soldiers who testified at trial and establishing how old approximately they must have been at the time they were part of the FPLC.

[106] *Prosecutor v. Thomas Lubanga Dyilo*, Prosecution Closing Statement (2011, p. 20).

[107] Rome Statute (2002).

[108] Recruitment and/or use by an armed group or force of children *of any age* for the purpose of their participating in the commission of international crimes (as was the situation with the FPLC) is in any case unlawful.

[109] Rome Statute (2002).

[110] Assuming that is that the armed force or group is lawful and abiding by the rules of war.

or condoning of such activity. Furthermore, the particular element of the crime pertaining to the Article 8 war crimes proved in *Lubanga* (namely that the perpetrator 'knew or *should have known*' that some of the children recruited or participating actively in the hostilities for the FPLC were under age 15 years) amounts *in practice* to a caution under the Rome Statute[111] to decline to recruit and use in combat children of any age (persons under age 18). This is the case given the difficulty of determining the age of the child 'recruit'; particularly in the conflict theatre. The practice in the conflict theatre in cases that have come or potentially will come before the ICC is that of recruiting and using child soldiers without any regard for or effective means of age determination such that under 15s are recruited and used for active participation in the hostilities. That children under 15 were recruited by the UPC/FPLC was corroborated by the Prosecution not simply by former commanders and impartial NGO and UN child protection witnesses, teachers and family members but by scientific evidence:

> Lastly, your Honour, we submit that the age of these children can be determined by the testimony of the Prosecution's former child soldier witnesses, corroborated by scientific assessments of their bone and dental growth. In some cases, the testimony of these child soldiers was corroborated by their parents or by other witnesses. The expert scientific analysis of each of these witness's growth maturity corroborates their age. *In some cases the scientific data provides a precise age. In other case it is provides an age range, and in yet other cases a minimum age, but all of these various age assessments can put those children under the age of 15 and corroborates their testimony.*[112]

The Trial Chamber hence accepted the Prosecution evidence in regards to the recruitment and use by the FPLC of under 15s; the latter constituting a war crime under the Rome Statute.[113]

3.1.5 Gender Crimes and the 'Genocidal Forcible Transfer of Children'

3.1.5.1 Gender Violence as Integral to FPLC 'Recruitment' of Girls

It is here contended, as explained, that the children appropriated by the UPC/FPLC cannot be considered simply as recruited (whether by conscription or enlistment) as normally the term 'recruitment' is understood. Rather, the UPC/FPLC systematically and intentionally, according to a well thought out premeditated plan formulated at the highest levels of the organization, and with great malice aforethought, perpetrated genocidal forcible transfer in respect of these children. This was accomplished,

---

[111] Rome Statute (2002).

[112] *Prosecutor v. Thomas Lubanga Dyilo*, Prosecution Closing Statement (2011, p. 19, emphasis added).

[113] Rome Statute (2002).

in part, by having the children themselves commit atrocities (including procuring sex slaves for FPLC commanders; committing rapes on civilians etc.) as part of the FPLC; an armed force perpetrating systematic mass atrocities. This genocidal forcible transfer of the children (so-called FPLC child soldiers)[114] is evidenced, in addition, by the gendered crimes of sexual violence involved in the FPLC 'recruitment' process in the first instance (i.e. such as rapes perpetrated by other FPLC child soldiers and FPLC commanders against girls targeted for recruitment to the FPLC. That sexual violence continued also after recruitment for most of the girls, if not all, in some form or fashion).

Gendered violence was, according to the Prosecution; as argued before the Trial Court in *Lubanga*, an integral part of the FPLC 'recruitment' of under 15s to the FPLC. While no doubt sexual violence was correlated with the war crimes charged in Lubanga (pertaining to recruitment and use of under 15s for active participation in hostilities); the current author views sexual violence also as yet another vehicle for the genocidal forcible transfer of children (persons under age 18) to the FPLC. The FPLC gendered violence targeted children and youth in particular though not exclusively. The OTP submissions contained the following statement in this regard:

> ... girls who were recruited were even in a worse situation than boys, as they were used as sex slaves and were subject to systematic sexual abuse. *This resulted in pregnancies, abortions and a psychological state that is quite catastrophic.*[115]

Note that systematic mass forced pregnancy perpetrated against women and girls of a targeted victim group has been regarded by other international criminal forums as an aspect of genocide perpetrated against a particular protected group.[116] In the DRC situation, Hema girls transferred to the FPLC as so-called bush wives/child soldiers (sex slaves) suffered such systematic sexual violation resulting often in forced pregnancies that also serve as a marker for genocide (just as was the case for the women and girls of the Lendu and Nigiti protected perceived ethnic groups who were targeted by the FPLC for sexual violence).

The Prosecution in *Lubanga* took note of these gender crimes in its closing statement commenting as follows:

> States from all over the world decided that child recruitment is one of the most serious crimes of concern for the international community as a whole... [and] they [States] provided a special mandate to the Prosecution to pay particular attention to *gender crimes* and crimes against children. For the first time, Mr. President, these crimes were codified. And in furtherance of such specific mandate, the Prosecution presents its first case, a case focusing exclusively on crimes committed against the most vulnerable, the weakest, our children. The Prosecution is giving a voice to those children that Mr. Thomas Lubanga

[114] The current author has argued that children who are the victims of such genocidal forcible transfer to an armed group or force perpetrating mass atrocities and/or genocide must be considered to retain their civilian status (See Grover 2012) notwithstanding the colloquial term 'child soldier' that, though not part of the legal lexicon, is most often applied to them.

[115] *Prosecutor v. Thomas Lubanga Dyilo*, Prosecution Closing Statement (2011, p. 55, emphasis added).

[116] Carpenter (2000).

conscripted on their way to school; those children that Mr. Lubanga transformed into killers; *those girls that Mr. Lubanga offered to his commanders as sexual slaves.*[117]

As the evidence showed, girls were particularly singled out for particular abuse. They were either raped by fellow soldiers or were handed over to Lubanga's commanders as sexual slaves and forced to be wives to these commanders.[118]

Despite the Prosecution acknowledging before the ICC that there was rampant sexual violence perpetrated against the UPC/FPLC child recruits; especially girls, Lubanga was not charged with crimes of mass and systematic sexual violence as a vehicle for genocide[119] (i.e. namely the 'genocidal forcible transfer of children'; causing severe mental and physical harm to the children and to the group of origin; reducing the reproductive capacity of the group of origin thus destroying the group of origin in part etc.). In regards to mass sexual violence as a form of genocide note that the raped girls would no longer be marriageable or accepted members in their ethnic and religious communities. Such girls, furthermore, would be at risk of severe physical damage due to gang rape in some instances that would interfere with their reproductive capacity as well as being at high risk for HIV/AIDS thus reducing the viability of the group of origin even if the FPLC girl victims returned to that group (mainstream Hema civilian society). Lubanga, furthermore, was *not* charged with: (1) crimes against humanity[120] in connection with the sexual violence perpetrated by the FPLC under his command (i.e. widespread and systematic rape, forced pregnancy etc. as crimes against humanity etc.) nor with (2) sexual violence crimes as specific separate categories of war crimes[121] in addition to those war crimes charged relating to recruiting and/or using of children (under 15s) for active participation in the hostilities.

This author argues then that since the rape of girl children by the UPC/FPLC male members and the appropriation of girl children by the commanders as UPC/FPLC 'bush wives' (sex slaves) tends, in most instances, to significantly alienate the home communities from these girl soldier members of the UPC/FPLC and vice versa (even should these children somehow become freed from the armed group) such sexual violence perpetrated by the UPC/FPLC against the children recruited amounts to the genocidal forcible transfer of children (ultimately causing severe harms to the larger protected group to which those children belong defined in terms of ethnic, religious, national, and/or so-called racial dimensions and other characteristics such as perpetrator perceived political identity):

To function as genocide, the children (and the mothers who bore children "of the enemy") must be seen by the group [of origin] as alien to the group. ***It is the rejection of raped mothers and their children that destabilizes and destroys the group*** [i.e. the group of origin of the children]. . .[122]

---

[117] *Prosecutor v. Thomas Lubanga Dyilo*, Prosecution Closing Statement (2011, pp. 8–9, emphasis added).

[118] *Prosecutor v. Thomas Lubanga Dyilo*, Prosecution Closing Statement (2011, p. 9, emphasis added).

[119] Rome Statute (2002, Article 6(b)(d)(e)).

[120] Rome Statute (2002, Article 7(g)(k)).

[121] Rome Statute (2002, Article 8(2)(b)(xxii) and Article 8(2)(e)(vi).

[122] Carpenter (2000, p. 444, emphasis added).

The UPC/FPLC was well aware of how the removal of the girl children from their group of origin and the permanent stigmatization of these children as the result of rape and other factors would undermine the viability of the group of origin hence meeting the specific intent requirement for genocide (these girls even if returned to their home communities would not be considered by potential spouses as a viable marriage prospect and someone with whom to start a family).

3.1.5.2 Child Soldiers Procuring Sex Slaves for FPLC Commanders

Ms. Samson's[123] View on Whether Sexual Procurement Constitutes "Active Participation" in Armed Hostilities

The issue arose during *Lubanga* whether child recruits of the UPC/FPLC who were ordered to procure girls as sex slaves for the FPLC commanders were, in so doing, actively participating in the armed hostilities. Note the following exchange on this issue between Presiding Judge Fulford and Ms. Samson (one of the counsel representing the ICC Prosecutor's office):

> **PRESIDING JUDGE FULFORD**: Just before you do, Ms. Samson, and it's a point of clarification only... you advance the submission that as one of the ingredients of participating actively in hostilities, Witness 0294 sought out girls for commanders to sleep with... *Now, I want there to be no confusion about this. You are saying – is this right? – that if an individual is sent out to select women, young women, for commanders to sleep with, that falls on the side of the dividing line of participating actively in hostilities.*[124]
> **MS. SAMSON**: Your Honour, the Prosecution's position is this: That there are child soldiers, in this instance Witness 0294, who had a variety of tasks that he was requested to do at the behest of the commander. This is a witness who had, in fact, participated directly in combat. He had also, according to his testimony, been a body-guard to a commander. He was actively participating in hostilities in the sense that he was in a noncombat, sometimes a combat, related activity but one that is protected.[125]
> **PRESIDING JUDGE FULFORD**: Now, this may be something of importance, so dividing up the ways individually, *am I right in understanding you are, in fact,* ***not*** *saying that selecting young women* ***by itself*** *constitutes participating in hostilities, but you have to look at the position in the round. Is that right?*
> **MS. SAMSON**: *That's correct, your Honour.*[126]

The contention of the current author is that the above quoted courtroom exchange demonstrates the conundrums that unnecessarily emerge in the case analysis when the child 'recruits' to the UPC/FPLC are wrongly characterized as 'child soldiers' (engaged in 'soldiering' since the term soldiering is normally

[123] Counsel with the ICC Office of the Prosecutor.

[124] *Prosecutor v. Thomas Lubanga Dyilo*, Prosecution Closing Statement (2011, p. 22, emphasis added).

[125] *Prosecutor v. Thomas Lubanga Dyilo*, Prosecution Closing Statement (2011, pp. 22–23).

[126] *Prosecutor v. Thomas Lubanga Dyilo*, Prosecution Closing Statement (2011, p. 23, emphasis added).

understood to involve lawful conflict-related activities and not planned intentional systematic mass atrocities perpetrated pursuant to implementation of a common plan). In fact these so-called child soldier 'recruits' were victims of the 'genocidal forcible transfer of children' by the UPC/FPLC. The children were transferred to the FPLC for the express purpose of having these children perpetrate atrocities in the context of an armed conflict (i.e. committing war crimes such as capturing girl children in order that these girl captives could be routinely sexually violated by FPLC commanders; committing murders of civilians etc.).

With respect, from the quotes immediately above; it appears that both the Trial Court in *Lubanga* and Ms. Samson of the ICC OTP *incorrectly* characterized procurement of sex slaves for FPLC commanders by child soldiers as an activity that fell *outside* the boundaries of what could be considered child soldier "active participation" in armed hostilities. In fact, however, FPLC child recruits who were used to capture girls for forced sex with FPLC commanders *were*, on the analysis here, actively engaged in the armed hostilities through such an activity *in itself* (contrary to the view of the Court and the Counsel for the ICC Prosecution, Ms. Samson). The FPLC child soldier sex slave procurers were actively engaged in hostilities as FPLC perpetrators of mass atrocity (including facilitating the rape and sexual enslavement of women and girls). The latter was accomplished, in part, through bringing women and girls to FPLC commanders to be sexually abused and violated (that activity then also facilitating the genocidal forcible transfer of these girl children to the FPLC).[127] Perpetrating grave mass atrocities of various sorts (including procurement of women and girls as sex slaves) reflects a key FPLC combat and psychological tactic and serves one of the central FPLC military objectives; namely terrorizing the general population in order to keep a stronghold over territory under FPLC control. The FPLC was an unlawful force systematically and routinely flouting the rules of war during the relevant period covered in *Lubanga*. Hence, its activities (including that of child soldier members procuring sex slaves for FPLC commanders) did *not* constitute 'soldiering.' Rather, all of this conduct amounted to active participation in hostilities directed to perpetrating genocide; that is destroying in part not just the Lendu and Ngiti but mainstream Hema society as well.

3.1.5.3 The Women's Initiatives for Gender Justice

The Women's Initiatives for Gender Justice notes that one of the remarkable features of the Lubanga case is the fact that Lubanga was not charged with gender-based crimes though the FPLC was and is well known for perpetrating rape, sexual enslavement and other forms of sexual violence.[128]

[127] This constituted the crime of genocidal forcible transfer of children under Article 6(e) of the Rome Statute (2002).

[128] The Women's Initiatives for Gender Justice (2011, p. 2).

> The DRC has one of the highest rates of sexual violence in the world. The Ituri region, where the UPC operates, continues to experience ongoing conflict and militia attacks, and eastern DRC has been described by Margot Wallström, the United Nations Secretary-General's Special Representative on Sexual Violence in Conflict, as the 'rape capital of the world'.[129]

In August, 2006, 'The Women's Initiatives for Gender Justice' presented a dossier of evidence to the ICC Office of the Prosecutor (OTP) relating to gender-based crimes committed by the UPC/FPLC and other militia in Ituri (Lubanga had been in the custody of the ICC since March, 2006). At no point, however, did the OTP investigate these gender crimes in the context of the Lubanga case or bring charges in relation to such crimes against Lubanga or respond to the dossier.[130] This was the case despite the fact that, according to The Women's Initiatives for Gender Justice:

> The dossier provided information about the commission of these crimes, indicated that *sexual violence appeared to be an integral component of the attacks against the civilian population*, provided material suggesting a pattern of rape, abduction, sexual slavery and torture by the UPC, and confirmed that women victims/survivors were willing to be interviewed by the ICC.[131]

The Women's Initiatives for Gender Justice attempted to have the Pre-Trial Chamber in *Lubanga* consider whether the charges could be broadened to include certain gender-based crimes but were unsuccessful in this attempt. At the time of the Pre-Trial confirmation hearing, there were only four victim witnesses.[132]

Note that in 2009 the representatives of the 'Victim Participants' in the Lubanga case did petition the Trial Court for a legal re-characterization of the original facts considered by the Pre-Trial Chamber that would fit, in addition, with the criteria relating to the crimes of cruel and inhuman treatment and sexual slavery. This in that the OTP would not investigate the FPLC gender-based sex crimes even in relation to child soldiers[133] and the Pre-Trial Chamber declined to invite the OTP to do so.[134] The Women's Initiatives for Gender Justice turned its attention to investigating and explicating the role of sexual violence in the conscription of girls to the UPC/FPLC:

> Since the beginning of 2008, we have advocated that *rape and other forms of sexual violence were an integral component of the UPC conscription process for girls, particularly during the initial abduction phase and period of military training. The perpetration of sexual violence, primarily against girls, was an inherent feature of the UPC's conscription practises.* This is borne out in the interviews from our documentation missions as well as our victims' participation programme involving former child soldiers.[135]

---

129 The Women's Initiatives for Gender Justice (2011, p. 2).

130 The Women's Initiatives for Gender Justice (2011, p. 2).

131 The Women's Initiatives for Gender Justice (2011, p. 3, emphasis added).

132 The Women's Initiatives for Gender Justice (2011, p. 3).

133 The Women's Initiatives for Gender Justice (2011, p. 4).

134 The Women's Initiatives for Gender Justice (2011, p. 4).

135 The Women's Initiatives for Gender Justice (2011, p. 4, emphasis added).

The argument advanced by the current author is that rape and other sexual violence as an integral part of the initial abduction and initiation into the UPC/FPLC is completely consistent with a view of such so-called 'recruitment' as also fitting the criteria for the genocidal forcible transfer of these girl children to the UPC/FPLC. That genocidal forcible transfer of the girl children involved UPC/FPLC commanders regarding these new 'recruits' as being the permanent property of the UPC/FPLC to do with as these commanders and others (with the permission of commanders) in the armed group saw fit:

> The girls were regularly raped, many from the moment of abduction and throughout their time with the UPC, with the most intense period reportedly occurring during the initial abduction phase and once they were relocated to the training camps. *Rape and sexual slavery were integral to induction into the militia group to the extent that* ***rape could be considered an indicator of conscription for girls***. .... Being raped, witnessing rape, being forced to rape were regular occurrences especially during the training phase of new conscriptees. It is clear and certain, that conscription of children by the UPC was not gender-neutral.[136]

It is here contended that the rape and other sexual violence perpetrated by FPLC commanders and other FPLC members against: (1) the girl FPLC 'child soldiers' and against (2) the new girls during the recruitment phase, and subsequently, was not "an indicator of conscription" *in any ordinary sense* (i.e. if conscription is understood to refer to lawful forced recruitment for military service with a group or force recognized as comprised of 'soldiers'; the latter being defined under international and military law as lawful belligerents. That (lawful) conscription of children 15 and over, further, being only for the period of the armed conflict). Rather, the FPLC sexual violence against girl child soldier recruits was and is an indicia of the genocidal forcible transfer of children to the UPC/FPLC (a group of unlawful belligerents with no regard for abiding by international humanitarian law) where:

> The sexual violence was used as an effective mechanism for demonstrating control and ***ownership*** over [so-called] child soldiers by the UPC and for ***severing attachment with their lives prior to abduction*** [for an indefinite period].[137]

The child 'recruits' sexually violated by the UPC/FPLC commanders had become effectively 'children of the enemy' as is the intent with the *genocidal forcible transfer of children* and suffered grave physical and psychological harms due to the transfer and all that it entailed:

> The suffering and torment of the UPC child soldiers was and is immense. Their rights to a childhood, to safety, protection, to physical and bodily integrity, to education, to exercising their reproductive rights and health, and to sexual autonomy were denied and destroyed. Many of those raped by the UPC subsequently tested positive for HIV, suffered multiple internal and external injuries, some of the young women had unwanted pregnancies, and ***some were rejected by their families or communities upon their return, because they were known to have been with the UPC militia – a group recognised as a source of violence and suffering by thousands of people***.[138]

---

[136] The Women's Initiatives for Gender Justice (2011, p. 4, emphasis added)).

[137] The Women's Initiatives for Gender Justice (2011, p. 4, emphasis added).

[138] The Women's Initiatives for Gender Justice (2011, p. 5, emphasis added).

Such genocidal forcible transfer of girl children through the mechanism of abduction to an armed group and sexual violence perpetrated against the children transferred can properly be said to have destroyed: (1) the children transferred as a protected group in their own right and also (2) the children's protected ethnic and national group of origin; at least in part.

3.1.6 The Legal Re-Characterization of the Facts Controversy in Lubanga

The Legal Representatives for Victims on 22 May, 2009 jointly petitioned the ICC Trial Chamber in *Lubanga* to allow for legal re-characterization of the facts and circumstances to include crimes relating to cruel and inhuman treatment and sexual slavery along with the original charges relating to the recruitment ('conscription' and 'enlistment') and use of children under 15 years to actively participate in armed hostilities. The 'Victim Participant' group was asking the ICC Trial Chamber to consider, more specifically, whether the facts and circumstances described in the existing charges confirmed by the Pre-Trial Chamber in *Lubanga* supported a legal re-characterization of the FPLC co-perpetrators' acts as including also: (1) inhuman treatment as a war crime; (2) cruel treatment as a war crime; (3) sexual slavery as a war crime and (4) sexual slavery as a crime against humanity. The legal representatives of the victim participants in *Lubanga* were forced into taking this step before the Trial Chamber as the OTP had: (1) declined to file separate charges relating to sexual slavery and cruel and inhuman treatment and at the Pre-Trial Confirmation of Charges hearing to make the aforementioned specific pleadings and (2) declined, in the alternative, to request at a Pre-Trial hearing to amend the charges to add sexual slavery and cruel and inhuman treatment crimes to the existing charges. (Nevertheless, the Prosecutor presented extensive evidence at trial pertaining to the use of girl FPLC soldiers as sex slaves and cruel and inhuman treatment by the FPLC of their child soldiers). The ICC Trial Chamber in *Lubanga* conceded to this victim participant request for a hearing regarding legal re-characterization of the facts and circumstances consistent with charges of sexual slavery and cruel and inhuman treatment but that decision was overturned by the ICC Lubanga Appeal Chamber.

Many of the Prosecution witnesses in *Lubanga* at trial had testified about regular and systematic sexual violence, including rape, perpetrated against girl 'child soldier' recruits by UPC/FPLC commanders and other UPC/FPLC members. Therefore, any existing cultural taboos regarding discussing sex in a public forum, such as a courtroom, were, as pointed out by the Women's Initiatives for Gender Justice, apparently not an insurmountable burden for the OTP in *Lubanga* (and would not then have been such either at the Pre-Trial stage in presenting this type of evidence):

> Although there are no charges for gender-based crimes in the Lubanga case, *the gender dimensions of enlistment and conscription of children have been referenced by every actor in this trial.* At least 21 out of 25 witnesses who testified during the presentation of the Prosecution's case in 2009, mentioned the presence of girl soldiers within the UPC. *A significant number of prosecution witnesses, at least 15, also testified explicitly about gender-based violence, in particular the rape and sexual slavery of girl soldiers within the UPC by other combatants and commanders.*[139]

The ICC Appeal Court agreed with the Victim Participant group legal representatives in *Lubanga* that the legal characterization of facts and circumstances can be changed to better accord with one or more of the crimes listed under Rome Statute Articles 6, 7 or 8 (genocide, crimes against humanity or war crimes) and/or with the form of the defendant's participation in the crime(s) as set out under Articles 25 (individual responsibility) and 28 (responsibility as commander or other superior). However, the Appeal Court made clear that this legal re-characterization of the facts and circumstances cannot exceed the facts and circumstances that were set out in the charges and any amendment to those charges.[140] The Appeal Court's perspective was that the judgment must be based on acts alleged in the charges or amendments thereto[141] but that, at the same time, the facts substantiating the occurrence of these acts, their nature and the circumstances surrounding these acts could be subject to legal re-characterization. Potentially the facts could even be legally re-characterized as being consistent with more serious crimes in addition to or instead of the original crimes charged[142] and this would *not* contradict Article 74(2) of the Rome Statute[143] which reads as follows:

> **Rome Statute**
>
> **Article 74**
>
> **Requirements for the decision**
>
> ...
>
> 2. The Trial Chamber's decision shall be based on its evaluation of the evidence and the entire proceedings. *The decision shall not exceed the facts and circumstances*

[139] The Women's Initiatives for Gender Justice (2011, p. 5, emphasis added).

[140] *Prosecutor v. Thomas Lubanga Dyilo*, Appeal Court judgment December 2009 on Trial Chamber I July 2009 decision regarding legal re-characterization of the facts (2009, p. 33, para 91).

[141] *Prosecutor v. Thomas Lubanga Dyilo*, Appeal Court judgment December 2009 on Trial Chamber I July 2009 decision regarding legal re-characterization of the facts (2009, p. 33, para 91).

[142] *Prosecutor v. Thomas Lubanga Dyilo*, Appeal Court judgment December 2009 on Trial Chamber I July 2009 decision regarding legal re-characterization of the facts (2009, p. 36, para 99–100).

[143] *Prosecutor v. Thomas Lubanga Dyilo*, Appeal Court judgment December 2009 on Trial Chamber I July 2009 decision regarding legal re-characterization of the facts (2009, p. 34, para 93).

> *described in the charges and any amendments to the charges*. The Court may base its decision only on evidence submitted and discussed before it at the trial.[144]
>
> [...]

The ICC Appeal Court further noted that there is a procedure for the Prosecutor to add additional facts and circumstances not described in the original charges (i.e. through amended charges presented for confirmation to the Pre-Trial Chamber) under a procedure set out at Article 61(9) of the Rome Statute:

> *After the charges are confirmed and before the trial has begun*, the Prosecutor may, with the permission of the Pre-Trial Chamber and after notice to the accused, amend the charges. If the Prosecutor seeks to add additional charges or to substitute more serious charges, a hearing under this article to confirm those charges must be held. After commencement of the trial, the Prosecutor may, with the permission of the Trial Chamber, withdraw the charges.[145]

The Appeal Court thus objected to the *alleged* implication of the Trial Chamber's analysis on the issue of legal re-characterization of the facts and circumstances in *Lubanga* which it took to be that "the Trial Chamber [had] the power *to extend* proprio motu the scope of a trial *to facts and circumstances not alleged by the Prosecutor*."[146] The latter approach, in the view of the Lubanga Appeal Chamber, would be inconsistent with the distribution of powers under the Rome Statute.[147] Put differently, the ICC Appeal Court in *Lubanga* held that the ICC Trial Chamber could not alter the original statement of facts and circumstances proffered by the Prosecutor, but only the legal characterization of those same facts and circumstances already contained in the description of the original confirmed charges or any amendments thereto.[148] The Appeal Chamber, however, left open the question as to whether the facts and circumstances in the confirmed charges or any amendments thereto in *Lubanga* (i.e. the factual allegations made by the Prosecutor in the first instance) could be legally re-characterized to include crimes under Articles 7(l)(g), 8(2)(b)(xxii), 8(2)(e)(vi) (sexual slavery), and Articles 8(2)(a)(ii) (inhuman treatment) and 8(2)(c)(i) of the Statute (cruel treatment).[149] The Women's Initiative for Gender Justice was in fact hopeful that:

---

[144] Rome Statute (2002, Article 74(2), emphasis added).

[145] Rome Statute (2002, Article 61(9)).

[146] At the same time: "The Appeals Chamber found that Article 61(9) did not foreclose the possibility that a trial chamber can modify the *legal characterization* of the facts *sua sponte*" [as long as those facts and circumstances were already established as underlying the confirmed or amended charges]. Further, the Appeals Chamber held that any new charges based on new facts and circumstances would require a new confirmation hearing pursuant to Article 61(9) (See Senier, A., 2010, p. 3, emphasis added).

[147] *Prosecutor v. Thomas Lubanga Dyilo*, Appeal Court judgment December 2009 on Trial Chamber I July 2009 decision regarding legal re-characterization of the facts (2009, p. 34, para 94).

[148] Senier, A., (2010, p. 4).

[149] Rome Statute (2002).

> *A decision which recognises the gender dimensions of enlistment, conscription and the forced participation of children in hostilities*, [i.e. a decision that acknowledges systematic rape of girl 'child soldier' recruits, forced marriage of these girls to UPC FPLC commanders etc. as an aspect of the initiation and conscription process] could provide justice for children utilised by the UPC, transform the legal definition of child soldiers [i.e. to include in the definition of 'child soldier' also child sex slaves appropriated by armed groups or forces] and pave the way for future prosecutions.[150]

The Lubanga Trial Chamber, however, given the Appeal Court ruling on the matter of legal re-characterization of the facts and circumstances, was not, in its view, permitted to consider the sexual violence evidence or that regarding cruel and inhuman treatment (presented allegedly for the first time at trial) as a basis for the Trial Court engaging in a legal re-characterization of the facts and circumstances to potentially support separate charges also of sexual slavery and cruel and inhuman treatment:

> In accordance with the jurisprudence of the Appeal Chamber, the Trial Chamber's Article 74 decision shall not exceed the ...factual allegations described in the charges and any amendments to them. The Trial Chamber has earlier pointed out that "factual allegations potentially supporting sexual slavery are simply not referred to at any stage in the Decision on the Confirmation of Charges". *Regardless whether sexual violence may properly be included within the scope of "using [children under the age of 15] to participate actively in hostilities"* ***as a matter of law, because the facts relating to sexual violence were not included in the Decision on the Confirmation of Charges, it would be impermissible for the Chamber to base its Decision pursuant to Article 74(2) on the evidence introduced during the trial that is relevant to this issue***.[151]

It is here argued, however, that the Pre-Trial Chamber Decision on the Confirmation of Charges[152] in *Lubanga* did in fact, in part, rely on factual allegations relating to sexual violence perpetrated against girl soldiers (factual allegations that, for instance, supported a charge of sexual slavery) and, hence, that the Defence

---

[150] The Women's Initiatives for Gender Justice (2011, p. 7, emphasis added).

[151] See Prosecutor v Thomas Lubanga Dyilo, Final Trial Judgment Pursuant to Article 74 of the Rome Statute (14 March, 2012, pp. 287–288, para 630). Whether facts (factual allegations relating to each of the legal elements of the crime) were presented relating to cruel and inhuman treatment of the children in the Lubanga Decision on the Confirmation of Charges (29 January, 2007) is a matter for debate in that the very use of children in hostilities in any manner can be considered cruel and inhuman treatment *per se* especially when it is use by a group such as the FPLC engaging children to observe and participate in atrocity. Certainly the International Committee of the Red Cross considers that children's involvement in hostilities constitutes inhumane treatment. Thus, arguably detailed evidence presented at trial regarding the tortuous and cruel conditions of FPLC training in the military camps should have been considered in rendering the final judgment and allowed for a legal re-characterization to support a charge of cruel and inhuman treatment.

[152] See *Prosecutor v. Thomas Lubanga Dyilo* Decision on the Confirmation of Charges (29 January, 2007).

would have had some notice in that regard even though the Prosecution did not specifically charge separate international crimes relating to sexual violence. For instance, the Pre-Trial Chamber in *Lubanga* in its Decision on Confirmation of Charges had relied, in part, on the United Nations Organization Mission in the Democratic Republic of the Congo (MONUC) *Special Report on Events in Ituri January 2002–December 2003*.[153] That report confirmed that all the armed groups in Ituri were recruiting girl soldiers (including the UPC/FPLC) and that frequently these girls were sexually violated as child soldiers and were essentially also used as sex slaves/'bush wives':

> For many, however, entry into an armed group meant being subjected to sexual abuse. A number of accounts indicate that the sexual abuse started in the training camps, with instructors being responsible and persisted throughout the training.... In some cases, sexual abuse when it did occur, was of limited duration or was carried out in a sporadic manner, with different perpetrators depending on the situation at hand. Other girls were subjected to a more regular pattern of sexual abuse, effectively ***repeated rape over longer periods***, assigned to one military officer for example. These girls are commonly referred to as "***war wives***". ***In many ways the girls suffer a double jeopardy, many reportedly serving both as fighting elements in active combat and concomitantly being used to satisfy the sexual appetites of their commanders. Some, however, were reportedly abducted solely for use as sexual slaves.***[154]
>
> A 15-year-old girl allegedly abducted in April 2002 in Luguba ***by UPC*** described how she was handed over to a commander ***"as his wife"*** as soon as she arrived at Bule training camp. ...[155]

This systematic pattern of sexual violation of girl recruits by UPC/FPLC commanders continued it appears throughout the relevant period covered by the Lubanga case and beyond:

> In October and November 2003, the Child Protection Section received information that ***UPC*** forcibly abducted girls in another part of Djugu territory. On one occasion, a witness reported that a woman was beaten to death trying to prevent her 15-year-old daughter from being forcibly taken.[156]

The Pre-Trial Chamber also referred to the Human Rights Watch Report: *Ituri: "Covered in Blood" Ethnically Targeted Violence in Northeastern DR Congo*

---

[153] See *Prosecutor v. Thomas Lubanga Dyilo* Decision on the Confirmation of Charges (29 January, 2007, p. 82, FN 312).

[154] United Nations Organization Mission in the Democratic Republic of the Congo (MONUC) *Special Report on Events in Ituri January 2002–December 2003* (16 July, 2004, p. 43, para 152, emphasis added).

[155] United Nations Organization Mission in the Democratic Republic of the Congo (MONUC) *Special Report on Events in Ituri January 2002–December 2003* (16 July, 2004, p. 43, para 153, emphasis added).

[156] United Nations Organization Mission in the Democratic Republic of the Congo (MONUC) *Special Report on Events in Ituri January 2002–December 2003* (16 July, 2004, p. 43, para 153, emphasis added).

(DRC-OTP -0163-0344) which included a detailed section on systematic mass sexual violence in Ituri perpetrated by various armed groups in the region during the relevant period.[157] The reliance on reports that detailed sexual violence perpetrated against UPC/FPLC child soldiers (and those belonging to other armed groups) during the relevant period occurred in the context of the Pre-Trial Chamber's consideration of the war crimes charged in *Lubanga* relating to so-called child soldiering ('conscription', 'enlistment' and 'use') during the Confirmation of Charges hearing.

In addition, evidence was relied upon in the Pre-Trial Chamber Decision on Confirmation of Charges in *Lubanga* regarding cruel and inhuman treatment accorded FPLC child soldiers by FPLC commanders and others in the FPLC while at the military training camps:

> ***UPC***...were provided with military advisers and undertook the establishment of more stable camps. ***By all accounts, training conditions were generally physically gruelling and extremely hard, in terms of food rations and punishment regimes (children cited death threats, beatings and in one case an execution).*** At times trainers were minors themselves.[158]

Such cruel and inhuman treatment also included: (1) the FPLC child soldiers serving as bodyguards for commanders at the risk of their own lives and (2) sending the child soldiers to the frontlines after only two months training clearly ill-equipped in terms of military skills thus decreasing significantly their chances for survival or escape from grievous injury.[159] The use of under 15s for active participation (direct or indirect) in hostilities by State or non-State armed forces is in any case considered inhumane as reflected in the prohibition in this regard in the Additional Protocol II to the 1949 Geneva Conventions.[160] The aforementioned Pre-Trial Confirmation of Charges Decision also described evidence of Lubanga's knowledge of the details of what occurred with the child soldiers at these military training camps and in respect of the use of children (including under 15s) as bodyguards (some in his own Presidential guard). Further, there was evidence described of a pattern with the FPLC of the continued use of children for the

[157] See *Prosecutor v. Thomas Lubanga Dyilo* Decision on the Confirmation of Charges (29 January, 2007, FN 323, p. 86).

[158] United Nations Organization Mission in the Democratic Republic of the Congo (MONUC) *Special Report on Events in Ituri January 2002–December 2003* (16 July, 2004, p. 42, para 147, emphasis added).

[159] *Prosecutor v. Thomas Lubanga Dyilo*, Decision on Confirmation of Charges (29 January, 2007, p. 99, para 289).

[160] Additional Protocol II to the 1949 Geneva Conventions (1977).

inhumane practice of participating in the hostilities even after demobilization decrees[161] regarding the child soldiers.[162]

All of the foregoing evidence (*entered into the record and relied upon by the Pre-Trial Chamber in Lubanga in rendering its Decision on the Confirmation of Charges*) arguably supported holding a hearing on legal re-characterization of the facts and circumstances in consideration of potential separate charges of cruel and inhuman treatment of FPLC child soldiers and of sexual slavery of girl FPLC child soldiers. Thus, this author is in fact in accord with the Trial Chamber's *original position* that: (1) there was a basis for a hearing on the issue of legal re-characterization of the facts and circumstances in *Lubanga* to consider the consistency of this evidence with additional charges regarding crimes relating to sexual slavery and cruel and inhuman treatment. (On the analysis here this would have been justified, in part, since such evidence *was* relied upon at the Pre-Trial Confirmation of Charges hearing; though no pleadings were made at that stage for separate charges relating to sexual slavery of girl FPLC child soldiers or cruel and inhuman treatment of FPLC child soldiers) and that (2) evidence presented at

---

[161] Human Rights Watch Report: Ituri: "Covered in Blood" Ethnically Targeted Violence in Northeastern DR Congo (2003, p. 47): "The UPC has even mobilized child soldiers who were demobilized by efforts of UNICEF...

[162] On the issue of cruel and inhuman treatment: For instance, one witness testified that while at the military training camp Commander Bosco threatened the children recruited by the FPLC with death should they try to escape (*Prosecutor v. Thomas Lubanga Dyilo* Confirmation of Charges Decision 29 January, 2007, p. 141, para 389). Other evidence concerned Lubanga, in person, during a speech at a military training camp in February 2003 urging the child soldiers to endure the admitted "suffering" involved FPLC training so as to be able to go to the frontlines and fight after completion of the very short period of training of two months or less (*Prosecutor v. Thomas Lubanga Dyilo* Confirmation of Charges Decision 29 January, 2007, p. 143, para 391) and evidence was accepted that the children some much younger than 15 were subject to "strict military discipline" [Prosecutor *v. Thomas Lubanga Dyilo* Confirmation of Charges Decision 29 January, 2007, p. 133, para 379 (vi)]. Lubanga's knowledge of the details of what occurred with the child soldiers at these military training camps was referred to in Prosecutor *v. Thomas Lubanga Dyilo* Confirmation of Charges Decision 29 January, 2007, p. 153, FN 558, and p. 146, para 399). His knowledge of the use of children as bodyguards was also referred to (*Prosecutor v. Thomas Lubanga Dyilo* Confirmation of Charges Decision 29 January, 2007, pp. 143–144, para 393). The Pre-Trial Chamber relied on evidence of MONUC protection workers and NGOs who interviewed children at an FPLC training camp in March 2003 about their experiences there (Prosecutor *v. Thomas Lubanga Dyilo*, Confirmation of Charges Decision 29 January, 2007, p. 139, FN 513). There was also evidence relied on by the Pre-Trial Chamber regarding the use of active and former child soldiers aged mostly between 11-15 doing hazardous work in gold mines (forced labor) thus constituting cruel and inhuman treatment of these children as a *continuing crime* relating to their original recruitment for use by the FPLC (Prosecutor *v. Thomas Lubanga Dyilo*, Confirmation of Charges Decision 29 January, 2007, p. 81, FN 311). Further, there was evidence that Lubanga had appropriated the children permanently to the FPLC thus separating them from family and community indefinitely; this also constituting cruel and inhuman treatment of children. Lubanga and his co-perpetrators had no intention of releasing a majority or all of the FPLC children so as to forfeit the children's forced labor as so-called child soldiers, sex slaves or in any other capacity (Prosecutor *v. Thomas Lubanga Dyilo*, Confirmation of Charges Decision 29 January, 2007, p. 89, para 256).

trial regarding sexual violation of children in the FPLC and cruel and inhuman treatment of the FPLC child soldiers should be considered at such a hearing (i.e. in any case the Trial Court properly held this evidence presented at trial would only be considered if it was such as to "build a unity, from the procedural point of view, with the course of events described in the charges"). The contention here has been that:(1) the evidence on sexual slavery and cruel and inhuman treatment was in fact already relied upon in the Pre-Trial Decision on Confirmation of Charges (though not specifically labelled in that way nor set out in fine detail as to the elements of these crimes and their relation to the facts); and that (2) such a hearing on legal recharacterisation of certain facts and circumstances in *Lubanga* would *not* in any way compromise the defendant's due process rights[163] but rather was consistent with a fair assessment of the facts and circumstances of the case and the Trial Chamber's obligation to "search for the truth":

> In the view of the Majority of the Chamber, Regulation 55 is a unique device, carefully drafted blending different legal traditions while at the same time remaining consistent with recent human rights jurisprudence regarding the defendant's rights to a fair trial and satisfying the particular demands of international criminal justice and the interest in the search of the truth. Regulation 55 provides for a procedure that balances each of these concerns, thereby creating a unique procedural regime in accordance with the context of the Statute. As explained in the Majority Decision, Regulation 55(2) allows for the incorporation of additional facts and circumstances [to those described in the original charges] provided that notice to the participants is granted and an opportunity to make oral or written submissions concerning the proposed changes is afforded. Those "additional facts" must in any event have come to light during the trial and build a unity, from the procedural point of view, with the course of events described in the charges.[164]

The legal supportability of a hearing on legal re-characterization of the facts and circumstances in *Lubanga* in respect of possible additional charges regarding sexual slavery and cruel and inhuman treatment (and this author would add genocidal forcible transfer of children) seems all the more reasonable a proposition in that the scope of activities covered under the Rome Statute war crimes of 'conscription', 'enlistment' and 'use of under 15s for active participation in hostilities' is nowhere set out in the Rome Statute, The Elements of the Crimes or the Court Rules.[165]

---

[163] The International Federation for Human Rights (FIDH). Interview with Patricia Viseur Sellers (international criminal lawyer and former Legal Advisor for Gender and a Prosecutor at the International Criminal Tribunal for the Former Yugoslavia). Sellers has pointed out that: "The Prosecutor could have amended the indictment [to include charges related to sexual violence and cruel and inhuman treatment] at anytime prior to trial *or even at a reasonable moment during the presentation of the prosecution case* . . .the Trial Court could have allowed the accused whatever time he needed to prepare his case in light of the additional charges [thus ensuring him due process]. That is fairly standard procedure at other international tribunals." (16 March, 2012, p. 1).

[164] *Prosecutor v. Thomas Lubanga Dyilo* Trial Chamber I Clarification and further guidance to parties and participants in relation to the "Decision giving notice to the parties and participants that the legal characterisation of the facts may be subject to change in accordance with Regulation 55 (2) of the Regulations of the Court" (27 August, 2009).

[165] Prosecutor v Thomas Lubanga Dyilo, Final Trial Judgement Pursuant to Article 74 of the Rome Statute (2012, pp. 273–274, para 600).

Thus, consideration of facts and evidence relied on in the Pre-Trial Decision Confirmation of Charges relating to sexual slavery and cruel and inhuman treatment (and genocidal forcible transfer of children), as previously here discussed, as well as of evidence presented at trial in regards to the aforementioned international crimes, seems reasonable, on the analysis here, and in all likelihood legally permissible (contrary to the suggestion of the Appeal Court that, on the view here, with respect, (1) wrongly concluded or implied *in effect* that the facts and circumstances involved in conscription, enlistment and use of under 15s for active participation in hostilities by the FPLC (an armed group perpetrating systematic mass atrocities), as described and relied upon as evidence by the Pre-Trial Chamber in its confirmation of Charges Decision in *Lubanga*, did not include evidence of sexual slavery or cruel and inhuman treatment and that therefore (2) evidence presented in this regard at trial could not be considered for the purpose of possible legal re-characterization of the facts and circumstances consistent with certain possible additional charges).[166]

Further, it seems very counter-intuitive to suppose that such evidence as was excluded in regards to *legal re-characterization* of the facts and circumstances yet may, according to the Trial Chamber in *Lubanga*, be evaluated in determining sentence and reparations. The Prosecution argued for the same noting that the Defence had had a chance to cross-examine witnesses on these issues and had sufficient notice in this regard. Clearly if this evidence (on sexual slavery and cruel and inhuman treatment of FPLC child soldiers) is relevant to further assessing the nature and gravity of the crimes of 'conscription', 'enlistment' and 'use' of children under 15 in hostilities originally charged (as is the implication if it is to be used in the determination of sentence and reparations if any), then those same facts and circumstances should have been considered in regards to whether or not they support further separate charges (i.e. relating to sex slavery and cruel and inhuman treatment). On the view here; regulation 55 allowing legal re-characterization of facts and circumstances is *properly intended* to be a judicial check on the scope of the case as framed by the Prosecutor (*given the facts and circumstances of the case*) and has possible implications in terms of charges or the attributed form of participation of the defendant in the crimes alleged. In any case, the Trial Chamber did legally recharacterise the facts in Lubanga in respect to the nature of the armed conflict; declaring it internal during the period covered by the charges (September 2002 to August 2003).[167] Hence, any charges relating to cruel or inhuman treatment

[166] International Law Professor Dov Jacobs of Leiden University has pointed out in a posting 10 December, 2009 that the reasoning of the Appeal Court in Lubanga that the Trial Chamber's permitting new facts and circumstances to be considered circumvents Article 61(9) of the Rome Statute (2012) is not beyond criticism. Jacobs states that Article 61(9) mentions the Prosecutor's role regarding new charges not new facts and circumstances and that the distinction between the two is difficult in practice. Jacobs states: "Indeed, what would be the point of a recharacterisation [of facts and circumstances] if it did not affect the charges? Even if the Trial judges were to recharacterise facts already contained in the charges , it would probably affect the charges themselves . . .Article 61(9) is a common law approach giving more discretion to the Prosecutor wheras regulation 55 is civil law inspired by giving more to the judges."

[167] Prosecutor v Thomas Lubanga Dyilo, Final Trial Judgement Pursuant to Article 74 of the Rome Statute (2012, pp. 259–260, para 567).

as separate charges would have had to have been framed in terms of an internal conflict in the first instance or legally re-characterised as such [i.e. crimes against humanity (Article 7(1)(k)) "other inhumane acts causing great suffering, and/or the war crime of 'cruel treatment or torture (Article 8(2)(c)(i)) *pertaining to an internal conflict*)'"].[168]

It may be that the OTP's decision to decline to do: (1) an in-depth investigation of sexual violence allegations against the UPC/FPLC and decline to: (2) file separate charges against *Lubanga* in this regard (to be confirmed at the Pre-Trial stage) was perceived by the Prosecutor (incorrectly on the analysis here) as part of a necessary trial tactical strategy.[169] The Prosecutor took the position that sexual violation of FPLC girl soldiers, child soldiers abducting women and girls for sexual violation by FPLC commanders, repeated rape of FPLC girl soldiers by other FPLC child soldiers and commanders etc. was a regular part of the FPLC 'child soldiering' overall experience. However, when it came to more specifically considering just how sexual violence fit into the case and the existing charges; the OTP position on the matter was far from consistent. Recall in this regard the above noted exchange on this point between Presiding Judge Fulford and Ms. Samson of the OTP during which it was agreed that the Prosecution was allegedly *not* arguing that child soldiers selecting young women and girls for sexual violation by FPLC commanders constituted 'actively participating' in hostilities but rather that these were circumstances that also occurred *in addition to* the child sex slave procurers performing combat and other active participation duties.[170] At the same time, Prosecutor Moreno-Ocampo (as will be discussed in a later section in some detail) argued at trial in *Lubanga* that in fact such procuring, on order of FPLC commanders, of girl and women sex slaves *was* in fact in itself part and parcel of child soldier 'active participation' in the hostilities.

It would appear that the Prosecution calculated that: (1) such circumstances of systematic sexual violence involving so-called child soldiers in a myriad of ways would best be viewed by the Court as an *aggravating factor* relating to the war crimes actually charged in *Lubanga* (recruiting and using under 15s for active participation in the hostilities) and that (2) the war crimes charged would be considered to merit a heavier penalty than might otherwise be the case were there not one or more such aggravating factors[171] (another such factor being the cruel and

---

[168] Rome Statute (2002).

[169] The Prosecutor also opposed the victim's application at Trial for a legal re-characterization of the facts and circumstances to allow for sexual slavery and cruel and inhuman treatment charges. Insofar as the Prosecutor held that the Trial Chamber would be encroaching on the powers of the OTP should such a hearing materialize; the current author is disagreed for the reasons explained.

[170] *Prosecutor v. Thomas Lubanga Dyilo*, Prosecution Closing Statement (2011, p. 23).

[171] Note that the Trial Court indicated in its final judgement that sexual violence factors would be considered at the sentencing and reparation phase of the proceedings. (See *Prosecutor v. Thomas Lubanga Dyilo*), Final Trial Judgment Pursuant to Article 74 of the Rome Statute (14 March, 2012, p. 288, para 631).

inhuman treatment accorded children during their FPLC initiation and training and participation in hostilities). Indeed, it appears the Trial Chamber was prepared to consider the sexual violence evidence in sentencing and consideration of reparations to victims as indicated in its judgement on the finding on guilt.[172]

The OTP may have thought it was simpler conceptually to view: (1) sexual violence against; and cruel treatment of child soldier recruits (during FPLC recruitment/initiation; 'military' training; and participation in hostilities) and (2) FPLC commanders involving child soldiers in perpetrating sexual violence and procuring sex slaves as integral to the confirmed charges relating to the recruitment and use of child soldiers under age 15 and as aggravating factors. This in that the sexual violence aspect would emphasize the vulnerability of this age group (under 15s) and the forced aspect of their recruitment and active participation in hostilities regardless whether they had allegedly enlisted (consented to join)[173] with the UPC/FPLC or not. This then would highlight the children's protected group status under international human rights and humanitarian law thus further accentuating the gravity of the war crimes charged.

The contention of the current author is, however, that the sexual violence involving 'child soldiers' (persons under age 18)[174] was *also* another aspect integral to these children's 'genocidal forcible transfer' to the UPC/FPLC.[175] Such sexual violence was *not* merely then an 'aggravating factor' to the war crimes of recruiting and/or using under 15s for active participation in armed hostilities. Nor (with respect) was procurement of sex slaves for FPLC commanders by child soldiers, on the other hand, separate in itself from active participation in hostilities contrary to what Presiding Justice Fulford and counsel (Ms. Samson) of the OTP apparently maintained (procuring sex slaves on order of FPLC commanders was an aspect of the 'genocidal forcible transfer' of the child sex slave procurers and the sex slave victims both as the children's involvement in this regard, irrespective of the specifics of that involvement, marked them as tainted and as FPLC thus alienating them from their families and home communities). The 'genocidal forcible transfer of children' to the UPC/FPLC through sexual violence and through their use as 'child soldiers' to perpetrate atrocities on behalf of the FPLC was in fact a central aspect of UPC/FPLC military strategy.

---

[172] See also Prosecutor v. Thomas Lubanga Dyilo, Decision on Sentence Pursuant to Article 76 of the Statute (10 July, 2012).

[173] The Trial Court indicated in its judgement that children under 15, whether allegedly enlisted or conscripted, were both considered victims of the Article 8 war crimes relating to the recruitment and use of under 15s for active participation in hostilities. (*Prosecutor v. Thomas Lubanga Dyilo*), Summary Final Trial Judgment Pursuant to Article 74 of the Rome Statute (14 March, 2012, p. 9, para 23).

[174] In many instances these child soldiers were at once procurer (abducting females to serve as sex slaves for FPLC commanders) and/or rape victims and/or rape perpetrators themselves.

[175] Whether child soldier perpetrator or victim of FPLC sexual violence or both, such sexual violence serves to alienate the children from their families and communities and, hence, contributes to their genocidal forcible transfer to the UPC/FPLC.

3.1.6.1 More on What Constitutes 'Active Participation' in Armed Hostilities

The 'genocidal forcible transfer of children' during armed hostilities is accomplished, as has been discussed, often through their 'recruitment' into an armed force or group *perpetrating mass atrocities and/or genocide*. That genocidal forcible transfer is also, not infrequently, further solidified through the use of sexual violence in various ways as previously here described. The participation of the transferred children in perpetrating mass atrocities and/or genocide as 'child soldiers' amounts to the children's *direct* and 'active participation' in armed hostilities though such conduct is not in any sense 'soldiering.' 'Active participation' in armed hostilities is generally interpreted narrowly to mean performing a *direct* combat function or some support function *directly* related to combat and critical to advancing the military operation and objectives of the armed group or force. However, consider that the 'genocidal forcible transfer of children' (i.e. to the FPLC) in itself serves to devastate and demoralize the communities from which the children are 'recruited', suppress most, if not all, resistance in these communities and others, and reinforce the power of the perpetrator armed force psychologically and in concrete terms (the latter, in part, given the gain of the transferred children's forced labor). Thus, the child victims of 'genocidal forcible transfer' to an armed group or force perpetrating mass atrocities and/or genocide *indirectly* already *actively contribute* to the perpetrator's overall military strategic objectives in the armed hostilities *just through their appropriation* by the perpetrator group. This is the case ironically even though: (1) the children are rightfully considered passive victims of genocidal forcible transfer[176]and (2) it is the case that not all of the so-called child soldier members of the armed group or force may actually perform a direct combat or direct combat-related support function (i.e. some may exclusively be sex slaves or be forced to perform other non-combat related duties such as domestic chores though *most child soldiers function in multiple roles as was the case with the FPLC*).

Both (1) the children who are themselves the direct victims of sexual violence (i.e. FPLC girl child soldier victims of rape perpetrated by FPLC commanders etc.) and (2) the child soldiers who, on FPLC commander orders, abduct girl children for sexual slavery in the FPLC etc. have, as a result of their divergent involvement in the systematic sexual violence perpetrated by the FPLC, become victims of genocidal forcible transfer in part also through this sexual violence. That is, both these groups of children are stigmatized in their home communities and viewed as children of the FPLC (the perpetrator group) and no longer as children of their families and home communities as the result in part of their particular connection to the sexual violence.

[176] Even children who allegedly 'enlisted' in the FPLC (an arguable notion given the children's overall coercive circumstances and desperate attempts to survive by joining the FPLC) did not bargain for the inhuman treatment they received during their 'training' and subsequently and the reality that they were now FPLC captives in essence unable to leave or, in most instances, to escape; relegated to the status of quite expendable child soldiers.

The 'child soldiers' of the FPLC in contributing to the 'genocidal forcible transfer' of other children through sexual violence (i.e. through themselves committing rapes of other children abducted by the FPLC to become child soldiers; abducting child sex slaves for FPLC commanders etc. on FPLC command orders) were in fact actively *and directly* engaged in the armed hostilities in this manner. *This is the case in that the 'genocidal forcible transfer of children' carried out by various means is itself an intentional, widespread and systematic military conflict strategy*. Such a legal characterization of the facts as here presented then is contrary to the view taken by the OTP counsel Ms. Samson of the sexual violence evidence involving child soldiers in *Lubanga*. (Ms. Samson took the position that child soldiers' procurement through force, as per FPLC orders, of women and girls for commanders to sexually violate did *not* in itself in fact constitute 'active participation' in the armed hostilities).

On the analysis here, the FPLC girl child soldiers who were the victims of rape and, at a certain point, had not perpetrated any sexual violence of their own (if they ever did); were *indirect* but also 'active participants' in the armed hostilities. Their sexual victimization by the FPLC contributed to their genocidal forcible transfer to the FPLC. This genocidal forcible transfer of girl child soldiers in turn contributed to the military objectives of the FPLC (i.e. serving propaganda purposes in terrorizing the general population, weakening any potential opposition groups through appropriation of and defiling of their girls etc.) Both groups of children then (child soldier victims of rape by the FPLC and child perpetrators of sexual violence on order of the FPLC) were stigmatized by these involvements in sexual violence and are victims. Their chances for successful reintegration into their home communities should the chance have ever occurred (i.e. during a post-conflict period) were greatly diminished by the taint of their being victim of or victim perpetrator of FPLC sexual violence.

On the current author's view: (1) sexual violence was integral to the FPLC common plan targeting children as a protected group in their own right (whether this meant having child soldiers procure sex slaves for FPLC commanders or perpetrate their own additional sex crimes or whether it meant girl child soldiers being the victims of sexual violence by the FPLC etc.); and (2) sexual violence served as another vehicle for the genocidal forcible transfer of these children to the UPC/FPLC. The children as victims of genocidal forcible transfer to the UPC/FPLC during the period covered in *Lubanga* were pawns, as here described, contributing both directly and indirectly to the FPLC military objectives and operations. Note that as victims of genocidal forcible transfer to the UPC/FPLC; these children (*regardless of age*), even if directly involved in the hostilities (in a combat or direct combat-related support function) were entitled to be regarded as a protected group by any armed opposition. Thus, unless the opponent were in imminent significant danger as a result of the particular child's direct participation; the child's safety and well-being under international humanitarian law would need to be safeguarded. Further, as the Trial Court in *Lubanga* considered the conflict to be solely an internal one, the State had an obligation under international humanitarian law[177] to take all necessary means to ensure that children under age 15 were not recruited or used for direct participation in the conflict by State or non-State armed forces or groups.

3.1.6.2 Sexual Violence in *Lubanga*: An Analysis of ICC Prosecutor Moreno-Ocampo's View

On the Issue of No Separate Sexual Violence Charges

The Prosecutor in *Lubanga* advanced the position before the ICC Trial Chamber that gender crimes (the rape of girls etc.) were a routine and integral part of the FPLC 'conscription' process. The Prosecutor explained that the view of the OTP was that if the rapes and other sexual violence against girls conscripted into the FPLC were to be considered as *separate* from the conscription process then: (1) the girls might be viewed by the Court; not first and foremost as 'child soldiers' but rather as "wives" and (2) the girl children would erroneously *not* be viewed as amongst the FPLC child soldier members who needed to be rescued and demobilized and cared for:

> We believe the facts are that the girls were abused, used as sexual slaves and raped. ***We believe this suffering is part of the suffering of the conscription.*** We did not allege and will not present evidence linking Thomas Lubanga with rapes. We allege that he linked it with the conscription and he knows the harsh conditions. *So what we believe in this case is a different way to present the gender crimes. It presents the gender crimes not specific as rapes. Gender crimes were committed as part of the conscription of girls in – in the militias. And* ***it is important to have the charge as confined to the conscription****, because if not... if not, the girls are considered wife and ignored as people to be protected and demobilised and cared* [for]. ***That is why the Prosecutor decided to confine the charges – to present the suffering and the sexual abuse and the gender crime suffered by the girls in the camps just as conscription, showing this gender aspect of the crime*** **[of conscription]**.[178]

On the respectful view here, one troubling aspect of Prosecutor Ocampo's well-intentioned but misguided rationale (as he states it in the quote above) for *not* charging sexual violence crimes as *separate*[179] international crimes in *Lubanga*[180]

---

[177] Additional Protocol II to the 1949 Geneva Conventions (1977).

[178] *Prosecutor v. Thomas Lubanga Dyilo*, Prosecution Closing Statement (2011, p. 54, emphasis added).

[179] Ocampo stated that the OTP viewed such sexual violence as part and parcel of the FPLC conscription process and not separable therefrom as reflected in the Prosecution's case formulation. Hence, he did *not* charge Lubanga with sex crimes though evidence of such crimes was presented by the OTP in the case.

[180] The current author argues that sexual violence perpetrated against girl and boy so-called 'child soldiers' is a typical and systematic part of their appropriation to an armed group or force committing mass atrocities and/or genocide. Their appropriation by such armed forces or groups amounts, in fact, to the 'genocidal forcible transfer of children' thus rendering distinctions such as recruitment by 'enlistment' versus 'conscription' inapplicable and irrelevant.

(distinct from the conscription and use of under 15s charges) is his contention that the fact that FPLC girl 'child soldiers' have the perceived status also of 'wives' (even if but "bush wives") automatically poses a barrier to the Prosecution's ability to pursue separate charges of gender crimes (i.e. rape etc.). The quote from Prosecutor Moreno-Ocampo cited immediately above appears to suggest that his decision not to charge Lubanga also with international crimes relating to sexual violence was based on fears regarding the ICC taking a 'cultural relativist' stance on the issue of sexual violence perpetrated against FPLC girl soldier/bush wives. That is, the OTP appears to have considered that the mere fact that these FPLC girl soldiers also had the perceived status of 'bush wives' would: (1) counteract the perception of the forced nature of the sexual violation of these children (i.e. rape, forced impregnation and other such gendered sex crimes) and/or somehow undermine perceptions of the *illegitimacy* of the sexual violence perpetrated against the FPLC girls[181] and (2) detract from the fact that the girls too were FPLC child soldiers who most often also performed the same 'military' duties as the male child soldiers (i.e. serving as bodyguards and performing combat and combat support functions) in addition to performing forced sexual services for FPLC male perpetrators. These concerns of the OTP are reflected in the following admonition made at trial in *Lubanga* by one of the counsel for the Office of the Prosecutor:

> The Prosecution requests the Chamber to make clear that *these girls* ***are not the wives***, *are not the wives, of commanders.* ***They also are the victims of the crimes of recruitment*** and have to be particularly protected by the demobilisation programmes and by this Court.[182]

One would hope that the judiciary in *Lubanga* would *not* have been caught up in 'cultural relativist' ideology and any local context-specific misguided notions of 'political correctness' that in fact undermine universal human rights for any particular victim group(s) such as women and girls. There is no doubt that certain local norms detrimental to the fundamental rights of women and girls were still present to some degree in the DRC during the relevant period:

> The deployment of international troops in lturi in mid-2003 facilitated the release of some adolescent girls and access to support programmes to help them deal with some of the consequences [of child soldier recruitment and sexual victimization]...some of them had required medical and even hospital treatment for the consequences of violent abuse. Others are now child-mothers. But it is likely that many still remain within the groups. The question of the status of the undoubtedly numerous war wives is a serious one, ***as many traditional beliefs dictate that once a girl is sexually "taken" by a man, she is his property.*** The issue simply becomes one of payment to the family of a dowry. An FAPC colonel stated in an interview with the Child Protection Section on 9 November 2003, referring to these girl victims of abduction and sexual abuse within his ranks, that there would be *'... difficulties in taking these girls out of these forced 'marriages'.[183]

[181] There still are in fact some locales globally where sexual violence perpetrated against a wife by her husband is viewed as lawful under certain circumstances.

[182] Office of the Prosecutors Closing Statements (25 August, 2011, p. 10).

[183] United Nations Organization Mission in the Democratic Republic of the Congo (MONUC) *Special Report on Events in Ituri January 2002–December 2003* (16 July, 2004, p. 44, para 154, emphasis added).

The expectation then would be, hopefully justified, that the ICC would have been prepared in *Lubanga* to affirm at the Pre-Trial stage, and properly consider at trial; separate charges against Lubanga pertaining to international crimes involving acts of sex violence. The ICC then in addressing these charges would consider that: (1) the girl FPLC members have fundamental human rights to physical and psychological integrity regardless of their perceived status by some also as 'bush wives' (a status in reality of sexual enslavement) and that (2) these girls are entitled to a judicial remedy also for international crimes of a sexual nature perpetrated against them (by FPLC commanders and other members) including the holding to account under international criminal law (i.e. as per the Rome Statute[184]) of the perpetrators. Whether in fact ICC Prosecutor Moreno-Ocampo was or was not correct in *Lubanga* in his assessment that charging separate gendered crimes would lead the ICC Pre-Trial and Trial Chambers to a consideration of the FPLC girls only as 'bush wives' rather than as first and foremost 'child soldiers' remains an open question.

The OTP appears to have concluded that the forced nature of the sexual violations would only be a viable proposition for the Court if the sexual violence could be framed as an integral part of forced recruitment of girls ('conscription') to the FPLC. However, these girls, it is here contended, were entitled to have the FPLC perpetrators of the mass systematic sexual victimization of women and girls in the context of this armed conflict also prosecuted for these offences as *separate* international crimes (rape, forced pregnancy, sexual enslavement etc.) regardless of: (1) whether or not these girls were considered wives (or 'bush wives'/child brides) and (2) whether or not they were also considered to be child soldiers under a broad or more restrictive definition. To do otherwise is, on the view here, in practice to: (1) inadvertently downplay the gravity of these systematic sexual crimes (i.e. as independent grave crimes under the Rome Statute[185]) and (2) to unjustifiably contribute to impunity for such sexual violations when committed against women and girls assigned the status of 'bush wives' and/or child soldiers thus helping to perpetuate the powerlessness and dehumanization of these girls and women; especially once they are deemed "bush wives."

Note that the Prosecution in presenting its evidence in *Lubanga* went to great lengths to establish that the girl 'child soldiers' performed a variety of combat and combat-related support functions as members of the FPLC. The Prosecution's objective in taking this approach was apparently to persuade the Trial Chamber in *Lubanga* that these girls were in fact conscripted 'child soldiers' taking an active part in armed hostilities and not simply sexually abused child 'bush wives' allegedly removed from any participation in the hostilities (i.e. purportedly functionally non-child soldiers and, therefore, not in need of protection against child soldiering and all that that entails and not in need of demobilization).

On the view presented here, both the boys and girls 'recruited' by the FPLC; a group dedicated to perpetrating systematic mass atrocity, are viewed also as the victims of the 'genocidal forcible transfer of children.' As such, these children fulfilled

[184] Rome Statute (2002).

[185] Rome Statute (2002).

an ongoing FPLC military objective; namely serving as propaganda fodder communicating to the general population and the opposition the alleged unlimited power that the FPLC enjoyed (that power extending, for instance, to being able to appropriate children to their ranks). This propaganda function was served regardless whether the children's FPLC official day-today assigned specific duties were combat or non-combat related (the latter of which might include, for instance, being exclusively a bush wife/sex slave and not engaging in combat or any directly combat related support functions). Insofar as the children appropriated by the FPLC are advancing the FPLC military objectives, even as victims of the grave international crime of 'genocidal forcible transfer of children', they can be considered to be 'active participants' in the armed hostilities (such "active participation" then need *not* imply in all cases direct combat or closely combat-related support functions such as spying etc.).

Girls, as discussed, were the victims of genocidal forcible transfer to the FPLC in part due to their being raped by FPLC commanders or other members of the armed group, bearing children due to forced impregnation by FPLC commanders etc. or suffering other sexual violence (i.e. serving as a 'bush wives'/sex slaves to FPLC commanders). The genocidal forcible transfer of girls to the FPLC was accomplished then, in part, by the stigmatization of the girls and alienation from their families and home communities due to their sexual violation by FPLC. That alienation of the girls from their families and home communities was no doubt the objective in part and an anticipation of the FPLC in perpetrating the sexual violence against these girls in the first instance. These sexually violated Hema girls were thus ultimately perceived by themselves, by the FPLC perpetrators and by the children's families and home communities as FPLC 'child soldiers'.[186] On the respectful view here then (contrary to the suggestion of ICC Prosecutor Moreno-Ocampo in *Lubanga*); the girls' ancillary 'bush wives' status did *not* detract from the perception by all that they were FPLC child soldiers (and as such entitled to be rescued from the FPLC, demobilized and protected). The sexual violence perpetrated against the girls was not in fact part of a 'conscription' process[187] *as*

[186] Recall that the girls of the FPLC generally performed combat and combat- related functions (such as spying, serving as bodyguards etc.) as well sexual services thus contributing to the perception that they were FPLC child soldiers just as were the boys in the FPLC ranks.

[187] 'Conscription' is normally taken to mean 'forced recruitment' for the purpose of traditional *soldiering* functions. In the case of the FPLC, however, the boys and girls appropriated to their ranks were engaged in perpetrating mass atrocities and the girl FPLC soldiers also performed sexual services for the FPLC while the boy FPLC also procured sex slaves for the FPLC commanders and soldiers and were sometimes also themselves sexually victimized. Hence, the children of the FPLC were *not* engaged in 'soldiering' (though they were 'active participants' in the hostilities) and their induction process is not properly then characterized as 'recruitment' through 'conscription' or 'enlistment' *for the purpose of child soldiering*. Rather, the children were the victims of 'genocidal forcible transfer' to the FPLC. At the same time, however, the facts also support the war crimes charges involving conscription and use of under 15s for active participation in hostilities *if* 'conscription', in the context of the Lubanga case, is understood to refer to 'forcible recruitment' into an unlawful armed group and use in hostilities to participate as child civilians in perpetrating various international crimes that fall under ICC jurisdiction. (Enlistment is a term that is inapplicable in the context of these children's genocidal forcible transfer to the FPLC).

that term is normally understood; but rather a vehicle for the 'genocidal forcible transfer' of these girls to the FPLC. The Court thus properly should have been able to consider, as *separable* international crimes, the various acts of gendered sexual violence perpetrated against the girls in the context of their genocidal forcible transfer to the FPLC as child soldiers.

The same facts regarding sexual violence perpetrated against the girls appropriated by the FPLC, it is here argued, support a number of charges including, but not limited to: the 'genocidal forcible transfer of children'; the 'war crime' of rape as well as the 'crimes against humanity' of sexual slavery and, in some instances, the 'war crime' of forced pregnancy. Framed in terms of a vehicle for the genocidal forcible transfer of these girl children to the FPLC; it *is* in fact possible to justify specific *separate* gendered sexual violence charges as articulated under the Rome Statute[188] (i.e. as specific war crimes and/or particular crimes against humanity or even as certain genocidal acts[189]). Characterizing such FPLC sexual violence against girls as an aspect of '*conscription*' into the FPLC (as did the Prosecutor in *Lubanga*) improperly results in collapsing these gendered sex crimes into the latter offence category *such that they disappear* for all legal intents and purposes (except as perhaps 'aggravating factors' relating to the war crime of conscription of under 15s). It was (on the view here) thus critically important in terms of the 'interests of justice', as well as the legally supportability of the charges, that Prosecutor Moreno-Ocampo should have charged various sex crimes against Lubanga *in addition to* the war crimes charged. However that, of course, is not what occurred.

More on Sexual Violence, "Active Participation" in Hostilities, and 'Child Soldiers'

a) On FPLC Orders to Procure Sex Slaves: The Prosecutor's View

The position of the OTP on the specific relevance of sexual violence to the Lubanga case is somewhat complicated given conflicting presentations by representatives of the OTP. The ICC Trial Chamber, *based on the closing statements of Ms. Samson (counsel of the OTP)*, it will be recalled, concluded that the Prosecutor held that child soldiers procuring girls for FPLC commanders to take as "bush wives" and to routinely sexually violate was *not* part of the child soldier procurer's "active participation" in armed hostilities. However, the ICC Chief Prosecutor Moreno-Ocampo, speaking, in his view, as the official voice of the OTP as a whole, in fact articulated precisely the opposing view before the Trial Chamber. That is,

[188] Rome Statute (2002).

[189] The genocidal acts referred to here are, for instance, related to preventing births (where the raped girl FPLC members could no longer bear children due to the physical damage caused by repeated and/or gang rapes by FPLC commanders and other members), or causing the girls severe mental and physical harm such that the girl children as a protected group are destroyed in part as are their Hema home communities and families.

Prosecutor Moreno-Ocampo explained that the OTP viewed the 'child soldiers', *pursuant to orders by FPLC commanders*, procuring women and girls for commanders as 'bush wives' and sexual slaves to be raped, constituted these child soldier procurers being 'actively engaged' in hostilities (where *following commander orders* during armed hostilities is taken to be synonymous with "active participation" in hostilities as a child soldier):

> ...factually we believe when a commander ordered [the 'child soldier'] to abduct girls to use them as sexual slaves or rape them, ***this order is using the children*** [those so ordered] in hostility.... So to summarise, we agree with the Chamber there is a line, there's a border between hostilities and no hostilities, and cooking could be a good example, maybe, *but ordering to abduct girls in order to rape them is an order* to – and [amounts to the] use [of] children in hostilities.[190]

The current author is agreed with the former ICC Prosecutor Mr. Moreno-Ocampo that 'child soldiers' procuring girls for rape by FPLC commanders and other FPLC members does equate to the 'child soldier' procurers' "active participation" in hostilities. However, the current author does *not* hold that the children doing the procuring were functioning as child soldiers[191] *by virtue of, or as reflected in, their following the order* of FPLC commanders to procure sex slaves or bush wives for the FPLC commanders. This since, as has been previously here discussed, the FPLC was not engaged in 'soldiering' as that concept is understood in international law, but rather committing systematic mass atrocity and perpetrating all manner of international crimes. Hence, the command orders of the FPLC hierarchy, whether followed by the children or not, did not confer 'child soldier' status on the children nor help to characterize the scenario as military (soldiering activity) in some aspect in any ordinary sense. Rather, these children doing the procuring of girls for FPLC commanders and others in the armed group were actively participating in hostilities technically, from an international law perspective, *not* as (child) *soldiers* following orders, but, on the view here, as victims themselves of the 'genocidal forcible transfer of children' (now facilitating the genocidal transfer of these girls to the FPLC; an act that constituted an attack on the child victim, their families and on their home communities). These so-called child soldier procurers of sex slaves/bush wives were in fact, on the view here, acting as civilian members of a criminal organized armed group 'recruited' to commit grave international crimes and advance the UPC/FPLC 'military' cause in a myriad of ways.

b) 'Active Participation' in Hostilities Through One's Own Sexual Exploitation: The View of Radhika Coomaraswamy

The Special Representative of the U.N. Secretary-General on Children and Armed Conflict (Radhika Coomaraswamy), who submitted an amicus brief in the Lubanga case, took the view that the Trial Chamber should take a very broad view of what

---

[190] *Prosecutor v. Thomas Lubanga Dyilo*, Prosecution Closing Statement (2011, p. 55, emphasis added).

[191] The term 'child soldiers', as previously noted, is not a technical term with a precise definition recognized in international humanitarian law.

constitutes 'active participation' in armed hostilities. This would be in contrast to the position taken by the Pre-Trial Chamber that confirmed the charges against Lubanga. The Special Representative held that the Pre-Trial Chamber in *Lubanga* had erroneously used a 'bright-line' demarcation rule wherein there is no 'active participation' in hostilities, according to that Chamber, when the child's contribution is allegedly "manifestly without connection to the hostilities."[192] The Special Representative argued that children who were a part of the armed group providing support in any way to the armed group, *including through their own sexual exploitation*, were to be considered as being used for 'active participation' in hostilities. She, like the Prosecutor, emphasized that girls sexually exploited by the FPLC also performed combat and varied other duties more *directly* connected to the hostilities (i.e. serving as bodyguards to commanders).[193] The Special Representative (as did the Prosecutor Moreno-Ocampo in *Lubanga*) expressed the fear that if "active participation" in hostilities were too narrowly defined (that is, so as to exclude children travelling with armed groups and used in large part for sexual exploitation); girls who were members of the FPLC travelling with the armed force might be excluded from consideration as so-called 'child soldiers.'[194] The Special Representative summarized the issue of what under international law properly constitutes 'active participation' in hostilities thus:

> The Court should deliberately include any sexual acts perpetrated, in particular against girls, within its understanding of the "using" crime. The Special Representative underscores that during war, the use of girl children in particular includes sexual violence...The Special Representative explains that girl combatants are often invisible: "Because they are also wives and domestic aides, they either slip away or are not brought forward for DDR programs. *Commanders prefer to 'keep* ***their*** *women,' who often father their children, and even if the girls are combatants,* ***they are not released with the rest.*** Their complicated status makes them particularly vulnerable. ***They are recruited as child soldiers and sex slaves but are invisible when it comes to the counting.*** " As the above case illustrates, the actual experience of children in the DRC conflicts requires a more inclusive interpretation.[195]

The argument advanced by the current author is that sexually exploited girl members of the FPLC are to be considered as being 'used in hostilities' and also as 'participating actively' in hostilities as child soldiers[196] just as is the case for the boys. This ought to be the perspective regardless of whether or not the FPLC girls performed combat duties, bodyguard functions or other various support duties traditionally thought of as more directly related to the fighting *per se*. Children

---

[192] *Prosecutor v. Thomas Lubanga Dyilo*. Amicus Brief of Coomaraswamy, R. (United Nations Special Representative of the Secretary-General on Children and Armed Conflict), (2008, para 19).

[193] *Prosecutor v. Thomas Lubanga Dyilo*. Amicus Brief of Coomaraswamy, R. (United Nations Special Representative of the Secretary-General on Children and Armed Conflict), (2008, para 22–23).

[194] *Prosecutor v. Thomas Lubanga Dyilo*. Amicus Brief of Coomaraswamy, R. (United Nations Special Representative of the Secretary-General on Children and Armed Conflict), (2008, para 24).

[195] *Prosecutor v. Thomas Lubanga Dyilo*. Amicus Brief of Coomaraswamy, R. (United Nations Special Representative of the Secretary-General on Children and Armed Conflict), (2008, para 25–26, emphasis added).

[196] The term 'child soldiers' is used for convenience but as used by this author in the context of *Lubanga* refers to child civilian members of the FPLC who are victims of genocidal forcible transfer.

were/are being used by the FPLC to inflict *genocidal harms* on the children's groups of origin; the Hema (and not just targeted non-Hema ethnic groups such as the Lendu and Ngiti peoples). As such, the children are performing an *unlawful* military function. It is well understood by the UPC/FPLC what devastating effects on the Hema population/communities are wrought by the FPLC: (1) appropriating their children as so-called UPC/FPLC 'child soldiers' and (2) stigmatizing both the girl children through rape and the boy child soldiers by, for instance, having them procure sex slaves for FPLC commanders and by (3) ordering (or otherwise coercing) the children to commit a host of other international crimes (all of the aforementioned acts resulting in the genocidal forcible transfer of these so-called child soldiers to the FPLC) . This then amounts to *auto-genocide* in that the UPC/FPLC is dominated by commanders and a membership of Hema ethnic origin.[197]

c) Cruel and Inhuman Treatment and Sexual Violence as Allegedly Mere "Aggravating Factors" to the War Crimes Charged in Lubanga

The FPLC implemented a genocidal common plan to appropriate Hema children to the FPLC; including under 15s (i.e. through 'recruiting' them as 'child soldiers'; stigmatizing the girl children in the eyes of their home communities also through their sexual violation by FPLC commanders, torturing the children in so-called FPLC military training camps through cruel training that significantly harmed the children physically and psychologically, stigmatizing the boy child soldiers by having them procure sex slaves for the FPLC and commit other gendered atrocities etc.). Thus, the children were performing a forced function in the hostilities as victims of the genocidal forcible transfer of children to further the political and military strategic objectives of the UPC/FPLC. Yet, the OTP in *Lubanga* took the position that: (1) the cruel treatment of children in the FPLC training camps; (2) the sexual violence perpetrated in particular against FPLC girl 'child soldiers' as well as (3) the use of boy child soldiers, on FPLC command orders, to procure sex slaves for the FPLC commanders, were essentially but 'aggravating' factors to the war crimes charged (the latter relating to recruitment and use of under 15s for active participation in armed hostilities).

The identical position was taken by the Legal Representatives of the Victims in regards to FPLC sexual violence perpetrated against the child soldier 'recruits':

> Girls under the age of 15 were recruited . . .by the UPC and were used as sexual slaves, were deflowered at a very early age. Others sometimes became pregnant, had unwanted children. They were also submitted to household chores, and many of them were used as well in armed operations. . . in particular as scouts, in looting operations, killing, and fighting. *All of these criminal acts carried out against girls under the age of 15 should be considered as* ***aggravating circumstances*** *to the crime of enlistment, recruitment, and active participation of child soldiers under the age of 15 in hostilities during times of war.*[198]

---

[197] Note that nothing in the Genocide Convention (1951) disallows the notion of autogenocide (See Forster (2011)).

[198] *Prosecutor v. Thomas Lubanga Dyilo*, Legal Representatives of the Victims Closing Statement (2011, p. 71, emphasis added).

On the analysis of the current author (in contrast to the position taken by the OTP in *Lubanga*); sexual violation of FPLC girl 'child soldiers' is *not* an aspect of 'conscription' to an armed force *as the term is normally understood* under international law (i.e. compulsory induction into military service; that is, recruitment into 'soldiering' (as that term is normally understood in international law) for the duration of the conflict). Rather, sexual violation of the girl (and boy) 'child soldier' recruits and involving the boys in gendered crimes on FPLC commander orders is about: (1) the appropriation of persons (children) as if pieces of property (genocidal forcible transfer of children) and (2) moulding/grooming children to adopt the FPLC identity and aberrant norms and perpetrate atrocities as so-called child soldiers. Sexual violation of girl and boy 'child soldiers' and involving child soldiers in perpetrating procurement of sex slaves and committing other gendered crimes is, in fact, part of the 'genocidal forcible transfer' of these children. Sexual violence is thus integral to the latter crime; it is in itself one vehicle for the 'genocidal forcible transfer of children'. Sexual violence then is *not* just an aggravating factor related to appropriation and use of child soldiers (whether over or under age 15) for active participation in hostilities. Sexually violating the child soldiers and involving boy (or girl) child soldiers in perpetrating sexual violence is a vehicle also for cultural appropriation in that these child soldiers then become symbols of the norms set or endorsed by the FPLC rather than those of civilized society.

Such sexual violence against children, girls in particular (whether occurring in the context of what is in *Lubanga* characterized as or reduced only to 'conscription' or 'enlistment' into the FPLC)[199] occurs frequently in various armed conflict situations where mass atrocity and/or genocide is taking place and child soldiers are 'recruited' and used in hostilities. Such sexual violence is, in fact, another significant marker of the 'genocidal forcible transfer of children' in such contexts.

Given the analysis here (i.e. concluding that FPLC sexual violence against girls and boys was a vehicle for the *genocidal forcible transfer of the children*); the current author respectfully disputes the position of the OTP in *Lubanga* that sexual violence is best characterized as part of or resulting from 'conscription' as that term is normally understood.[200] The very fact that thousands of girls were subjected to the most violent sexual attacks by the FPLC, and even when they were *not* targeted for 'recruitment' to the FPLC as child soldiers; bolsters the point that such sexual violence by the FPLC directed against girl children in particular, though not

---

[199] The current author has already noted that the FPLC appropriation of children for the purpose of their participation in perpetrating international crimes as FPLC child soldier members cannot be considered recruitment in the normal sense but rather constitutes the genocidal forcible transfer of children.

[200] Note also that in the 'Second Report of the [ICC] Registry on Reparations' (1 September 2011): "[T]he Registry specifically includes sexual violence as a type of harm *caused as a result of child conscription*." (See 'Women's Initiatives for Gender Justice request for leave to participate in reparations proceedings'28 March, 2012, p. 10, para 25).

exclusively,[201] (whether Hema or non-Hema), had a genocidal intent (namely; the genocidal forcible transfer of children). Whether those girls sexually violated became FPLC child soldiers or not; and whether they were Hema or non-Hema child victims, in each case the girls were, due to the sexual victimization by the FPLC, now considered 'of the FPLC' (no longer part of mainstream civilized society).

Thus, while sexual violation of girl and boy children often coincided with the children's 'conscription' into the FPLC *as 'child soldiers'* and/or sex slaves (or was subsequent thereto); such sexual violence also occurred completely outside the context of 'conscription' or *alleged* enlistment as a 'child soldier'.[202] Put differently, it was the FPLC 'common plan' to perpetrate the genocidal transfer of children that caused both: (1) the sexual violence against the children and (2) the forced transfer of child civilians into a force perpetrating mass atrocities. In this regard, note that the FPLC made it perfectly clear that, in their view, they had every right to appropriate Hema children:

> MONUC, through its radio station, Radio Okapi, revealed that Mr. Lubanga had decreed that each family living in the areas under his control had to mandatorily contribute to the war effort by providing either a cow, money ***or a child*** to join the ranks of the rebels or the UPC militia.[203]

Clearly, were it the case that the children were simply 'recruited' to the UPC/FPLC to contribute to the war effort in a lawful manner as normally soldiers do (as opposed to being the victims of the 'genocidal forcible transfer of children'): (1) the cruel and inhuman treatment accorded the children in the FPLC 'military' training camps; (2) the sexual violation of the girls and boys 'recruited'[204] and (3) the routine use of child soldiers to procure girl sex slaves for FPLC commanders in the UPC/FPLC would not have been such a systemic integral part of the FPLC treatment of the children in its ranks. Note also that children's *alleged* consent or assent to sexual activity (i.e. as so-called 'bush wives') is irrelevant and inapplicable in a context in which sexual violence is a mechanism for the 'genocidal transfer of children' as was the case in the situation in the DRC for the period covered in *Lubanga*. Put differently, children of any age (persons under age 18), even domestic

---

[201] The Trust Fund for Victims' first report in the Lubanga case noted that "sexual violence was perpetrated widely *against girl and boy soldiers* during their conscription, enlistment and/or participation." (See 'Women's Initiatives for Gender Justice request for leave to participate in reparations proceedings'28 March, 2012, pp. 9–10, para 24).

[202] Thus, though conscription as a child soldier and sexual violation of the FPLC children 'recruited' by the FPLC were highly correlated events, conscription *per se did not cause* the sexual violation (contrast this view with that of the Legal Representative of the Victims in *Lubanga* who stated at Trial "sexual violence is indeed the result of the enlistment" [by which this author takes her to mean 'sexual violence is indeed the result of conscription and enlistment' given the context of her entire submission] (See Legal Representative of the Victims Closing Statements, Prosecutor v Lubanga 25 August, 2011, p. 71).

[203] Prosecutor v. Thomas Lubanga Dyilo, Legal Representatives of Victims Closing Statements (2011, p. 75).

[204] The children were often recruited by the FPLC subsequent to essentially forced surrender by the parents, and frequently by means of abduction.

legal age of sexual consent, *cannot* consent or assent under domestic or international law to their own genocidal forcible transfer via sexual victimization.[205]

d) An Inelegant Prosecution Argument Relating to FPLC Sexual Abuse of Girl Soldiers

It is here respectfully contended that it was neither necessary nor useful for the Prosecution in *Lubanga* to raise what, with respect, seems an inelegant argument in regards to FPLC sexual violence perpetrated against girls. The Prosecution argument referred to involved the claim that the girl children travelling with the FPLC (girls who were routinely sexually violated by FPLC officers and lower ranking members) were, *just by virtue of their providing forced sex*, performing an essential ***combat-related support function*** for the FPLC (a function that allegedly helped the FPLC in some way in its fighting operations *per se* in the conflict theatre and therefore, *for this reason*, in part these girl victims should be considered as 'child soldiers' entitled to the same protection as other child soldiers):

> In *Prosecutor v. Brima, Kamara and Kanu*,. . . the SCSL held that even the mere presence of children, regardless of their specific duties, in locations where crimes had been committed was found to constitute the use of children to participate actively in hostilities.
>
> [The SCSL in *Prosecutor v. Brima, Kamara and Kanu* determined] that participation in ***hostilities entails not only acts that put children's lives directly at risk in combat, but also any labour or support that gives effect to or helps maintain operations in a conflict***. . .[206]
>
> This wider interpretation is also supported by the testimony of the UN Special Representative of the Secretary General on Children and Armed conflict who stated that children performing roles as cooks, porters, nurses, translators ***and for sexual exploitation were considered essential support***, and that the Court must reject any interpretation [of child soldier] which excludes girls.[207]
>
> The Prosecution notes that while it is correct that the use of child soldiers in activities "clearly unrelated to the hostilities" falls outside the scope of the provision, **the use of children in a "*direct support function*" is considered to be included in the prohibition**. The Prosecution accordingly submits that in order to afford wider protection to child soldiers and to prevent any use of children in activities closely related to hostilities, *the Chamber* ***should approach the notion of "direct support" broadly, and include within the meaning of the term activities such as the ones described by the UN Special Representative [i.e. the activity of being sexual exploited]***.[208]

It has here been argued that all of these girl members of the FPLC were entitled under international law to the same protections as the boys. Thus, both girls and boy FPLC members are entitled to the same demobilization and re-integration services. This is the case in that *they are all child victims of genocidal forcible transfer to the*

---

[205] Indeed, the concept of assent or consent is inapplicable in the context of the genocidal transfer of any person of the group to the perpetrator group.

[206] *Prosecutor v. Thomas Lubanga Dyilo*, Prosecution closing brief (2011, p. 60, para 141, emphasis added).

[207] *Prosecutor v. Thomas Lubanga Dyilo*, Prosecution closing brief (2011, p. 61, para 142, emphasis added).

[208] *Prosecutor v. Thomas Lubanga Dyilo*, Prosecution closing brief (2011, p. 61, para 143, emphasis added).

FPLC who, due to coercive circumstances and/or more direct coercion, engaged in the fighting and/or performed combat related functions and/or provided ***non-combat*** *related services* including sexual favours. As child victims of genocidal forcible transfer; all of these children were integral to advancing FPLC military objectives (as living symbols for the general populace of FPLC power and as forced labor). The specific nature of these children's activities/duties within the FPLC are, therefore, irrelevant in terms of establishing their entitlements to: (1) NGO and UN services; and (2) their right to reparations as victims as well as to (3) the judicial remedy of prosecution of those FPLC individuals who perpetrated the severe and myriad harms the children have suffered and continue to suffer.

The current author is in accord with Navanethem Pillay (High Commissioner of Human Rights) that: "sexual violence is almost invariably the foreseeable consequence in situations of conflict and in a climate that fosters mass atrocities."[209] The present author would add that systematic and widespread sexual violence against *children* as highly prized target victims is also a foreseeable consequence in an armed conflict where: (1) one side or both is perpetrating mass atrocity and (2) children are the intended victims of *genocidal forcible transfer* to be used in part as so-called 'child soldiers' and/or sex slaves. From the latter perspective on the hostilities in Ituri, it is not surprising that the sexual violence perpetrated by the FPLC did *not* cease with the signing of a peace agreement in the DRC in 2002: "Instead it worsened with government soldiers and rebels raping hundreds of thousands of girls and women."[210] The FPLC continued to attempt the genocidal forcible transfer of child victims[211] through sexual violence to perpetuate a perception that they still had power; that they had the upper hand in the region. Such a genocidal mind set is difficult to eradicate; perhaps even more so than other precipitators of armed conflict and atrocity such as grandiose territorial ambitions.

3.1.7 On the Short Training Afforded FPLC Child Soldiers: Implications

Most often children in the FPLC were sent into combat with arguably wholly inadequate short-term training:

> *Upon completion of an intensive "short-term training", the recruits "would be ready for combat"*, given a weapon and a military uniform, and incorporated into military units (brigades, companies, battalions, or platoons).[212]

---

[209] Pillay, N. (2009).

[210] Tosh, C. and Chazan, Y. (Eds.) (2008, p. 4).

[211] Recall that genocidal forcible transfer of victims to the FPLC through sexual violation did not necessarily include in all instances of these mass sexual atrocities the physical transfer of the child victims to the FPLC as child soldiers or sex slaves. Thus, non-Hema children were sexually victimized by the FPLC and so *tainted forever as FPLC* in the perception of their home communities even though these children were not physically transferred to the FPLC to join the ranks.

[212] *Prosecutor v. Thomas Lubanga Dyilo*, Prosecution closing brief (2011, p. 85, para 207, emphasis added).

> On the evidence admitted for the purpose of the confirmation hearing, the Chamber considers that there are substantial grounds to believe that children under the age of fifteen years were enlisted and conscripted in order to undergo *a short military training lasting less than two months* . . .[213]

This exceedingly short training period for the child recruits is not surprising in that this was not about effective so-called 'military' training of children or instilling excellent '(child) soldiering' competencies, but rather directed to transforming the children (the so-called FPLC 'recruits') into perpetrators of mass atrocity regardless the cost to the so-called child 'recruits':

> As a result of the fighting, some of the child soldiers in the UPC/FPLC sustained injuries. Others died in the battle. ***Indeed, W-0038 said that children were more likely to be wounded or killed; compared to adults***, they run more slowly and could therefore be more easily shot at by the enemy. Children were also often put in the front line during combat. *According to the witnesses present on the battlefields, "[a] lot of children died."*[214]

Thus, a combination of factors, including importantly the short FPLC 'military' training the children received, contributed to the high number of FPLC child soldier injuries and deaths. It is here suggested, therefore, that the transfer of large numbers of children to the FPLC was more about communicating to the general populace that the group was willing and able to carry out a plan with genocidal intent than about building an effective strong 'military' force comprised largely of children and youths. The children then, as has here been explained, were the victims of genocidal forcible transfer to the FPLC and *not* of 'recruitment' if the latter is taken to mean recruitment as understood under international law i.e. a mechanism for becoming a member of a *bona fide* military soldiering armed group or force.

3.1.8 The 'Continuous Nature' of the International Crimes Perpetrated Against FPLC Child Soldiers

The appropriation of children to the UPC/FPLC by means that would leave these children forever identified with that armed group and largely or completely alienated from their home communities and families (i.e. raping the children, having the children commit atrocities etc.) was *not* classed as amongst the gravest of international crimes in *Lubanga* [i.e. the genocidal forcible transfer of children (persons under age 18)]; but only as a 'war crime' insofar as under 15s were victimized. In this regard; note that the current author is agreed with Frulli that (despite some protestations from certain academics to the contrary), in practice, the international judiciary regards 'crimes against humanity' (including 'genocide' as a

---

[213] *Prosecutor v. Thomas Lubanga Dyilo*, Decision on the Confirmation of Charges (2007, p. 99, para 289, emphasis added).

[214] *Prosecutor v. Thomas Lubanga Dyilo*, Prosecution closing brief (2011, p. 91, para 215, emphasis added).

separable independent category of the latter) as graver offences than are war crimes even where the latter are accompanied by aggravating factors.[215] Hence, it is here argued that the Lubanga case was *undercharged* in not also charging the defendant with the 'genocidal forcible transfer of children.'

The failure of the Prosecution to charge Lubanga additionally with the 'genocidal forcible transfer of children' likely contributed to the Prosecution erroneously limiting the scope of the 'continuous' nature of the FPLC crimes perpetrated against their own child soldier recruits. The Prosecution in *Lubanga* framed the issue of the continuous nature of the crimes perpetrated against children by the defendant and his co-perpetrators in the UPC/FPLC thus:

> The Prosecution submits that the war crime of enlisting and conscripting children under the age of 15 *is a crime of a continuous nature committed as long as the child remains in the armed group or is underage. The crime encompasses all the acts suffered by the child during the training and during the time they were forced to be a soldier.* This interpretation is particularly relevant to capture the gender abuse, a crucial part of the recruitment of girls.[216]

The contention is, on the current analysis, in contrast, that the 'continuous nature' of the crime of appropriating children to the UPC/FPLC[217] (to be raped, to have these children commit atrocity against other children both within and outside the UPC/FPLC ranks and against adult civilians etc.) extends well beyond the time that: (1) the children remain with the armed group or (2) that they were under age 15 and should thus be viewed through the lens of 'genocidal forcible transfer of children'. The continuous nature of crimes perpetrated against these children extend indefinitely (i.e. even after they leave the UPC/FPLC and/or are aged 15 or over) in that the children so victimized (i.e. despite the best efforts of NGOs in the post-conflict period) most often continue to be considered as perpetrators of atrocities in the view of their families and home communities and are thus alienated from the latter as was the intention of the UPC/FPLC. Furthermore, other significant harms are also of an indefinite continuing nature such as UPC/FPLC girl 'child soldiers' contracting HIV as the result of rape by UPC/FPLC commanders and other members of their armed units; girl FPLC soldiers having their reproductive capacity destroyed through sexual violence, other physical and psychological irreversible harms done to the FPLC male and female child soldiers by the FPLC command itself etc. The duration of certain of the crimes perpetrated by the UPC/FPLC against FPLC child soldier 'recruits' then *cannot* be delimited to

---

[215] Frulli (2001, pp. 332–333).

[216] *Prosecutor v. Thomas Lubanga Dyilo*, Prosecution Closing Statement (2011, p. 10, emphasis added).

[217] There is dispute as to whether or not the Rome Statute (2002) contemplates the notion of 'continuing crimes'. This author maintains that the Statute should be interpreted as doing so and that this is consistent with the purpose of the Statute and the ICC mandate to hold accountable those who commit the gravest of international crimes which generally are continuing crimes. Arguably the prohibition against the appropriation and use of other people's children has been a part of customary law for some time. For a discussion of the matter of continuing crimes under the Rome Statute see Nissel (2004).

the period "the child remains in the armed group or is underage."[218] This continuous nature of the crime *beyond* (1) the children's UPC/FPLC initiation, training and active participation in the group in some capacity while under 15 or (2) as children under age 15 having been or currently being an FPLC child soldier is a key feature of the genocidal forcible transfer of these children (a crime not charged in *Lubanga*).

In sum then the particular war crimes charged in *Lubanga* (recruitment and use of children under age 15 for active participation in armed hostilities) were considered by the ICC Prosecution to be continuous but yet delimited to the period in which the children were with the FPLC and/or were underage (given the elements of these particular war crimes under the Rome Statute[219]). The contention here has been that the continuous nature of the grave international crime of 'genocidal forcible transfer of children', in contrast, extends well beyond the delimited time frame carved out by the Prosecutor for the 'continuous' nature of the war crimes charged under Rome Statute Article 8(2)(b)(xxvi) or Article 8(2)(e)(vii)[220] in the Lubanga case.

Ironically, the Prosecution in *Lubanga* acknowledged at other points in its closing statement (consistent with the children having been the victims of genocidal forcible transfer to the UPC/FPLC; a crime not charged in the case) the ongoing nature of certain of the harms suffered by the UPC/FPLC child recruits which extended for years beyond the child's initiation and participation in the armed conflict [i.e. ongoing psychological trauma resulting directly from the children's UPC/FPLC initiation and 'training' as well as due to the children's active participation in armed conflict and what that entailed as a UPC/FPLC member (i.e. committing systematic atrocity)]:

> The Prosecution submits that even those children who survived the tortures suffered during training *continue to be tortured*, that those who have no visible scars of the wounds received *have internal scars that will remain with them for years to come*, that even if you see no blood on the body of a former child soldier, they are internally bleeding.[221]

The Hema children appropriated by the UPC/FPLC to become child soldiers were removed from their group of origin in the first instance as fully functional individuals who, in the ordinary course, would have contributed greatly to the vitality and sustainability of their families; home communities and group of origin (i.e. Hema civil mainstream society). However, in many instances, these so-called ex 'child soldiers' can no longer, for the most part, contribute as meaningfully and fully to the viability of their communities and group of origin as would normally be the case; if they can do so at all. This is the case due to the continuous nature of the crime of genocidal forcible transfer of children (here perpetrated through the

---

[218] *Prosecutor v. Thomas Lubanga Dyilo*, Prosecution Closing Statement (2011, p. 10).

[219] Rome Statute (2002).

[220] Rome Statute (2002).

[221] *Prosecutor v. Thomas Lubanga Dyilo*, Prosecution Closing Statement (2011, p. 10, emphasis added).

vehicle of appropriation and use by an armed group perpetrating systematic mass atrocities) as evidenced by: (1) the severe psychological and/or physical harms suffered by the children as ex members of the UPC/FPLC and (2) given the ex child soldiers/sex slaves frequent significant alienation from their families and home communities. The latter continuing harms are telling indicia of the occurrence of the genocidal forcible transfer of these children to the FPLC in that such genocidal transfer of children destroys the children's group of origin at least in part.

Given that the children were regarded by the UPC/FPLC as property of the armed group (the FPLC); it is not surprising that Lubanga's several decrees in which he directed that under 18s in the FPLC should be demobilized were, according to the Prosecution and its evidence, not vigorously enforced and were in fact, for the most part, actually sham attempts at demobilization of the children (i.e. The Prosecution evidence suggested that even after issuance of these demobilization decrees the FPLC continued to recruit children, including under 15s, and the child members of Lubanga's own protection unit were not demobilized):

> *Witness 0046, the senior child protection officer for the United Nations in Ituri*, visited Thomas Lubanga on the 30th of May, 2003, just 16 days before the 1st June 2003 order. She warned him specifically about the Rome Statute and the rights provided to children and the obligation not to use child soldiers. So on the 1st of June, it is not surprising that Thomas Lubanga again prohibited the use of children under the age of 18, *a prohibition that Witness 0046 described as a* ***masquerade***.[222]

Prosecution witnesses testified that: (1) the UPC/FPLC did not consider that the recruitment and use of children for active participation in armed hostilities (regardless of the age of the children) was a crime and that (2) the demobilisation decrees were just issued to placate the media and the international community but that no significant effort towards demobilizing the 'child soldier' members of the FPLC in fact took place. That the UPC/FPLC would not regard the recruitment and use of children for active participation in armed hostilities (regardless of age of the children involved) as a crime is consistent with the UPC/FPLC having the view that the children were now *bona fide* members of the armed group bearing all the normal responsibilities of that membership including perpetrating mass systemic atrocity. Such a perspective as held by the UPC/FPLC is quintessentially that of the perpetrators of genocidal forcible transfer of children.

3.1.8.1 FPLC Child Soldiers and Their Lack of Criminal Culpability

The Office of Public Counsel for Victims in *Lubanga*, through counsel Ms. Massidda, argued in its closing statement that the child soldiers of the FPLC were *not* individually criminally culpable under international criminal law for the crimes that they

---

[222] *Prosecutor v. Thomas Lubanga Dyilo*, Prosecution Closing Statement (2011, p. 35, emphasis added).

perpetrated (including for instance "murder, rape, mutilations or looting")[223] because the children at issue were under 15 and unable to give consent to being "soldiers":

> In addition, *children* ***under the age of 15*** *cannot reasonably give their consent to recruitment in an army, and all the more so, their consent cannot be used as consenting to be soldiers. Therefore, children* **cannot** *be considered responsible for any acts that result from their recruitment, and this applies throughout the period for which they remained within an armed group.*
>
> Therefore, the former child soldiers can only be considered as victims of the crimes that they were the victims of and can in no case be considered responsible for acts that they committed in that context.[224]

The current author advances the proposition, however, that *all* of the children (persons under age 18) who were members of the FPLC were the victims of 'genocidal forcible transfer' rather than recruitment as 'soldiers'. This since the FPLC cannot be considered a 'soldiering' (military) unit under international law given that the objective of the UPC/FPLC from the outset (during the period covered in *Lubanga*) was not to abide by international law during the conflict; but rather to adopt and implement a 'common plan' of mass atrocity which did in fact materialize on the ground. As a result, the child members of the FPLC were no longer accepted by their home communities and groups of origin but were instead perceived as perpetrators. Yet, the parties in the Lubanga case erroneously characterized the child victim members of the FPLC as holding the status of 'soldiers' simply based on the fact that they were members of the FPLC armed group[225] and, in most instances, actively and directly participated in its illegal armed activities:

> All of the former child soldiers participating in this trial have no doubt undergone psychological damage because they lived through an atrocious experience and traumatising ***because they were soldiers***. Many of them – many of these former child soldiers underwent physical damage and a wide range of injuries, violent acts against them including sexual violence. The parents of the former child soldiers have suffered moral damage, moral prejudice, and psychological suffering because of the abduction of their children, ***because of the enlistment of these children in the army*** and their participation in activities associated with adults at the risk of being killed or injured.[226]

The current author argues, in contrast, that children aged 15 and over (but under 18) could no more legally consent to their own 'genocidal forcible transfer'

[223] *Prosecutor v. Thomas Lubanga Dyilo*, Office of Public Counsel for Victims Closing Statement (2011, p. 60).

[224] *Prosecutor v. Thomas Lubanga Dyilo*, Office of Public Counsel for Victims Closing Statement (2011, p. 60).

[225] The war crimes charged in Lubanga were nevertheless proper and viable as there is no requirement in regards such charges under the Rome Statute (2002) that the 'recruitment' and/or use of under 15s be by an armed group or force that in other respects abides by the customary rules of war and international humanitarian law.

[226] *Prosecutor v. Thomas Lubanga Dyilo*, Office of Public Counsel for Victims Closing Statement (2011, p. 61).

to the FPLC (or other such groups or forces perpetrating mass atrocities and/or genocide) than could children under age 15.[227] Recall further that the genocidal forcible transfer of children under the Rome Statute Elements of the Crime[228] construction need not necessarily involve the use of physical force; but can involve any form of coercion, psychological or other such as intimidation of family members, creating circumstances where not joining the group would pose a more immediate physical danger than joining etc. (all of which were employed by the FPLC as so-called recruitment strategies). Thus, children aged 15 and over also cannot be held criminally responsible for being a part of the FPLC or for the acts (international crimes) that foreseeably flowed from their membership in such an armed force as the FPLC.

Recall that the FPLC accomplished the genocidal forcible transfer of children to its ranks *initially* through abductions, pressuring families to surrender their children to the FPLC and through propaganda campaigns that made it clear, for instance, that joining the FPLC was allegedly a means to survival for the individual, their family and village. However, that genocidal forcible transfer of the children, as has been explained, was also accomplished by then having the children, after a period of very brief 'training', engage in mass atrocities against both moderate Hema and specific targeted ethnic groups such as the Lendu. This in order to increase the likelihood that: (1) these children would be pariahs in their own families and communities even in a post-conflict period and that they would (2) forever be identified as FPLC 'soldiers' who committed heinous atrocities also against their own communities. The latter then the FPLC calculated no doubt would increase the likelihood of these children retaining their loyalty to the UPC/FPLC.

As the mass atrocities committed by these children were part and parcel of *their own genocidal forcible transfer to the FPLC*, they cannot justifiably be held criminally responsible for the international crimes they may have perpetrated. Recall in this regard that: (1) the 'genocidal forcible transfer of children' involves persons under age 18 according to the Rome Statute Elements of the Crime[229] and that (2) the Rome Statute *excludes* from its jurisdiction persons who were children (under age 18) at the time of committing the international crimes articulated in the Statute.[230] The latter exclusion is thus consistent with the proposition advanced here that children commit these mass atrocities generally as victims of genocidal forcible transfer to an unlawful armed group or force perpetrating mass atrocities and/or genocide and are, therefore, non-culpable under international criminal law.

---

[227] Grover (2012).

[228] Rome Statute Elements of the Crime (2002).

[229] Rome Statute Elements of the Crime (2002).

[230] This author has argued elsewhere that the exclusion of Rome Statute jurisdiction over persons who were children (under age 18) at the time of committing the international crimes articulated in the Rome Statute (2002) was formulated as a general principle of Rome Statute criminal law and not simply a jurisdictional discretionary choice (See Grover 2012, pp. 76–79).

3.1.8.2 The Current Situation in the DRC Regarding Child Soldiering

The 'Office of Public Counsel for Victims' in *Lubanga* stressed the fact that ex FPLC child soldiers who co-operated with the OTP and came forward to testify at trial as victim witnesses did so at great personal risk:

> For most victims the decision to participate in this case has not been an easy decision. It meant major sacrifices, in particular as regards their security, in particular for victims who accepted to co-operate with the Office of the Prosecutor and to participate in this trial as witnesses for the Prosecution. Indeed, the victims participating in this trial as well as the victims benefiting from dual status as witnesses and victims are all from the Ituri region, this region where supporting the accused and his political and military movement is still today very, very strong.[231]

Indeed, counsel for the 'Office of Public Counsel for Victims' noted that: (1) many of the former FPLC child soldiers who cooperated with the OTP and were prepared to testify had been threatened and that (2) families of these victims disassociated, in many instances, from their children due to the ex child soldiers agreeing to participate in the ICC process.[232] It seems reasonable to assume that these families feared retribution from the FPLC should their children cooperate with the ICC Office of the Prosecutor and testify at trial in *Lubanga*. Afterall, the Prosecution had presented evidence at trial in *Lubanga* that families and village peoples were often pressured to surrender their children to the FPLC on pain of risking the security of their families and villages. The basis of support for the UPC/FPLC thus seems intricately linked to its brutal and inhuman tactics. Indeed, the U.N. Committee on the Rights of the Child (CRC) (in its comments of 18 January, 2012 concerning the DRC initial report to the Committee regarding purported progress in complying with the Optional Protocol to the Convention on the Rights of the Child concerning children involved in armed conflict)[233] noted that there was continued impunity in the DRC for perpetrators of grave violations of children's human rights. That impunity is likely based on fear of retribution should there be attempted prosecutions:

> Ms. Lee [a Committee on the Rights of the Child expert who questioned DRC representatives on the report submitted in 2012 to the Committee] expressed serious concern about *continued impunity for perpetrators of child rights violations, including some senior military officers*. For example...Perpetrators with an International Criminal Court arrest warrant, such as General Bosco Ntaganda, who had been listed by the United Nations Security Council, and others ....remained in the Armed Forces of the Democratic Republic of the Congo (FARDC); there had been no prosecutions or convictions. *The Committee was concerned that threats of reprisal may be the very reason why cases were not brought against many high-ranking officers.*[234]

---

[231] Prosecutor v. Thomas Lubanga Dyilo, Office of Public Counsel for Victim Closing Statement (2011, p. 63).

[232] Prosecutor v. Thomas Lubanga Dyilo, Office of Public Counsel for Victim Closing Statement (2011, p. 63).

[233] Optional Protocol to the Convention on the Rights of the Child concerning children involved in armed conflict (2002).

[234] Committee on the Rights of the Child Concluding Observations on the Report of the DRC regarding its compliance with the Optional Protocol to the Convention on the Rights of the Child concerning children involved in armed conflict (2012, emphasis added).

Note that General Bosco Ntaganda is charged by the ICC with three counts of war crimes: enlistment of children under the age of 15; conscription of children under the age of 15; and using children under the age of 15 to participate actively in hostilities.

It is the case that, according to Committee on the Rights of the Child (CRC) expert Lee: "The Democratic Republic of the Congo had the highest number of children used and recruited by armed groups and the national military force of any country in the world."[235] The representative from the DRC government took the position before the CRC reviewing the DRC report that there were children amongst the armed troops but that they were being recruited not by the Armed Forces of the Democratic Republic of the Congo (FARDC; the national armed forces), but rather supposedly exclusively by rebel armed groups resisting the peace process.[236] The representative of the DRC noted that the legal age of recruitment into the national army of the DRC at present is 18; claimed that forced recruitment of minors into the national army had ended as a practice or accepted policy; and reminded the committee that according to the government of the DRC; 30,000 children had been removed from the ranks of varied armed groups and that this effort was continuing.[237] However, another expert of the Committee on the Rights of the Child stated that:

> ...official reports showed there had been 127 additional enlistments of children into the Armed Forces of the Democratic Republic of the Congo (FARDC).[238]

It would appear then that there is no debate that the recruitment and use of children for active participation in hostilities, including those under 15, is ongoing in the DRC. There is, however, dispute regarding just who is responsible and to which groups or forces the children are being recruited. According to the 2011 shadow report to the Committee on the Rights of the Child submitted by the 'Coalition to Stop the Use of Child Soldiers' (a report intended to provide some guidance to the Committee in regards to its consideration of the first report of the DRC on DRC compliance with the Optional Protocol to the Convention on the Rights of the Child on the involvement of children in armed conflict[239]); despite large numbers of children being demobilized as child soldiers in the DRC; on the whole:

---

[235] Committee on the Rights of the Child Concluding Observations on the Report of the DRC regarding its compliance with the Optional Protocol to the Convention on the Rights of the Child concerning children involved in armed conflict (2012).

[236] Committee on the Rights of the Child Concluding Observations on the Report of the DRC regarding its compliance with the Optional Protocol to the Convention on the Rights of the Child concerning children involved in armed conflict (2012).

[237] Committee on the Rights of the Child Concluding Observations on the Report of the DRC regarding its compliance with the Optional Protocol to the Convention on the Rights of the Child concerning children involved in armed conflict (2012).

[238] Committee on the Rights of the Child Concluding Observations on the Report of the DRC regarding its compliance with the Optional Protocol to the Convention on the Rights of the Child concerning children involved in armed conflict (2012).

[239] Optional Protocol to the Convention on the Rights of the Child on the involvement of children in armed conflict (2002).

. . .the situation for child soldiers, those at risk of recruitment or re-recruitment, and those attempting to rebuild their lives following release, remains substantially unchanged, especially in the eastern provinces where armed conflict persists.[240]

Hundreds of children remain in the ranks of the national armed forces (Forces armées de la Republique Démocratique du Congo, FARDC) despite legal and policy obligations to release them and government pledges to do so. Active recruitment – although reduced – is ongoing, and children have been recruited into other government security forces such as the Republican Guard. Some child soldiers captured by the FARDC have been unlawfully detained and in some cases ill-treated or tortured. Others have been harassed or used for intelligence gathering purposes, exposing them to the risk of reprisals by armed groups. Hundreds, perhaps thousands, of children are in the ranks of armed groups. Many more children are at risk of recruitment and use in conditions of chronic insecurity where child protection mechanisms are virtually non-existent.[241]

Despite legal obligations to ensure that child soldiers are released and provided with assistance for their recovery and reintegration, *the DRC government has consistently failed to develop or implement an effective national strategy to identify and release child soldiers or provide them with assistance for their reintegration.* Programs which do exist remain UN and NGO-led and are inadequate to address the scale of the problem.[242]

It is here suggested that the lack of adequate progress in demobilizing so-called child soldiers from the national army and from rebel armed groups in the DRC is importantly related to the fact that the children are viewed by these armed entities *not* as 'child soldier recruits' to be rescued and released; but rather as property (i.e. of the FARDC or of the various rebel armed groups of which they are a part). The psychology that allows for the appropriation of children in this way *where combined with the common plan of committing systematic mass atrocities*, as was the case with the UPC/FPLC, is that of the *genocidaire* perpetrating the 'genocidal forcible transfer of these children'. Indeed, one might quite reasonably contend that the appropriation of 'child soldiers' on a large scale by armed entities is a harbinger of an increased likelihood that mass atrocities and/or genocide may occur if this is not already the case. This is the case in that appropriating large numbers of children (especially those under 15 as well) to child 'soldiering' reflects a general lack of concern for humane practice.

3.1.9 The Defence Closing and the Prosecution Reply: Selected Issues Arising

3.1.9.1 False Rationales for the Recruitment of 'Child Soldiers'

The Prosecution in *Lubanga* (in its reply to the Defence Closing Brief) challenged the Defence contention that the risk of recruitment of under 15s was justified and

[240] Coalition to Stop the Use of Child Soldiers (2011, p. 1).

[241] Coalition to Stop the Use of Child Soldiers (2011, p. 1).

[242] Coalition to Stop the Use of Child Soldiers (2011, p. 1, emphasis added).

legally supportable since it occurred at a time of an alleged national security threat. The Prosecution stated in its reply to the Defence Closing Brief, furthermore, that the Defence had in fact conceded various key aspects of the Prosecution case:

> *With respect to leadership and responsibility, the Defence appears to concede significant aspects of the case*: . . .despite its [the Defence] claim that the UPC/FPLC did not set out to recruit children, *the known risk that recruitment drives would snare children under the age of 15 was in any event justified and accepted* – because the obligation to constitute an army sufficient to meet the security threat was [allegedly] more pressing than his [Lubanga Dyilo's] duty to observe the law against recruiting child soldiers, and in a conflict between the two duties the former took precedence [according to Lubanga and his co-perpetrators]. . . and . . . when it suited his purpose the Accused issued untrue official documents as propaganda . . . as the Prosecution argues was the case for the [child soldier] demobilisation documents[243]
>
> Additionally, the Defence also suggests . . .a theory of justification – that the duty of a political or military leader to constitute an army sufficient to meet the security threat was more pressing than the duty to observe the law against recruiting child soldiers, and in a conflict between the two duties the former took precedence. ***While the conclusion itself is legally invalid,*** *the argument appears to concede that the Accused – even under his protestation that he was a political and not a military leader – was responsible and accepted the "risk" that his recruitment drives would sweep up underage children.*[244]

In sum then the Defence in: (1) making the claim that recruitment of under 15s was justified in the alleged circumstance (where there was a purported national security threat), though allegedly not intended by the UPC/FPLC; and (2) affirming then, by implication, that the UPC/FPLC would not have relented on its indiscriminate child recruitment tactics despite international pressure had, in effect, conceded that Lubanga as head of the UPC/FPLC: (1) did know or should have known that under 15s would likely be recruited to the FPLC and that (2) he and the other UPC/FPLC leadership found this to be acceptable and not something to be assiduously avoided. Thus, the ICC Prosecution through this and other evidence made out, in the view of the ICC Trial Court, that: (1) the UPC/FPLC did not (in order to comply with international law) at any point change its child recruitment tactics during the period covered in *Lubanga* to prevent recruitment and use of under 15s; and that (2) the FPLC did not under Lubanga's political/military leadership and command release significant numbers of child soldiers since the intention all along was to transfer to FPLC ranks as many children as possible even those under 15. The Trial Court further concluded that Lubanga made an essential contribution to the common plan as *both* political and military head of the UPC/FPLC and that the common plan included child recruitment regardless of the children's age (i.e. even if under 15):

> The evidence establishes that he [Lubanga] not only condoned the recruitment policy but he also played an active role in its implementation, and ***he approved the recruitment of children below the age of 15.*** The statement of his personal secretary . . .that the accused

[243] *Prosecutor v. Thomas Lubanga Dyilo*, Prosecution's Reply to the Conclusions finales de la Défense (2011, p. 3, para 3).

[244] Prosecutor v. Thomas Lubanga Dyilo, Prosecution's Reply to the Conclusions finales de la Défense (2011, p. 63, para 43.

would have had an interest in mobilising troops, rather than demobilising them, supports the conclusion that the accused was informed about, and actively influenced, the decisions on recruitment.[245]

Let us digress here for a moment to note that a rationale such as that proffered by Lubanga for recruitment of under 15s is similar, in some respects, to the grounds offered for the reservation by the United Kingdom to Article 1 of the Optional Protocol to the Convention on the Rights of the Child on the involvement of children in armed conflict (OP-CRC-AC) regarding the UK use of 16 and 17 years olds for active participation in hostilities.[246] *Of course the UK army, unlike the FPLC, relies on voluntary recruitment exclusively and does not intentionally or knowingly recruit or use under 15s.* The UK reservation to Article I of the OP-CRC-AC allows, in certain very narrow circumstances, for 16 and 17-year-old voluntary recruits to the UK national forces to be deployed to conflict zones:

United Kingdom of Great Britain and Northern Ireland Declaration made upon signature and confirmed upon ratification of the Optional Protocol to the Convention on the Rights of the Child on the involvement of children in armed conflict (Declaration made 7 Sept., 2000 and confirmed 24 June, 2003 respectively):

The United Kingdom of Great Britain and Northern Ireland will take all feasible measures to ensure that members of its armed forces who have not attained the age of 18 years do not take a direct part in hostilities.

The United Kingdom understands that article 1 of the Optional Protocol would *not* exclude the deployment of members of its armed forces under the age of 18 to take a direct part in hostilities where:

a) there is a genuine military need to deploy their unit or ship to an area in which hostilities are taking place;

and

b) by reason of the nature and urgency of the situation:

i) it is not practicable to withdraw such persons before deployment; or

ii) to do so would undermine the operational effectiveness of their ship or unit, and thereby put at risk the successful completion of the military mission and/or the safety of other personnel."

Upon ratification:
Declaration:

".....in accordance with Article 3, paragraph 2, of the Optional Protocol:

- The minimum age at which individuals may join the UK Armed Forces is 16 years. ... Parental consent is required in all cases of recruitment under the age of 18 years.

The United Kingdom maintains the following safeguards in respect of voluntary recruitment into the armed forces:

1. The United Kingdom Armed Forces are manned solely by volunteers; there is no compulsory recruitment.

---

[245] *Prosecutor v. Thomas Lubanga Dyilo* Final Trial Judgement Pursuant to Article 74 of the Rome Statute (14 March, 2012, pp. 529–530, para 1234).

[246] Optional Protocol to the Convention on the Rights of the Child on the involvement of children in armed conflict (OP-CRC-AC) (2002).

2. A declaration of age, backed by an authoritative, objective proof (typically the production of an authentic birth certificate) is an integral and early requirement in the recruitment process. Should an individual volunteering to enter the United Kingdom Armed Forces be found either by their own declaration or by inspection of supporting evidence of age to be under 18 years of age, special procedures are adopted. These procedures include:

- the involvement of the parent(s) or legal guardian(s) of the potential recruits:

- clear and precise explanation of the nature of duties involved in military service to the both the individual and their parent(s)/guardian(s); and

- as well as explaining the demands of military life to the individual volunteer and establishing that he/she remains a genuine volunteer, the requirement that the parent(s) or guardian(s), having been similarly informed, freely consent to the individual's entry into the Armed Forces and duly countersign the appropriate application or other appropriate recruitment process forms.[247]

Returning then to the previous discussion, note that the Defence in *Lubanga*, by implication, erroneously argued that children; even persons under age 15 (persons who have no political power and cannot vote in the DRC[248] and are considered a special protected group under international humanitarian and human rights law) are obligated under international law to defend the nation when there is a significant security threat. The latter Defence proposition would have to be true (which is not the case) in order to argue (as did the Defence in *Lubanga*) that: (1) Lubanga had a compelling obligation and a legal right to build an 'army' using children; *even under 15s*, where he deemed this necessary for national security reasons[249] and that (2) doing so did not violate international law. In regards to the FPLC alleged intent to build a strong 'army', note that the FPLC perpetrating systematic mass atrocity as part of a common plan negates any characterization of the FPLC as an army comprised of '*soldiers*' (including so-called child soldiers who received 'military training') as the terms 'soldiers' and 'army' are understood under international humanitarian law:

> ...child soldiers,...committed ***as part of their military experience*** certain crimes such as ***murder, rape, mutilations, or looting.***[250]

---

[247] United Kingdom of Great Britain and Northern Ireland Declaration articulating a reservation to OP-CRC-AC (Declaration made 7 Sept., 2000 and confirmed on ratification of the OP-CRC-AC 24 June, 2003).

[248] Watchlist on Children and Armed Conflict (Report by the Women's Refugee Commission) (June, 2003, p. 1).

[249] In any case, international humanitarian law does *not* legitimize the recruitment and use of children of any age by any armed group or national armed force perpetrating grave international crimes as was the case for the FPLC in the period covered in *Lubanga*. While the Additional Protocol to the 1949 Geneva Conventions (Protocol I) (1977) does not absolutely prohibit the use of children of any age in an international conflict by a national armed force abiding by international law, by the same token it urges at Article 77(2) that States parties take all feasible measures not to use under 15s for direct participation in hostilities. The prohibition on recruitment of under 15s was incorporated but there was no express mention of refusing volunteers (See the ICRC commentary on Protocol I, Article 77(2)(1977). The DRC as party to the Rome Statute (2002) further was obligated not to use or recruit under 15s (the DRC ratified the Rome Statute 11 April, 2002).

[250] *Prosecutor v. Thomas Lubanga Dyilo*, Office of the Public Council for Victims Closing Statement (2011, p.60, emphasis added).

Thus, though the children in the FPLC may have worn army uniforms; learned how to assemble and disassemble military weapons, march, adhere to the rigid FPLC hierarchical command structure, and carry out certain reconnaissance manoeuvres etc., their FPLC training yet *cannot* be considered 'military' training in the ordinary meaning of the term. This is the case since the prime focus of FPLC training was on how effectively to perpetrate mass atrocity and otherwise gain control of Ituri by unlawful means. In fact, perpetrating mass atrocity as part of an FPLC 'common plan' sets the FPLC training and so-called 'military experience' for its members as something quite separate from military experience as the term is normally understood under international law. Rather, the so-called 'military experience' for the FPLC 'child soldier' recruits, for instance, was that of being the victim of the 'genocidal forcible transfer of children.' These child soldier victims of genocidal forcible transfer to the FPLC were expected to perpetrate atrocities against targeted civilians and others. This in order to ensure also that these child soldiers (both the survivors and those who died in battle) would have a perceived permanent tie to and identification with the FPLC; one forged in part in the blood of the child soldiers' victims and, in many cases, also their own.

3.1.9.2 Implications of Children's Special Protected Status

The Prosecution in *Lubanga* contested the Defence claim that the rebel UPC/FPLC, with Lubanga as head, had as its purpose to lawfully protect the DRC Ituri region from a legitimate national security threat and had no intent to recruit underage minors as child soldiers. Instead, the Prosecution alleged a UPC/FPLC common plan to take unlawful control of the Ituri region relying knowingly and intentionally on a force comprised largely of children including under 15s:

> ... the accused and co-perpetrators agreed to build an army to take over Bunia and to expand their [FPLC] territorial control throughout Ituri; that ...plan involved the enlistment, conscription and use in hostilities of young persons, *regardless of age...*[251]

Let us consider for the moment, however, a basic first order question: 'Does the commander-in-chief of a political/military organization have an *obligation* to utilize children for participation in an armed conflict to allegedly protect national security where this would be a major military asset or is allegedly a military necessity?' It is to be emphasized in that regard that children retain the right of 'special protection' under international humanitarian law *even should there be a national security threat*. That special protected status logically then must include, to some extent, protection from the grave harms that may ensue from their recruitment and use for active participation (direct or indirect) in armed hostilities. International human rights and humanitarian treaty law in fact carves out a principle/zone of special protection for children during armed conflict while balancing the latter in

[251] *Prosecutor v. Thomas Lubanga Dyilo*, Prosecution's Reply to the Conclusions finales de la Défense (2011, p. 3, para 4, emphasis added).

various ways against the purported military interests of the State Parties.[252] Recall that the DRC ratified the 1977 Additional Protocols I and II to the 1949 Geneva Conventions that set out the special protected status of children at Article 77 and Article 4(3) respectively.[253] Further, recall that the DRC ratified the Convention on the Rights of the Child (CRC) on 27/09/1990 and the Optional Protocol to the Convention on the Rights of the Child on the involvement of children in armed conflict (OP-CRC-AC) on 11 November, 2001.[254] The Optional Protocol entered into force 12 February, 2002 thus predating the relevant period for the Lubanga case which was from early September 2002 to 13 August 2003. That Optional Protocol to the CRC requires, amongst other things, that States Parties take all feasible measures to ensure that members of their national forces under age 18 do not take direct part in armed hostilities and that under 18s are not compulsorily recruited into the State national force. Further the OP-CRC-AC at Article 4 stipulates that armed *non-State* groups (such as the UPC/FPLC)[255] are prohibited from the recruitment of children or their use in any manner in hostilities. The FPLC (during the relevant period in *Lubanga*), as here previously described, blatantly violated, in the most egregious fashion, the notion of the special protected status of children as articulated in the aforementioned treaties.[256]

This author has argued elsewhere that the special protected status of children during armed conflict extends to all persons under age 18 and not only to under 15s.[257] While the Additional Protocols to the 1949 Geneva Conventions[258] do not explicitly ban the recruitment and use of children *15 and over* for direct or active participation in hostilities (international or internal) by State national armed forces; neither is this endorsed in those treaties.[259] Further, the use of under 15s for direct

---

[252] The current author not surprisingly supports the notion of an *inviolable* special protected status for children during armed conflict (international or internal) that would absolutely prohibit the recruitment or use of *under 18s* for active participation (*direct or indirect*) in hostilities by State or non-State armed entities.

[253] DRC ratified Protocol I and II Additional to the 1949 Geneva Conventions 3/06/1982 and 12/12/2002 respectively.

[254] Ratifications of the Optional Protocol to the Convention on the Rights of the child on the involvement of children in armed conflict (Status as of 31 May, 2012).

[255] Optional Protocol to the Convention on the Rights of the child on the involvement of children in armed conflict (2002).

[256] Non-State entities are not parties to the international human rights and humanitarian law treaties discussed. However, the treaties in articulating the legal concept of the special protected status of children have in fact codified an aspect of customary law with which non-State parties must comply.

[257] Grover (2012).

[258] Additional Protocols I and II to the 1949 Geneva Conventions (1977).

[259] For instance, Protocol I Additional to the 1949 Geneva Conventions (1977) requires States to recruit from the oldest first amongst persons under 18 but at least 15 years in age. This clearly suggests that recruitment of children 15 and older is *not* unreservedly endorsed under international humanitarian law and that the goal is to protect children generally; and with the youngest in any group receiving the most protection; particularly the under 15s.

involvement in hostilities by State national forces in an *international* conflict is not banned but is strongly discouraged (i.e. the State is required to take *all feasible measures* to prevent the same under Protocol I Additional to the 1949 Geneva Conventions).[260] Protocol II Additional to the 1949 Geneva Conventions,[261] however, prohibits both the State and non-State armed force or group from recruiting or using under 15s in hostilities for any type of participation. It is reasonable to conclude then that there is no support; express or implied, in international humanitarian or international human rights law (given the constraints on child soldiering discussed) for either the proposition that: (1) children (persons of any age under 18) are *obligated* in any context to serve in the State national military or non-State armed group or participate (directly or indirectly) in armed hostilities as child soldier members of a State or non-State armed force or group or that (2) commanders are *obliged* to recruit and use children of any age, including under 15s, for active participation (direct or indirect) in hostilities where there is an alleged security threat or for any other purported compelling reason relating to alleged military necessity. Put differently, there is *no* support (express or implied) in international humanitarian or international human rights law for Lubanga's contention that the commander-in-chief (the political/military head) is *obliged* to use children (*notwithstanding their special protected status under international law*) for active participation in armed conflict where there is a purported national security threat and 'military necessity' in that regard to build up the armed force or group.

Relevant international human rights and humanitarian treaty law (such as that here referenced) collectively, in part, simply reflects: (1) political compromises in the treaty drafting process and (2) the 'realities on the ground' in terms of State recruitment and use of children in armed hostilities (though there has been an evolution of sorts in international law in terms of increased protection for children during armed conflict i.e. as reflected in the OP-CRC-AC).[262] At the same time, the aforementioned humanitarian and human rights international treaties highlight the State and non-State armed forces' obligation to respect children's special protected status during armed conflict *at a minimum* to the degree articulated in the relevant treaties and/or as per customary law.[263] Furthermore, an armed force that is engaged in grave violations of international law, such as was the FPLC, cannot

[260] Protocol I Additional to the 1949 Geneva Conventions (1977).

[261] Protocol II Additional to the 1949 Geneva Conventions (1977).

[262] Optional Protocol to the Convention on the Rights of the child on the involvement of children in armed conflict (2002).

[263] Protocol II to the 1949 Geneva Conventions (1977), by implication, sets out the States Parties' obligation to ensure that non-State armed groups respect children's special protected status and do not recruit or use under 15s in hostilities. Further, as the Additional Protocols I and II to the 1949 Geneva Conventions have arguably achieved the status of customary law; non-States Parties are also bound by their provisions including that regarding the special protected status of children which notion in fact predates these treaties.

lawfully recruit and use children (persons under age 18) for active participation in hostilities (direct or indirect) whether in an international or internal conflict in any case.[264]

Protocol I Additional to the 1949 Geneva Conventions then simply deals with the 'realities on the ground' in referring to *children 15 and over* participating in hostilities and sets out certain safeguards under the treaty for these children as well as for under 15s:

Protocol I Additional to the 1949 Geneva Conventions

Article 77: Protection of children

1. *Children [no age specified] shall be the object of special respect* and shall be protected against any form of indecent assault. *The Parties to the conflict shall provide them with the care and aid they require, whether because of their age or for any other reason.*
2. The Parties to the conflict shall take all feasible measures in order that children who have not attained the age of fifteen years do not take a direct part in hostilities and, in particular, they shall refrain from recruiting them into their armed forces. In recruiting among those persons who have attained the age of fifteen years but who have not attained the age of eighteen years the Parties to the conflict shall endeavour to give priority to those who are oldest.[265]

The Rome Statute[266] has not yet developed to be consistent with international human rights law in explicitly prohibiting the use of children at any age (persons under age 18) for direct participation in hostilities (as per Article 1 of the Optional Protocol to the Convention on the Rights of the Child on children involved in armed conflict).[267] (The Rome Statute,[268] as discussed, declares as war crimes the recruitment of children and their use for active participation in hostilities in respect only of under 15s). However, neither does the Rome Statute[269] regard children (persons under age 18) participating in hostilities as so-called child soldiers individually criminally culpable for crimes under ICC jurisdiction which they perpetrated

---

[264] The armed force is under those circumstances a criminal organization. Recruitment and use of persons of any age with the objective of committing systematic and widespread grave international crimes as alleged 'military strategy' is, of course, legally impermissible and that fact cannot be masked or justified with reference to a perceived national security threat. See also the prohibition on the recruitment and use of children *under 15s* in internal hostilities articulated in Protocol II Additional to the 1949 Geneva Conventions (1977) as well as the Optional Protocol to the Convention on the Rights of the Child on the involvement of children in armed conflict (OPCRC-AC) (2002) which prohibits non-State parties from all recruitment and use of child soldiers (persons under 18) in any armed conflict.

[265] Protocol Additional to the Geneva Conventions of 12 August 1949, and relating to the Protection of Victims of International Armed Conflicts (Protocol I), (8 June 1977, emphasis added).

[266] Rome Statute (2002).

[267] Optional Protocol to the Convention on the Rights of the Child on the involvement of children in armed conflict (OPCRC-AC) (2002, Article 1).

[268] Rome Statute (2002).

[269] Rome Statute (2002).

as children. The current author has argued elsewhere that the exclusion of children from individual criminal responsibility under the Rome Statute[270] constitutes substantive law and is therefore listed under the Rome Statute Part 3: General Principles of Criminal Law rather than under Part 2 of the Rome Statute dealing with jurisdictional matters and applicable law.[271] This is an indicator also that children's participation in armed conflict is considered an aberration under international law and that their acts as members of an armed force or group are ultimately therefore the State's responsibility (due to the State's 'failure to protect' children as a special protected group (persons under age 18) from recruitment and use in hostilities by either or both State or non-State armed forces or groups). Let us turn now to the matter of Lubanga's failure to demobilize most or all of the child soldiers from the FPLC and Lubanga's reliance on the issue of a perceived national security threat as alleged justification for the unrealized FPLC child soldier demobilization.

The Defence in *Lubanga* argued that the failure to fully demobilize children in the FPLC ranks (especially those under 15) was consistent with Lubanga's alleged *higher obligation* to defend against a purported security threat and restore order in the Ituri region under the UPC/FPLC.[272] However, it is noteworthy that after Lubanga's issuing of a child soldier demobilization decree; the 'recruitment' of children actually increased:

> In fact, the witness testified that the demobilisation programmes were not followed up and more importantly that the numbers of child soldiers *increased*.[273]

This ***increase*** in the numbers of children being appropriated to FPLC ranks *after* Lubanga's demobilization decrees is consistent with a common plan to implement the 'genocidal forcible transfer of children' as opposed to ridding FPLC ranks of children, especially under 15s (the latter supposedly 'recruited' inadvertently):

> ***W-0024 also established that the UPC/FPLC's demobilisation was a sham.*** Following the purported demobilisation in October 2002 he continued to see UPC/FPLC child soldiers between the ages of 9–18, armed and in uniform, in towns and cities, threatening everybody. *Though, as he testified, some UPC/FPLC demobilisations occurred, they "concerned a limited number of children"*. . .[274]
>
> In fact, in May 2003, when the UPC/FPLC regained Bunia, far from being dismantled, the kadogo unit [comprised of children including those under 15] was incorporated into the main staff headquarters. Some of the child soldiers were briefly disarmed under the pressure of external actors, but for "not more than ten days." [then re-armed].[275]

---

[270] Rome Statute (2002).

[271] Grover (2012).

[272] *Prosecutor v. Thomas Lubanga Dyilo,* Defence Closing Brief (2011, p. 273, para 880).

[273] *Prosecutor v. Thomas Lubanga Dyilo*, Prosecution's Reply to the Conclusions finales de la Défense (2011, p. 19, para 52).

[274] *Prosecutor v. Thomas Lubanga Dyilo*, Prosecution's Reply to the Conclusions finales de la Défense (2011, p. 19, para 53, emphasis added).

[275] *Prosecutor v. Thomas Lubanga Dyilo*, Prosecution's Reply to the Conclusions finales de la Défense (2011, p. 20, para 55).

The Prosecutor argued that these sham decrees regarding the purported order for demobilization of all 'child soldiers' from the FPLC were in response to Lubanga being notified time and again by NGOs and others that there were under 15s in his forces in violation of international law. The Prosecutor maintained that the "sham" decrees and the failure to fully demobilize FPLC child soldiers reveal that: (1) Lubanga was well aware that there were child soldiers in the ranks of the FPLC, including under 15s, and that (2) this situation was in fact consistent with the UPC/FPLC common plan (to which his contribution was essential) to build a an 'army' using in large part children; which plan he intended to continue to pursue[276]:

> There is direct evidence that the Accused and co-perpetrators agreed upon a plan and acted together since 2000, with greater intensity after April 2002, ***to build an army of predominantly young persons***.[277]

It is here contended, however, that Lubanga's failure to honour his own demobilization of FPLC child soldier decrees is probative not simply in terms (as the Prosecution argued) of providing evidence of: (1) Lubanga's knowledge that the FPLC had children, even under 15s, in its ranks and (2) Lubanga's intent to maintain large numbers of children in the FPLC and to continue to 'recruit' them into that force to build an "army" constituted of "predominately young persons" without due regard to age. The failure of Lubanga and his co-perpetrators to effectively demobilize FPLC child soldiers despite the strong urgings from NGOs in the field and the international community generally, combined with the other evidence here discussed, is another indicia of the 'genocidal transfer of children' to the FPLC (an armed group committing systematic mass atrocity). That genocidal forcible transfer of the children to the FPLC constituted a grave attack on the psychological and physical well being of the children so transferred, their families and their home communities. In transferring large numbers of Hema children, even under 15s, to the FPLC ranks; Lubanga had severely *undermined* the viability of the Hema general populace in the Ituri region (*contrary* to Lubanga's stated purported objective of enhancing the sustainability of Hema in the Ituri region in the face of an alleged national security threat). This is evident in that to maintain the viability of a people it is necessary as a priority to protect the lives and good development of their children. The UPC/FPLC ***itself*** then posed a grave internal threat to the general populace in Ituri by appropriating Hema children and destroying, by various means, the children of the Lendu and other targeted ethnic groups. The UPC/FPLC common plan then was quite *inconsistent* with Lubanga's purported concern for the survivability of the Hema and any other *allegedly* UPC/FPLC favoured group.

To build an 'army' of *predominately* young people who are poorly trained and physically weaker than adults, as were the children, including under 15s 'recruited' into the FPLC, makes little sense from a military standpoint. It does make sense, however, if the common plan is to oppress the general populace in large part through the genocidal forcible transfer of its children. The FPLC (including its

---

[276] *Prosecutor v. Thomas Lubanga Dyilo*, Prosecution's Reply to the Conclusions finales de la Défense (2011, p. 11, para 28).

[277] *Prosecutor v. Thomas Lubanga Dyilo*, Prosecution's Closing Brief (2011, p. 40, para 74).

child soldier contingent), as discussed, was in fact *not* engaged in 'soldiering' but rather in perpetrating mass atrocity and the FPLC child soldiers were regarded by their high command as but expendable tools of which there was/is a ready supply given the large child population in the DRC.

The Prosecution pointed out that documentary evidence entered at trial indicated that the UPC had agreed to leave *one-quarter* of the children to the population in the villages.[278] The Prosecution argued from this evidence that the villagers were reluctant to surrender their children. Indeed, even when children, including under 15s, were surrendered by villagers to the FPLC; most of the time these villagers expected that the children would be trained and return to help defend the villages from Lendu attacks. However, this did not occur. For example:

> DW-007 said he sent young boys to be trained with the UPC/FPLC in Mandro. Although they wanted those youths to return to villages upon completion of training, these recruits were integrated into the UPC/FPLC army and did not return.[279]

The Prosecution thus presented evidence that villagers were being forced to surrender their children in large numbers and that the villagers had expected the children's return at the completion of the children's FPLC 'training' in order that these 'child soldiers' would help defend the Hema villages. Respectfully, the Prosecution, however, on the analysis here, ought to have argued also that this massive so-called 'recruitment' of most children from the Hema population to the FPLC constituted a specific targeting of children which amounted to a 'genocidal forcible transfer of children'. The fact that the UPC would purport to be committed to leaving one-quarter of the children to the general populace indicates that the group was well aware that the *complete* transfer of the children would be clearly intuited by the general populace to be a genocide. This, as villagers need *not* be schooled on the precise legal meanings of 'genocide' under international law to understand that the complete transfer of their children to the FPLC would be a deathblow to their communities and culture. However, the objective of transferring *en masse* such a large a segment of the child population of Ituri (three-quarters of the Hema child population) to the FPLC as part of the UPC/FPLC 'common plan' clearly constituted the genocidal forcible transfer of children. The UPC/FPLC child recruitment and use strategy, as a central part of the common plan, led, and foreseeably so, to the partial destruction of the Hema communities and undermined significantly the viability of the Hema (a perceived distinct ethnic/cultural group in the DRC Ituri region).

There was indisputable evidence, further, that children under 15 were in fact part of Lubanga's personal bodyguard contingent. The Prosecution argued that:

> As head of the UPC/FPLC the Accused used children under the age of 15, setting by example the means by which Ituri was to be conquered.[280]

---

[278] *Prosecutor v. Thomas Lubanga Dyilo*, Prosecution's Reply to the Conclusions finales de la Défense (2011, p. 13, para 32).

[279] *Prosecutor v. Thomas Lubanga Dyilo*, Prosecution's Closing Brief (1 June, 2011, p. 142, para 353).

[280] *Prosecutor v. Thomas Lubanga Dyilo*, Prosecution's Reply to the Conclusions finales de la Défense (2011, p. 14, para 36).

> The Defence cannot reasonably dispute that children under the age of 15 were present in the FPLC, and specifically within the Accused's personal guard. W-0016 testified that the Presidential guard included children under the age of 15, and as to that evidence the Defence only contests the exact number.[281]
>
> W-0017, W-0055 and W-0038 testified that the term kadogo included children under the age of 15 and, concerning the composition of the kadogo unit, W-0017 stated that "people knew they were kadogos", meaning "[t]hey were less than 15 years old". Contrary to the Defence assertions . . .W-0017 described at length the military training underwent by the children composing this unit, and particularly referred to "their commanders", who ensured that they did not "run away into the bush".[282]

The current author argues that the genocidal forcible transfer of huge numbers of children to the FPLC (including under 15s) was *in itself*, in large part, the means by which the FPLC intended "Ituri to be conquered." That is, the appropriation of the children by the FPLC *in itself* had already resulted in the partial decimation and complete intimidation of the general populace and its subjugation to the UPC/FPLC (even aside from the other international crimes perpetrated on the peoples in the region by these children as FPLC 'child soldiers' and by the other FPLC members). Clearly, the evidence in Lubanga pointed to an intentional and knowing transfer of children to the FPLC, even under 15s, to serve as child soldiers in varied capacities; some involving, in part, close; even intimate contact with commanders.

Since the 'genocidal forcible transfer of children' was a major part of the UPC/FPLC common plan; it can be argued that Lubanga and his co-perpetrators of necessity knew and intended that children, including those under 15, would be 'recruited' into the FPLC. The *mens rea* (consistent with that relating to the genocidal forcible transfer of children) goes beyond simply knowing that large numbers of children were being recruited and that, therefore, there was a likelihood that some under 15s would end up in the ranks of the FPLC. According to the Defence; those numbers of children were being recruited because there was an alleged security threat that required building up a strong army and this then purportedly justified: (1) the use of child soldiers and (2) provided justification for excusing the lack of age verification by the FPLC to ensure under 15s were not recruited. Put differently, the Defence suggested that the recruitment of children was a last resort given an emergency situation allegedly not of the UPC/FPLC making with under 15s being included in the so-called 'recruitment' purportedly inadvertently. The argument here has been, in contrast, that the UPC/FPLC political/military leadership acted intentionally, unrelentingly and with careful deliberation *to specifically target children of all ages* for appropriation to the FPLC as their common plan included, as a major component, the 'genocidal forcible transfer of children' to their armed group.

---

[281] *Prosecutor v. Thomas Lubanga Dyilo*, Prosecution's Reply to the Conclusions finales de la Défense (2011, p. 14, para 37).

[282] *Prosecutor v. Thomas Lubanga Dyilo*, Prosecution's Reply to the Conclusions finales de la Défense (2011, p. 23, para 65).

The Prosecution set out in its reply to the Defence's final conclusions that the co-perpetrators of the common plan in *Lubanga* "accepted the *likelihood*" that the common plan would result in the war crimes charged:

> The specific *mens rea* required for the crime of enlistment, as stipulated in Article 8 of the Rome Statute, is *inapplicable* in this case where the Accused is charged with co-perpetration based on joint control over the crimes. That the Accused, and all co-perpetrators, must be *mutually aware of and accept* ***the likelihood*** that implementing the common plan would result in the execution of the objective elements of the crimes, renders the "should have known" standard redundant.[283]

In the Prosecution Closing Brief, the Prosecution argued clearly that the accused and his co-perpetrators in fact "knew" that the war crimes charged would be committed as the result of implementing the common plan:

> In this case, the Prosecution argues that the Accused ***knew that children under the age of 15 would be conscripted, enlisted or used to participate actively in hostilities*** as a result of the implementation of the Common Plan.[284]

Note that in the Prosecution Closing Brief, the Prosecution, at another point, clearly indicates that it is advancing the notion also that Lubanga 'intended ***or at least accepted***' that the FPLC common plan of recruiting children *en masse* would result in the recruitment and use in hostilities of children under 15:

> The sheer number of children recruited, trained and used by the UPC/FPLC throughout the period of the charges, including children under the age of 15, demonstrates that the co-perpetrators intentionally cast a wide net in their recruitment campaigns *and intended* ***(or at least accepted)*** that as a result they were recruiting, training and using children under the age of 15.[285]

The Prosecution advancing (in its closing brief)[286] the proposition that Lubanga and his co-perpetrators may have simply been operating at the level of: (1) '*accepting*', rather than 'intending', that under 15s *would be* recruited and used for active participation in hostilities or (2) '*accepting*', rather than intending, that under 15s *would likely* be recruited and used in hostilities as a result of the common plan (which involved huge numbers of Hema children being transferred to the FPLC) is, on the analysis here, with respect, highly unfortunate and inaccurate on the facts. On the analysis here, the UPC/FPLC common plan (as evidenced by the facts presented at trial regarding intent as revealed in videos of Lubanga's speeches to armed FPLC units with child soldiers members clearly not of age, internal official command communiqués regarding child soldiers, FPLC recruitment strategies, failure to demobilize child soldiers, the FPLC perpetration of mass atrocities and

[283] *Prosecutor v. Thomas Lubanga Dyilo*, Prosecution's Reply to the Conclusions finales de la Défense (2011, pp. 14–15, para 39, emphasis added).

[284] *Prosecutor v. Thomas Lubanga Dyilo*, Prosecution closing brief (2011, p. 39, FN 123).

[285] *Prosecutor v. Thomas Lubanga Dyilo,* Prosecution Closing Brief (2011, pp. 65–66, para 154, emphasis added).

[286] *Prosecutor v. Thomas Lubanga Dyilo,* Prosecution Closing Brief (2011, pp. 65–66, para 154, emphasis added).

use of child soldiers also in the latter regard etc.) was, in large part, a genocidal one involving the objective of forcible transfer of a large segment of the Hema child population to the FPLC by various means. The genocidal transfer of children generally is *not* restrictive in terms of the ages of the children so transferred as was also the case here with the implementation of the FPLC common plan. Hence, the FPLC commanders accomplished this genocidal forcible transfer of children of all ages by intentional acts such as raping children of all ages, including those under age 15, transferring large numbers of Hema children of all ages (including under 15s) to the fighting force to perform a variety of functions even when numbers of these children were too young and weak to be able to carry weapons or perform the FPLC combat training exercises etc.

To recap briefly then, the 'genocidal forcible transfer of children' to the FPLC constituted a large part of the UPC/FPLC common plan. Hence, the FPLC perpetrators would not have been expected to be concerned, and were in fact *not* concerned, with avoiding the transfer ('recruitment') also of children under age 15 to the FPLC (and instead selecting only older, physically stronger children). Thus, the FPLC common plan under Lubanga; encompassing as it did the genocidal forcible transfer of children', involved the architects and co-perpetrators of this plan having a *specific intent* to transfer children of all ages and physical/health status, including under 15s, to the FPLC (and not merely 'accepting' that 'recruiting' under 15s and not exclusively children 15 and over would be or would likely be an eventuality in implementing the common plan). It is respectfully contended here, as a consequence, that this 'specific genocidal intent' *cannot* then (contrary to the suggestion made by the Prosecutor) on any proper analysis be reduced to simply a "mutual awareness" and "acceptance" amongst the co-perpetrators that if the UPC/FPLC common plan of recruiting children *en masse* to the FPLC were implemented; there was a "likelihood" or even a certainty that under 15s would be amongst them (an entirely foreseeable but *allegedly unintended* consequence of the FPLC broad 'recruitment' strategy). The current analysis thus reveals that in the particular case (as here) where the common plan involves the genocidal forcible transfer of children—*a specific intent crime*—the *mens rea* element of the war crimes relating to the recruitment and use of child soldiers (where also charged) involving both 'knew' *and* 'should have known' that under 15s are in fact also being appropriated and used actively in hostilities is also met.[287] More specifically, the FPLC commanders 'knew' *and* 'should have known' that under 15s would also being 'recruited' along with other children as a consequence of FPLC *blanket sweeps* of villages looking for children to 'recruit' and in abductions of groups children in other settings all with no regard for the children's ages (i.e. at school or on the way to and from school etc.). This blanket 'recruitment' of children was an integral part of what happened in Ituri in the time frame covered by the Lubanga case and was key to the FPLC common plan because the

[287] *Prosecutor v. Thomas Lubanga Dyilo*, Prosecution's Reply to the Conclusions finales de la Défense (2011, pp. 14–15, para 39, emphasis added).

goal was in fact the genocidal transfer of children aged both over and under age 15 to the FPLC. The facts then go much beyond the FPLC simply accepting the risk of recruiting under 15s due to the nature of the common plan being as it was indiscriminate (contrary to the Defence position and also, at points, the Prosecution argument):

> The argument [of the Defence] appears to concede that the Accused – even under his protestation that he was a political and not a military leader – was responsible and ***accepted the "risk"*** *that his recruitment drives would sweep up underage children.*[288]

Recall that the same facts can ground more than one international crime. In *Lubanga* those crimes, it is here contended, include but are not limited to: (1) the war crimes of 'recruiting' under 15s and using these children for active participation in armed hostilities; (2) the genocidal forcible transfer of children (persons under age 18) to the FPLC to act also as perpetrators of atrocity as per the FPLC so-called 'military' strategy of systematic mass atrocity (as well for the purpose of fulfilling other roles such as bodyguards, sex slaves etc. depending on the particular children involved) and (3) various sex crimes perpetrated against children, mostly girls, as crimes against humanity and war crimes:

> The Accused's own witnesses confirmed that the UN and other international organisations complained in October 2002 about the UPC/FPLC's recruitment of children.[289]

Note that all of the FPLC child soldiers, regardless of their age as children (persons under age 18), must be considered in law, on the view here, as having suffered a ***forced*** 'recruitment' to the FPLC. This was not just the case then for the *under 15s* contrary to the implication of the Trial Court judgement in *Lubanga* which includes the following:

> The Chamber has concluded that the crimes of conscription *and enlistment* are committed at the moment a child *under the age of 15* is enrolled into *or joins* an armed force or group, *with or without compulsion*.[290]
>
> The Chamber finds that between 1 September 2002 and 13 August 2003, the armed wing of the UPC/FPLC was responsible for the widespread recruitment of young people, including children under the age of 15, on an enforced as well as a "voluntary" basis.[291]

That in the situation covered in *Lubanga* all of the children recruited into the FPLC, *regardless of age*, were *forcibly recruited* is a function of the fact that they were all the victims of the *genocidal forcible transfer of children to the FPLC* as illustrated by varied evidence admitted at Trial as previously here discussed. Just as

---

[288] *Prosecutor v. Thomas Lubanga Dyilo*, Prosecution's Reply to the Conclusions finales de la Défense (2011, p. 16, para 43, emphasis added).

[289] *Prosecutor v. Thomas Lubanga Dyilo*, Prosecution's Reply to the Conclusions finales de la Défense (2011, p. 18, para 48).

[290] *Prosecutor v. Thomas Lubanga Dyilo* Summary of the "Judgment pursuant to Article 74 of the Statute (14 March, 2012, p. 9, para 23).

[291] *Prosecutor v. Thomas Lubanga Dyilo* Summary of the "Judgment pursuant to Article 74 of the Statute (14 March, 2012, p. 10, para 27).

under 15s cannot in law consent to being child soldiers so, too, in law *under 18s* cannot consent to their genocidal forcible transfer as children to an armed group or force perpetrating mass atrocities and/or genocide. In each case then the context negates *in law* the possibility of child 'enlistment' to an armed group such as the FPLC perpetrating grave international crimes on a systematic basis and renders all child recruitment and use forced.

The Prosecution presented evidence that the FPLC *did not turn away children of any age*. The latter is another indicia of the occurrence of the genocidal forcible transfer of children by the FPLC when considered in the context of all the other evidence pertaining to FPLC conduct relating to children:

> W-0055 [an experienced FPLC officer] ....testified that children too young to carry a weapon would be assigned to headquarters. And he explained that "there were children who could not undergo training, and children like that were sent off to carry out other tasks". ***In other words, his evidence does not establish a practice to "drive away" underage children; to the contrary, they remained in the FPLC***. Moreover, DW-0011 – called by the Defence presumably for his insider knowledge on the issues – ***testified that he was not aware of any official procedure to verify the ages of children***.[292]

Recall also that so-called voluntary enlistment in the FPLC occurred in a context where parents were being threatened for their lives if they did not surrender their children and facilitate their joining the FPLC. This may have been viewed as the only viable option for protecting one's family and village from decimation by the FPLC or another party to the conflict. Such pressures as the aforementioned applied to these children and the families are here considered also to constitute the application of 'force' as understood in the definition of the genocidal forcible transfer of children under the Rome Statute.[293]

3.1.9.3 The Judgment Regarding Lubanga's Conviction at the Trial Level (14 March, 2012)

Sexual Violence Against FPLC Girl Child Soldiers Perpetrated by UPC/FPLC Commanders

The Trial Chamber found that certain witnesses including P-0055, P-0017 and P-0038 and P-0046 had testified credibly regarding the fact that the UPC/FPLC had recruited children including those under age 15 [either through forced

---

[292] *Prosecutor v. Thomas Lubanga Dyilo*, Prosecution's Reply to the Conclusions finales de la Défense (2011, pp. 16–17, para 45, emphasis added).

[293] Rome Statute, Elements of the Crime (2002, Article 6(e)(FN 5): "The term 'forcibly' is not restricted to physical force, but may include threat of force or coercion, such as that caused by fear of violence, duress, detention, psychological oppression or abuse of power, against such person or persons or another person, or by taking advantage of a coercive environment".

recruitment (conscription) or alleged voluntary enlistment] and sent them to the headquarters in Bunia or 'military' training camps in a variety of locations.[294] Four of these credible witnesses also testified that:

> ...girl child soldiers were subjected to sexual violence and rape. P-0046 and P-0038 specifically referred to girls under the age of 15 who were subjected to sexual violence by UPC commanders.[295]

Notwithstanding the testimony of witnesses who, in the estimation of the Trial Chamber, were credible; the Trial Chamber (based on an Appeal Court ruling in *Lubanga* on the issue of whether sexual violence evidence and evidence on cruel and inhuman treatment presented at trial could be considered in rendering judgement) took the position that sexual violence was *not* within the scope of the case and that, therefore, it would not be proper to rule on the matter. In this regard the Trial Chamber stated:

> ...sexual violence does not form part of the charges against the accused, and the Chamber has *not* made any findings of fact on the issue, particularly as to whether responsibility is to be attributed to the accused (for the sexual violence perpetrated against child soldiers of the UPC/FPLC).[296]

This author would argue that: (1) sexual violence against children (here girl child soldiers in particular) is another hallmark of and vehicle for the genocidal forcible transfer of these children to the FPLC as previously discussed and that (2) the latter charge (the genocidal forcible transfer of children) should have been one of the charges filed against Lubanga by the ICC Prosecutor in the first instance. Girls becoming 'child bush wives'/sex slaves to FPLC commanders, girl FPLC child soldiers being routinely raped by FPLC members and other international crimes of sexual violence committed by the FPLC against girls in particular, when viewed as a vehicle for genocidal forcible transfer of the girls to the FPLC, allows for consideration of these facts as central to an international crime (the genocidal forcible transfer of children) and not simply as an 'aggravating factor' (i.e. in *Lubanga*; sexual violence was treated by the Prosecutor, and ultimately the Trial Court, as but an aggravating factor to the war crimes of conscripting and using under 15s for active participation in hostilities such that this factor may affect the Trial judgement only in respect of sentencing and reparations).

This author then contends in sum that the facts and circumstances regarding sexual violence against and cruel and inhuman treatment of children during recruitment and after transfer to the FPLC ranks should have been presented at the Pre-Trial stage in *Lubanga* in support of: (1) separate relevant war crimes and crimes against humanity charges and (2) in support of the charge of the genocidal forcible transfer of children to the UPC/FPLC.

---

[294] Prosecutor v Thomas Lubanga Dyilo, Final Trial Judgement Pursuant to Article 74 of the Rome Statute (2012, p. 398, para 912).

[295] Prosecutor v Thomas Lubanga Dyilo, Final Trial Judgement Pursuant to Article 74 of the Rome Statute (2012, p. 398, para 913).

[296] Prosecutor v Thomas Lubanga Dyilo, Final Trial Judgement Pursuant to Article 74 of the Rome Statute (2012, p. 398, para 913, emphasis added).

It should be recalled that, as the Trial Court in *Lubanga* noted, the concepts of conscription, enlistment and use of under 15s for active participation in hostilities are nowhere defined in the Rome Statute, the Elements of the Crime or the Court Rules.[297] The current author argues that the charge of 'recruitment' (conscription or enlistment) of under 15s[298] into an armed force such as the FPLC *that is committing systematic mass atrocities* has embedded into that charge the notion that the children will be *appropriated* by the group through unlawful means. Sexual violence is one possible and common means by which the children are so appropriated and used as was the case with the FPLC. Like sexual violence, other cruel and inhuman treatment of the child recruits by FPLC commanders and officers served to break down the children's personal identity and actualize their genocidal forcible transfer to the UPC/FPLC on a psychological level and not just in the physical sense of their 'joining' the FPLC ranks.

'Recruitment' (conscription or alleged enlistment) in the instance of children transferred to an armed force such as the FPLC that is committing widespread and systematic mass atrocities, furthermore, is *not* a single event occurring at the point of an abduction, conscription or *alleged* voluntary enlistment or at even at the point of an initiation rite into the group. Rather, 'recruitment' is an *ongoing process* of indoctrination and appropriation of the children which process routinely involves *repeated violence*; sexual and non-sexual and, in actual fact, constitutes the genocidal forcible transfer of the children physically, and over time, in terms of the children's transformed psychology or state of mind. The Trial Chamber in fact affirmed that the crimes charged are continuous (the crimes ending, in the Trial Court's view, only when the child leaves the armed group or force or reaches age 15).[299]

Therefore, it is here respectfully contended that the Appeal Chamber in *Lubanga*: (1) erred in not allowing the Trial Chamber to consider the facts in *Lubanga* presented at trial pertaining to the alleged sexual violence against and inhuman and cruel treatment of UPC/FPLC child soldiers[300] as an aspect of the

[297] Prosecutor v Thomas Lubanga Dyilo, Final Trial Judgement Pursuant to Article 74 of the Rome Statute (2012, pp. 273–274, para 600).

[298] The Trial Court in *Lubanga* held that the conceptual distinction between conscription and enlistment is irrelevant when it comes to the recruitment of under 15s and the Rome Statute (2002) Article 8 war crime in regards to recruitment of under 15s. On the view here, children (persons under 18) appropriated by an armed force or group such as the FPLC committing systematic mass atrocity is considered genocidal forcible transfer and hence the conceptual distinction between conscription and enlistment is inapplicable in the context of this forced transfer.

[299] *Prosecutor v. Thomas Lubanga Dyilo* Summary of the "Judgment pursuant to Article 74 of the Statute (14 March, 2012, p. 9, para 23). This author has argued that these crimes are continuous beyond the point suggested by the Trial Court where children are appropriated and used by an armed force or group committing mass atrocity and/or genocide. This is the case given the long-term adverse effects of these traumatic experiences on the victims and the victims' continued perceived identification with the perpetrator armed force or group and alienation from family and community.

[300] Note that on the analysis suggested there is no need to establish that girl child soldiers of the UPC/FPLC being sexually violated by UPC/FPLC commanders or others within the armed group constitutes a *combat* related function.

conscription, enlistment and use of children by the FPLC; and (2) erred in not allowing the Trial Chamber (in response to the victim participants' 2009 joint application[301]) to consider legally re-characterizing the facts and circumstances so as to take proper account of the evidence regarding: (a) sexual violence against UPC/FPLC girl child soldiers in particular and that (b) pertaining to the cruel and inhuman treatment accorded the child soldiers in UPC/FPLC ranks (the issue of the Appeal Court reversal of the Trial Court's decision in Lubanga to hold a hearing on legal re-characterization of the facts and circumstances pertaining to sexual slavery and cruel and inhuman treatment was here discussed in detail previously).

Sexual violence perpetrated by FPLC members against children and cruel and inhuman treatment of the new FPLC child recruits were key aspects of the child recruitment process into this murderous armed group (recruitment and use that in fact amounts to genocidal forcible transfer of children to an armed group perpetrating mass atrocities). However, there was, for the reasons explained, a failure to attribute responsibility or lack of responsibility to Lubanga as per the facts respecting sexual violence crimes (as war crimes and or crimes against humanity) and the war crime of cruel and inhuman treatment of the child soldiers. With respect, on the view here, ideally the Prosecutor should have, at the Pre-Trial stage advanced *separate charges* supported by specific factual allegations regarding sexual violence (i.e. rape, and sexual slavery as war crimes and crimes against humanity) and cruel and inhuman treatment as a war crime. Further, the Prosecutor should have, on the analysis here, filed a charge of genocidal forcible transfer of children to the FPLC explaining how sexual brutalization; cruel and inhuman treatment; and transfer to an armed group to participate in mass atrocities as child soldiers contributes to that genocidal forcible transfer of the children.[302]

Child Soldiers as UPC/FPLC Mascots

It is here contended that another indication that 'recruitment' by the FPLC of children translated into much more than what is normally meant by the term 'recruitment' is the fact that many child soldiers, especially young children under 15, were essentially used as mascots by the FPLC. The term mascot is defined in the Oxford Dictionary as "a person or thing that is supposed to bring good luck, especially one linked to a particular organization or event."[303] In this particular case, the Trial Chamber made a finding of fact that children, frequently including

[301] The Women's Initiatives for Gender Justice (2011, p. 4).
Prosecutor v Thomas Lubanga Dyilo, Final Trial Judgement Pursuant to Article 74 of the Rome Statute (2012, pp. 273–274, para 600).
[302] The children through such victimization lose their identity, become alienated from family and community and integrate into the FPLC.
[303] Oxford Dictionary Online (2012).

also children under 15, were the *preferred choice* for use as bodyguards by the FPLC and that there existed within the UPC/FPLC a military unit *comprised entirely* of young children mostly those under age 15:

> The testimony of [list of witnesses identified by code numbers] and the documentary evidence has demonstrated that children under the age of 15 were within the ranks of the UPC/FPLC between 1 September 2002 and 13 August 2003. The evidence [list of witnesses identified by code numbers] proves that children were deployed as soldiers. . . and took part in fighting. . . ***The evidence [list of witnesses identified by code numbers] establishes that the UPC used children under the age of 15 as military guards. The evidence of P-0017 reveals that a special "Kadogo Unit" was formed, which was comprised principally of children under the age of 15.*** The evidence of [list of witnesses identified by code numbers] as well as the video footage . . .demonstrates that *commanders in the UPC/FPLC* ***frequently used children under the age of 15 as [personal] bodyguards.*** *The accounts of [list of witnesses identified by code numbers], along with the video evidence, clearly prove that children under 15 acted as bodyguards or served with the presidential guard of Mr. Lubanga.*[304]

The contention of this author is that the child FPLC personal bodyguards and the children of the FPLC "Kadogo Unit" served also a symbolic function as mascots who would purportedly bring good fortune to the UPC/FPLC in their armed initiatives. The children then symbolized the image (real or imagined) of vigor and *esprit du corps* of the UPC/FPLC that the political/military group wished to portray to the Hema citizenry of the Ituri region as well as to its opposition. Given such a UPC/FPLC perspective as here contemplated; it is *not* surprising then that: (1) children under the age of 15 would have been frequently used as personal bodyguards by the FPLC commanders and by the President of the UPC/FPLC Lubanga himself despite these children *not* being amongst the most able and strongest 'recruits'; and that (2) the FPLC would be highly reluctant to demobilize these child soldier perceived human embodiments of 'good luck charms.' As mascots for the UPC/FPLC; these child soldiers had been *appropriated* in part thus to symbolize or express irrational psychological fantasies about the anticipated future political and military success and longevity of the UPC/FPLC. Hence, the children were not 'recruits' in any simple sense of the word as that term is normally understood but rather children fully appropriated in every sense indefinitely to the UPC/FPLC.

On What Constitutes 'Active Participation' in Hostilities: Underlying Presumptions

The Trial Chamber found that beyond a reasonable doubt Lubanga "by virtue of his position as President and Commander-in-Chief from September 2002 onwards, was able to shape the policies of the UPC/FPLC and to direct the activities of his alleged co-perpetrators. . .and that he was kept fully informed throughout the relevant

[304] Prosecutor v Thomas Lubanga Dyilo, Final Trial Judgement Pursuant to Article 74 of the Rome Statute (2012, p. 399, para 915, emphasis added).

period and he issued instructions relating to the implementation of the common plan [and]. . .personally assisted in the military affairs of the UPC/FPLC in a variety of ways."[305] It is noteworthy also that the Trial Chamber affirmed the fact that:

> . . .the accused [Lubanga] and other commanders were protected by guards, some of whom were below 15, [and that] *the use of children as bodyguards for the commanders amounts to their use to participate actively in hostilities.*[306]

The Trial Chamber in Lubanga thus decided that being a bodyguard amounted to "active participation" in hostilities. Let us consider then (1) how the Trial Chamber reached this conclusion, (2) where, with all due respect, the Chamber erred in its reasoning though reaching the proper conclusion, and (3) what are the broader implications of the Chamber's conclusion in regards to what constitutes "active participation" in hostilities.

The Trial Chamber states that:

> . . .the prohibition against using them to participate actively in hostilities is generally intended to protect children from the risks that are associated with armed conflict.[307]
>
> The prohibition against using children under the age of 15 to participate actively in hostilities is *not* dependent on the individuals concerned having been earlier conscripted or enlisted into the relevant armed force or group.[308]

The position of the current author is, as has been discussed here previously in some detail, that the recruitment and/or use of children in armed hostilities by a State or non-State armed force or group *committing genocide and/or mass atrocities* constitutes the genocidal forcible transfer of those children to the armed force or group. That is, the children's 'recruitment' *and/or* participation with such a force or group known to perpetrate mass atrocities and/or genocide means that the children acquire the identity of the armed group or force and forfeit, for all intents and purposes, any identity separate and distinct from that armed force or group (this is especially the case where the children themselves also commit atrocity, as for instance with the FPLC, although the latter is *not* a necessary condition for the children being properly considered as *bona fide* victims of the genocidal forcible transfer to the armed group or force). Hence, recruitment to such a murderous armed State or non-State force or group encompasses itself, in the first instance, 'active participation in hostilities' whether the children actually engage in the fighting or not and regardless whether they commit atrocities. This is the case in that 'recruitment' of children into such an armed force or group (which 'recruitment' amounts in fact to the genocidal forcible transfer of children to the armed

[305] Prosecutor v Thomas Lubanga Dyilo, Final Trial Judgement Pursuant to Article 74 of the Rome Statute (2012, para 1270, p. 547).

[306] Prosecutor v Thomas Lubanga Dyilo, Final Trial Judgement Pursuant to Article 74 of the Rome Statute (2012, para 1270, p. 548, emphasis added).

[307] Prosecutor v Thomas Lubanga Dyilo, Final Trial Judgement Pursuant to Article 74 of the Rome Statute (2012, p. 282, para 619).

[308] Prosecutor v Thomas Lubanga Dyilo, Final Trial Judgement Pursuant to Article 74 of the Rome Statute (2012, p. 282, para 620, emphasis added).

force or group) necessarily involves the children's full integration and stigmatization in terms of the perception of the child, the armed group or force involved and the regional society at large. The harms that flow from that integration are substantial for the children; exposure to violence during recruitment and 'training', witnessing grave international crimes including commonly also within the so-called military training camps (as was the case with the UPC/FPLC training camps), alienation from family and community, psychological and physical suffering of the children etc. Further, the children now appropriated (i.e. by the FPLC) become symbols of the power of the murderous armed group or force (i.e. the FPLC) even before they participate in the hostilities; if they ever do. All of this amounts to *active participation* in hostilities. In sum then the current author argues that regardless of the task or specific duty assigned to a child 'recruited' (forcibly transferred) to an armed group or force perpetrating genocide and/or mass atrocities; the presence of each and every child transferred to the armed group or force is essential to the functioning of the armed group or force. This is the reality in that the children 'recruited' (transferred) are first and foremost fundamentally propaganda symbols fulfilling a psychological function for the armed group or force communicating to the general population and the opposition the armed group's genocidal intent and the power of the armed group or force perpetrating this appropriation of children. The children's transfer to the perpetrator group[309] in itself helps to undermine peace and security in the region, further fuels the armed conflict and perpetuates it; and thus also for these reasons in itself constitutes 'active participation' in the hostilities.

Further, note that the current author's perspective on the issue of what constitutes "active participation in hostilities"(as per Article 8 of the Rome Statute)[310]—specifically the scope of the term-differs from that of the Trial Chamber in *Lubanga* as will be here discussed shortly. Recall that the Prosecution in Lubanga limited the protection afforded child soldiers under the Rome Statute[311] prohibition against use of children under 15 for active participation in armed conflict to include only those children whose activities are "essential to the functioning of the armed group":

> . . .the protection is not restricted to those children who actively fight, but rather it includes *any child whose role is essential to the functioning of the armed group*, for instance by working as a cook, porter, messenger *or when individuals are used for sexual purposes*, including by way of forced marriage. . .[or through] direct participation in combat, as well as combat-related activities such as scouting, spying, sabotage and . . .children [participating] at military checkpoints or as decoys and couriers. . . or. . .as the body guards of military commanders.[312]

---

[309] Sexual violence can be a vehicle for the genocidal forcible transfer of children to the perpetrator group as can recruitment of children as child soldiers to the armed group or force perpetrating systematic mass atrocities.

[310] Rome Statute (2002).

[311] Rome Statute (2002).

[312] Prosecutor v Thomas Lubanga Dyilo, Final Trial Judgement Pursuant to Article 74 of the Rome Statute (2012, p. 264, para 574–575, emphasis added).

> The prosecution accepts the pre-Trial Chamber's ruling that *activities that are clearly unrelated to hostilities, such as delivering food to an airbase and working as domestic staff in the officers' quarters, are excluded* [from protection under the Article 8 Rome Statute prohibitions regarding the use of children for active participation in armed conflict].[313]

The current author disputes the notion that *any child* associated with the armed group or force perpetrating genocide and/or mass atrocities can be excluded (i.e. based on their task assignment within the armed group or force) from the protections afforded under the Rome Statute[314] to children with respect to: (1) the prohibition against the use of children under 15 for active participation in armed hostilities and (2) the genocidal transfer of the children (that is, persons under age 18) to that armed group or force (State or non-State). Hence, even children performing 'non-combat' duties such as being a domestic to commanders or delivering food to the armed group's airbase would in fact, on the view here, be considered 'active participants' in hostilities if the children were considered by the perpetrators and the others in society to be a part of the armed unit serving in *any* capacity (including a support capacity far removed from combat support).[315] This is the case in that, as mentioned, *all* of the children transferred to the murderous armed group or force serve a symbolic and not just a labor function. *All* children's (persons under 18) genocidal forcible transfer (erroneously referred to by the moniker 'recruitment') to the armed group or force perpetrating genocide and/or mass atrocities communicates the genocidal intent of the armed group or force involved and, hence, serves military propaganda functions contributing, for instance, to the terrorizing of the general populace. The latter functions are clearly ones constituting the children's: (1) "active participation" in hostilities and (2) essential contribution to the armed group or force despite the ostensible roles of certain children being removed to some degree from *direct* participation in the fighting itself.

The Defence in *Lubanga* argued that in the context of *criminal* proceedings; children fulfilling roles that are not direct support roles for the fighting or roles constituting active combat functions in themselves should *not* be classified as child soldiers (and hence that these children not be entitled to benefit from the prohibitions against recruitment of children under 15 to State or non-State armed

---

[313] Prosecutor v Thomas Lubanga Dyilo, Final Trial Judgement Pursuant to Article 74 of the Rome Statute (2012, p. 264, para 575, emphasis added).

[314] Rome Statute (2012).

[315] It appears entirely arbitrary that the ICC Prosecutor makes a distinction between: (1) girl child soldiers who sexually service UPC/FPLC commanders and, in some cases, are also the commanders' forced bush wives *versus* for instance (2) girl child domestics who work in the households of these commanders. The latter group of female children are also generally sexually violated. Furthermore, both groups of children are perceived by the perpetrators to be part of the UPC/FPLC support system though not necessarily in each case in relation to any clear direct support for the fighting per se and irrespective of any combat functions that they may or may not perform. Both child groups then are comprised of children who are the victims of genocidal forcible transfer to the perpetrator armed group and as such are contributing to the hostilities via the symbolic and propaganda value of their transfer.

groups or forces).[316] The Defence, however, maintained that this limitation need not be imposed in the context of international human rights proceedings concerning violations of human rights instruments intended to provide the broadest protections possible to children. The current author, however, contends (in opposition to the Lubanga Defence arguments regarding who is a child soldier engaged in active participation in the hostilities) that the ICC criminal proceedings, too, are fundamentally about human rights and should afford all the children 'recruited' to the armed group or force perpetrating mass atrocities (such as the FPLC) the broadest possible protection (i.e. as per the Rome Statute[317] provisions regarding the genocidal forcible transfer of children and the Article 8 war crimes provisions regarding the prohibition on recruitment and/or use of children under 15 for active participation in hostilities). That protection, in practice, is intricately tied to holding to account perpetrators of the international crimes relating to recruitment and/or use of children under 15 for active participation in hostilities and the genocidal transfer of children (persons under age 18).

More specifically, the Defence in Lubanga stated the following on the issue of who, in their view, was properly designated a child soldier covered by the prohibition under the Rome Statute regarding recruitment of children into State or non-State armed forces:

> The critical distinction suggested by the defence is *between* ***those children who are integrated into an armed group as soldiers and who undertake military functions****, and those who do not perform a military role and are not assigned any functions connected with the hostilities* (although they are within the armed group). The latter, it is submitted, should not be treated as having been enlisted.[318]

The current author has argued that *all* children 'recruited' into an armed State or non-State group or force such as the UPC/FPLC perpetrating mass atrocities and/or genocide (as per a common plan) are in fact *automatically integrated* into that armed group and tainted by that group in the perception of the community at large and in their own eyes. This is the case regardless whether the children engage in combat functions, function exclusively as bodyguards or perform any other assigned duty such as bringing food to an airbase or being a sex slave. The children 'recruited' into such armed forces or groups are in fact the victims of genocidal forcible transfer and, as such, all the children so transferred serve the *military function* of demoralizing and terrorizing: (1) the general population through the usurpation of the group of origin's right to their own children; and (2) the opposing belligerent armed group through serving as a reminder that the latter's children are at risk of being sexually violated or otherwise brutalized by the adversary. The transferred children become the symbol simultaneously of the power of the perpetrator group on the one hand and the loss of hope for the future viability of the

---

[316] Prosecutor v Thomas Lubanga Dyilo, Final Trial Judgement Pursuant to Article 74 of the Rome Statute (2012, pp. 266–267, para 579–582).

[317] Rome Statute (2002).

[318] Prosecutor v Thomas Lubanga Dyilo, Final Trial Judgement Pursuant to Article 74 of the Rome Statute (2012, p. 267, para 582, emphasis added).

children's group of origin/home communities and of the loss of autonomy and self-governance of those communities on the other. The distinction between direct and indirect participation in hostilities thus breaks down in this context[319] as *all* the child victims of genocidal forcible transfer to the armed group: (1) perform, at the very least, a vital military propaganda function just by virtue of their transfer and (2) have been harmed by the suffering and inevitable virtual permanent alienation from family and community that such a genocidal transfer (recruitment) most often entails.[320] Given the ongoing alienation from family and community and the long-term traumatic effects resultant from the children having been an integral part of an armed group or force perpetrating mass atrocity and/or genocide, it is here argued that the offences of: (1) recruiting children to an *armed group or force committing mass atrocities and/or genocide* and/or (2) using them for active participation in hostilities in such armed groups or forces continue well beyond age 15 and beyond the point at which the individual has physically left the armed group or force for any period or reached age 15. The latter position thus differs from that of the Prosecution and even victim participant groups in *Lubanga*.[321]

One last point on the Trial Court's view regarding what constitutes "active participation in hostilities" must be discussed. Consider the following statement from the Trial Court summary of the judgement in *Lubanga*:

> As regards the offence of using children under the age of 15 to participate actively in hostilities, the Chamber has concluded that this includes a wide range of activities, from those children on the front line (who participate directly) through to the boys or girls who are involved in a myriad of roles that support the combatants. All of these activities, which cover either direct or indirect participation, have an underlying common feature: ***the child concerned is, at the very least, a potential target. The decisive factor, therefore, in deciding if an "indirect" role is to be treated as active participation in hostilities is whether the support provided by the child to the combatants exposed him or her to real danger as a potential target. In the judgment of the Chamber these combined factors – the child's support and this level of consequential risk – mean that although absent from the immediate scene of the hostilities, the individual was nonetheless actively involved in them.***[322]

The point the current author would make then is that as victims of the genocidal forcible transfer of children: (1) all of the children 'recruited' to the FPLC were targets

---

[319] Note that Article 8 of the Rome Statute uses the expression "participating actively in hostilities" rather than the phrase "taking a direct part" used in Additional Protocol I to the Geneva Convention. That distinction according to the victim submission in Lubanga was intended to encompass a wider range of activities that children are prohibited from engaging in during armed conflict. (See Prosecutor v Thomas Lubanga Dyilo, Final Trial Judgement Pursuant to Article 74 of the Rome Statute (2012, p. 270, para 590).

[320] The Defence in Lubanga had argued that Article 8 of the Rome Statute in regards to the use for "active participation" in hostilities prohibition respecting children was intended to punish only those who use children (under 15s) for "direct participation" in hostilities (See Prosecutor v Thomas Lubanga Dyilo, Final Trial Judgement Pursuant to Article 74 of the Rome Statute (2012, pp. 268–269, para 586).

[321] Prosecutor v Thomas Lubanga Dyilo, Final Trial Judgement Pursuant to Article 74 of the Rome Statute (2012, p. 272, para 597).

[322] *Prosecutor v. Thomas Lubanga Dyilo* Summary of the "Judgment pursuant to Article 74 of the Statute (14 March, 2012, pp. 9–10, para 24).

who were at severe risk of harm both physically and psychologically and (2) all did suffer these harms in a myriad of ways. This was the case regardless of whether the children forcibly transferred to the FPLC participated in the combat; or performed combat support functions; or were domestics; or functioned primarily in some other role such as sex slave or did so in combination with combat roles or direct or indirect combat support functions they performed for the FPLC. Most if not all the children travelled with the FPLC and were thus at risk of severe harm or death from the opposing belligerents due to that fact as well as from their own armed unit. Further, as mentioned, the perceived enduring association and identification of the transferred children with the FPLC (their stigmatization), regardless of their specific role with the FPLC, served a vital FPLC propaganda function for the armed group that amounts to the children's 'active participation' in hostilities. On this account, the current author respectfully disputes the Lubanga Trial Chamber contention that "Sexual violence does not form part of the charges against the accused…"[323] relating to the recruitment and/or use of children for active participation in the hostilities. The view here is, in contrast, that children sexually violated by the FPLC have, in fact, become the victims of the genocidal forcible transfer to the armed group in this way (through stigmatization and the resulting alienation from family and home community). The facts in this regard, insofar as under 15s are concerned, also fit the elements of the war crimes of recruitment and use of under 15s (the latter being charged in *Lubanga*). These sexually violated children, furthermore, are 'active participants' in the hostilities, not via performing forced sexual services for the FPLC *per se* (on an alleged awkward FPLC 'support function' theory); but rather due to the propaganda value for the FPLC of the children's sexual and other victimization. The current author then respectfully contests the alleged legal supportability of the Trial Chamber in *Lubanga* not making any findings in regards to the sexual violence, how it relates to the charges and contributes to the Article 8 crimes actually charged.[324]

More on the Concept of 'Child Soldiers' and Their Recruitment

The Defence in Lubanga relied in its argument as to who purportedly qualifies as a child soldier[325] and who does not on the Dissenting Opinion of Justice Robertson at the SCSL who stated:

---

[323] *Prosecutor v. Thomas Lubanga Dyilo* Summary of the "Judgment pursuant to Article 74 of the Statute (14 March, 2012, p8, para 29). Of course it is the case that *separate* sex crimes charges were not put forward in *Lubanga*.

[324] *Prosecutor v. Thomas Lubanga Dyilo* Summary of the "Judgment pursuant to Article 74 of the Statute (14 March, 2012, p8, para 29).

[325] The current author contends that the term 'child soldier' is a misnomer since soldiers have an unqualified right to participate in armed hostilities while no such right exists for children and international law views children's participation in hostilities as an anomaly to be discouraged (See Grover 2008, 2012). This author favours the expression "children associated with armed forces or groups"; a term that is increasingly coming to replace the term 'child soldier'. However, the latter term is used here for ease of reference. (See Prosecutor v Thomas Lubanga Dyilo, Final Trial Judgement Pursuant to Article 74 of the Rome Statute (2012, p. 270, para 589, "Victims Submissions").

> Forcible recruitment is always wrong, but enlistment of child volunteers might be excused if they are accepted into the force only for non-combatant tasks, behind the front lines.[326]

The current author, in opposition to the Lubanga Defence position (the latter reflecting the perspective of Justice Robertson of the SCSL), contends that since so-called 'recruitment' into an armed force or group committing mass atrocity and/or genocide (such as the FPLC) constitutes the genocidal forcible transfer of children (for the reasons previously discussed), no child so transferred can be considered to have 'enlisted.'[327] To suggest otherwise is to *erroneously* contend that: (1) children can consent or assent to their own genocidal forcible transfer to such an armed group or force and that (2) alleged consent or assent is a potential defence to the integration of children (persons under age 18) into armed groups or forces systematically perpetrating grave international crimes (especially, it would seem, according to Justice Robertson of the SCSL if they are performing alleged "non-combatant tasks").[328]

Further, the current author maintains that it is *manifestly unlawful* to 'recruit' children (persons under age 18) into an armed group or force perpetrating mass atrocities or genocide (doing so constitutes the genocidal forcible transfer of children). Hence, there is no possibility of a violation of the *nullem crimen* when individuals responsible for such 'recruitment' are held individually criminally liable.[329] In any case, there is clear evidence that prior to 1996 there existed a customary law prohibition on recruitment of children under 15s to armed groups or forces and that a violation of the same could result in individual criminal liability.[330]

3.1.9.4 Further Commentary on the Lubanga Trial Chamber's Analysis and Conclusions

Analysis of Dissenting Judge Odio Benito's View

The ICC Trial Chamber in *Lubanga* highlighted the critical fact that the acts comprising the three offences with which Lubanga was charged are

---

[326] Prosecutor v Thomas Lubanga Dyilo, Final Trial Judgement Pursuant to Article 74 of the Rome Statute (2012, p. 267, para 582).

[327] Note that in *Lubanga*, the Trial Chamber held that : "the crimes of conscription and enlistment are committed at the moment a child under the age of 15 is enrolled into or joins an armed force or group, ***with or without compulsion***." (*Prosecutor v. Thomas Lubanga Dyilo* Summary of the "Judgment pursuant to Article 74 of the Statute (14 March, 2012, p. 9, para 23).

[328] Distinctions between (1) those children who 'enlist' and those who are 'forced recruits' and between (2) children assigned military roles versus children assigned non-military functions post-recruitment arguably may be possible when children are members of armed groups or forces that, as a matter of policy and practice, do adhere to international humanitarian law.

[329] Justice Robertson of the SCSL in his Dissenting Opinion in *Prosecutor v Norman* took the view that *nullem crimen* had been violated in prosecuting Norman for 'recruitment' of children. (See Dissenting Opinion of Justice Robertson in *Prosecutor v Samuel Hinga Norman* (31 May, 2004).

[330] SCSL *Prosecutor versus Samuel Hinga Norman*, Appeals Chamber, Fourth Defence Preliminary Motion Based on Lack of Jurisdiction (Child Recruitment) Amicus Curiae Brief of the United Nations Children's Fund (UNICEF) (21 January, 2004).

actually ***not*** defined under the Rome Statute[331]; the Rules or the Elements of the Crime:

> ***Addressing the three relevant acts, namely conscripting, enlisting children under the age of 15 or using them to participate actively in hostilities, in each instance the conduct is not defined in the Statute, the Rules or the Elements of the Crimes.*** Accordingly, the scope of the activities covered by Article 8(2)(e)(vii) of the Statute must be determined in accordance with Articles 21 and 22(2) of the Statute. . .[332]

Given the absence of definitions of the three acts referred to in the confirmed charges in *Lubanga*, (i.e. the lack of clarity as to the scope of activities these acts include) the Trial Court, in order to interpret and apply the law correctly, would importantly also have to rely in part on:

(i) Interpretive rules set out in the Vienna Convention on the Law of Treaties[333]:

> The Appeals Chamber has established that the interpretation of the Statute is governed by the Vienna Convention on the Law of Treaties. . .[334]

(ii) Rome Statute Article 21(3) on applicable law[335];
(iii) The General Principle of Law articulated at Article 22(2) of the Rome Statute.[336]

Respectfully, the contention of the current author is that the final ICC Trial judgement in *Lubanga* in respect of the meaning of enlistment; conscription and use of children under 15 for active participation in armed hostilities is *not* fully consistent with respect for internationally recognized human rights contrary to the requirements of Article 21(3) of the Rome Statute[337] concerning applicable law and despite the best intentions of the Court. This in that the Trial Court judgment (1) excludes various groups of children unjustifiably from the protections afforded by the prohibition against the recruitment and use of under 15s for active participation in hostilities and (2) girls are disproportionately affected in this

---

[331] Rome Statute (2002).

[332] Prosecutor v Thomas Lubanga Dyilo, Final Trial Judgement Pursuant to Article 74 of the Rome Statute (2012, pp. 273–274, para 600).

[333] Vienna Convention on the Law of Treaties (1980). Article 31(1): "A treaty shall be interpreted in good faith in accordance with the ordinary meaning to be given to the terms of the treaty in their context and in the light of its object and purpose."

[334] Prosecutor v Thomas Lubanga Dyilo, Final Trial Judgement Pursuant to Article 74 of the Rome Statute (14 March, 2012, p. 274, para 601).

[335] Rome Statute (2012): Article 21(3): "The application and interpretation of law pursuant to this article must be consistent with internationally recognized human rights, and be without any adverse distinction founded on grounds such as gender as defined in article 7, paragraph 3, *age*, race, colour, language, religion or belief, political or other opinion, national, ethnic or social origin, wealth, birth or *other status*." (emphasis added).

[336] Rome Statute (2012). Article 22(2):" The definition of a crime shall be strictly construed and shall not be extended by analogy. In case of ambiguity, the definition shall be interpreted in favour of the person being investigated, prosecuted or convicted."

[337] Rome Statute (2002).

exclusion from protection (this amounting to adverse impact systematic discrimination based on gender due to the court's particular interpretation of the Article 8 Rome Statute[338] war crimes charged in Lubanga). The current author thus is agreed with Dissenting Judge Odio Benito of the Lubanga Trial Court that:

> Since neither the Statute nor the Elements of the Crime define further these three criminal conducts [enlistment, conscription and use of children under 15 to participate actively in the hostilities], the Chamber is required to define them taking into consideration other applicable law. Furthermore, pursuant to Article 21(3) of the Rome Statute, the Chamber is compelled to interpret and apply the law consistent with internationally recognized human rights.. . . .*It would consequently be contrary to "the object and purpose" of the Rome Statute,*[339] *contrary to international recognized human rights and discriminatory* under Article 21 (3), not to define the legal concepts of enlistment, conscription and use to participate actively in the hostilities. . .[340]

Given the current author's position on the legal supportability of there having been a legal re-characterization of the facts and circumstances in Lubanga consistent with additional and separate charges relating to sexual slavery and cruel and inhuman treatment (as discussed previously in some detail); it is also here held that: (1) the interpretation of these latter crimes and of (2) the elements of the crimes of enlistment, conscription and use of children under 15 to participate actively in the hostilities should have been based in part on evidence presented at the Pre-Trial (i.e. in MONUC and Human Rights Watch reports etc.) and at trial through witnesses, experts and other sources *relating to sexual violence and cruel and inhuman treatment*.

The current author applauds Dissenting Judge Odio Benito for highlighting in *Lubanga* a crucial matter that is often overlooked in the heat of adversarial wrangling amongst the parties involved in an ICC case and in the Court's assiduous care in affording the defendant his or her proper entitlement to due process in an international criminal proceeding (namely the victims' basic human rights that are implicated in the Rome Statute[341] provisions at issue in the case). This key matter she addresses as follows:

> ***Although the Rome Statute's provisions are applied and interpreted in relation to specific charges brought against individuals, the Chamber must not disregard the interests that these provisions are meant to protect. In the present case, the statutory provisions are meant to protect the life and personal integrity of children under the age of 15***. It would thus be impermissible for a Chamber to decline to enter a comprehensive legal definition of a crime and leave it open to case-by-case analysis or the limited scope of the charges brought against the accused. This would be a step backwards in the progressive development of international law.[342]

---

[338] Rome Statute (2002).

[339] Compare Article 31(1) Vienna Convention on the Law of Treaties (1980).

[340] Dissenting Opinion of Judge Odio Benito Prosecutor v Thomas Lubanga Dyilo, Final Trial Judgement Pursuant to Article 74 of the Rome Statute (14 March, 2012, pp. 2–3, para 6).

[341] Rome Statute (2012).

[342] Dissenting Opinion of Judge Odio Benito Prosecutor v Thomas Lubanga Dyilo, Final Trial Judgement Pursuant to Article 74 of the Rome Statute (14 March, 2012, p. 3, para 7, emphasis added).

> …this case-by-case determination [regarding what constitutes 'use to participate actively in hostilities'] can produce a limited and potentially ***discriminatory assessment*** of the risks and harms suffered by the child….[343]
>
> …By failing to deliberately include within the legal concept of 'use to participate actively in hostilities' the sexual violence and other ill-treatment suffered by boys and girls, the Majority of the Chamber is making this critical aspect of the crime invisible. *Invisibility of sexual violence in the legal concept leads to* **discrimination** *against the victims of enlistment, conscription and use who systematically suffer from this crime [sexual violence and cruel and inhuman treatment] as an intrinsic part of the involvement with the armed group.*[344]
>
> …Sexual violence committed against children in the armed groups causes irreparable harms and is a direct and inherent consequence to their involvement with the armed group. *Sexual violence is an intrinsic element of the criminal conduct of "use to participate actively in the hostilities*" Girls who are used as sex slaves or "wives" of commanders or other members of the armed group *provide an essential support function to the armed groups.*[345]
>
> It is ***discriminatory*** to exclude sexual violence which shows a clear gender differential impact ….The use of young girls and boys bodies within ***or outside the group*** is a war crime and as such ***encoded in the charges against the accused.***[346]

Yet, in Lubanga, the Trial Chamber did just what Judge Odio Benito admonishes against. This by leaving vague who precisely is included as protected from 'use for active participation in hostilities'(that is, clarifying which children performing which roles within an armed group or force such as the FPLC are protected from 'use for active participation in hostilities').

> As regards the offence of using children under the age of 15 to participate actively in hostilities, the Chamber has concluded that this includes a wide range of activities, from those children on the front line (who participate directly) through to the boys or girls who are involved in a myriad of roles that support the combatants. ***All of these activities, which cover either direct or indirect participation, have an underlying common feature: the child concerned is, at the very least, a potential target. The decisive factor, therefore, in deciding if an "indirect" role is to be treated as active participation in hostilities is***

---

[343] Dissenting Opinion of Judge Odio Benito Prosecutor v Thomas Lubanga Dyilo, Final Trial Judgement Pursuant to Article 74 of the Rome Statute (14 March, 2012, p. 6, para 15, emphasis added).

[344] Dissenting Opinion of Judge Odio Benito Prosecutor v Thomas Lubanga Dyilo, Final Trial Judgement Pursuant to Article 74 of the Rome Statute (14 March, 2012, p. 6, para 16, emphasis added).

[345] Dissenting Opinion of Judge Odio Benito Prosecutor v Thomas Lubanga Dyilo, Final Trial Judgement Pursuant to Article 74 of the Rome Statute (14 March, 2012, p. 7, para 20). Note that the current author holds that it is unnecessary and awkward; to say the least, to argue that the child recruits providing sex is an "essential support function to the armed group." Rather, the sexual violence is better viewed as falling with the 'use' crime as a correlate of conscription and a vehicle for 'genocidal forcible transfer of children' to the armed group with such appropriation of children serving the military and propaganda objectives of the armed group as previously here discussed.

[346] The genocidal forcible transfer of children by the FPLC, it has here been argued, was also implemented through sexual violation of non-Hema children, mostly girls, who did not in fact become FPLC child soldiers as part of the FPLC ranks. Such sexual violation yet is embedded in the notion of conscription and use by an armed group or force perpetrating mass atrocities and/or genocide (inasmuch as these sexually violated girls are now considered tainted and hence on that account part of the enemy perpetrator group).

> ***whether the support provided by the child to the combatants exposed him or her to real danger as a potential target.*** In the judgment of the Chamber these combined factors – the child's support and this level of consequential risk – mean that although absent from the immediate scene of the hostilities, the individual was nonetheless actively involved in them.[347]

The above statement from the Trial Court majority judgment leaves to the discretion of a particular judicial panel, based on its evaluation of the evidence in a specific case, which children under age 15, if any, through their support activities [indirect participation in hostilities] with an armed group or force were "exposed... to real danger as a potential target."[348] Some judicial panels, therefore, may decide at their discretion, for instance, that: (1) girls allegedly used only as sex slaves or domestics by such an armed group or force as the FPLC were allegedly *not* exposed to such actual high risk as a "potential target" (*as if* they were on the frontlines) and (2) that these girls are therefore not considered part of the protected group implicated in the Rome Statute[349] prohibitions against recruitment and use of under 15s for active participation in hostilities. This latter approach, however, is erroneous as it does not consider the following:

> Children are protected from child recruitment not only because they can be at risk for being a potential target to the "enemy" but also because *they will be at risk from their "own" armed group who has recruited them and will subject these children to brutal trainings, torture and ill-treatment, sexual violence and other activities and living conditions that are incompatible and in violation to these children's fundamental rights.* The risk for children who are enlisted, conscripted or used by an armed group inevitably also comes from within the same armed group.[350]

Note that the majority Trial Chamber in *Lubanga* as to the question of which children, given their *indirect participation*, are protected (due to the Rome Statute[351] prohibition against under 15s' *active participation* in hostilities) opined that to be part of the protected group; the risk to the child of these indirect participation activities must be equivalent to that which would be incurred by a child soldier at the frontlines (insofar as these activities constituting indirect participation make these children also "potential targets" of the enemy). In other words, 'use for active participation in hostilities', in respect of indirect participation, on the aforementioned Trial Court majority view in *Lubanga* must have the child perceived as a child soldier legitimate target by the enemy. In contrast, Judge Odio Benito's views regarding 'use' for active participation in hostilities' (whether direct or indirect participation) are much more inclusive considering *harms that result per se from transfer of*

---

[347] *Prosecutor v. Thomas Lubanga Dyilo* Summary of the "Judgment pursuant to Article 74 of the Statute (14 March, 2012, pp. 9–10, para 24).

[348] *Prosecutor v. Thomas Lubanga Dyilo* Summary of the "Judgment pursuant to Article 74 of the Statute (14 March, 2012, pp. 9–10, para 24).

[349] Rome Statute (2012).

[350] Dissenting Opinion of Judge Odio Benito Prosecutor v Thomas Lubanga Dyilo, Final Trial Judgement Pursuant to Article 74 of the Rome Statute (14 March, 2012, p. 7, para 19).

[351] Rome Statute (2012).

children to an armed group or force such as the FPLC and, in particular, due to the sexual violation perpetrated against the children recruited that is endemic within such armed groups or forces that appropriate children under 15 (and in fact, on the available evidence, it is here pointed out, is endemic amongst such armed groups or forces that 'recruit' children of any age). Judge Odio Benito's inclusive approach to conceptualizing which children are protected under the prohibition against use of under 15s for active participation in hostilities insofar as it better considers the full range of harms suffered by these children (whether they are perceived by the enemy as child soldiers or simply sex slaves or whatever) comes close to the notion of such 'recruitment' and 'use' constituting the 'genocidal forcible transfer of children' to an armed group or force (State or non-State) perpetrating mass atrocities and/or genocide. The current author is wholeheartedly agreed with Judge Odio Benito then that:

> It becomes irrelevant . . .if the prosecution submitted the charges as separate crimes [sexual slavery as a separate war crime and crime against humanity and cruel and inhuman treatment as a separate war crime] or rightfully including [sic] them as *embedded* in the crimes of which Mr. Lubanga is accused.[352] The harm suffered victims is not only reserved for reparations [and sentencing] proceedings, but *should be a fundamental aspect of the Chamber's evaluation of the crimes committed.*[353]

The suggestion by Judge Odio Benito, furthermore, that sexual violence and cruel and inhuman treatment are "an *intrinsic part* of the [children's] involvement with the armed group" [specifically their 'use for active participation in hostilities'][354] and that: "The risk for children who are enlisted, conscripted or used by an armed group inevitably also comes from within the same armed group"[355] also comes closer (if unintentionally) to the view here that the children were the victims of 'genocidal forcible transfer.' This is the case in that sexual violence and cruel and inhuman treatment are significant markers for the 'genocidal forcible transfer of children' as opposed to recruitment and use of children for the purpose strictly of child soldiering (the latter in the sense of participating in combat and direct combat related functions (such as spying, sabotage, being a courier, being a personal bodyguard for commanders etc.) that are undertaken consistent with the rules of war and thus lawful *if undertaken by a person of age* who is purportedly a 'soldier' (or a civilian in a popular uprising directed to overthrowing dictatorial and/or colonial/imperial rule in which fundamental human rights were

---

[352] Dissenting Opinion of Judge Odio Benito Prosecutor v Thomas Lubanga Dyilo, Final Trial Judgement Pursuant to Article 74 of the Rome Statute (14 March, 2012, pp. 3–4, para 8).

[353] Dissenting Opinion of Judge Odio Benito Prosecutor v Thomas Lubanga Dyilo, Final Trial Judgement Pursuant to Article 74 of the Rome Statute (14 March, 2012, pp. 3–4, para 8, emphasis added).

[354] Dissenting Opinion of Judge Odio Benito Prosecutor v Thomas Lubanga Dyilo, Final Trial Judgement Pursuant to Article 74 of the Rome Statute (14 March, 2012, p. 6, para 16, emphasis added).

[355] Dissenting Opinion of Judge Odio Benito Prosecutor v Thomas Lubanga Dyilo, Final Trial Judgement Pursuant to Article 74 of the Rome Statute (14 March, 2012, p. 7, para 19, emphasis added).

trampled). Thus, sexual violence and cruel and inhuman treatment of children (the latter beyond their actual participation in combat *per se* through direct or indirect typical activities associated with engaging with the enemy) typically occur in the context of transfer ('recruitment') and 'use' by an armed group or force perpetrating mass atrocities and/or genocide (on the view here transfer to an unlawful armed criminal organization whether euphemistically designated a State 'army' or a non-State armed group or so-called 'army'). Thus, the current author is agreed with Judge Odio Benito's assertion that: ". . .the concept of enlistment, conscription and use in both Article 8(2)(b)(xxvi) and Article8(2)(e)(vii) of the Rome Statute should be understood as encompassing *any type of armed group or force*, regardless of the nature of the armed conflict in which it occurs".[356]

This potential exclusion of certain children from protection (i.e. girl sex slaves of the FPLC) arose, in part, it would appear, due to the reversal decision by the Appeal Court which prevented the Trial Court from considering facts and circumstances relevant to potential separate charges of sexual slavery and cruel and inhuman treatment. Further, it resulted, on the view here, due to the failure of the Prosecutor to charge Lubanga additionally with genocidal forcible transfer of Hema children to the UPC/FPLC to serve as child soldiers and/or sex slaves or in other capacities and the genocidal forcible transfer of non-Hema children to the FPLC through their sexual victimization.[357] The result was that the Trial Court ultimately *in effect* potentially excluded various groups of children from the protections due them arising from: (1) the prohibition against recruitment ('conscription' or 'enlistment')[358] and use of under 15s for active participation in hostilities and (2) the prohibition against the 'genocidal forcible transfer of children' stipulated under the relevant subsections of Article 8 and Article 6(e) of the Rome Statute, respectively.[359]

On Article 31 of the Vienna Convention on the Law of Treaties

Respectfully, what is here viewed as a narrow and *under-inclusive* interpretation of Article 8 of the Rome Statute[360] (regarding recruitment and use of under 15s for

---

[356] Dissenting Opinion of Judge Odio Benito Prosecutor v Thomas Lubanga Dyilo, Final Trial Judgement Pursuant to Article 74 of the Rome Statute (14 March, 2012, p. 5, para 14, emphasis added).

[357] This is not at all to suggest that Lubanga should not also have been charged with war crimes in relation to the systematic mass sexual victimization of women by the FPLC, particularly but not exclusively non-Hema women; a topic that is simply beyond the scope of the present work.

[358] *If* child sex slaves/child domestics/child' bush wives' appropriated by the FPLC and travelling with the FPLC are *not* regarded by the Majority in *Lubanga* as protected 'child soldier' high value 'potential targets' of the enemy (whether or not they were on the frontlines) then it is difficult to understand how the majority can conclude either that they were conscripted or enlisted within the ordinary meaning of the Article 8 Rome Statute notions of 'conscription' and 'enlistment' in an armed conflict situation.

[359] Rome Statute (2002).

[360] Rome Statute (2002).

active participation in hostilities) adopted by the majority Trial Chamber panel in *Lubanga*, on the analysis here, violates the rules of interpretation as set out in Article 31 of the Vienna Convention on the Law of Treaties.[361] The Trial Chamber in *Lubanga* summarized the rules of interpretation of treaties as per Article 31 of the Vienna Convention on the Law of Treaties as follows:

> The rule governing the interpretation of a section of the law is its wording read in context and in light of its object and purpose. The context of a given legislative provision is defined by the particular sub-section of the law read as whole in conjunction with the section of the enactment in its entirety. *Its objects may be gathered from the chapter of the law in which the particular section is included and its purposes from the wider aims of the law as may be gathered from its preamble and the general tenor of the treaty.*[362]

In regards to the issue of the broader purpose of the Rome Statute[363] Article 8 prohibitions (regarding 'conscription' or 'enlistment' and/or 'use of under 15s for active participation in hostilities'); consider the matter of cultural bonds between the children so affected and their community. 'Culture' and 'cultural diversity' are replaced, due to the recruitment and use of children by armed groups or forces committing mass atrocities, by one thing and one thing only; namely systematic mass violence perpetrated against designated targeted groups and any opposition (regardless if the opposition is coming from moderate segments of the same national or ethnic group etc. or from outside). Preserving cultural bonds and cultural diversity is a prime objective of the Rome Statute:

> Conscious that all peoples are united by common bonds, their cultures pieced together in a shared heritage, and concerned that this delicate mosaic may be shattered at any time...[364]

Consider further that preserving cultural bonds and cultural diversity necessarily means protecting the right of parents to rear their children (and do so in accord with their traditions where the latter do not violate the fundamental rights of the child). There is then a fundamental right of families and communities, in the normal course, to have their children as an integral part of these groupings. In addition, the children, in the normal course, have a fundamental right to their personal identity, their parents, and to be an integral part of their primary caretaking family and their home communities. Such rights are explicitly set out in various international instruments including in the following provisions of the Convention on the Rights of the Child (CRC)[365] and the International Covenant on Civil and Political Rights (CCPR)[366]as follows:

---

[361] Vienna Convention on the Law of Treaties (1980).

[362] Prosecutor v Thomas Lubanga Dyilo, Final Trial Judgement Pursuant to Article 74 of the Rome Statute (2012, pp. 274–275, para 601, citing a 2006 ICC Appeal decision in *Situation in the Democratic Republic of Congo* (see footnote 1766 of the Final Trial Judgment in *Lubanga*, 20 March, 2012, emphasis added).

[363] Rome Statute (2002).

[364] Rome Statute (2002, Preamble).

[365] Convention on the Rights of the Child (1990).

[366] International Covenant on Civil and Political Rights (1976).

CRC: Article 5

States Parties shall respect the responsibilities, rights and duties of parents or, where applicable, the members of the extended family or community as provided for by local custom, legal guardians or other persons legally responsible for the child, to provide, in a manner consistent with the evolving capacities of the child, appropriate direction and guidance in the exercise by the child of the rights recognized in the present Convention.[367]

CRC: Article 8

1. States Parties undertake to respect the right of the child to preserve his or her identity, including nationality, name and family relations as recognized by law without unlawful interference.
2. Where a child is illegally deprived of some or all of the elements of his or her identity, States Parties shall provide appropriate assistance and protection, with a view to re-establishing speedily his or her identity.[368]

CRC: Article 9

1. *States Parties shall ensure that a child shall not be separated from his or her parents against their will, except when competent authorities subject to judicial review determine, in accordance with applicable law and procedures, that such separation is necessary for the best interests of the child.* Such determination may be necessary in a particular case such as one involving abuse or neglect of the child by the parents, or one where the parents are living separately and a decision must be made as to the child's place of residence.[369]

   . . .

CCPR: Article 23

(1) ***The family is the natural and fundamental group unit of society and is entitled to protection by society and the State*. . .**[370]

Note that the Democratic Republic of Congo (DRC) ratified the Convention on the Rights of the Child 27 September, 1990 and acceded to the International Covenant on Civil and Political Rights 1 November, 1976. The relevant time period covered in the Lubanga ICC case according to the ICC Trial Chamber was early September 2002 to 13 August 2003 with respect to international crimes committed in the context of the non-international (internal) conflict in the DRC.

In addition, well established humanitarian law, arguably of customary law status, established the right of children (no age specified) to special care and respect in the context of armed conflict which is of course inconsistent with appropriation/transfer of a child of any age (persons under age 18) to an armed group or force perpetrating mass atrocities and/or genocide to serve in any capacity (see, for instance, Article 77, Protocol I Additional to the Geneva Conventions concerning international conflict and Article 4 Protocol II Additional to the Geneva Conventions concerning non-international conflict situations).[371] The right of

---

[367] Convention on the Rights of the Child (1990).

[368] Convention on the Rights of the Child (1990).

[369] Convention on the Rights of the Child (1990)

[370] International Covenant on Civil and Political Rights (1976).

[371] Protocols I and II Additional to the Geneva Conventions (1977).

children to their parents and families and vice versa during armed conflict is also recognized in Protocol I and II Additional to the 1949 Geneva Conventions and can be considered another aspect of the respect and care owed children as a special protected group. There is reference in Protocol II to temporary removal of children from hot conflict zones and separation from parents only where necessary for the children's safety with reunion of families as soon as possible being the objective:

Protocol II Additional to the Geneva Conventions

Part II: Humane Treatment
Article 4: Fundamental Guarantees
(3) Children shall be provided with the care and aid they require, and in particular:
b) ***all appropriate steps shall be taken to facilitate the reunion of families*** temporarily separated;

[. . .]

e) measures shall be taken, if necessary, and whenever possible with the consent of their parents or persons who by law or custom are primarily responsible for their care, to remove children temporarily from the area in which hostilities are taking place to a safer area within the country and *ensure that they are accompanied by persons responsible for their safety and well-being*.[372]

Protocol I Additional to the Geneva Conventions also places a high priority on maintaining the integrity of families during armed conflict wherever feasible:

Protocol I Additional to the Geneva Conventions

Article 74 – Reunion of dispersed families
The High Contracting Parties and the Parties to the conflict ***shall facilitate in every possible way the reunion of families dispersed as a result of armed conflicts*** and shall encourage in particular the work of the humanitarian organizations engaged in this task in accordance with the provisions of the Conventions and of this Protocol and in conformity with their respective security regulations.[373]

It is quite evident then that there existed at the time of the international crimes committed by *Lubanga* international humanitarian and human rights legal principles regarding: (1) the high duty of care owed to children as a special protected group in times of armed conflict; (2) children's right to their personal identity, family and home community as well as (3) the parents' right to rear their children and the community's right to enjoy the benefits that derive from having a young generation amongst their members.[374] The contention here is that the latter fundamental rights are very broad and necessitate an interpretation of the central

---

[372] Protocols II Additional to the Geneva Conventions (1977, emphasis added).

[373] Protocols I Additional to the Geneva Conventions (1977, emphasis added).

[374] The Trial Chamber in Lubanga made reference to prohibitions in various international human rights and humanitarian law instruments against the use of under 15s as an attempt not just to protect children from violence but also from trauma resulting from i.e. "separating children from their families." (See Prosecutor v Thomas Lubanga Dyilo, Final Trial Judgement Pursuant to Article 74 of the Rome Statute (2012, p. 277, para 605). The Trial Chamber, however, did not consider how the latter might play into the occurrence not just of war crimes relating to the recruitment and use of child soldiers so-called but also the genocidal forcible transfer of children.

facts, contextual circumstances and the law in *Lubanga* as indicating that Lubanga and his co-perpetrators violated these rights through: (1) the recruitment and use of Hema children by the FPLC for active participation in hostilities (which included their use as sex slaves and in other non-combat roles) and (2) the perpetrating of mass atrocities and arguably also genocide against the Lendu and Ngiti and other peoples of Ituri and the targeting of the children of these groups for particularly heinous brutality (such as but not limited to sexual victimization).

It is noteworthy that the Trial Court in *Lubanga*, in its analysis of the facts and the law (including established human rights and humanitarian principles); focused its attention exclusively on the right of under 15s to be protected against recruitment and use for active participation in armed hostilities. Thus, the Trial Chamber looked to international human rights and humanitarian law instruments only in respect of the prohibitions on the recruitment and use of under 15s for active participation in hostilities incorporated in those treaties and conventions.[375] That is, there was no consideration, in addition, of the violation of the right of the transferred children to their original identity, their family and community all of which are, as has here been discussed, well established rights also entrenched in several of the aforementioned international law instruments which predate the Rome Statute[376] (some of which instruments arguably have the status of customary law). It is here argued that consideration of how the facts and circumstances in *Lubanga* pertaining to the confirmed charges [namely; recruitment to the FPLC (including sexual violation of girl child soldiers as an aspect of conscription) and use of children for active participation in hostilities by the FPLC (including using child soldiers to procure sex slaves for FPLC commanders)] relate to violation of the transferred children's rights to their identity, family and community properly could have provided the grounding for the legal re-characterization of the facts as also consistent with 'genocidal forcible transfer of children' to the FPLC (a force perpetrating mass atrocities as part of a 'common plan').[377]

It was, it should be noted, not only Hema children under age 15 whose aforementioned rights to family, community and their identity were violated by their genocidal forcible transfer to the FPLC but also: (1) child members of the FPLC over age 15; (2) all children of the FPLC whatever their designated role in the FPLC may have been and whether they were perceived by the ICC as 'child soldiers' or something separate and apart from being a child soldier as well as (3) FPLC sexually victimized non-Hema children. The facts, evidence and surrounding circumstances described as underlying the Article 8 confirmed charges in *Lubanga*, it is here

---

[375] For instance the Trial Court in Lubanga refers to Article 4(3)(c) of Additional Protocol II to the Geneva Conventions pertaining to an absolute prohibitions on recruitment and use of under 15s in hostilities (See Prosecutor v Thomas Lubanga Dyilo, Final Trial Judgement Pursuant to Article 74 of the Rome Statute (2012, p. 276, para 604).

[376] Rome Statute (2002).

[377] Note also that humanitarian agencies are increasingly coming to realize the importance for children's welfare of keeping families together and reuniting separated families in times of armed conflict and in other emergency situations (i.e. See Doyle, J., 2010).

contended, when properly legally characterized, then would also support a charge of 'genocidal forcible transfer of children'; referring here to persons under age 18.

As previously explained, segments of the FPLC child contingent aged under 15 cannot be properly be excluded from consideration as victims of the Rome Statute Article 8 "use" charges (children used to participate actively in hostilities) confirmed by the Pre-Trial Chamber. That erroneous potential exclusion by the Trial Court of certain FPLC children as victims of the crime of being used for "active participation" in hostilities would be based simply on these children's designated roles in the FPLC (i.e. as bush wives/sex slaves/domestics etc. allegedly performing no combat or closely combat-related function)".[378] In fact, to the contrary, all the children, as members of the FPLC subsequent to their genocidal forcible transfer, served a military and propaganda function (that is, the FPLC children symbolized the vitality and alleged power in perpetuity of the FPLC given their ability to appropriate an endless supply of children to their ranks). In this way, amongst many others, the appropriation of these children helped to prolong the armed hostilities. Thus, all children who were the victims of recruitment and use (also amounting to the 'genocidal forcible transfer of children') to the FPLC were being used for "active participation" in the armed hostilities.

In the final analysis then the facts and circumstances in *Lubanga*, it is here argued, should have been; and would have been properly legally re-characterized if sexual violence committed against girls were viewed as both: (1) a vehicle for the genocidal forcible transfer of children to the FPLC (a crime under Article 6(e) of the Rome Statute addressing genocide) and as (2) an aspect of conscription and use (as per the crimes of 'conscription' and 'use' of under 15s articulated in Article 8 of the Rome Statute[379] dealing with war crimes). In addition, using child soldiers to procure sex slaves for FPLC commanders and other FPLC should have been viewed as: (1) an aspect of 'using children to participate actively in hostilities' for the reasons here discussed earlier and as also (2) a vehicle for 'genocidal forcible transfer' of the child soldier procurers and their child victims to the FPLC. Further, the facts regarding various sex crimes (rape, forced pregnancy etc.) committed by the FPLC should have been legally re-characterized in *Lubanga* to provide the grounding for separate war crimes and/or crimes against humanity charges as per the relevant Rome Statute[380] provisions in that the same facts underlying the confirmed Article 8 charges fit these multiple additional offences as well.

The cruel and inhuman treatment accorded the FPLC child soldiers on order of FPLC commanders should have been considered; it is here contended, as an aspect of both: (1) the children's recruitment (i.e. brutal treatment during the children's abduction and forced recruitment and/or during 'military' training etc.) and (2) their

[378] The evidence in Lubanga however demonstrated, as will be recalled, that girl FPLC members most often performed both the duties of bush wives/sex slaves and those routine child soldier duties such as being a bodyguard for commanders, scouting etc. (See for instance *Prosecutor v. Thomas Lubanga Dyilo*, Amicus Brief of Coomaraswamy, R. (United Nations Special Representative of the Secretary-General on Children and Armed Conflict), (2008, para 25–26).

[379] Rome Statute (2002).

[380] Rome Statute (2002).

'use for active participation in hostilities' by the FPLC (forcing the children to commit atrocities against their own families and communities and other civilians etc). The facts regarding cruel and inhuman treatment (that were already in evidence to support the confirmed charges of recruitment and use of under 15s in hostilities and presented at trial) should have been legally re-characterized as substantiating also the charge of genocidal forcible transfer of children by the FPLC. This in that such cruel and inhuman treatment served to destroy the children's identities, and alienate them from their families and communities. In addition, the relevant facts in evidence should have been legally re-characterized to fit the charge of cruel and inhuman treatment of the FPLC 'child soldiers' as separate war crimes charges. The ICC Appeal Chamber, however, quashed the possibility of any legal re-characterization of the facts pertaining to sexual violence and cruel and inhuman treatment in *Lubanga* and, therefore, also the potential for a any further charges in that regard.

Keeping the former points in mind regarding: (1) the rights of all children to their personal identity, family and community, and (2) their right to special protection in times of armed conflict let us briefly recap. The argument is that a proper interpretation of Rome Statute[381] Article 8 (pertaining to the recruitment (conscription or enlistment) and/or use of children under age 15 for active participation in armed hostilities) and of Article 6 (e) (referring to the bar against the 'genocidal forcible transfer of children' (persons under age 18)) requires that: (1) *all children* (persons under age 18) appropriated by armed groups or forces such as the UPC/FPLC perpetrating mass atrocities and/or genocide be considered as victims of the 'genocidal forcible transfer of children' *regardless their assigned role/function in the group or force* if any and that (2) the under 15s are to be regarded, in addition, as the victims of war crimes under the Rome Statute Article 8 provision pertaining to child soldiering (conscription and use) including children used as sex slaves or for any other purpose (in the latter case the children regardless of age are also the victims of separate war crimes and/or crimes against humanity pertaining to sexual violence). In addition, all children transferred to the armed group and suffering cruel and inhuman treatment are the victims of separate war crimes in regards to the latter. This foregoing interpretation and application of the law is consistent with the established international human rights and humanitarian law principles here previously discussed pertaining to: (1) the special protected status of children (persons under age 18) also in times of armed conflict; and (2) children's right to their identity, family and community. The fact that the Rome Statute[382] is in part intended, as is clear from the preamble, to: (1) protect cultural diversity and hence the cultural bond between children, their families and their communities and, by implication, (2) preserve the children's personal identity in all its aspects also supports such an interpretation and application of the relevant Rome Statute[383] provisions in the Lubanga case.

---

[381] Rome Statute (2002).

[382] Rome Statute (2002).

[383] Rome Statute (2002).

It is here contended that the fact that the Rome Statute contains a special provision regarding the prohibition against the genocidal forcible transfer of children (persons under age 18) of the group to another group establishes the importance that the drafters intended to place on one's right to his or her identity, and to one's family and home community in part as a means to maintaining the integrity of one's group of origin. The prohibition against the 'genocidal forcible transfer of children' amounts (notwithstanding some of the debates in the preparatory work for the Rome Statute[384] regarding the need to omit *explicit references* to culture or political group in Article 6) also to the right to preserve one's cultural heritage and personal identity.[385]

Failure to Consider the Plight of Child Soldiers Over 15

The failure to consider that appropriation[386] of children by armed groups or forces *committing mass atrocities and/or genocide* constitutes the 'genocidal forcible transfer of children'[387] means that children 15 and over (but under age 18), in practice, have little if any protection under the Rome Statute[388] in regards to their 'recruitment' and transfer as child soldiers to such murderous armed groups or forces.[389] This is the case since the relevant Article 8 war crimes provisions pertaining to the prohibition on recruitment ('conscription' or 'enlistment') and/or 'use of children for active participation in armed hostilities' pertain only to children *under age 15 years*. The exclusion *in practice* of children 15 and over from protection under the Rome Statute[390] against appropriation by armed groups or forces committing mass atrocities and/or genocide amounts to age discrimination

[384] Rome Statute (2002).

[385] The need for a broader interpretation of 'protected group' as stipulated in Article 6 of the Rome Statute was here previously discussed. Note that 'ethnic group' (included in the Rome Statute enumeration of protected groups) in fact implies cultural identity as expressed in language, tradition and other distinctive characteristics that distinguish the identified group from others.

[386] Appropriation of children by armed groups or forces committing mass atrocities and/or genocide refers here to recruitment and/or use of children (persons under age 18) for active participation in armed hostilities by such groups or forces.

[387] See also Grover (2012).

[388] Rome Statute (2002).

[389] As discussed, in Lubanga, no separate charges were advanced or confirmed in regards to specific war crimes or crimes against humanity such as rape that could have included also the children over 15 who were victims. Note that the crime against humanity of forcible transfer of a population (Article 7(d) of the Rome Statute) and unlawful transfer of a person or persons as an Article 8 Rome Statute war crime are not child- specific crimes unlike the genocidal forcible transfer of children (Article 6(e) Rome Statute (2002). Furthermore , "unlawful transfer" under the Article 7 and 8 Rome Statute provisions refer to "forced displacement" and hence does not entirely capture the conduct described in Article 6(e) pertaining to the forcible transfer of a child or children of the group to another group in terms of the meaning of 'forcible transfer'.

[390] Rome Statute (2002).

against older children[391] in terms of their right to have their fundamental human rights protected in such a context. This age discrimination contradicts the objective of the Rome Statute[392] to provide non-discriminatory protection against the most serious international crimes. Respectfully then it is here suggested that the Prosecutorial approach in this regard in *Lubanga* violates Rome Statute Article 21(3):

Rome Statute: Article 21

Applicable law
1. The Court shall apply:
[. . .]
2. [. . .]
3. ***The application and interpretation of law pursuant to this article must be consistent with internationally recognized human rights, and be without any adverse distinction founded on grounds such as*** gender as defined in article 7, paragraph 3, ***age,*** race, colour, language, religion or belief, political or other opinion, national, ethnic or social origin, wealth, birth or other status.[393]

The failure to protect children 15 and over (given the scope of the cases brought to the ICC respecting the use of child soldiers) from genocidal forcible transfer to armed groups or forces such as the UPC/FPLC committing mass atrocities and/or genocide is the flip side of the fact that perpetrators are not held individually criminally responsible for the appropriation of these older children as in *Lubanga* (for instance via (1) charges of the 'genocidal forcible transfer of children (persons under age 18) to the FPLC and (2) war crimes and/or crimes against humanity charges related to the sexual violence and cruel and inhuman treatment perpetrated against children of all ages appropriated as child soldiers and sex slaves, domestics and in other capacities by the FPLC). This is in violation of the Rome Statute[394] stated objective to ensure that "the most serious crimes of concern to the international community as a whole . . .not go unpunished[395] [and that discriminatory factors do not influence the interpretation and implementation of the Rome Statute provisions]".

It is noteworthy that both the Prosecutor and the ICC Trial Court in *Lubanga* gave no particular consideration to the appropriation of children 15 and over by the FPLC. This was the case despite the fact that there was evidence introduced and accepted by the Trial Court that children 'recruited' and used for active participation in hostilities by the FPLC included those aged under 15 and those aged 15 and over but under 18. It is here argued that the evidence of recruitment and use by the

---

[391] Such exclusion of protection for older children occurs in cases such as *Lubanga* where only Article 8 charges regarding the recruitment and use of under 15s are pursued as opposed to also charges pertaining to the genocidal forcible transfer of children (persons under age 18) to such an armed group or force perpetrating mass atrocities and/or genocide.

[392] Rome Statute (2002).

[393] Rome Statute (2002, Article 21(3), emphasis added).

[394] Rome Statute (2002).

[395] Rome Statute (2002, Preamble).

FPLC also of children 15 and over should have highlighted the need to legally re-characterize the facts in this specific regard (amongst others) to ensure that these older child soldiers also received justice through the vehicle of the Lubanga ICC trial.[396] Indeed, the 2012 Trial Court judgment in *Lubanga* makes reference only to provisions in other legal instruments such as the Convention on the Rights of the Child (CRC) that address prohibitions regarding child soldiering with respect to *under 15s*:

> ...In addition, the Convention on the Rights of the Child, a widely ratified human rights treaty, requires the States Parties to "take all feasible measures to ensure that persons who have not attained the age of fifteen years do not take a direct part in hostilities," and "refrain from recruiting any person who has not attained the age of fifteen years into their armed forces" in all types of conflicts ("armed conflicts which are relevant to the child").[397]

There was reference only in two footnotes,[398] for instance, to the Optional Protocol to the Convention on the Rights of the Child on the involvement of children in armed conflict which affords certain protections to children (persons under age 18) including those 15 and over regarding child soldiering:

> **Article 1**
>
> States Parties shall take all feasible measures to ensure that members of their armed forces who have not attained the age of 18 years do not take a direct part in hostilities.
>
> **Article 2**
>
> States Parties shall ensure that persons who have not attained the age of 18 years are not compulsorily recruited into their armed forces.
>
> **Article 4**
>
> 1. Armed groups that are distinct from the armed forces of a State should not, under any circumstances, recruit or use in hostilities persons under the age of 18 years.
> 2. States Parties shall take all feasible measures to prevent such recruitment and use, including the adoption of legal measures necessary to prohibit and criminalize such practices...[399]

This failure to consider in particular also the plight of FPLC child soldiers 15 and over was due to the fact that: (1) the war crime Article 8 charges[400] brought by the Prosecutor and confirmed by the Pre-Trial Chamber in *Lubanga* only pertained to

[396] Such a legal re-characterization of the facts already introduced in the Lubanga case to support the confirmed charges would, as discussed, fit the charge of genocidal forcible transfer of children and thus apply also to those children over 15 recruited and/or used for active participation in hostilities by the FPLC.

[397] Prosecutor v Thomas Lubanga Dyilo, Final Trial Judgement Pursuant to Article 74 of the Rome Statute (2012, p. 276, para 604).

[398] Prosecutor v Thomas Lubanga Dyilo, Final Trial Judgment Pursuant to Article 74 of the Rome Statute (14 March, 2012, p. 276, FN 1770).

[399] Optional Protocol to the Convention on the Rights of the Child on the involvement of children in armed conflict (OPCRC-AC) (2002). Note that the DRC ratified OPCRC-AC 11 Nov, 2001.

[400] Rome Statute (2002 Article 8(2)(b)(xxvi) and Article 8(2)(e)(vii)).

under 15s and that (2) the Trial Chamber in *Lubanga* did not, on its own motion, consider the pressing need (based on the evidence presented in support of the existing confirmed charges that children over and under age 15 comprised a large segment of the FPLC force) for a legal re-characterization of the facts to include children 15 and over as child soldier victims of the FPLC (i.e. through a legal re-characterization of the facts consistent with 'genocidal forcible transfer of children' (persons under 18) as well as sexual violence and cruel and inhuman treatment of the children (where child refers to person under age 18). Certainly, it adds insult to injury for the victims, at least on the current analysis, to have the Trial Court in *Lubanga* refer to the vulnerability of under 15s (in the context of discussing the CRC[401] and Article 4(3)(c) of Additional Protocol II to the Geneva Conventions)[402] while virtually disregarding the fact that children 15 and over were also the victims of appropriation by the FPLC with consequent severe psychological and physical suffering:

> These provisions recognize that "children are particularly vulnerable [and] require privileged treatment in comparison to the rest of the civilian population." The principle objective underlying these prohibitions . . .is to protect children *under the age of 15* from the risks that are associated with armed conflict, and first and foremost they are directed at securing their physical and psychological well-being.[403]

Respectfully, on the view here, the (improperly) under-inclusive charging by the ICC Prosecutor in *Lubanga* and the failure, in the alternative, to legally re-characterize the existing facts and evidence underlying the confirmed charges in *Lubanga* so as to cover also the victim children aged 15 and over[404] serves to: (1) undermine the fundamental human right of children 15 and over also to be protected from recruitment and use for active participation in armed hostilities by armed groups and forces committing mass atrocities and/or genocide and (2) contributes to the impunity of the perpetrators that also victimize older children in this way.

The FPLC 'Common Plan' as Intrinsically Criminal

The Pre-Trial Chamber in *Lubanga* confirmed that Lubanga had been a direct co-perpetrator of the crimes charged regarding the recruitment and use of under 15s for active participation in hostilities.[405] The Pre-Trial Chamber further found that there

---

[401] Convention on the Rights of the Child (CRC) (1990).

[402] Additional Protocol II to the 1949 Geneva Conventions (1977).

[403] Prosecutor v Thomas Lubanga Dyilo, Final Trial Judgement Pursuant to Article 74 of the Rome Statute (2012, pp. 276–277, para 605, emphasis added).

[404] There is no suggestion here that charges should not also have been brought in relation to adult victims of the FPLC in regards to rape, forced pregnancy, cruel and inhuman treatment and various other war crimes and crimes against humanity applicable given the evidence in the case. The latter topic is simply beyond the scope of this work.

[405] Prosecutor v Thomas Lubanga Dyilo, Final Trial Judgement Pursuant to Article 74 of the Rome Statute (2012, p. 423, para 978).

must, under the theory of co-perpetration, have been a 'common plan' amongst the co-perpetrators in order that they can be held jointly criminally liable for the crime(s).[406] Further, the Pre-Trial Chamber held that the common plan must have "an element of criminality" but that it "need not be specifically directed at the commission of a crime."[407] What was needed in terms of the 'common plan', according to the Pre-Trial Chamber, to establish joint liability was instead:

> (i) that the co-perpetrators have agreed (a) to start the implementation of the common plan to achieve a non-criminal goal, and (b) to only commit the crime if certain conditions are met; *or*
> (ii) that the co-perpetrators (a) are aware of the risk that implementing the common plan (that is specifically directed at the achievement of a non-criminal goal) will result in the commission of a crime, and (b) accept such outcome.[408]

The Prosecution accepted the Pre-Trial Chamber's interpretation of what constitutes the elements regarding joint liability while the Defence argued that: (1) liability under a theory of co-perpetration required that the common plan be "intrinsically criminal" and that (2) simply knowing that there was a risk that the common plan *might* lead to the commission of a crime was not sufficient to establish criminal liability for the co-perpetrators of the common plan[409] The Trial Chamber in *Lubanga* affirmed the Pre-Trial Chamber's position that the 'common plan' need *not* be inherently criminal but that what was required for joint criminal liability was only that "its implementation embodied a *sufficient risk* that, if events followed the ordinary course, a crime *will be* committed."[410] Ultimately the Trial Chamber held in *Lubanga* that:

> …the enlistment of children under the age of 15 and using them to participate actively in hostilities was the result of the implementation of the common plan …*it is* ***not*** *necessary for the plan to have been* ***directed*** *specifically at committing the crime in question*, and the [Trial] Chamber has considered the issue on this basis.[411]

The current author, in any case, contends that the UPC/FPLC 'common plan' to recruit and use children for active participation in hostilities carried out by Lubanga and his co-perpetrators *was* inherently criminal ('manifestly unlawful') regardless the age of the children recruited and used. Thus, it is here argued that the common plan was intrinsically criminal even if: (1) Lubanga and his co-perpetrators did not

---

[406] Prosecutor v Thomas Lubanga Dyilo, Final Trial Judgement Pursuant to Article 74 of the Rome Statute (2012, pp. 424–425, para 981).

[407] Prosecutor v Thomas Lubanga Dyilo, Final Trial Judgement Pursuant to Article 74 of the Rome Statute (2012, p. 425, para 982).

[408] Prosecutor v Thomas Lubanga Dyilo, Final Trial Judgement Pursuant to Article 74 of the Rome Statute (2012, p. 425, para 982).

[409] Prosecutor v Thomas Lubanga Dyilo, Final Trial Judgement Pursuant to Article 74 of the Rome Statute (2012, p. 425, para 983).

[410] Prosecutor v Thomas Lubanga Dyilo, Final Trial Judgement Pursuant to Article 74 of the Rome Statute (2012, pp. 425–426, para 984, emphasis added).

[411] Prosecutor v Thomas Lubanga Dyilo, Final Trial Judgement Pursuant to Article 74 of the Rome Statute (2012, p. 440, para 1021).

specifically set out to recruit and use also under 15s for active participation in the armed hostilities (which claim the current author disputes) and (2) the crime in regard to the recruitment and use of under 15s in hostilities occurred instead simply with the co-perpetrators knowing that widespread FPLC recruitment of young people without verifying their ages would, in the normal course, result also in the recruitment and use of under 15s (meeting the 'should have known' test). The FPLC common plan, it is here argued, regarding recruitment and use of Hema children for active participation in hostilities constituted an 'auto-genocide' involving the 'genocidal forcible transfer' of Hema children from civilized society to a fringe group outside of mainstream society (namely transfer to the FPLC, an armed group committing mass atrocities and arguably also genocide against the Lendu and Ngiti peoples and certain other perceived ethnic groups). Since the genocidal forcible transfer of children is "manifestly unlawful" (intrinsically criminal); the common plan of Lubanga and his UPC/FPLC co-perpetrators to systematically and unlawfully appropriate three-quarters of the Hema child population in Ituri region consequently was manifestly unlawful as well. To suggest (expressly or by implication) that recruitment and use of children for active participation in armed hostilities *by an armed group or force committing systematic mass atrocities and/or genocide* such as the FPLC is not intrinsically criminal if the children are *15 and over* is to make a fundamental interpretive error. The FPLC was an unlawful organized armed group in no small part since it disregarded international humanitarian and human rights law as well as the customary rules of war insofar, for instance, as its treatment of children was concerned. Thus, while the Rome Statute articulated Article 8 war crimes pertaining to recruitment and use of children for active participation in hostilities protect only under 15s, this limitation of the relevant Article 8 provisions should *not* be taken to mean that recruitment to and use by an unlawful armed group such as the FPLC perpetrating grave international crimes is lawful in certain cases depending on the age of the children involved. The latter would be inconsistent with the need to hold accountable those who commit grave international crimes that shock the conscience of humanity. Certainly, it is the case that the 'genocidal forcible transfer of children' (whether over or under 15) by whatever means to an armed group or force such as the FPLC committing mass atrocities offends the sensibilities of the international community in no small part since: (1) transfer of children to such armed groups or forces inevitably involves children in the commission of grave international crimes as well as was the case with FPLC child soldiers and (2) leads to the enduring stigmatization of the children and loss of their identity as well as the severing of the children's bonds with their families and communities which bonds often times are not successfully re-established.

Since the transfer of children to the FPLC was accomplished through a common plan implemented on a systemic widespread basis notwithstanding the children's ages; it can be inferred that the *intent* was to appropriate to the FPLC children falling into a broad age range; including older children of at least 15 and very young children. In this way, it was clear to the Hema peoples that no child was safe from transfer to the FPLC whether 15 and over or under age 15. This then served to add to the terror inflicted by the FPLC on the general population and reinforced the view that the FPLC had unlimited and unrestrained power.

The position argued here then is that the evidence in *Lubanga* reveals that recruitment of and use of under 15s for active participation in the hostilities was intentional and an essential integral part of the FPLC common plan. The fact that: (1) the FPLC did not release all children or at least all those who were clearly much younger than 15 (children i.e. aged 10, 11 and 12), and/or those children who were physically weak and small in stature as a function of their young age (even after so called demobilization decrees); and that (2) some of these younger children under 15 were intentionally killed by FPLC commanders as these children could not, in many instances, endure the FPLC training and that (3) many of these younger children under 15 were used in the hostilities serving in various 'military' functions illustrates that another integral part of the common plan was in fact to 'recruit' and integrate children under age 15 into the FPLC and use them for various purposes. Were this not the case then one might reasonably expect that at least children who were to any casual observer *obviously under 15* and who were yet caught up in the FPLC indiscriminate recruitment dragnet would be released. One also then would expect that obviously physically weak and small children (factors generally correlated with a young age well under 15) would not be recruited in the first instance; however; this was not the case as was previously discussed. In this regard note that the Prosecution held that Lubanga should be convicted based on the fact that he actually knew there were under 15s in the FPLC ranks and being used for active participation in hostilities and the Trial Chamber proceeded on that basis.[412]

"Children Associated With Armed Conflict"

The Trial Chamber held that Lubanga (President of the UPC and Commander-in-Chief of its armed wing the FPLC) did make an "essential contribution" to the common plan during the period covered by the confirmed charges (That common plan resulted foreseeably, and in the ordinary course of implementing the plan, in the recruitment and use of under 15s for active participation in hostilities):

> Viewed in its entirety, the evidence demonstrates that the accused and his alleged co-perpetrators ...worked together and each of them made an essential contribution to the common plan that resulted in the enlistment, conscription and the use of children under the age of 15 to participate actively in hostilities.[413]

[414]The Trial Chamber also accepted the evidence that Lubanga relied in part on children under age 15 to ensure his personal security in their role as bodyguards[415]:

[412] Prosecutor v Thomas Lubanga Dyilo, Final Trial Judgement Pursuant to Article 74 of the Rome Statute (2012, p. 437, para 1015).

[413] Prosecutor v Thomas Lubanga Dyilo, Final Trial Judgement Pursuant to Article 74 of the Rome Statute (2012, p. 548, para 1271).

[414] Prosecutor v Thomas Lubanga Dyilo, Final Trial Judgement Pursuant to Article 74 of the Rome Statute (2012, p. 548, para 1271).

[415] Prosecutor v Thomas Lubanga Dyilo, Final Trial Judgement Pursuant to Article 74 of the Rome Statute (2012, p. 543, para 1262).

> . . .the accused and other commanders were protected by guards, some of whom were below 15. . ..the use of children as bodyguards for the commanders amounts to their use to participate actively in hostilities. . .the implementation of the common plan would not have been possible without his [Lubanga's] contribution.[416]

The argument of the current author has been, for the reasons previously discussed, that the evidence on the record in *Lubanga* supports a legal re-characterization of the facts to support additional charges of: (1) genocidal forcible transfer of children and of (2) various crimes of sexual violence and cruel and inhuman treatment under the Rome Statute[417] provisions concerned with war crimes and crimes against humanity offences. The concept of 'genocidal forcible transfer of children' to an armed group or force committing mass atrocities and/or genocide, as explained: (1) applies to children of all ages transferred to armed groups or forces (by whatever means) which systematically ignore international humanitarian law in a most egregious fashion and (2) applies regardless of the specific role the children may or may not have played in such an armed group or force (i.e. child soldiers who engaged directly in the hostilities, sex slaves, couriers etc.). Note that in order to convey the notion that children under age 15 who had been sexually enslaved and/or used as domestics or cooks or in some other non-combat role by Lubanga's FPLC should yet be considered as victims of "use for active participation in hostilities" (an Article 8 war crime); several of the amicus curiae in the case used the more inclusive expression "children associated with armed conflict" or "children associated with armed forces or armed groups."[418]

The current author maintains that the expression "children associated with armed conflict" captures something of the essence of the war crimes of recruitment (conscription or enlistment) and use for active participation in hostilities when the children are appropriated by an armed group or force committing mass atrocities and/or genocide.[419] Any child associated with such an armed group or force, as previously discussed, is automatically stigmatized and integrated into that group and most often also alienated from the home community *whether performing so-called traditional child soldier combat or closely related combat support functions or not*. In fact none of the activities performed by children as members of an armed group or force such as the FPLC can be regarded, on the view here, as 'soldiering' in that such armed groups or forces, as a pattern and practice, defy international law and the customary rules of war. These children then are not in fact 'soldiers' (lawful non-civilian belligerents), it is here contended, but rather victims of the genocidal forcible transfer of children. The children transferred are playing out various roles

[416] Prosecutor v Thomas Lubanga Dyilo, Final Trial Judgement Pursuant to Article 74 of the Rome Statute (2012, p. 548, para 1270).

[417] Rome Statute (2012).

[418] Aptel, C. (18 March, 2012).

[419] The term "children associated with armed conflict" is useful also in including as 'actively participating in hostilities' children associated with armed forces or groups regardless the children's roles with these armed forces or groups or the degree to which those armed forces or groups abide by international humanitarian and human rights law.

for the armed group or force perpetrating international crimes but they are nevertheless all serving a symbolic propaganda function communicating to the opposition and to the general populace that the perpetrators who appropriated the children are not only ruthless and inhumane but that they have indefinite staying power given their virtually unlimited supply of young people to draw upon.[420] Thus, all of these children are being used for "active participation in hostilities" and arguably even "direct participation" in hostilities in that they are fulfilling an FPLC military propaganda objective above and beyond any specific labor function they may be assigned and perform. Furthermore, all of these children, as victims of genocidal forcible transfer to an armed group or force perpetrating mass atrocities, are endangered psychologically and physically (i.e. given their witnessing atrocity, their being in many if not most cases exposed to sexual violation, being separated from family and community for an indefinite period, being stigmatized through their association with the UPC/FPLC, being subjected to cruel and inhuman treatment etc.) regardless whether they were or were not directly involved in the fighting or in performing a closely combat -related function.[421]

The Trial Chamber found that the FPLC and Lubanga as Commander-in-Chief in fact placed a heavy emphasis on 'recruiting' children to the FPLC and Lubanga was aware that under 15s were present in the FPLC even as members of the Presidential Guard:

> The evidence presented to the Chamber establishes that the accused [Lubanga] ... frequently tried to convince the population . . .to make youngsters available in order to join, and to train with, the army of the UPC/FPLC. . .the Chamber concludes that he was aware that children under the age of 15 formed part of their personal escorts.[422]
>
> Irrespective of whether there was a policy of verifying the ages of the recruits, it has been established that the accused [Lubanga] was aware that the FPLC was recruiting and using child soldiers who were clearly below the age of 15 and he condoned, and he took steps to implement, this policy, along with his co-perpetrators.[423]

With great respect, it is here contended that the Trial Chamber unwittingly interpreted the Article 8 Rome Statute[424] charges against Lubanga *in effect* as if the charges referred to recruitment and use by an armed group or force that was engaged in 'soldiering' as that term is understood under international humanitarian

---

[420] Recall that there is in the DRC and in many African countries a very large child and youth population. Large numbers of these children are being used for active participation in hostilities in various of these states.

[421] This contrasts with the defence view in *Lubanga* that the Rome Statute war crimes provisions under which Lubanga was charged were focused on children under 15 *who had more directly participated in the hostilities* and that the provisions were directed to prohibiting the endangerment of the latter group only (See Prosecutor v Thomas Lubanga Dyilo, Final Trial Judgement Pursuant to Article 74 of the Rome Statute (2012, p. 269, para 587).

[422] Prosecutor v Thomas Lubanga Dyilo, Final Trial Judgement Pursuant to Article 74 of the Rome Statute (2012, pp. 551–552, para 1277).

[423] Prosecutor v Thomas Lubanga Dyilo, Final Trial Judgement Pursuant to Article 74 of the Rome Statute (2012, p. 552, para 1278).

[424] Rome Statute (2002).

law (as if the FPLC did not have a common plan to perpetrate mass atrocities and or genocide). This erroneous interpretation of Article 8 by the Trial Chamber is reflected in the fact, for instance, that: (1) sexual exploitation of the child members of the FPLC was *not* viewed by the Trial Chamber in *Lubanga* as an integral aspect of recruitment or use under Article 8 and (2) child members of the FPLC ordered to procure sex slaves for FPLC commanders were *not* viewed as actively engaged in hostilities when performing this function. However, recruitment and participating actively in armed hostilities takes on a different meaning in the context of transfer of children to an armed group or force committing mass atrocities and/or genocide. In the latter context, all the child members are considered as *forcibly* transferred ('conscripted') and all are fulfilling a military objective through that very transfer (and hence being 'used for active participation in hostilities') regardless whatever other function they may or may not be assigned by the perpetrator armed group or force.

The Trial Court stated

> It is to be noted that ***the potentially broad concept of "children associated with armed conflict" was referred to throughout the trial***. This expression does ***not*** form part of the wording of any of the charges the accused faces, but instead, as is submitted by the defence-it is clearly designed to afford children the greatest possible protection. Although ***it is to be stressed that the [Trial] Chamber has applied the provisions of the Statute as opposed to this more general concept***[425]

It is here respectfully contended then that a proper reading of the Article 8 Rome Statute[426] provisions under which Lubanga was charged requires a broader view such that all children under 15 are covered by the protections afforded under the relevant Article 8 provisions[427] regardless the specific role/duty officially assigned to the children by their FPLC commanders and other FPLC superiors. This is the case since the FPLC was an armed group perpetrating mass atrocities during the period covered by the charges and, hence, the interpretation of 'recruitment' and 'use of under 15s for active participation in hostilities' must reflect the realities of each in *this* context. On the view here, the Trial Chamber in not having utilized the broader concept of "children associated with armed conflict" (in *interpreting* the Article 8 charges against Lubanga) had, contrary to the claim of the Trial Chamber, also *not* in fact applied the relevant provisions of the Statute. This was the case insofar as Article 8 was misinterpreted given the failure to consider the implications for interpretation of that Article (namely the scope of the acts covered under 'conscription', 'enlistment' and 'use for active participation in hostilities') in a context where children were appropriated by an armed group perpetrating mass atrocities as part of a common plan. In the latter instance, as explained, the systematic mass transfer itself of children to the armed group perpetrating mass

---

[425] Prosecutor v Thomas Lubanga Dyilo, Final Trial Judgement Pursuant to Article 74 of the Rome Statute (2012, p. 277, para 606, emphasis added).

[426] Rome Statute (2002).

[427] Conscription, enlistment and use for active participation in hostilities.

atrocities serves a vital propaganda and military function and serves to empower the armed group and disempower the general populace. Hence, the children associated with armed conflict (the children associated with armed forces or groups) in such a context of mass atrocity as created in part by the FPLC are all to be properly considered as forcibly transferred (conscripted) and being used for active participation in hostilities (and as victims of the genocidal forcible transfer of children to an armed group).

FPLC Resistance to Demobilization of Their 'Child Soldiers'

The fact that transfer of children to an armed group such as the FPLC perpetrating mass atrocities is not 'recruitment' and 'use' of so-called 'child soldiers' in any ordinary sense is evidenced, in part, by the reluctance to release these FPLC children even after peace processes were initiated. These children were *not* recruited by the UPC/FPLC for a time-limited combat or support service but rather fully appropriated for an indefinite period. This then fits a conceptualization of FPLC so-called child 'recruitment' and 'use' as in fact genocidal forcible transfer of children (mostly directed at children of a perceived distinct ethnic group; the Hema).

There were many compelling pieces of evidence presented at trial in *Lubanga* (and accepted as credible by the Trial Chamber) regarding FPLC resistance to the demobilization of its child soldiers. Some of this evidence is referred to in the following excerpts from the 2012 Trial conviction judgment:

> . . .there was . . .evidence to the effect that individuals working in the field of demobilization were threatened by the UPC/FPLC. . .[Witness] P-0046 . . .added that in 2002 several individuals belonging to humanitarian organizations were arrested by the administration of the UPC. . ..[Witness] P-0116 said the [humanitarian] organization only received threats from Mr. Lubanga's group, and he suggested this was because they were witnessing , and reporting on, the recruitment of children, and working to raise awareness on this issue. They were considered a nuisance because their activities were having an impact.[428]
>
> . . .the evidence [according to the Trial Chamber] demonstrates the UPC/FPLC attempted to impede the work of the organizations which were involved in helping child soldiers during the period of the charges [against Lubanga].[429]

[There was] a wealth of evidence demonstrating that recruitment [of children] continued unabated in spite of the demobilization orders. . ..[430] The evidence proves that child recruitment continued regardless of the external pressure [from NGOs, the UN etc. to demobilize minors who were part of the FPLC] and [notwithstanding]

---

[428] Prosecutor v Thomas Lubanga Dyilo, Final Trial Judgement Pursuant to Article 74 of the Rome Statute (2012, pp. 556–557, para 1287).

[429] Prosecutor v Thomas Lubanga Dyilo, Final Trial Judgement Pursuant to Article 74 of the Rome Statute (2012, p. 559, para 1290).

[430] Prosecutor v Thomas Lubanga Dyilo, Final Trial Judgement Pursuant to Article 74 of the Rome Statute (2012, p. 563, para 1299).

internal orders to demobilize.[431] There was also evidence accepted by the Trial Chamber that demobilized child soldiers of the FPLC were, in instances, re-armed by the FPLC and sent into combat.[432] The Trial Chamber concluded that "the [FPLC] demobilization [of minors] orders were *not* genuinely implemented"[433]:

> . . .whether or not some the demobilization orders were implemented for some of the children under the age of 15, others were simultaneously recruited, re-recruited and used by the FPLC throughout the timeframe of the charges. The demobilization orders additionally prove that Lubanga knew that the recruitment of children was prohibited and that children remained amongst the ranks of the UPC/FPLC in spite of the prohibition.[434]

The current author contends that the intent of Lubanga and his co-perpetrators in recruiting and re-recruiting children (both under and over age 15) to the FPLC and in arming and re-arming them throughout the period covered by the charges cannot be reduced simply to an alleged attempt, as the Trial Chamber suggests, to "ensure that the UPC/FPLC had an army *strong enough* to achieve its political and military aims."[435] The intent was primarily rather that of 'genocidal forcible transfer of the children' to the UPC/FPLC with the knowledge that these children would remain appropriated by this group: (1) even after the UPC/FPLC had achieved military control of Ituri if it did; (2) despite any international law prohibiting such appropriation of children to an armed group perpetrating mass atrocities[436] and (3) notwithstanding the devastating effect such appropriation of children had on the general Hema population (the latter adverse impact was in fact part of the common plan). Given this genocidal intent; all children appropriated by the FPLC were considered valuable for *recruitment* regardless of their young age or weak physical status or ill health and none were rejected for transfer based on their severe limitations regarding their military potential or inability to carry out designated roles.[437]

---

[431] Prosecutor v Thomas Lubanga Dyilo, Final Trial Judgement Pursuant to Article 74 of the Rome Statute (2012, p. 571, para 1321).

[432] Prosecutor v Thomas Lubanga Dyilo, Final Trial Judgement Pursuant to Article 74 of the Rome Statute (2012, pp. 572–573, para 1323).

[433] Prosecutor v Thomas Lubanga Dyilo, Final Trial Judgement Pursuant to Article 74 of the Rome Statute (2012, p. 584, para 1345).

[434] Prosecutor v Thomas Lubanga Dyilo, Final Trial Judgement Pursuant to Article 74 of the Rome Statute (2012, pp. 584–585, para 1346).

[435] Prosecutor v Thomas Lubanga Dyilo, Final Trial Judgement Pursuant to Article 74 of the Rome Statute (2012, p. 585, para 1347).

[436] The FPLC, of course, also disregarded the Rome Statute (2002) prohibition against recruiting and using for active participation in hostilities under 15s.

[437] Although some children were killed by FPLC because they were too weak physically to complete military training and were made an example of, the FPLC had yet recruited them in the first instance consistent with their genocidal intent to appropriate indiscriminately three-quarters of the Hema child population.

Literature, Materials and Cases

Literature

Carpenter C (2000) Surfacing children: limitations of genocidal rape discourse. Hum Rights Q 22:428–477

Charny IW (2009) The definition of genocide. In: Totten S, Bartrop PR (eds) The genocide studies reader. Routledge, New York, pp 36–40

Forster TK (2011) The Khmer Rouge and the crime of genocide: issues of genocidal intent with regard to the Khmer Rouge mass atrocities. http://www.cambodiatribunal.org/sites/default/files/reports/KHMER%20ROUGE%20AND%20THE%20CRIMES%20OF%20GENOCIDE.pdf. Accessed 18 Jun 2012

Frulli M (2001) Are crimes against humanity more serious than war crimes? Eur J Int Law 12:239–350

Grover S (2012) Child soldier victims of genocidal forcible transfer: exonerating child soldiers charged with grave conflict-related international crimes. Springer, Berlin

Grover S (2008) Child soldiers as non-combatants: The inapplicability of the refugee convention exclusion clause. *International Journal of Human Rights*, 12(1), 53–65

Kuper L (1981) Genocide: its political use in the twentieth century. Penguin, London

Nissel AT (2004) Continuing crimes in the Rome Statute. Mich J Int Law 25(653). http://papers.ssrn.com/sol3/papers.cfm?abstract_id=2070212. Accessed 16 Jun 2012

Materials

American Society of International Law (ASIL Insights) (2010) The ICC Appeals Chamber judgment on the legal characterization of the facts in Prosecutor v Lubanga (8 January, 2010, Vol. 14(1)). http://www.asil.org/insights100108.cfm. Accessed 4 Jun 2012

Coalition to Stop the Use of Child Soldiers (2011) Democratic Republic of Congo: OPAC Shadow Report to the Committee on the Rights of the Child. http://www2.ohchr.org/english/bodies/crc/crcs59.htm. Accessed 27 Jan 2012

Committee on the Rights of the Child Concluding Observations on the Report of the DRC regarding its compliance with the Optional Protocol to the Convention on the Rights of the Child concerning children involved in armed conflict (18 January, 2012). http://www.ohchr.org/en/NewsEvents/Pages/DisplayNews.aspx?NewsID=11766&LangID=E. Accessed 27 Jan 2012

Convention on the Prevention and Punishment of the Crime of Genocide (1951) (Entry into force 1951). http://www.preventgenocide.org/law/convention/text.htm. Accessed 3 Feb 2012

Convention on the Rights of the Child (1990) (Entry into force 2 September, 1990). http://www2.ohchr.org/english/law/crc.htm. Accessed 24 Mar 2012

Doyle J (2010) Misguided Kindness: Making the right decisions for children in emergencies (A report prepared by J. Doyle, Child Protection Technical Adviser to Save the Children UK). http://www.crin.org/docs/Misguided_Kindness.pdf. Accessed 28 Mar 2012

Geneva Conventions (1949) and their Additional Protocols (1977) http://www.icrc.org/eng/war-and-law/treaties-customary-law/geneva-conventions/index.jsp. Accessed 24 May 2012

Human Rights Watch (2003) Ituri: "Covered in blood" (Ethnically Targeted violence in North-eastern DR Congo). http://www.hrw.org/reports/2003/ituri0703/DRC0703.pdf. Accessed 28 Jan 2012

International Committee of the Red Cross (ICRC) (2005) Commentary on Protocol I additional to the 1949 Geneva Conventions. http://www.icrc.org/ihl.nsf/COM/470-750099?OpenDocument. Accessed 5 Feb 2012

International Covenant on Civil and Political Rights (CCPR) (1976) (Entry into force 23 March 1976). http://www.hrweb.org/legal/cpr.html. Accessed 24 Mar 2012

IRIN (The humanitarian news and analysis service of the UN Office for the Coordination of Humanitarian Affairs) (2002) In depth: Ituri Eastern DRC (25 November, 2002). http://www.irinnews.org/InDepthMain.aspx?InDepthId=33&ReportId=70762. Accessed 3 Feb 2012

Jacobs D (10 December, 2009) Commentary on the ICC Appeal Court reversal of the Trial Chamber's decision on the legal recharacterisation of the facts. http://dovjacobs.blogspot.ca. Accessed 6 Jun 2012

Optional Protocol to the Convention on the Rights of the Child on the involvement of children in armed conflict (OPCRC-AC) (2002) Entry into force 12 February 2002. http://www2.ohchr.org/english/law/crc-conflict.htm. Accessed 22 Dec 2010

Oxford Dictionary Online http://oxforddictionaries.com/definition/mascot. Accessed 20 Mar 2012

Pillay N (2009) Statement of Ms. Navanethem Pillay United Nations High Commissioner for Human Rights at the 12th session of the Human Rights Council (15 September, 2009). http://www.ohchr.org/EN/NewsEvents/Pages/DisplayNews.aspx?NewsID=87&LangID=E. Accessed 27 Jan 2012

Protocol Additional to the 1949 Geneva Conventions relating to the protection of victims of international armed conflicts (Protocol I) (8 June, 1977) http://www.icrc.org/ihl.nsf/FULL/470?OpenDocument. Accessed 18 Jan 2012

Protocol Additional to the 1949 Geneva Conventions Relating to the Protection of victims of non-international armed conflicts (Protocol II) (8 June, 1977) http://www.icrc.org/ihl.nsf/INTRO/475. Accessed 18 Jan 2012

Ratifications of the Optional Protocol to the Convention on the Rights of the child on the involvement of children in armed conflict (Status as of 31 May, 2012). http://treaties.un.org/Pages/ViewDetails.aspx?src=TREATY&mtdsg_no=IV-11-b&chapter=4&lang=en.

Rome Statute (2002) (entered into force 7 January, 2002) http://untreaty.un.org/cod/icc/statute/romefra.htm. Accessed 14 Jan 2012

Rome Statute Elements of the Crime (2002) http://www.icc-cpi.int/NR/rdonlyres/9CAEE830-38CF-41D6-AB0B-68E5F9082543/0/Element_of_Crimes_English.pdf. Accessed 18 Jan 2012

Senier, A. The ICC Appeals Chamber Judgment on the Legal Characterization of the Facts in *Prosecutor v. Lubanga,* (American Society of International Law) *ASIL Insight* , January 8, 2010, Vol. 14(1), 1-8 http://www.asil.org/insights100108.cfm (Accessed 24 March, 2012).

The International Federation for Human Rights (FIDH) (2012) Crimes of sexual violence and the Lubanga case: interview with Patricia Viseur Sellers (16 March, 2012). http://www.fidh.org/Crimes-of-sexual-violence-and-the. Accessed 8 Jun 2012

The Women's Initiatives for Gender Justice (2011) Reflection: gender issues and child soldiers (the case of *Prosecutor v Thomas Lubanga Dyilo*). http://www.peacewomen.org/assets/file/Resources/NGO/hr-vaw_childsoldiers_gender_icc_womensinitiativeforgenderjustice_2011.pdf. Accessed 20 Jan 2012

The Women's Initiatives for Gender Justice Request for leave to participate in reparations proceedings' (2012) (*Prosecutor v. Thomas Lubanga Dyilo*) (28 March, 2012). http://www.iccwomen.org/documents/Womens-Initiatives-request-Lubanga-reparations.pdf. Accessed 30 May 2012

Tosh C, Chizan Y (eds) (2008) Special report: sexual violence in the Democratic Republic of the Congo (Institute for War and Peace Reporting). http://www.ceipaz.org/images/contenido/Sexual%20violence%20in%20the%20Democratic%20Republic%20of%20Congo.pdf. Accessed 27 Jan 2012

United Kingdom of Great Britain and Northern Ireland Declaration articulating a reservation to the Optional Protocol to the Convention on the Rights of the Child on the involvement of children in armed conflict (OP-CRC-AC) http://treaties.un.org/Pages/ViewDetails.aspx?src=TREATY&mtdsg_no=IV-11-b&chapter=4&lang=en#EndDec. Accessed 28 Jan 2012

United Nations Organization Mission in the Democratic Republic of the Congo (MONUC) (2004) Special Report on Events in Ituri January 2002–December 2003 (16 July, 2004). http://reliefweb.int/sites/reliefweb.int/files/resources/93F81A37C5B409E785256EEC00679CE1-unsc-drc-16jul.pdf. Accessed 7 Jun 2012

Vienna Convention on the Law of Treaties (1980) Entered into force 27 January, 1980. http://untreaty.un.org/ilc/texts/instruments/english/conventions/1_1_1969.pdf. Accessed 24 Mar 2012

Watchlist on Children and Armed Conflict (June, 2003) (Report by the Women's Refugee Commission) The Impact of armed conflict on children in the Democratic Republic of Congo (DRC). http://www.watchlist.org/reports/pdf/dr_congo.report.pdf. Accessed 31 May 2012

Cases

Prosecutor v Samuel Hinga Norman Dissenting Opinion of Justice Robertson in (31 May, 2004) (SCSL-04-14-AR72(E)) http://www.sc-sl.org/LinkClick.aspx?fileticket=z1qWROwTItg%3D&tabid=193. Accessed 23 Mar 2012

Prosecutor v. Thomas Lubanga Dyilo, Amicus brief of Coomaraswamy, R. (United Nations Special Representative of the Secretary-General on Children and Armed Conflict) (2008) http://www.un.org/children/conflict/_documents/AmicuscuriaeICCLubanga.pdf. Accessed 14 Jan 2012

Prosecutor v. Thomas Lubanga Dyilo, Appeal Court judgment, 8 December, 2009 decision on the ICC Trial Chamber I July, 2009 decision regarding legal re-characterization of the facts http://www.icc-cpi.int/iccdocs/doc/doc790147.pdf. Accessed 23 Jan 2012

Prosecutor v. Thomas Lubanga Dyilo (Trial Chamber I) Clarification and further guidance to parties and participants in relation to the "Decision giving notice to the parties and participants that the legal characterisation of the facts may be subject to change in accordance with Regulation 55(2) of the Regulations of the Court" (27 August, 2009, pp. 6–7, para 8) http://www.iclklamberg.com/Caselaw/DRC/Dyilo/TCI/2093.pdf. Accessed 6 Jun 2012

Prosecutor v. Thomas Lubanga Dyilo, Decision on Confirmation of Charges (29 January, 2007) http://www.icc-cpi.int/iccdocs/doc/doc266175.PDF. Accessed 14 Jan 2012

Prosecutor v. Thomas Lubanga Dyilo, Decision on Sentence Pursuant to Article 76 of the Statute (10 July, 2012) http://www.icc-cpi.int/iccdocs/doc/doc1438370.pdf. Accessed 13 Oct 2012

Prosecutor v. Thomas Lubanga Dyilo, Defense Closing Brief of 15 July, 2011 http://www.icc-cpi.int/iccdocs/doc/doc1325997.pdf. Accessed 29 Jan 2012

Prosecutor v. Thomas Lubanga Dyilo, Defense Closing Statement of 26 August, 2011 http://www.icc-cpi.int/iccdocs/doc/doc1211991.pdf. Accessed 29 Jan 2012

Prosecutor v Thomas Lubanga Dyilo, Dissenting Opinion of Judge Odio Benito Final Trial Judgement Pursuant to Article 74 of the Rome Statute (14 March, 2012) http://www.icc-cpi.int/iccdocs/doc/doc1379838.pdf. Accessed 20 Mar 2012

Prosecutor v Thomas Lubanga Dyilo, Final Trial Judgement Pursuant to Article 74 of the Rome Statute (14 March, 2012) http://www.icc-cpi.int/iccdocs/doc/doc1379838.pdf. Accessed 20 Mar 2012

Prosecutor v Thomas Lubanga Dyilo, Joint Application of the Legal Representatives of the Victims for the Implementation of the Procedure under Regulation 55 of the Regulations of the Court, 22 May, 2009 http://www.icc-cpi.int/iccdocs/doc/doc712021.pdf. Accessed 21 Mar 2012

Prosecutor v. Thomas Lubanga Dyilo, Legal Representatives of Victims Closing Statements (25 August, 2011) http://212.159.242.181/iccdocs/doc/doc1210316.pdf. Accessed 14 Jan 2012

Prosecutor v. Thomas Lubanga Dyilo, Office of Public Counsel for Victims Closing Statement (25 August, 2011) http://212.159.242.181/iccdocs/doc/doc1210316.pdf. Accessed 14 Jan 2012

Prosecutor v. Thomas Lubanga Dyilo, Prosecution Closing Brief (1 June, 2011) http://www.icc-cpi.int/iccdocs/doc/doc1123809.pdf. Accessed 14 Jan 2012

Prosecutor v. Thomas Lubanga Dyilo, Prosecution Closing Statements (25 August, 2011) http://212.159.242.181/iccdocs/doc/doc1210316.pdf. Accessed 14 Jan 2012

Prosecutor v. Thomas Lubanga Dyilo, Prosecution's Reply to the Conclusions finales de la Défense, 1 August, 2011. http://www.icc-cpi.int/NR/exeres/7A274DFF-7D95-424F-95B8-9EADF0CC6DA1.htm. Accessed 3 Feb 2012

Prosecutor v. Thomas Lubanga Dyilo Summary of the "Judgment pursuant to Article 74 of the Statute (14 March, 2012) http://micro5.mscc.huji.ac.il/~gharpaz/admins/uploads/lubanga_judgment_summary.pdf. Accessed 3 Jun 2012

Special Court of Sierra Leone (SCSL) Prosecutor versus Samuel Hinga Norman, Appeals Chamber, Fourth Defence Preliminary Motion Based on Lack of Jurisdiction (Child Recruitment) Amicus Curiae Brief of the United Nations Children's Fund (UNICEF) (21 January, 2004) http://www.unhcr.org/refworld/docid/49aba9462.html. Accessed 23 Mar 2012

Chapter 4
Case 2: Prosecutor v. Germain Katanga and Mathieu Ngudjolo Chui

4.1 Confirmed Charges

Germain Katanga and Mathieu Ngudjolo Chui allegedly jointly[1] committed, through other persons, the following crimes falling under ICC jurisdiction:

War crimes:

a) using children under the age of fifteen to take active part in the hostilities, under article 8(2)(b)(xxvi) of the Statute;
b) directing an attack against a civilian population as such or against individual civilians not taking direct part in hostilities under article 8(2)(b)(i) of the Statute;
c) wilful killings under article 8(2)(a)(i) of the Statute;
d) destruction of property under article 8(2)(b)(xiii) of the Statute;
e) pillaging under article 8(2)(b)(xvi) of the Statute;
f) sexual slavery under article 8(2)(b)(xxii) of the Statute.
g) rape under article 8(2)(b)(xxii) of the Statute

Crimes against humanity:

a) murder under article 7(1)(a) of the Statute;
b) rape under article 7(1)(g) of the Statute.
c) sexual slavery under article 7(1)(g) of the Statute.[2]

The Pre-Trial Chamber confirmed that Katanga and Chui were aware from August 2002–May 2003 of the factual circumstances that constituted an armed conflict of an international character and that from August 2002–May 2003, they

[1] The two groups (FNI under Chui and FRPI under Katanga) later integrated into the *Forces Armées de la République Démocratique du Congo* ("the FARDC") headed by Katanga as Brigadier-Général.

[2] Prosecutor v Germain Katanga and Mathieu Ngudjolo Chui (Decision on Confirmation of Charges 26 September, 2008).

S.C. Grover, *Humanity's Children*, DOI 10.1007/978-3-642-32501-4_4,

were aware also of "the nexus between the common plan to "wipe out" the Bogoro village and the armed conflict taking place in Ituri."[3]

4.2 The Prosecution Opening Statement

The Prosecutor alleged that Katanga and Chui were responsible jointly as principals (leaders of their respective militias) for crimes against humanity and war crimes committed in Bogoro, in the Democratic Republic of Congo (DRC), on 24 February 2003 and in the aftermath of the attack. The attack on Bogoro was part of a common plan[4] coordinated between the two defendants and occurred, according to the Prosecution, in the context of the widespread systemic attack on Hema civilians in Ituri region of the DRC (those widespread attacks, according to the Prosecution, had resulted in 8,000 civilian deaths and 600,000 persons being internally displaced).[5] The Prosecutor alleged that these two defendants:

> . . .used children [under 15] as soldiers [to attack Bogoro]. . .killed more than 200 civilians in a few hours [in Bogoro]. . .raped women, girls and elderly. . .looted the entire village and . . .transformed women into sexual slaves.[6]

The defendants were described by the Prosecution as leaders of the militias comprised of Lendu and Ngiti who were fighting the UPC/FPLC militia led by Lubanga (the UPC/FPLC being comprised of Hema). The Prosecution put it to the Chamber that Katanga and Chui had attacked Bogoro since the UPC militia wing had a military camp there in the centre of the village and that the defendants wished to "open the Bunia-Kasenyi road, and prevent UPC attacks on nearby Lendu and Ngiti villages."[7] The Prosecution alleged that the plan was to destroy the entire village rather than just the UPC military camp.[8] The defendants' forces did not distinguish between FPLC forces and non-forces and attacked villagers indiscriminately killing them in various horrific manners[9] and committed a range of additional grave international crimes. The Prosecution quoted a witness of the Bogoro attack

[3] Prosecutor v Germain Katanga and Mathieu Ngudjolo Chui (Decision on Confirmation of Charges 26 September, 2008, pp. 204–205, para 573).

[4] Prosecutor v Germain Katanga and Mathieu Ngudjolo Chui, Prosecution Opening Statement (2009, p. 14).

[5] Prosecutor v Germain Katanga and Mathieu Ngudjolo Chui, Prosecution Opening Statement (2009, p. 11).

[6] Prosecutor v Germain Katanga and Mathieu Ngudjolo Chui, Prosecution Opening Statement (2009, p. 2).

[7] Prosecutor v Germain Katanga and Mathieu Ngudjolo Chui, Prosecution Opening Statement (2009, p. 4).

[8] Prosecutor v Germain Katanga and Mathieu Ngudjolo Chui, Prosecution Opening Statement (2009, p. 4).

[9] Prosecutor v Germain Katanga and Mathieu Ngudjolo Chui, Prosecution Opening Statement (2009, p. 5).

who stated: "They [Katanga's and Chui's forces] killed everyone; they didn't make any distinction between men, women, children and the elderly."[10]

4.3 Charging Sexual Violence Crimes Under the Rome Statute

The Prosecution in its opening statement made specific reference to sexual crimes perpetrated against women and girls:

> The joint attack achieved its goal. But horror was not over yet for the *women* of Bogoro. Once captured, some *women* hid their Hema identity to save their lives. Those later revealed as Hema were killed, the others were raped and forced into marriage as combatants' "wives" or detained to serve as sexual slaves by Katanga or Ngudjolo's soldiers. All these women were victimized on the basis of their gender: they were attacked in particular because they were women.[11]
>
> ...during the earlier attacks on Bogoro in 2001 and 2002, ***young girls*** were abducted and ***forced to become the "wives"*** of combatants. During the Nyankunde attack, many ***young girls were raped, and either killed or taken to Ngiti or Lendu camps to become sexual slaves***. During later attacks, *women* were often used to carry looted goods to the camps and remained captive, were raped and deprived of their identity and liberty. Their existence was reduced to being the *"forced wives" or sexual slaves* of soldiers.[12]

Unlike the situation in *Lubanga*, Katanga and Chui faced separate charges also regarding sexual slavery[13] and rape[14] pursuant to: (1) Article 7(1)(g) of the Rome Statute as 'crimes against humanity'. (Article 7(1)(g) sets as 'crimes against humanity' the following: "Rape, sexual slavery, enforced prostitution, forced pregnancy, enforced sterilization, or any other form of sexual violence of comparable gravity."[15]) and (2) war crimes per Articles 8(2)(b)(xxii) (sexual slavery) and Article 8(2)(b)(xxii) (rape). Note that many of the sexual slaves taken, women and girls, in fact, bore children fathered by the FNI/FRPI perpetrators. The Prosecution charged that the defendants Katanga and Chui:

> [...] committed, jointly with others, or each ordered the commission of crimes against humanity which in fact occurred, namely, the sexual enslavement of ***civilian female***

[10] Prosecutor v Germain Katanga and Mathieu Ngudjolo Chui, Prosecution Opening Statement (2009, p. 5).

[11] Prosecutor v Germain Katanga and Mathieu Ngudjolo Chui, Prosecution Opening Statement (2009, p. 6, emphasis added).

[12] Prosecutor v Germain Katanga and Mathieu Ngudjolo Chui, Prosecution Opening Statement (2009, p. 12, emphasis added).

[13] Prosecutor v Germain Katanga and Mathieu Ngudjolo Chui, Decision on Confirmation of Charges (2008, p. 143, para 428).

[14] Prosecutor v Germain Katanga and Mathieu Ngudjolo Chui, Decision on Confirmation of Charges (2008, p. 147, para 437).

[15] Rome Statute (2002).

> ***residents*** *or civilian women* present at Bogoro village, in the Bahema Sud collectivité, Irumu territory, Ituri district, including W-132 and W-249.[16]

The Pre-Trial Chamber confirmed: (1) the charges of 'crimes against humanity' and 'war crimes' involving *sexual slavery*; as well (2) the charges of 'crimes against humanity' and 'war crimes' involving *rape* against both Katanga and Chui (the victims involved in the aforementioned international crimes included not only adult female victims but also child female victims; including also those under age 15).

There was recognition that these women and girls were often abducted and taken to the military camps to be used as sex slaves:

> The Chamber finds that there is sufficient evidence to establish substantial grounds to believe that before and in the aftermath of the joint FRPI/FNI attack against the village of Bogoro on 24 February 2003, combatants from the FRPI and the FNI: (i) abducted ***women and/or girls*** from villages or areas surrounding the camps for the purpose of using them as their "wives"; (ii) forced and threatened ***women and/or girls*** to engage in sexual intercourse with combatants and to serve as ***sexual slaves*** for combatants and commanders alike; and (iii) ***captured and imprisoned women and/or girls to work in a military camp servicing the soldiers***...[17]
>
> In conclusion, the Chamber finds that there are substantial grounds to believe that the crime against humanity of ***sexual slavery***, as detailed in article 7(1)(g) of the Statute, was committed by FNI/FRPI members in the aftermath of the 24 February 2003 attack on Bogoro village.[18]
>
> The Chamber finds that there is sufficient evidence to establish substantial grounds to believe that members of the FNI and FRPI, by force or threat, invaded the body, or parts of it, of ***women and girls*** abducted before, during and after the February 2003 attack on the village of Bogoro...[19]
>
> In conclusion, the Chamber finds that there are substantial grounds to believe that the crime against humanity of ***rape,*** as detailed in article 7(1)(g) of the Statute, was committed by FNI/FRPI members in the aftermath of the 24 February 2003 attack on Bogoro village.[20]

The Pre-Trial Chamber affirmed that in regards to the war crime of 'using children under 15 to participate actively in hostilities'; that this crime can be committed by a perpetrator also against individuals in his own party to the conflict:

> this war crime can be committed by a perpetrator against individuals in his own party to the conflict. Thus, *the allegiance of the child who is used in hostilities is not relevant for the purposes of this provision*, as long as the child in question is under the age of fifteen.[21]

[16] Prosecutor v Germain Katanga and Mathieu Ngudjolo Chui, Decision on Confirmation of Charges (2008, p. 143, para 428, emphasis added). Those female residents sexually violated and taken as sex slaves, on the evidence of witnesses, included also girls regardless of age.

[17] Prosecutor v Germain Katanga and Mathieu Ngudjolo Chui, Decision on Confirmation of Charges (2008, pp. 145–146, para 434, emphasis added).

[18] Prosecutor v Germain Katanga and Mathieu Ngudjolo Chui, Decision on Confirmation of Charges (2008, p. 147, para 436, emphasis added).

[19] Prosecutor v Germain Katanga and Mathieu Ngudjolo Chui, Decision on Confirmation of Charges (2008, p. 148, para 442, emphasis added).

[20] Prosecutor v Germain Katanga and Mathieu Ngudjolo Chui, Decision on Confirmation of Charges (2008, p. 149, para 444, emphasis added).

[21] Prosecutor v Germain Katanga and Mathieu Ngudjolo Chui, Decision on Confirmation of Charges (2008, p., para 248, emphasis added).

It would seem that such a view properly allows for considering child members of the FNI/FRPI (under 15s) who are the victims of sexual violence as 'conscripted' and 'used for active participation in hostilities' as Article 8 Rome Statute[22] war crimes (even though they may share the same perceived ethnicity as their abductors). The current author regards girls serving primarily or exclusively as sex slaves, domestics or in any other capacity (or serving multiple roles) with armed groups or forces such as the FNI/FRPI perpetrating systematic international crimes as also child solders conscripted for 'use for active participation in hostilities.' The appropriation of these girl sex slaves/bush wives to the FNI/FRPI contributed to the military objective of spreading terror amongst the general populace and exposed the children 'recruited' as sex slaves to severe harm both physically and psychologically (for the reasons explained previously in earlier chapters such 'conscription' amounts also to the 'genocidal forcible transfer of children' to the FNI/FRPI). As the crimes of rape and sex slavery in *Katanga and Chui* were advanced by the ICC Prosecutor as separate 'crimes against humanity' charges under Article 7 and separate 'war crimes' under Article 8(2)(b) (and *not* also in terms of separate counts of Rome Statute[23] Article 8 war crimes pertaining to' the conscription' and 'use of under 15s for active participation in hostilities'); there was no need to establish clearly the precise age or close approximate age of the girl victims in regards to these separate sexual violence charges. Nonetheless, there was ample evidence presented and accepted by the Pre-Trial Chamber in *Katanga and Chui* regarding the Article 8(2)(b)(xxvi) war crimes charges that under 15s were integrated into and used by the FNI/FRPI and this would then, on the analysis here, include also those girls used by the FNI/FRPI as sex slaves.

The same sort of facts were alleged by the Prosecutor in *Lubanga* i.e. women and girls (girls including under 15s) being forced to perform sexual services for commanders and lower rank fighters in the FPLC (sexual slavery), and being forced to travel with the armed group and act as 'bush wives' to be routinely raped. Also in *Lubanga;* as in *Katanga and Chui*, the women and girls were taken as captives to the 'military' encampments to travel with the armed group and often to also act as 'soldiers' (including female children under 15) providing combat and closely combat-related support functions and to serve as bodyguards as well as to provide a range of other forced services including domestic and sexual services. Yet, the crimes of sexual enslavement and rape [and for that matter forced pregnancy] were not charged as separate crimes in the Lubanga case. The Prosecutor argued in *Lubanga*, it will be recalled, that: (1) gender crimes involving sexual violence against girls were simply part of the FPLC child soldier recruitment process for female child soldiers[24] and that (2) charging such gender crimes involving sexual slavery and rape as *separate charges* would (allegedly) undermine the view of these

---

[22] Rome Statute (2002).

[23] Rome Statute (2002).

[24] Note that there is no intent to imply here that the crimes against humanity and war crimes of rape and sexual enslavement are intrinsically gender specific to female victims in every context.

girls as child soldiers entitled to justice in respect of: (a) holding to account those most responsible for their conscription and use for active participation in hostilities and (b) their entitlement to any and all equivalent compensation to which male FPLC child soldiers were entitled. The argument for not advancing separate charges respecting sexual violence in *Lubanga* falls flat in part in that it is inconsistent with the Prosecutor's approach in *Katanga and Chui*, The charges against Katanga and Chui, as in *Lubanga*, also involved (pursuant to Article 8(2)(b)(xxvi) of the Rome Statute[25] relating to an international armed conflict in *Katanga and Chui*)[26] charges relating to the recruitment ('conscription' or 'enlistment') of and 'use for active participation in hostilities of children under the age of 15' (though in *Lubanga* the Trial Chamber re-characterised the armed conflict as exclusively an internal one). More specifically, the ICC Prosecution in *Katanga and Chui* filed *separate charges* relating to sexual violence and also alleged that the conduct of Katanga and Chui involved; amongst other things:

> [...] the use of children under the age of fifteen to participate actively in hostilities, including W-28 and W-157, during the attack at Bogoro village in the Bahema Sud collectivité, Irumu territory, Ituri district.[27]

However, in both cases (*Katanga and Chui (tried jointly) and Lubanga*), sexual violence against girls under 15 (taken to military encampments to be used as sex slaves and raped) was *not* charged by the ICC Prosecutor as separate counts of 'conscription' and of 'use of under 15s for participation in hostilities' (Rome Statute[28] Article 8 war crimes) (that is rape as a method of 'conscription' and 'use of under 15s for active participation in hostilities' and sexual slavery as a method of 'conscription' and 'use of under 15s for active participation in hostilities' were not charged in either case).[29] Thus, it appears to be the case that Lendu girl sex slaves[30] and Ngiti girl sex slaves[31,32] under age 15 (as well as any Hema girl sex slaves under 15 appropriated by these armed groups) were *not* regarded as entitled, as under 15s, to the protections deriving from the Article 8 Rome Statute[33] prohibitions against

---

[25] Rome Statute (2002).

[26] Rome Statute (2002).

[27] Prosecutor v Germain Katanga and Mathieu Ngudjolo Chui, Decision on Confirmation of Charges (2008, p. 76, para 246).

[28] Rome Statute (2002).

[29] In *Lubanga*; Prosecutor Moreno-Ocampo argued that sexual violence against girls under 15 was part of the FPLC conscription process and constituted also active use in hostilities of these sexual violence victims once they were 'child soldier' members of the FPLC. However, no sexual violence crimes were charged under any ICC offence category.

[30] These girls were those conscripted into the *Front des Nationalistes et Intégrationnistes* ("the FNI") headed by Chui.

[31] These girls were those conscripted into the *Force de Résistance Patriotique en Ituri* ("the FRPI"), headed by Katanga.

[32] The two groups (FNI and FRPI) later integrated into the *Forces Armées de la République Démocratique du Congo* ("the FARDC") headed by Katanga as Brigadier-Général.

[33] Rome Statute (2002).

'conscription' and 'use of under 15s for active participation in hostilities' *based on their sexual victimization per se* by the FNI/FRPI or FPLC (contrary to the situation for children who benefited from those protections due to the fact that they were allegedly more clearly perceived by the enemy as legitimate potential targets as 'child soldiers').[34] This was the case despite the fact that the Pre-Trial Chamber in *Katanga and Chui* confirmed the charge of 'using children under 15 to participate actively in hostilities' as a war crime under Article 8(2)(b)(xxvi).[35] (Recall in *Lubanga* that the Trial Chamber held that: "The decisive factor. . .in deciding if an "indirect" role is to be treated as 'active participation in hostilities' is whether the support provided by the child to the armed group or force exposed him or her to real danger as a potential target" [of the enemy]).[36]

Such an approach as adopted by the ICC Prosecutor regarding sexual violence against children under 15 serving as sex slaves/'bush wives' to armed forces or groups (respectfully, on the view here inadvertently) undermines the rights of the children to be more fully protected from sexual violence; including in respect of gender-specific sexual violence crimes affecting girls in particular though not exclusively (harms perpetrated not just by the enemy but also by members of the armed group or force into which the girl child has been fully integrated). This as a result of the discriminatory adverse impact on girls who were used as sex slaves but yet do not benefit from their full entitlement to the protection afforded by the prohibitions against 'conscription' and 'use of children under 15 for participation in hostilities'. In both the *Katanga and Chui (tried jointly) and Lubanga* cases there was a disregard then for the fact that these girl sex slaves/bush wives were in fact also child soldiers exposed to severe psychological and physical harms as a result of their conscription and use by the armed forces in question for active participation in hostilities; armed forces committing mass atrocities amounting to grave international crimes (These girls were exposed to actual and high risk harms posed by both the armed forces of which they were members and by enemy forces).

The Pre-Trial Chamber in the Katanga and Chui case referred several times to *Lubanga* and endorsed the views expressed by the Pre-Trial Chamber in *Lubanga*, for instance, in relation to the charges pertaining to child soldiering (i.e. the definition adopted in *Lubanga* regarding the meaning of 'active participation in hostilities' as pertains to the war crimes set out at Article 8 of the Rome Statute regarding the recruitment and use of children in armed hostilities):

> The Chamber considers that the definition of the phrase "active participation in hostilities" set out in the Lubanga Decision is relevant to this Decision. With regard to the specific

[34] Further, there was no initiative taken in *Katanga and Chui* at the trial stage regarding a legal re-characterization of the facts that would have allowed girls under 15 used as sex slaves by the FNI and FRPI to be regarded also as victims of 'conscription' and 'use for active participation in hostilities' as Article 8 Rome Statute (2002) war crimes.

[35] Prosecutor v Germain Katanga and Mathieu Ngudjolo Chui, Decision on Confirmation of Charges (2008, p. 210).

[36] *Prosecutor v. Thomas Lubanga Dyilo* Summary of the "Judgment pursuant to Article 74 of the Statute (14 March, 2012, pp. 9–10, para 24).

context of the war crime of using children in hostilities, the phrase applies to cases in which:

> [. . .] children are used to guard military objectives, such as military quarters of the various units of the parties to the conflict, or to safeguard the physical safety of military commanders (in particular, where children are used as bodyguards). These activities are indeed related to hostilities in so far as (i) the military commanders are in a position to take all necessary decisions regarding the conduct of hostilities; (ii) they have a direct impact on the level of logistic resources and on the organisation of operations required by the other party to the conflict whose aim is to attack such military objectives.[37] [Citing the Lubanga Pre-Trial Confirmation of Charges Decision 29 January, 2007 (ICC-01/04-01/06-803-tEN, para. 263)].

It is noteworthy then that no mention was made, however, by the Pre-Trial Chamber in the Katanga and Chui case of the fact that the Prosecution had opted to charge separate sexual violence crimes perpetrated against women *and girls* in the Katanga and Chui case but did not do so in respect of girl child soldiers in *Lubanga*. Further, there was no consideration in *Katanga and Chui* of: (1) sexual violence against girl soldiers in particular in terms of it being a routine correlate of their 'conscription' and 'use for active participation in hostilities' and (2) the consequent grounds also for *separate counts* of rape and sexual slavery charges in connection with war crimes under Article 8(2)(b)(xxvi) pertaining to international conflict.

4.4 The Genocidal Forcible Transfer of Children as "Child Soldiers"

4.4.1 The FNI/FRPI Appropriation of Children as the 'Genocidal Forcible Transfer of Children'

Recall that the ICC Pre-Trial Chamber in the Katanga and Chui case made a finding, as mentioned previously, that it is possible to commit, *against one's own party*, the war crime of recruiting under 15s and using them for active participation in armed hostilities:

> *The Chamber observes that this war crime can be committed by a perpetrator against individuals in his own party to the conflict*. Thus, the allegiance of the child who is used in hostilities is not relevant for the purposes of this provision, as long as the child in question is under the age of fifteen.[38]

The Pre-Trial Chamber in *Katanga and Chui* appears to have made the aforementioned assertion to highlight its view that if children *under 15* claim allegiance to a particular armed group or force this would be irrelevant in terms of mitigating the

---

[37] Prosecutor v Germain Katanga and Mathieu Ngudjolo Chui, Decision on Confirmation of Charges (2008, pp. 76–77, para 250).

[38] Prosecutor v Germain Katanga and Mathieu Ngudjolo Chui, Confirmation of Charges (2008, p. 76, Para 248).

criminal responsibility of the perpetrators for war crimes involving the recruitment and use of children (under 15s) for active participation in hostilities. It has here been argued that recruitment ('conscription' or 'enlistment') and 'use of children for active participation in armed hostilities' (whether involving direct or indirect participation) by armed groups or forces committing mass atrocities and/or genocide is 'genocidal forcible transfer of children'. This is the case whether the children involved are the same or different from the perpetrators recruiting them in terms of nationality, religion, ethnicity, or 'race' or along some other dimension. The forcible transfer of children to murderous armed groups such as the FNI/FRPI may constitute: (1) 'autogenocide' where the children appropriated share certain key characteristics such as ethnicity with the perpetrators (i.e. the transfer of Lendu children to the FNI (comprised of Lendu) to serve as sex slaves and/or child soldiers engaged in the hostilities in a combat or combat support function) or (2) genocide against a distinct group distinguishable from the perpetrator group in some central way such as in terms of ethnicity, religion etc. (i.e. the WW II Lebensborn program of the Nazis where children transferred to Germany to be raised in Nazi households or in specialized institutions were of non-German nationality and ethnic descent but nonetheless deemed to have desirable so-called 'Aryan' characteristics). The genocidal forcible transfer of children to these armed groups or forces committing grave international crimes destroys in part the group of origin of the children (that group of origin being, on the analysis here, a protected ethnic, religious, so-called racial or national group or one defined along some other perpetrator targeted dimension such as a political one which generally overlaps with one or more of the protected group categories listed at Article 6 of the Rome Statute[39]).

With respect, it is here argued that the following *Katanga and Chui* Pre-Trial Chamber line in the Decision on the Confirmation of Charges is misleading ("The Chamber observes that this war crime ['use of children under 15 for active participation in hostilities'] can be committed by a perpetrator against individuals *in his own party to the conflict*"].[40] The phrase is misleading in that though children who are recruited and used by an armed group or force *committing mass atrocity and/or genocide*, may be: (1) of the same cultural and ethnic background as the perpetrator group that recruited them into their ranks and (2) fully integrated into that armed force or group, these children are *not*, on the view here, of the "same party to the conflict." This is the case in that under international law these victims of the 'genocidal forcible transfer of children' to an armed group or force do *not* 'belong' to ***any*** party to the conflict. Recall that 'children' under international humanitarian law (i.e. Additional Protocol I and II to the 1949 Geneva Conventions[41]) and under international human rights law (i.e. the Optional Protocol to the Convention on the

---

[39] Rome Statute (2002).

[40] Prosecutor v Germain Katanga and Mathieu Ngudjolo Chui, Confirmation of Charges (2008, p. 76, Para 248, emphasis added).

[41] Additional Protocol I and II to the 1949 Geneva Conventions (1977).

Rights of the Child on the involvement of children in armed conflict)[42] are first and foremost a *protected group* entitled to special care and respect during armed conflict ('children' here referring to persons under 18).[43] Furthermore, and most importantly in regards to the foregoing issue, children (persons under age 18) as a protected group are to be safeguarded against their becoming the victims of genocidal forcible transfer (i.e. to an armed group or force committing systematic mass atrocities and/or genocide). Child victims of 'genocidal forcible transfer' to an armed group or force systematically committing mass atrocities and/or genocide (notwithstanding the fact that the children may be fully integrated into that group physically and psychologically and performing functions; combat and otherwise on behalf of the perpetrator group) do *not* 'belong' to the perpetrator group. To suggest otherwise is unwittingly to accept as accomplished the *genocidaire's* transformation of the child victims' original personal identity (shaped by family and home community) to one reduced to and restricted to 'child soldier member of the perpetrator group' (i.e. FNI/FRPI child soldier and/or sex slave etc.).

The perpetrators (here referring exclusively to the commanders of armed groups or forces systematically violating international law as a 'common plan') who ostensibly use child members *of their own armed group* (including under 15s) to participate actively in hostilities are, in actuality, using victims of the 'genocidal forcible transfer of children' who do *not* in law 'belong' to any armed party to the conflict. These children then retain their status under international law as being civilian victims of the perpetrator group (notwithstanding perpetrator manufactured alienation of the transferred children from their families and home communities, the fact that the children generally come to think of themselves as 'belonging' to the armed perpetrator group and the fact that the general community in the main may perceive them as child members 'of'/belonging to the perpetrator group in every sense and no longer members of their original communities). As discussed in earlier chapters, forcing the children to commit atrocities is also a typical method employed by such armed groups as the FNI/FRPI to facilitate the community perception that these child victims of genocidal forcible transfer are members 'belonging' to the perpetrator group. However, it can no more legitimately be said that these children belong to the party to the conflict which perpetrated their genocidal forcible transfer to that armed group or force than it is to say that victims of Nazi forced labor camps 'belong' to the Nazi armed party to the conflict.

The recruitment and use of children under 15 in armed hostilities is not in accord with customary law though it does occur and arguably has seen something of a resurgence especially, though not exclusively, in some developing States. Recall in regard to children's protected status in times of armed conflict that in its

[42] Optional Protocol to the Convention on the Rights of the Child on the involvement of children in armed conflict) (entry into force 12 February, 2002).

[43] Such care and respect provisions then contradict the prohibition on use of children in hostilities insofar as the latter pertain only to under 15s in the Additional Protocols to the 1949 Geneva Conventions (1977).

commentary on Additional Protocol I to the 1949 Geneva Conventions, the International Committee of the Red Cross stated: "Participation of children *and adolescents* in combat is an *inhumane practice* and the ICRC considered that it should come to an end."[44] Note that the ICRC did *no*t hold the position then that only under 15s ought not participate in hostilities (the ICRC view was that *under 18s* should not be participants in hostilities but, of course, compromises were made in the final drafting of Additional Protocol I and II to the 1949 Geneva Conventions).[45] Thus, the ICRC advocated, for instance, that the parties to the Additional Protocols to the 1949 Geneva Conventions negotiate maximum protection for all 'children' during armed conflict wherever feasible. The term 'children' was, for instance, purposely left undefined and no age range given for the provision in paragraph one of Article 77 of Additional Protocol I so as to afford maximum protection in regards to this provision to children of all ages:

> Children shall be the object of special respect and shall be protected against any form of indecent assault. The Parties to the conflict shall provide them with the care and aid they require, whether because of their age or for any other reason.[46]

Hence, though children over or under 15 may, in practice, end up in the ranks of an armed group or force perpetrating mass atrocities and/or genocide, this reality does not render these children a party to the conflict as members of a particular group of belligerents. This is the case since the children's transfer to an armed group or force perpetrating mass atrocity and/or genocide constitutes genocidal forcible transfer of children to which the children cannot be considered to have lawfully consented.[47] The child victims of genocidal forcible transfer to an armed group or force are "protected persons" who are no more genuine members of that force than are any other group of protected persons forcibly transferred. In this regard, for instance, recall Article 8(2)(a)(v) of the Rome Statute setting out the war crime of: "Compelling a prisoner of war *or other protected person* to serve in the forces of a hostile Power."[48] The point the current author is making here then is that fighting on the same side as the armed group to which one was appropriated does not result in assignment of the status of *bona fide* lawful member of that fighting force nor does it confer the status of being party to the conflict in any legal sense under international law. It is here argued then that all children (persons under age 18 years) who have been transferred to armed groups or forces committing mass atrocity and/or genocide are to be regarded as protected persons who are the victims of genocidal forcible transfer whether recruited through conscription or alleged enlistment.

---

[44] International Committee of the Red Cross (ICRC) Commentary on Protocol I additional to the 1949 Geneva Conventions (2005).

[45] Additional Protocol I to the 1949 Geneva Conventions (1977).

[46] International Committee of the Red Cross (ICRC). Commentary on Protocol I additional to the 1949 Geneva Conventions (2005).

[47] Grover (2012).

[48] Rome Statute (2002).

It was pointed out previously that such children allegedly 'enlisted' are in any case not normally free to leave the armed group or force into which they were recruited except in exceptional circumstances (i.e. to relieve international pressure on the group or force some children are released to NGOs as a token gesture). Note that "...rates of abduction [of children for child soldiering] near 50 percent of the overall population in war affected regions, such as e.g. ...parts of the Democratic Republic of Congo..."[49] One marker of this genocidal forcible transfer of children (under 15s) to armed groups such as the FNI/FRPI or UPC/FPLC that: (1) distinguishes such an appropriation of children from *recruitment* of children who are of age (as per international humanitarian law) into a lawful armed force and (2) sets it out as resulting in a form of captivity or enslavement of children is the fact that typically measures are taken by such unlawful armed groups or forces to block the appropriated children ever returning and successfully re-integrating into their home communities:

> In many cases child soldiers are forced to commit atrocities against civilians [as in the DRC in the time period relevant to the Lubanga and Ktanaga and Chui cases amongst others], at times against own family- and community members; ***so as to cut-off return routes*** and inflict increased terror and psychological harm also on home communities.[50]

The Pre-Trial Chamber in the Katanga and Chui case held that the context of the armed conflict in that case was international and that the charges regarding child recruitment and use should therefore pertain to Article 8(2)(b)(xxvi) (conscription or enlistment of under 15s into a *national force* and the use of children for active participation in armed hostilities).[51] The assumption then was in the Katanga and Chui case, as in *Lubanga*, that the children recruited and used for active participation in hostilities were functioning as 'child soldiers' and that they had received 'military training' and could be regarded as "part of the militias":

> In the view of the Chamber, the evidence demonstrates that the training of *child soldiers* took place in FRPI333 and FNI334 camps. The evidence further shows that some of the children learned how to handle weapons, and received "armes blanches" (e.g. machetes and spears), or guns at the end of their training.[52]
>
> Many children in FRPI and FNI camps were visibly under fifteen years of age, received *military training* pursuant to the orders of Germain Katanga and Mathieu Ngudjolo Chui, and were often paraded in their presence.[53]
>
> As previously found, there are substantial grounds to believe that, in addition to ***having been fully integrated into the militias*** during the attack on the village of Bogoro on 24 February 2003...[54]

[49] Schauer (2009, p. 34).

[50] Schauer (2009, p. 29, emphasis added).

[51] Prosecutor v Germain Katanga and Mathieu Ngudjolo Chui, Decision on Confirmation of Charges (2008, p. 76, para 249).

[52] Prosecutor v Germain Katanga and Mathieu Ngudjolo Chui, Decision on Confirmation of Charges (2008, p. 79, para 255).

[53] Prosecutor v Germain Katanga and Mathieu Ngudjolo Chui, Decision on Confirmation of Charges (2008, p. 83, para 261).

[54] Prosecutor v Germain Katanga and Mathieu Ngudjolo Chui, Decision on Confirmation of Charges (2008, p. 81, para 258, emphasis added).

In contrast, the view here is advanced that the children were not fundamentally being trained to be soldiers but to be perpetrators of systematic international crimes with mass victims; conduct that is anathema to what constitutes 'soldiering' as understood under international humanitarian law. Their training then cannot be considered military training even if they learned how to use weapons and parade etc. Consider in this regard the following excerpt from the confirmation of charges decision in *Katanga and Chui*:

> More specifically, the evidence shows that during the attack on the village of Bogoro on 24 February 2003, ***some combatants*** were identified by the inhabitants of Bogoro as children who were visibly under the age of fifteen years. These children attacked the village of Bogoro killing civilians, destroying properties, and pillaging goods.[55]

Thus, the war crime of recruitment (conscription or enlistment) and use of children (under 15s) for active participation in armed hostilities does *not*, it is here argued, presuppose that the children have been recruited into a soldiering unit; whether State or non-State. Put somewhat differently, the war crimes set out at Article 8(2)(b)(xxvi) and Article 8(2)(e)(vii)of the Rome Statute[56] involving recruiting children under age 15 and their use for active participation in international and non-international armed hostilities respectively do not presuppose those child victims hold the status of 'child soldiers.' Furthermore, it is *not* a legal element of these war crimes that these children hold the status of 'child soldier' in any legal sense or even in terms of the perception of the parties involved. Rather, these children are under international law, in respect of conscription or enlistment and/or their use for active participation by armed groups or forces perpetrating atrocities, it has here been argued, the victims of genocidal forcible transfer and are not in any sense functioning as 'child soldiers'. Their integration into the armed forces in question in the context of the DRC conflict is as the victims of genocidal forcible transfer and not as a result of normal recruitment and integration through 'military training' and exercises associated with soldiering as the term is understood in international law. Respectfully then it is here contended that the fact that children under age 15 fought alongside adult members of the FNI/FRPI and participated in perpetrating grave international crimes against the civilians of Bogoro does *not* at all mean that these children can be considered *"combatants"* as the term is understood under international humanitarian law as related to international conflicts contrary to the suggestion of the Pre-Trial Chamber:

> As previously found by the Chamber, there is sufficient evidence to establish substantial grounds to believe that a large number of FNI/FRPI ***combatants*** who participated in hostilities were under the age of fifteen.[57]

---

[55] Prosecutor v Germain Katanga and Mathieu Ngudjolo Chui, Decision on Confirmation of Charges (2008, p. 80, para 257, emphasis added).

[56] Rome Statute (2002).

[57] Prosecutor v Germain Katanga and Mathieu Ngudjolo Chui, Decision on Confirmation of Charges (2008, p. 81, para 259, emphasis added).

In fact, these child victims of genocidal forcible transfer whose protected status was so gravely violated retained their civilian child protected status though appropriated by the armed forces in question to participate in the conflict in large part by perpetrating atrocities.

Since it is here argued that the children recruited and used by the FNI/FRPI were the victims of genocidal forcible transfer; it is irrelevant in order to *substantiate the commission of the latter crime* to establish whether the child victims were 15 and over or under age 15. Had all the children 'recruited' by the FNI/FRPI been 15 or over; their so-called recruitment into a group committing mass atrocity still constituted a grave international crime; namely the genocidal forcible transfer of children to that armed group. The children so transferred are forever stigmatized and perceived in their communities as members of a perpetrator group (i.e. FNI/FRPI etc.); especially where these children are known to have or suspected of having perpetrated atrocity against their own home communities. In the latter cases their re-integration into regular society is tenuous at best in many if not most instances:

> Social isolation and the *formation of ex-combatants as a distinct civilian sub-group* is a consequence of the combined effects of factors which include host communities' negative attitudes towards ex-combatants and their [ex child soldiers'] psychological problems causing difficulties in social interaction.[58]

4.4.2 Cruel and Inhuman Treatment of FNI/FRPI 'Child Soldiers'

The defendants Katanga and Chui were *not* charged with war crimes under Article 8(2)(a)(ii) of 'inhuman treatment' or 'outrages upon person dignity' (Article 8(2)(b)(xxi)) *directed to the children recruited and used for active participation in armed hostilities by the FNI/FRPI*. Consider then the implication of omitting children appropriated to the FNI/FRPI fighting forces in light of the Pre-Trial Chamber's reference to inhuman treatment being a war crime inflicted on any 'protected persons':

> The war crime provided for in article 8(2)(a)(ii)-2 of the Elements of Crimes is defined as the infliction of "inhuman treatment" ***upon any persons protected*** under the 1949 Geneva Conventions.[59]

[58] Schauer (2009, p. 32–33). As mentioned here previously; the term 'combatants'—if used in the legal sense (as understood under international humanitarian law)—is erroneously applied to the child victims of genocidal forcible transfer appropriated by armed groups or forces perpetrating mass atrocities and/or genocide. These children are child civilian victims of genocidal forcible transfer and retain that status even while integrated into the perpetrator armed group or force.

[59] Prosecutor v Germain Katanga and Mathieu Ngudjolo Chui, Decision on Confirmation of Charges (2008, p. 115, para 356).

The implication of the omission of child 'members' of the FNI/FRPI from the group of victims suffering 'inhuman treatment' at the hands of the FNI/FRPI is that the children so 'recruited' were held by the Prosecutor and the Chamber *erroneously* to be 'child soldiers' not in a colloquial sense (meaning children participating in the fighting under duress or 'voluntarily') but in some legal sense referring to these children *allegedly* having lost their protected status as civilian children insofar as the war crimes relating to inhuman treatment and outrages on their personal dignity are concerned. It has here been argued in opposition that the children recruited and used by the FNI/FRPI were in fact the victims of genocidal forcible transfer of children and as such retained their *protected status* under Additional Protocol I Article 77 as children and under Additional Protocol I Article 75 and Geneva Convention IV Article 13 as civilians in the power of a party to the conflict as well. They were then as victims of the genocidal forcible transfer of children "*in the hands of* a party to the conflict" and not to be regarded as (combatant) 'members' of the FNI/FRPI as the term 'member' is normally understood:

> Article 8(2)(a)(ii) of the Statute therefore applies to those situations in which *protected civilians* are inhumanely treated *"in the hands of" a party to the conflict*, and thus also applies to the inhuman treatment of the protected persons by an attacking force, when such conduct occurs after the overall attack has ended, and defeat or full control of the targeted village has been secured.[60]

The so-called 'child soldier' constituent of the FNI/FRPI was forcibly transferred to these armed groups in the context of armed attacks on villages and on random groups of children walking to and from school and at school and in other locales. The inhuman treatment they suffered occurred also during their so-called 'military training' subsequent to these attacks in which the children were 'recruited', and in the course of their assigned roles as so-called child soldiers of the FNI/FRPI. For instance, these child soldiers were expected to inflict heinous injuries on civilians intended to cause extreme suffering and death and did so at the village of Bogoro (the attack involved the use of machetes, burning people alive and other such horrific acts).[61] In fact the attack at Bogoro was directed at the Hema ethnic group and the intent was to commit mass murder and eliminate all Hema in the village (a genocidal intent). In participating in mass atrocity as the victims of forcible genocidal transfer by the FNI/FRPI for the purpose of child soldiering, the children perpetrating these acts themselves suffered grave mental and often physical harms. One of the experts in the Lubanga trial testified to the suffering and trauma that child soldiers experience and the long-term effects:

> Among a number of at risk populations, children of war and child soldiers are a particularly vulnerable group and often suffer from devastating long-term consequences of experienced or witnessed acts of violence. Child war survivors have to cope with *repeated traumatic life*

[60] Prosecutor v Germain Katanga and Mathieu Ngudjolo Chui, Decision on Confirmation of Charges (2008, p. 116, para 358, emphasis added).

[61] Prosecutor v Germain Katanga and Mathieu Ngudjolo Chui, Decision on Confirmation of Charges (2008, pp. 154–155, para 462).

> *events*, exposure to combat, shelling and other life threatening events, acts of abuse such as torture or rape, violent death of a parent or friend, witnessing loved ones being tortured or injured, separation from family, being abducted or held in detention, insufficient adult care, lack of safe drinking water and food, inadequate shelter, explosive devices and dangerous building ruins in proximity, marching or being transported in crowded vehicles over long distances and spending months in transit camps. . .These experiences can hamper children's healthy development and their ability to function fully even once the violence has ceased.[62]
>
> When children are recruited into combat and servitude, they experience sexual violence and exploitation and are exposed to explosives, combat situations and the experience and witnessing of killings. Reports abound from conflict zones of girls and boys being abducted and forced into sexual slavery by militias or rebel groups. . .Countries especially named for sexual exploitation of child soldiers – this includes boys as well as girls – are:..Congo. . .[63]
>
> [Child] perpetrator events, as well as surviving rape and cruel torture, seem to have a predictive power in terms of likelihood of development of psychopathology.[64]

The expert reported that various empirical interview studies with former child soldiers found high rates of post-traumatic stress disorder (PTSD); multiple co-occurring psychological disorders and long-term adverse physical effects of child soldiering experiences.[65] (PTSD is a debilitating condition for many creating long-term suffering and reliving of their war-time traumas).[66] Note also that clinical evidence demonstrates that:

> Psychological exposure and suffering from trauma can cripple individuals and families even into the next generations.[67]

In addition to the traumas resulting from their experiences of so-called child soldiering causing long term psychological suffering; there are also higher mortality rates amongst ex child soldiers than the general war affected population.

> Beyond psychological suffering from the symptoms of PTSD, traumatized populations [such as ex child soldiers] show significantly elevated levels of physical morbidity and mortality[68] [the latter also including high rates of suicide amongst former child soldiers].[69]
>
> They [ex child soldiers] are victimised two-fold, since they first are exposed to traumatic experiences and later are blamed and stigmatised for the atrocities they have committed.[70]

The contention here then is that Katanga and Chui ought to have been charged with separate counts of war crimes relating to inhuman treatment of the FNI/FRPI child soldier population in particular as a separate protected group of children/child civilians. This should have been the case in that these child soldier recruits were

---

[62] Schauer (2009, p. 3).

[63] Schauer (2009, p. 6).

[64] Schauer(2009, p. 16).

[65] Schauer (2009, pp. 12–20).

[66] Schauer (2009, p. 16).

[67] Schauer (2009, p. 25).

[68] Schauer (2009, p. 16).

[69] Schauer (2009, p. 20).

[70] Schauer (2009, p. 29).

specifically targeted for special forms of inhuman treatment. Their genocidal forcible transfer to murderous armed groups or forces, as discussed, does not negate their child civilian protected status and itself constitutes inhuman treatment under Article 8(2)(a)(ii).[71] The FNI/FRPI had no regard whatsoever for the life and well-being of the children they appropriated to their ranks. These separate counts of inhuman treatment charges in *Katanga and Chui* would then be in addition to the counts of inhuman treatment of the civilian population in the villages such as Bogoro attacked by FNI/FRPI. It is also here argued that war crimes charges of "outrages upon personal dignity" under Article 8(2)(b)(xxi)[72] should have been advanced in regards to the treatment accorded the FNI/FRPI child soldier population. These children were stripped of their personal identity and transformed into perpetrators of atrocity, often used as sex slaves, physically and psychologically abused and humiliated, tortured or even killed if they resisted all of which amounts to outrages upon personal dignity.

4.4.3 Mens Rea and the Appropriation of Children to the FNI/FRPI

The Pre-Trial Chamber found that Katanga and Chui knew or should have known that they were 'recruiting' under 15s and using them for active participation in hostilities. It is apparent that these defendants and their co-perpetrators were aware that these children under 15 were 'protected persons' given their status as children (the latter principle being one of customary law). It is here argued that the children 15 and over were also child civilian victims of genocidal forcible transfer to the FNI/FRPI and that the commanders of these armed groups in fact were well aware of this. Thus, these children (persons under 18 appropriated by the FNI/FRPI) were civilian victims in the power of a party to the conflict used to participate actively in the conflict despite the fact that they, according to international humanitarian law, were to be considered protected persons affected by armed conflict. The FNI/FRPI appropriation of these children as 'child soldiers' does *not* confer on such children legal 'combatant' (non-civilian) status given that: (1) these armed groups systematically did not abide by international law and cannot be considered legitimate armed forces; (2) many of the children 'recruited' were under 15 in contravention of Protocol I Additional to the 1949 Geneva Conventions and customary international law (Protocol I also being considered customary law) and (3) the *alleged* 'enlistment' of the children aged 15 and over occurred in the context of highly coercive circumstances given the mass atrocities that the FNI/FRPI as well as the opposing forces were perpetrating in the relevant time frame. Thus, the children (over and under age 15) appropriated by the FNI/FRPI were

[71] Rome Statute (2002).

[72] Rome Statute(2002).

unlawfully recruited and used regardless the children's ages and, for the reasons discussed, were all the victims of the genocidal forcible transfer of children.

4.4.4 Genocidal Forcible Transfer of Children; Nationality and the Protected Status of Children

Note that the nationality of the children in the custody and control of the FNI/FRPI (children appropriated in order to serve as so-called FNI/FRPI 'child soldiers') is irrelevant to a determination of their protected status. The children do *not* lose their protected status as both civilians and as children under international humanitarian law as a function of the fact that they may share the same nationality as the perpetrators of their genocidal forcible transfer to a national armed group committing mass atrocity as part of a common plan. Nor do these children, whether considered 'of age' or not, have an obligation to participate as 'child soldiers' in an armed group or force (whether perceived as a national army or not) which has lost its legitimacy due to its systematic violation of international law. (This author has noted elsewhere, in any case, that children—persons under age 18—have no unqualified right to participate in hostilities).[73] Rather, the children's active participation in hostilities is instead considered exceptional under customary and international humanitarian treaty law. (The latter fact has now been codified in Article 1 of the Optional Protocol to the Convention on the Rights of the Child on the Involvement of Children in Armed Conflict).[74] Consider in this regard the commentary of the International Committee of the Red Cross (ICRC) on the issue of nationality and the protection guarantees under Protocol I Additional to the 1949 Geneva Conventions[75] to be afforded to civilians as 'protected persons': "...the question of whether the [protection] guarantee will be applied will not depend on this fact alone [nationality], *for international law [the humanitarian protection guarantee] overrides the criterion of nationality*."[76] Put somewhat differently; here with specific reference to the context of child soldiering, the foregoing ICRC commentary translates to the following: 'Children of the same nationality as the perpetrator of the genocidal forcible transfer of those same children (i.e. here children in the power or "in the hands of" the FNI/FRPI, a party to the conflict committing mass atrocity) do *not* lose their civilian child protected status regardless of the fact that they are perceived as FNI/FRPI 'child soldiers' by the local community and are so designated by the party to the conflict which has them in its power.

[73] Grover (2008).

[74] Optional Protocol to the Convention of the Rights of the Child on the Involvement of Children in Armed Conflict.

[75] Protocol I Additional to the 1949 Geneva Conventions (1977).

[76] International Committee of the Red Cross (ICRC) to Additional Protocol I to the 1949 Geneva Conventions (2005, emphasis added).

4.4.5 More on Outrages on Personal Dignity

The Chamber in the Katanga and Chui case noted that the elements required for the charge of 'outrages on personal dignity' include: (1) a nexus between an armed conflict and the crime; (2) the perpetrator's awareness of the factual circumstances that establish the existence of such an armed conflict and (3) a violation of the person's dignity that reaches to the level of being an outrage on the individual's personal dignity.[77] In addition:

> This war crime requires that the perpetrator, by action or omission, caused the humiliation, degradation, or violation of the personal dignity of individuals: (i) who are aligned or whose allegiance is to a party to the conflict who is adverse or hostile to the perpetrator; and (ii) who are in the hands of the party to the conflict to which the perpetrator belongs. . .The types of actions or omissions which could constitute [this] crime [under the Rome Statute] were left undefined.[78]

Note that the Pre-Trial Chamber *dismissed* the charges of outrages on personal dignity under Article 8(2)(b)(xxi) and inhuman treatment under Article 8(2)(a)(ii) in *Katanga and Chui* due to alleged lack of sufficient evidence.[79] It is here contended, however, that children who were appropriated by the FNI/FRPI (or children who are the victims of such a genocidal forcible transfer to *any* armed group or force perpetrating mass atrocity and/or genocide) are automatically the victims of outrages on their personal dignity and inhuman treatment. For instance, children appropriated by such groups to be child soldiers are typically subjected to brutal training involving what can only be described as torture, etc. and compelled through direct and indirect means to commit atrocity. They are separated from their families and communities to become expendable tools of war and, especially with respect to girl soldiers, forced to provide other degrading services such as to function as sex slaves. While there is no question that the children transferred from their home communities to these armed groups or forces are "in the hands of the party to which the perpetrator [of outrages on the children's personal dignity] belongs"; the question arises regarding the other element of the crime specifying that the victim be someone who is "aligned or whose allegiance is to a party to the conflict who is adverse or hostile to the perpetrator."[80] The contention here is that children appropriated by armed groups or forces committing mass atrocity and/or genocide must be regarded as non-consenting under international humanitarian law as their transfer constitutes the genocidal forcible transfer of children for the reasons explained. As such any allegiance that the children may or may not profess

[77] Prosecutor v Germain Katanga and Mathieu Ngudjolo Chui, Decision on Confirmation of Charges (2008, p. 119, para 367).

[78] Prosecutor v Germain Katanga and Mathieu Ngudjolo Chui, Decision on Confirmation of Charges (2008, p. 119, para 368).

[79] Prosecutor v Germain Katanga and Mathieu Ngudjolo Chui, Decision on Confirmation of Charges (2008, p. 206, para 577).

[80] Rome Statute; Elements of the Crime: War Crime 8(2)(b)(xxi) (2002).

to the armed group or force that has committed this outrage on the children's personal dignity is irrelevant since the children cannot be considered to have consented to their own genocidal forcible transfer (i.e. any professed allegiance to the perpetrator group who appropriated them is not probative or relevant). The children properly then must be regarded as belonging to the civilian population being subjected to systematic attack by these same armed perpetrators who appropriated the children of these communities to become so-called child soldiers As previously discussed, such child soldier victims of genocidal forcible transfer do not in fact in law belong to any of the armed parties to the conflict; they are simply children who belong to a protected group under international humanitarian law. Further, they must be considered in law, as a result of their genocidal forcible transfer, for all practical purposes, to be in the hands of an adversary.

Literature, Materials and Cases

Literature

Grover S (2012) Child soldier victims of genocidal forcible transfer: exonerating child soldiers charged with grave conflict-related international crimes. Springer, Berlin

Grover SC (2008) 'Child Soldiers' as 'Non-Combatants': the inapplicability of the refugee convention exclusion clause. Int J Hum Rights 12(1):53–65

Materials

Geneva Convention IV Relative to the Protection of Civilian Persons in Times of War, 12 August, 1949 http://www.icrc.org/ihl.nsf/full/380 Accessed 17 Oct 2012

International Committee of the Red Cross (ICRC) Commentary on Protocol I additional to the 1949 Geneva Conventions (2005) http://www.icrc.org/ihl.nsf/COM/470-750099?OpenDocument. Accessed 5 Feb 2012

Optional Protocol to the Convention on the Rights of the Child on the involvement of children in armed conflict (2002) (Entry into force 12 February, 2002). http://www2.ohchr.org/english/law/crc-conflict.htm. Accessed 10 Jun 2012

Protocol Additional to the 1949 Geneva Conventions relating to the protection of victims of international armed conflicts (Protocol I) (8 June, 1977). http://www.icrc.org/ihl.nsf/FULL/470?OpenDocument. Accessed 18 Jan 2012

Protocol Additional to the 1949 Geneva Conventions relating to the protection of victims of non-international armed conflicts ((Protocol II) 1977) (8 June, 1977). http://www.icrc.org/ihl.nsf/full/475?opendocument. Accessed 10 Jun 2012

Rome Statute (2002) Entered into force 7 January, 2002. http://untreaty.un.org/cod/icc/statute/romefra.htm. Accessed 14 Jan 2012

Schauer E (2009) The psychological impact of child soldiering (Expert testimony before the ICC, 25 February, 2009) 212.159.242.181/iccdocs/doc/doc636752.pdf. Accessed 12 Feb 2012

Cases

Prosecutor v Germain Katanga and Mathieu Ngudjolo Chui, Decision on the Confirmation of Charges (Pre-Trial Chamber I) (26 September 2008) http://www.icc-cpi.int/iccdocs/doc/doc571253.pdf. Accessed 9 Feb 2012

Prosecutor v Germain Katanga and Mathieu Ngudjolo Chui, Prosecution Opening Statement (Trial Chamber II) (24 November 2009) http://www.icc-cpi.int/NR/rdonlyres/D8F34FB0-DEAD-431A-8F80-54757F418EAC/281274/091124KatangaOpeningStatementformatted1.pdf. Accessed 7 Feb 2012

Prosecutor v. Thomas Lubanga Dyilo Summary of the "Judgment pursuant to Article 74 of the Statute" (14 March, 2012)

Chapter 5
Case 3: Prosecutor v Omar Hassan Ahmad Al Bashir

5.1 Background

> ***The Confirmed Charges***
> Mr Al Bashir is allegedly criminally responsible on ten counts on the basis of his individual criminal responsibility under Article 25(3)(a) of the Rome Statute as an indirect co-perpetrator including:
> **five counts of crimes against humanity:** murder – Article 7(1)(a); extermination – Article 7 (1)(b); forcible transfer – Article 7(1)(d); torture – Article 7(1)(f); and rape – Article 7(1)(g);
> **two counts of war crimes**: intentionally directing attacks against a civilian population as such or against individual civilians not taking part in hostilities – Article 8(2)(e)(i); and pillaging – Article 8(2)(e)(v).
> **Three counts of genocide**: genocide by killing (article 6-a), genocide by causing serious bodily or mental harm (article 6-b) and genocide by deliberately inflicting on each target group conditions of life calculated to bring about the group's physical destruction (article 6-c).[1]

The Pre-Trial Chamber in *Prosecutor v Omar Hassan Ahmad Al Bashir* found that between March, 2003 to at least 14 July 2008, there was a *non-international* armed conflict occurring in Darfur between the Government of Sudan (GoS) and several rebel groups including but limited to the Sudanese Liberation Movement/Army (SLM/A) and the Justice and Equality Movement (JEM). The Pre-Trial Chamber found there was evidence to substantiate that Al Bashir along with other top ranking Sudanese government officials and commanders entered into a common plan to attack the civilian population of Fur, Masalit and Zaghawa ethnicity perceived as supporters of the rebels. The GoS attacks were carried out with the genocidal intent to destroy, at least in part, these perceived distinct ethnic groups. The GoS attacks on civilians were carried out by the GoS forces, including the Sudanese Armed Forces and their allied *Janjaweed* militia, the Sudanese Police Forces, the National Intelligence and Security Service (NISS) and the Humanitarian Aid Commission (HAC).

[1] ICC Charges (Counts) against Omar Hassan Ahmad Al Bashir (International Criminal Bureau, 15 July, 2010).

S.C. Grover, *Humanity's Children*, DOI 10.1007/978-3-642-32501-4_5,

The common plan as implemented involved crimes against humanity, genocide, and war crimes and was either directly coordinated and implemented by Al Bashir as *de jure* and *de facto* President of the State of Sudan and Commander-in-Chief of the Sudanese Armed Forces or he is responsible as he was "in control of all branches of the 'apparatus' of the State of Sudan and used such control to secure the implementation of the [so-called] counter-insurgency campaign."[2]

5.2 The Prosecutor's ICC Application for an Arrest Warrant Re Omar Hassan Ahmad Al Bashir (14 July, 2008)

5.2.1 On Whether Darfur Involved 'Autogenocide' and Whether Correctly Answering that Question Matters

In the initial application for an ICC arrest warrant pertaining to Al Bashir, the Prosecutor alleged the accused was criminally responsible for various counts of genocide, crimes against humanity and war crimes occurring between March 2003 to July 14, 2008. The Darfur situation had been referred by the UN Security Council in 2005 and the Al Bashir case, amongst others relating to Darfur, were developed subsequent to the aforementioned referral. The Prosecutor alleged that Al Bashir fuelled ethnic tensions that later facilitated acts of genocide:

> He promoted the idea of a polarization between tribes aligned with him, whom he labelled "Arabs" and the three ethnic groups he perceived as the main threats, the Fur, Masalit and Zaghawa (hereafter "target groups"), who became derogatorily referred to as "Zurgas" or "Africans".[3]

Note that the Prosecutor stressed that in reality in Darfur: "Both, victims and perpetrators are "Africans" and speak Arabic."[4] Recall in this regard that it has been argued here and by certain other scholars that it is possible to have perpetrator groups commit genocide against a target group which, *objectively speaking*, is fundamentally ethnically and culturally the same as the perpetrator group though perhaps perceived by the perpetrators as distinguishable in some way on some dimension. It is debatable whether all of the 120 different tribes living in the rural areas of Darfur can be considered to be different ethnic groups on any objective basis today (given the extent of intermarriage between the groups and their co-existence[5] in the same territories). Thus, though the groups (tribes) perceive

[2] Statement of the Spokesperson of the ICC, Laurence Blairon (4 March, 2009, p. 2).

[3] Prosecutor v Omar Hassan Ahmad Al Bashir, Public Redacted Version of the Prosecutions' application under Article 58 (2008, ANNEX, p. 7, para 5).

[4] Prosecutor v Omar Hassan Ahmad Al Bashir, Public Redacted Version of the Prosecutions' application under Article 58 (2008, ANNEX, p. 7, para 5).

[5] Prosecutor v Omar Hassan Ahmad Al Bashir, Public Redacted Version of the Prosecutions' application under Article 58 (2008, ANNEX, p. 7, para 6).

themselves to be different ethnically, it is here argued that the genocide charges would be feasible also were the Al Bashir perpetrator group considered objectively to be the same as the victim groups (the latter being the Fur, Masalit and Zaghawa tribal peoples). If the case were framed as involving peoples (perpetrators and victims) who are in contemporary times essentially ethnically/culturally the same; the genocide charges would pertain to an 'autogenocide' and, on the analysis here, still be viable.

5.2.2 *Motive, Genocide and Child Soldiering*

The Prosecutor alleged that Al Bashir used as an excuse or camouflage of his genocidal intent to destroy the Fur, Masalit and Zaghawa, the pretence that he was simply trying to quell an insurgency. The Prosecutor pointed out, however, that according to existing international criminal law jurisprudence: "in genocide cases, the reason why the accused sought to destroy the victim group has no bearing on guilt."[6] This author is in accord with the view that motive for genocide is irrelevant to guilt (where 'motive' is to be distinguished from 'genocidal intent'). However, notwithstanding the foregoing, the contention here is that in one particular set of circumstances this principle (the need to ignore motive in genocide cases) is unjustly *not* actually applied in practice. The circumstances referred to are those involving the recruitment and use of children (persons under 18) to participate actively with armed groups or forces *committing mass atrocity and/or genocide* (the appropriation of children in the latter context amounts to the 'genocidal forcible transfer of children' as previously here discussed). The latter perpetrator conduct has *not* to date been considered by the ICC (or other international criminal tribunals for that matter) to constitute 'genocide' (namely the 'genocidal forcible transfer of children'). Thus, it is the case, in practice, that alleged motive for such 'genocidal forcible transfer of children' (as so-called child soldiers and/or supports) to armed groups or forces perpetrating mass atrocities and/or genocide has led to no accountability for the perpetrators for this genocidal crime (i.e. those motives being framed in various allegedly righteous terms such as the State interest in maintaining the stability of the State and quashing a purported unjustified insurgency as in the Al Bashir case).

By the ICC Prosecutor not designating the transfer of children to armed groups or forces *committing systematic mass atrocity and/or genocide* (as occurred in Darfur) as itself a form of genocide (the genocidal forcible transfer of children'); children aged 15 and over have no protection against such transfer deriving from Rome Statute[7] prohibitions against recruitment or use of children for active

[6] Prosecutor v Omar Hassan Ahmad Al Bashir, Public Redacted Version of the Prosecutions' application under Article 58 (2008, ANNEX, p. 7, para 8).

[7] Rome Statute (2002).

participation in hostilities (i.e. since the latter prohibitions protect only under 15s). The Rome Statute[8] war crimes provisions pertaining to the recruitment and use of children *under 15s* are so drafted as to afford, by implication, the State armed force (and allied militia) and the non-State rebel armed groups complete discretion in terms of determining whether the use of child soldiers ***aged 15 and over*** is justified *notwithstanding the fact that the State or non-State armed force or group is perpetrating systematic mass atrocity or genocide* (and notwithstanding the fact that agents of the State or non-State armed group or force may be charged with various Rome Statute[9] offences relating to their perpetrating widespread systematic attacks and atrocities on the civilian population and/or genocide as well as committing offences under the Rome Statute[10] against enemy belligerents). Respectfully, it is here contended that the interests of justice require that the appropriation of children (conscription or alleged enlistment and use for active participation in hostilities of children) by State or non-State armed forces or groups perpetrating systematic mass atrocity or genocide *not* be viewed exclusively through the war crimes lens of the Rome Statute[11] but also be properly legally characterized as constituting the genocidal forcible transfer of children. Let us consider the latter point then in further detail.

Note that the Rome Statute war crime involving the recruitment and use of under 15s in hostilities is in part premised on the notion that children under age 15 cannot legally consent to participate in armed hostilities. Recall however that children (*persons under age 18)* are protected from transfer to an armed group or force perpetrating mass atrocity and/or genocide given that: (1) children (persons under age 18) under international humanitarian law are members of a *protected group as children* during armed conflict and are owed a high duty of care and respect; and (2) such armed groups or forces as described are operating in an unlawful manner and hence *the children's recruitment or use by these perpetrator groups or forces is unlawful* (where children refers to persons under 18). The crime of genocidal forcible transfer of children thus, on the analysis here, includes, but is not limited to, the recruitment and use of children (persons under 18) for active participation (direct or indirect)[12] in hostilities by a State or non-State armed force or group perpetrating systematic mass atrocity and/or genocide as part of a common plan. Children (persons under age 18) thus cannot be considered in law to have consented to appropriation or use by such unlawful armed groups or forces perpetrating grave international crimes as part of a common plan as: (1) such consent would be equivalent in law to consenting to one's own genocidal forcible transfer; and (2) the latter is clearly an absurd result that is inconsistent with the very concept of the 'genocidal forcible transfer of children'.

[8] Rome Statute (2002).

[9] Rome Statute (2002).

[10] Rome Statute (2002).

[11] Rome Statute (2002).

[12] On the view here, children used as sex slaves, domestics, cooks or in any other capacity by armed groups or forces perpetrating systematic mass atrocities and/or genocide are included as victims of the genocidal transfer of children to these perpetrator groups or forces.

In sum then the appropriation ('recruitment) and use in any capacity of children of any age (persons under age 18) properly can be regarded, on the view here, as constituting the genocidal forcible transfer of children *where the children's transfer is to an armed force (State or non-State) committing systematic mass atrocities and/ or genocide as part of a common plan.* Yet, those most responsible as commanders of such State or non-State armed groups or forces hold that the recruitment and use for active participation in armed conflict of *children* 15 or 16 and over is lawful (i.e. though such *use* of children, persons under 18, by State armed forces for direct participation in armed hostilities is in contravention of the Optional Protocol to the Convention on the Rights of the Child on children involved in armed conflict[13] no explicit prohibition is included in Rome Statute[14] Article 8 in this regard as pertains to children 15 and over as discussed[15]). The international criminal law community has *not* adopted an unqualified helpful approach then; especially considering that children 15 and over who are the victims of the genocidal forcible transfer of children to armed groups or forces committing mass atrocity and/or genocide receive no protection benefit from the war crimes provisions of the Rome Statute[16] pertaining to the recruitment and use of *under 15s* for active participation in hostilities. The genocidal forcible transfer of children as child soldiers and sex slaves etc. to an armed force (State or non-State) committing systematic mass atrocities and/or genocide is an especially persistent and widespread problem where: (1) the State itself is responsible in large part for such grave violations of the children's basic right to security under international law and (2) the national government is not making genuine or any efforts to end the recruitment and use of children in armed hostilities by either State or non-State armed forces in its jurisdiction or under its effective control (Note that the State has a responsibility under international humanitarian and human rights law to protect children also from unlawful recruitment and use by non-State armed forces).

To date no charges have been filed by the Prosecutor against Al Bashir pertaining specifically to the recruitment and use of children by State armed forces (GoS) and allied militias committing grave human rights violations against civilians on a massive scale including genocide. To date, in ICC case law, the matter of child soldiers serving in State or non-State armed groups or forces which are perpetrating grave international crimes as part of a common plan has been addressed only in terms of war crime charges against the perpetrators of child recruitment and use of

[13] Optional Protocol to the Convention on the Rights of the Child on children involved in armed conflict (OP-CRC-AC) (2002).

[14] Rome Statute (2002).

[15] Article I of the OP-CRC-AC (2002) requires States to "take all feasible measures to ensure that members of their armed forces who have not attained the age of 18 years do not take a direct part in hostilities". Article 2 requires States not to conscript under 18s. Article 4 (1) states that "Armed groups that are distinct from the armed forces of a State should not, under any circumstances, recruit or use in hostilities persons under the age of 18 years" and Article 4(2) requires States to "take all feasible measures to prevent such recruitment and use."

[16] Rome Statute (2002).

children *under 15*. This is the case though all such children regardless of age, on the view here, are the victims of the genocidal forcible transfer of children[17]; an offence under the Rome Statute.[18]

Consider the following telling statement by the ICC Prosecutor in the Al Bashir case:

> There is a right for a Government to use force to control its territory, but it cannot use genocide or crimes against humanity as means to do so. *The crimes covered in the Application are not the collateral damages of a military campaign*. Since 2003 Al Bashir's forces *specifically and purposefully targeted civilians*, in particular a substantial part of the target groups, *who were not participants to any conflict*.[19]

The point to be made is that: (1) Al Bashir also targeted child civilians over and under age 15 who belonged to the so-called Arab ethnic group to become 'child soldiers' in the Government of Sudan forces; namely in the national armed forces and in the militia/Janjaweed[20] (as is discussed in more detail in a later section) and that (2) the recruitment and use of children whether aged 15 and over or under 15 for active participation in armed conflict and the perpetrating of mass atrocities and genocide also *cannot* be considered part of the "collateral damages" of a military campaign or the untoward consequences of alleged military exigencies. Instead, involving children of any age in the armed conflict as child soldiers for an armed group or force perpetrating systematic grave international crimes as part of a common plan must be regarded as a form of genocide in itself; namely the genocidal forcible transfer of children (such that the children are in effect appropriated by the armed force or group indefinitely to participate in some capacity with the armed force or group which is perpetrating mass grave international crimes).

5.2.3 The Targeting of So-Called 'Arab' Children of Darfur for Child Soldiering as an Act of Genocide

The ICC Prosecutor in *Al Bashir* highlighted for the Pre-Trial Chamber that Al Bashir "intended to destroy in substantial part the Fur, Masalit and Zaghawa ethnic groups as such."[21] However, there was no consideration given in the charges to the genocidal forcible transfer of children to GoS forces as a key means to the destruction of the so-called Arab tribal peoples of Darfur as well (via the

---

[17] Grover (2012).

[18] Rome Statute (2002).

[19] Prosecutor v Omar Hassan Ahmad Al Bashir, Public Redacted Version of the Prosecutions' application under Article 58 (2008, ANNEX, pp. 7–8, para 9).

[20] Coalition to Stop the Use of Child Soldiers (Child Soldiers Global Report (2008)): "Military officials acknowledged that children from armed forces were transferred into their forces... in May 2006, child soldiers were seen in a newly integrated SAF unit." (p. 316).

[21] Prosecutor v Omar Hassan Ahmad Al Bashir, Public Redacted Version of the Prosecutions' application under Article 58 (2008, ANNEX, p. 8, para 10).

subsequent loss of reproductive capacity, loss of talent, demoralization and grief and mental suffering caused by the loss of their children to the murderous GoS forces and allied militias).

It is noteworthy that the Prosecutor in *Al Bashir* in arguing that genocide had occurred due to the actions of the GoS forces; highlighted that the civilians had nowhere to go to escape; that they were essentially under the control of the GoS forces and subject to attacks even in IDP camps (camps for internally displaced persons):

> **AL BASHIR** thus ***forced the displacement of a substantial part of the target groups and then continued to target them in the camps for internally displaced persons*** (hereafter "IDPs"), *causing serious bodily and mental harm* – through rapes, tortures and forced displacement in traumatising conditions – and deliberately inflicting on a substantial part of those groups conditions of life calculated to bring about their physical destruction, in particular by obstructing the delivery of humanitarian assistance.[22]
>
> through 2004, he [Al Bashir] organized the process of strangulation of the displaced communities, denying them any meaningful assistance, preventing the returns, forcing the UN and others to set up the largest humanitarian operation in the world, and yet obstructing each step of their work.[23]

The ICC Prosecutor thus argued that: (1) the forcible transfer by Al Bashir forces of large segments of the targeted ethnic communities (Fur, Masalit and Zaghawa) and (2) denying the victims the means for survival provided grounds for a reasonable inference of genocidal intent. The Prosecutor did not, however, also consider a separate count of genocide relating to the "genocidal forcible transfer of children" of perpetrator perceived 'Arab' ethnicity. With respect, it is here argued that the latter separate count of genocide is legally supportable given that the children's recruitment and use was by a State armed force and allied militia perpetrating mass atrocities and genocide. The children appropriated thus by the Al Bashir forces as child soldiers are in fact, for all intents and purposes, 'forcibly displaced persons' and in many instances permanently displaced (many children appropriated and used in a variety of ways by such forces are never returned to their families and home communities). These children were also unable to access humanitarian assistance for their release during the time period covered by the Al Bashir indictment and even now NGOs have been unable to successfully negotiate the children's release from the GoS forces and allied pro-government Janjaweed militia. The so-called Arab children recruited and used for active participation in the hostilities by the GoS and allied militia also, as a result, had their right to survival and good development put at grave risk.

During the early period covered by the indictment in 2003, Al Bashir outrageously denied access to humanitarian aid (in respect of a host of basic necessities for survival) to persons in the IDP camps amongst others. (Some of those in the IDP camps were undoubtedly escaped child soldiers from pro-government and from rebel militias).

[22] Prosecutor v Omar Hassan Ahmad Al Bashir, Public Redacted Version of the Prosecutions' application under Article 58 (2008, ANEX, p. 8, para 10, emphasis added).

[23] Prosecutor v Omar Hassan Ahmad Al Bashir, Prosecution Document in Support of Appeal against the "Decision on the Prosecution's Application for a Warrant of Arrest against Omar Hassan Ahmad Al Bashir" (2009, p. 4 para 6).

Sudan backed Janjaweed militia attacked villages near Kartum in May 2006 and their number included many child soldiers.[24] Further, Janjaweed militia were witnessed to have recruited child soldiers from Sudanese refugee camps in Chad in May 2006.[25] One witness who visited Darfur during the relevant time period expressed *shock* at the conditions in IDP camps, and observed that "denial of access was the single [greatest] impediment to humanitarian efforts in Darfur."[26]

Alfredson makes the important point that child soldier recruits though displaced from the families and communities are rarely counted among the displaced by the international community:

> Almost all children under the age of 18 who enlist, are conscripted or forced to serve in armed forces or armed groups become 'separated' children—removed from their families and/or home environment...They are physically relocated, often at great distances from their homes and often to dangerous zones. Not only are they not free to return to their family or community at will (or lack the knowledge or support for their right to do so where legislation on conscientious objection to military service exists), they also often lack the means to return without facing serious dangers, or because their families or communities have also been displaced. *They are essentially in a state of displacement and as such are even more at the mercy of the armed forces or groups that have recruited them.*
>
> ***Unfortunately, the commonly accepted concept of displacement has not encompassed children in these situations, even those forcibly recruited, abducted or pressured to 'volunteer' against their will. As a result, a huge population of displaced children [child* soldiers*] has 'fallen through the cracks'***, perhaps in support of the view that militaries have the right to recruit and use children as soldiers—a view increasingly falling out of fashion.
>
> However, it is becoming clear that ***adults or children who are recruited, whether forcibly or voluntarily, fit the displaced definition*** insofar as they are *compelled* to leave their homes and/or are *prevented* from returning at their own will, particularly during conflict situations.[27]

It has here been argued, however, that not only are the child soldier 'recruits' to those armed forces or groups committing grave violations of international law *displaced* children[28]; but they are also children who are the victims of genocidal forcible transfer. Put somewhat differently; the children who become child soldier[29]

[24] Coalition to Stop the Use of Child Soldiers (Child Soldiers Global Report, 2008, p. 316).

[25] Coalition to Stop the Use of Child Soldiers (Child Soldiers Global Report, 2008, p. 316).

[26] Prosecutor v Omar Hassan Ahmad Al Bashir, Public Redacted Version of the Prosecutions' application under Article 58 (2008, ANNEX, p. 54, para 186).

[27] Alfredson (2002, emphasis added).

[28] Whether or not child recruits (aged 15 and over) to armed forces or groups that abide by international humanitarian law are displaced is a matter beyond the scope of this book though note that Alfredson (2002) considers that all child soldiers are 'displaced' even if members of armed forces or groups that abide by international law.

[29] The term 'child soldiers' as used here includes all children serving in armed groups or forces perpetrating mass atrocity and/or genocide including domestics, cooks, sex slaves etc. in that they have all been alienated from their communities and families as a result of their genocidal forcible transfer to these armed groups or forces and most often perform multiple combat and non-combat functions.

'members' of armed groups or forces perpetrating mass atrocity and/or genocide have been displaced from their families and home communities to travel with these armed groups or forces (i.e. the GoS and allied militia forces or the rebel forces with their very lives under constant threat). The latter facts then meet the criteria for genocide also in terms of "deliberately inflicting on the group conditions of life calculated to bring about its physical destruction in whole or in part" as per Rome Statute Article 6 (c)[30] (on the analysis here the protected groups implicated are both the child group transferred to the GoS and Janjaweed or rebel forces in the thousands to become child soldiers and the larger civilian group of origin of these children now destroyed in part due to the loss of their children to the aforementioned armed forces or groups). Recall, however, that Al Bashir was not charged with a separate count of genocide under Rome Statute Article 6(e)[31] relating to the genocidal forcible transfer of children to the GoS armed forces and Janjaweed militia over which he had control (their each being in effect an apparatus of the State).

As members of the GoS and Janjaweed, the 'child soldiers' are purposefully, incited to commit atrocities on the explicit and standing orders of GoS or allied militia commanders. Further, these 'child soldiers' themselves suffered (i.e. as a direct consequence of their involvement in perpetrating mass atrocity on behalf of their pro-government commanders, due to their brutalization during military training etc.). The children thus are effectively stigmatized; traumatized and moulded to accept a new false *perceived* identity (i.e. ruthless SAF (child) 'soldiers' or Janjaweed militia as opposed to child civilian victims of genocidal forcible transfer whose right under international humanitarian law as children is to be protected from recruitment to and use by murderous State or non-State armed forces or groups).

Involving the children in the commission of atrocities is itself degrading and inhumane treatment of these children (where 'children' refers to the child soldier 'members' of the GoS forces and allied militias). However, Al Bashir was not charged under Rome Statute Article 7(1)(k)[32] with inhumane treatment (as a crime against humanity causing great mental suffering) of the children appropriated in large numbers into the ranks of the GoS and allied militias (i.e. the Janjaweed) to participate in mass atrocity. In the Child Soldier 2008 Global Report the widespread targeting of children by the Janjaweed ***as a proxy for the GoS*** and the government's responsibility for this grave violation of children's rights under international law was noted:

> ***In Sudan*...*.responsibility for ending the widespread use in hostilities of children by the government-backed Janjaweed militias rests squarely with the Sudanese authorities*.**[33]

It is unacceptable that Al Bashir and his co-perpetrators most responsible should to date have potential impunity for their war crimes including the alleged

---

[30] Rome Statute (2002).

[31] Rome Statute (2002).

[32] Rome Statute (2002)

[33] Coalition to Stop the Use of Child Soldiers (Child Soldier Global Report 2008, emphasis added).

recruitment and use of children *under 15* as so-called child soldiers to participate in mass atrocity and genocide and for the crime of 'genocidal forcible transfer of children' (under 18s). Of course the same is true in regards to commanders of rebel armed groups (i.e. the Sudanese Liberation Army of South Sudan) using thousands of child soldiers in the Darfur conflict as they did during the relevant period covered by the Al Bashir case.[34]

5.2.4 Sexual Violence as a Vehicle for the Genocidal Forcible Transfer of Children

The SAF (Sudanese Armed Forces) and allied Janjaweed, it is alleged by i.e. NGOs and other observers on the ground and the ICC Prosecutor, had a proclivity for perpetrating sexual violence in Darfur (particularly against women and girls)[35] during the period covered in *Al Bashir* as did armed opposition groups:

> ***Thousands of women and girls belonging to the target groups were and continue to be raped in all three States of Darfur by members of the Militia/Janjaweed and Armed Forces since 2003****. Girls as young as 5 years old have been raped. A third of the rapes are rapes of children.*[36]
>
> Gender-based violence, in its most horrific form, is used as a calculated strategic device of war. *When sexual violence is employed as a military stratagem* and an instrument of war, the types of violence deployed are calculated to maximize horror and demoralization. Targeting young girls achieves this most simply and effectively. They are not armed. They pose no physical threat. *And targeting them, both government soldiers and rebel groups have found, can be a very effective means of intimidating and humiliating, terrorizing and demoralizing an entire population. The younger the victim, the greater the impact.* For example, human rights organizations have documented rape and sexual violence used to terrorize and displace rural communities throughout the Darfur region of Sudan, where girls as young as seven and eight years old have been victims.[37]

In 2006, UN Secretary-General Kofi Anan warned that sexual violence was escalating against women and girls in Darfur and that the SAF and Janjaweed in

---

[34] The Sudanese People's Liberation Army (SPLA) acknowledged that it had child soldiers in its ranks and in 2007 the UN confirmed the presence of children in the SPLA forces in Southern Sudan. The SLA (Sudanese Liberation Army) in cooperation with the Chadian government recruited 4700 Sudanese refugees including many hundreds of children in March 2006. (See Coalition to Stop the Use of Child Soldiers, 2008, p. 316 and p. 319).

[35] The UN reported that IDP camps in Darfur were sites of great sexual violence and in 2006–2007, for instance, there were many reports of sexual violence perpetrated by Sudanese Armed Forces, the central reserve police and the Janjaweed against women and girls in the Darfur IDP camps (Coalition to Stop the Use of Child Soldiers (2008, p. 317)).

[36] Office of the Prosecutor. Situation in Darfur: Summary of the Case (Prosecution application for warrant of arrest under Article 58 against Omar Hassan Ahmad Al Bashir) (p. 5, emphasis added).

[37] Office of the Prosecutor. Situation in Darfur: Summary of the Case (Prosecution application for warrant of arrest under Article 58 against Omar Hassan Ahmad Al Bashir) (p. 5, emphasis added).

particular were amongst the worst offenders.[38] Anan further noted that: "Girls have been targeted in inter-ethnic conflicts [in Darfur] as *a deliberate form of humiliation of a group*, and as a means of ethnic cleansing. Rape has been used to force displacement."[39] It is here argued, however, that such sexual violence in fact was *also* a vehicle for the 'genocidal forcible transfer of children' as the women and girls raped and those who suffered forced pregnancies were no longer accepted in the main by their communities. The intent was to transfer *the identity* of these sexually victimized women and girls and that of any offspring from forced pregnancy to the perpetrator group in the perceptions of the community and often to also use the females including young girls as sex slaves at military encampments (their use as sex slaves also contributed to identification of these sexual violence victims with the perpetrator group in the eyes of the community). The comments routinely made, for instance, during the sexual violence perpetrated by the SAF and Janjaweed against particular targeted ethnic groups such as the Fur reflect this intent to perpetrate also a genocidal forcible transfer of any children that resulted from the sexual victimization of women and girls:

> After they [sexually] abused us, they told us now ***we would have Arab babies*** and if they could find any Fur woman, they would rape them again to change the colour of their children.[40]

This 'genocidal forcible transfer of children' through sexual victimization by perpetrator armed groups or forces in Darfur (parties to the conflict during the relevant period covered in *Al Bashir*), it is here contended, includes but is not limited to: (1) children of all ethnic groups (including children of so-called Arab ethnic groups) sexually victimized by Al Bashir State armed forces and allied militia or by opposition armed groups and (2) sexually victimized children who were killed as well as those taken to military camps to serve as sex slaves and/or child soldiers as well as any offspring resulting from this sexual victimization. There is every indication that such sexual violence was likely also perpetrated by SAF, Janjaweed and other pro Al Bashir forces also against girls perceived as of Arab descent; especially those who were associated with these forces as child soldiers and/or sex slaves. Sexual violence also against one's perceived 'own' is a typical pattern amongst armed groups or forces perpetrating mass atrocities and/or genocide (i.e. note, for instance, that many of the villages attacked by the SAF and Janjaweed were *not* exclusively comprised of so-called non-Arabs[41] and children were abducted

---

[38] UN Office for the Coordination of Humanitarian Affairs (IRIN) Sudan: Children still victims of war (23 August, 2006). Many women and girls raped were unable to stay with their families if the families moved to a safer location as they were ostracized.

[39] UN Office for the Coordination of Humanitarian Affairs (IRIN) Sudan: Children still victims of war (23 August, 2006, emphasis added).

[40] Office of the Prosecutor. Situation in Darfur: Summary of the Case (Prosecution application for warrant of arrest under Article 58 against Omar Hassan Ahmad Al Bashir) (p. 9).

[41] Office of the Prosecutor. Situation in Darfur: Summary of the Case (Prosecution application for warrant of arrest under Article 58 against Omar Hassan Ahmad Al Bashir): "The Armed Forces, often acting together with Militia/Janjaweed, singled out for attack those villages and small towns inhabited *mainly* by members of the target groups." (p. 3–4).

en masse from these villages as well. The likely result then was that so-called Arab children were also appropriated through force during these attacks on villages to serve as sex slaves). Yet, none of these children (so-called child soldier and/or sex slave members of Al Bashir's pro-government forces and militias)[42] were considered by the ICC prosecutor as the victims of genocide (i.e. the victims of genocidal forcible transfer of children; as a separate count of genocide). This despite the fact that having been raped by GoS or pro-government militia members would have stigmatized the children permanently and created enormous barriers (most often insurmountable) for re-integration into home communities if released or escaped from their pro-government or allied militia armed units (thus contributing to the long-term perceived identification of these children with GoS forces or allied militia (i.e. Janjaweed) and increasing the chances also for re-recruitment of these child soldier victims of genocidal forcible transfer).

There was then, on the view here, an under-inclusive categorization of rape victims considered by the ICC Prosecutor in the Darfur situation. For instance, rape as a crime against humanity was charged in *Al Bashir* in regards to women and girl members of the Fur, Masalit and Zaghawa communities attacked and raped in their villages and in IDP camps and taken often as sex slaves but not in respect of (1) the girl soldiers/sex slaves of so-called Arab ethnicity recruited into the ranks of the GoS and allied militias and sexually victimized or (2) women and girls raped in Eastern Chad by Sudanese rebel groups.[43]

Indeed, Al Bashir was not even charged with war crimes in respect to the international crimes of recruiting and using children under 15 for active participation in armed hostilities. This was the case though the ICC Prosecutor in 2009 had launched an investigation into UNICEF's allegations that up to 6,000 child soldiers, some as young as 11, had been recruited by both government and rebel forces in Darfur.[44] In 2009, UNICEF estimated "a total of 8000 child soldiers in Sudan, 6000 in Darfur and the rest in Southern Sudan"[45] At the time of writing, no indictments relating to charges of recruiting and using children under 15 for active participation in the hostilities have been filed by the Prosecutor in *Al Bashir* or, for that matter, in the other cases regarding the Sudan conflict against defendants from the rebel groups.[46] Nor have there been charges filed by the ICC Prosecutor relating to the

---

[42] Coalition to Stop the Use of Child Soldiers (Child Soldier Global Report 2008). This report noted the use of child soldiers by the SAF among other armed parties to the conflict in Darfur during the relevant period.

[43] Note that some girls in Eastern Chad which area had been dragged into the conflict in Sudan in fact joined the 'United Front for the Democratic Change' in the hopes of being protected from Sudanese Zaghawa (rebel) militias. (In 2010, Chad and Sudan ended their conflict that had been carried out by proxy rebel armed groups).

[44] Charbonneau (2009).

[45] Charbonneau (2009).

[46] The Director of ICC Watch in fact in a 2009 letter to the ICC Prosecutor (Mr. Moreno-Ocampo) stated: "It is extraordinary that you have failed to launch and investigation into the horrific activities of JEM (the Justice and Equality Movement; a Sudanese rebel group) in using child

'genocidal forcible transfer of children' (i.e. forcible transfer of children of the targeted ethnic groups of Fur, Masalit and Zaghawa to the so-called Arab group in the symbolic form of the SAF and allied Janjaweed militia to serve as sex slaves or in regards to the transfer of so-called Arab children to pro-government forces).

The ICC Prosecutor commented as follows in regards to the charges against Al Bashir:

> **AL BASHIR**'s conduct simultaneously constitutes genocide against the Fur, Masalit and Zaghawa ethnic groups, as well as crimes against humanity and war crimes against the civilian population in the area, including members of the target groups.[47]

It is here argued that just as these attacks on the Fur; Masalit and Zaghawa constitute genocide as well as other international crimes; so too is this the case with child recruitment and use of the so-called Arab children by Al Bashir forces. Consider, for instance, that the children born of the mass rape of the Fur; Masalit and Zaghawa were/are considered 'children of the enemy':

> ***Babies born as a result of these assaults have been termed "Janjaweed babies" and are rarely accepted as members of the community***. The high number of such unwanted babies has led to an explosion of infanticides and abandonment of babies in Darfur. As one victim explained: "they kill our males and dilute our blood with rape. [They]. . .want to finish us as a people, end our history".[48]

The fact is that just as the Fur; Masalit and Zaghawa children born of rape by Al Bashir armed forces and allied militia fighters are considered 'children of the enemy' so is this the case for child soldiers who fought with the Sudan Armed Forces or the Janjaweed militia and committed atrocity and for their offspring. There is a typical pattern of significant difficulties with re-integration efforts relating to ex child soldiers where these children are known or at least perceived to have committed conflict-related atrocities as members of genocidal forces (and for girl child soldiers who were raped including also those who had children). A significant proportion of their home communities often wish to exclude and punish the children for their commission of grave international crimes if any and erroneously regard the child victims of rape *in effect* as themselves culpable for their own victimization.[49]

Mass rape is now considered under international criminal law as a potential vehicle for genocide when directed to a targeted specific set of victim groups since rape is used to "kill the will, the spirit, and life itself".[50] It is indisputable, at the

---

soldiers and other forces operating in Darfur in using child soldiers given the current prosecution of Thomas Lubanga for precisely this crime" http://www.iccwatch.org/pressrelease_25feb09.html.

[47] Prosecutor v Omar Hassan Ahmad Al Bashir, Public Redacted Version of the Prosecutions' application under Article 58 (2008, ANNEX, p. 8, para 11).

[48] Prosecutor v Omar Hassan Ahmad Al Bashir, Public Redacted Version of the Prosecutions' application under Article 58 (2008, ANNEX, p. 12, para 26, emphasis added).

[49] Parmar et al. (2010).

[50] Prosecutor v Omar Hassan Ahmad Al Bashir, Public Redacted Version of the Prosecutions' application under Article 58 (2008, ANNEX, p. 12, para 28, Citation from ICTR Akayesu case).

same time, that using children (persons under age 18) as child soldiers and/or sex slaves (for active participation in a genocidal armed force committing mass atrocity) is also an effective tool for 'killing the spirit' of the children so recruited and used and that of their home communities.

5.2.5 The Recruitment and Use of Child Soldiers by the GoS During the Time Period Covered by the Al Bashir Case (March 2003 to July 14, 2008)

In a letter dated 1 December 2006 from the Chair of the U.N. Working Group on Children and Armed Conflict to the President of the UN Security Council it was noted that:

> The participants in the discussion [of the UN Working Group on Children and Armed Conflict] expressed their concern regarding violations cited in the report [by the UN Secretary General], such as killing and maiming of children, *their recruitment and use as soldiers by many armed forces and groups*, grave sexual violence, abductions, and denial of humanitarian access, that continued in the Sudan largely unabated. . .[51]

The letter went on to recommend in part that the President of the UN Security Council urge the Sudanese Government of National Unity and the Government of South Sudan:

> . . .take necessary corrective measures throughout the military hierarchy in order to prevent the recruitment and use of child soldiers in violation of applicable international law by the ***Sudanese armed forces, the Sudan Peoples Liberation Army and any armed group under their control and/or aligned with them***.[52]
>
> To take specific action to put an end to the continuous disregard of the Security Council resolutions on children and armed conflict by parties to the armed conflict in the Sudan, ***including the Janjaweed militias*** **[pro-government militias]**, and to fight against impunity. . .[53]

While there has been some progress in securing the release of child soldiers from former rebel groups, the recruitment and use of child soldiers in Sudan and in Darfur persists as the UN Secretary General's 2011 report on the matter attests.[54]

---

[51] De La Sablière, Jean-Marc. Letter dated 1 December 2006 to the President of the UN Security Council.

[52] De La Sablière, Jean-Marc. Letter dated 1 December 2006 to the President of the UN Security Council, emphasis added.

[53] De La Sablière, Jean-Marc. Letter dated 1 December 2006 to the President of the UN Security Council, emphasis added.

[54] UN Secretary-General's report on children and armed conflict in Sudan (5 July, 2011).

5.2.6 Report of the Secretary-General on Children and Armed Conflict in the Sudan (5 July, 2011)

The Secretary-General's report on children and armed conflict in Sudan referred to here covers the period January 2009 to February 2011 (beyond the period relating to the Al Bashir case indictments to date). The executive summary of the report states in part:

> ... ***the report shows the continued presence of children in the Sudanese Armed Forces (SAF), its associated forces, Sudanese police forces,*** the Sudan People's Liberation Army (SPLA), as well as several armed groups in Darfur, and the perpetration of other grave violations against children in the Sudan. ***Of particular concern are the killing and maiming of children, and sexual violence against children.***[55]

With regard to sexual violence against children in Darfur, the UN Secretary General's report noted that:

> Rape cases that are documented are often allegedly committed by men in uniform and attributed to military and police personnel, factions of armed groups and militia members.[56]
> A third of the victims of rape [by Al Bashir forces] are children.[57]

Given: (1) the numbers of children still retained by the SAF and allied militias (among other parties to the conflict in Darfur) as child soldiers in 2011 and (2) the general pattern of the various armed parties to the conflict in Darfur of perpetrating sexual violence against large numbers of civilians; including very young girls; it is highly likely that child soldier members of the Sudanese army and allied militias (as well as child soldier members of the rebel armed groups in Sudan) were also the victims of sexual violence.

The extent of the problem of child soldier recruitment and use by the Government in Northern Sudan[58] may be grossly underestimated in the UN Secretary-General's 2011 report given that:

> Reporting on violations continued to be significantly hampered by insecurity and lack of access to non-Government-controlled areas, as well as by Government restrictions, in particular in Darfur and the transitional areas.[59]

---

[55] UN Secretary-General's report on children and armed conflict in Sudan (Executive Summary) (5 July, 2011) (emphasis added).

[56] UN Secretary-General's report on children and armed conflict in Sudan (5 July, 2011, p. 9 para 36).

[57] Prosecutor v Omar Hassan Ahmad Al Bashir, Public Redacted Version of the Prosecutions' application under Article 58 (2008, ANNEX, p. 10, para 16).

[58] Note that Omar Al-Bashir was elected President of the Republic in 2010 national elections, and Salva Kiir Mayardit was elected President of the Government of Southern Sudan which became an independent State 9 July, 2011.

[59] UN Secretary-General's report on children and armed conflict in Sudan (Executive Summary) (5 July, 2011).

The Secretary-General's 2011 Report listed the following parties[60] (which included the Sudanese Armed Forces and allied pro-government militias) still recruiting and using children for active participation in armed conflict in Sudan during the period covered by his report:

Parties in the Sudan

I. Parties in southern Sudan
Lord's Resistance Army (LRA) *, †, ‡
Sudan People's Liberation Army (SPLA) *

II. Parties in Darfur *

1. Chadian armed opposition groups *
2. Police forces, including the Central Reserve Police and Border Intelligence Forces *
3. Popular Defence Forces *
4. ***Pro-Government militias*** *
5. ***Sudanese Armed Forces*** *
6. **Parties signatories to the Darfur Peace Agreement**:
   a) Justice and Equality Movement (Peace Wing) *
   b) Movement of Popular Force for Rights and Democracy *
   c) Sudan Liberation Army (SLA)/Mother Wing (Abu Gasim) *
   d) Sudan Liberation Army (SLA)/Free Will *
   e) Sudan Liberation Army (SLA)/Minni Minawi *
   f) Sudan Liberation Army (SLA)/Peace Wing *
7. **Parties not signatories to the Darfur Peace Agreement:**
   a) Justice and Equality Movement (JEM) *
   b) Sudan Liberation Army (SLA)/Abdul Wahid *
   c) Sudan Liberation Army (SLA)/Historical Leadership *
   d) Sudan Liberation Army (SLA)/Unity *

Code:
*** Parties that recruit and use children.**
† Parties that kill and maim children.
‡ Parties that commit rape and other forms of sexual violence against children

In the 2011 report of the UN Secretary-General regarding the situation of children affected by the armed conflict in Darfur, the Secretary General had the following to say in regards to the continued recruitment and use of children by the Sudanese Armed Forces and their allied militias:

> ***While SAF does not have a policy of recruiting children, the task force has expressed concern over the continued association of children with the armed force.*** On 23 May 2010 in Khartoum, the task force met with senior SAF officers to discuss the preparation of an action plan to end the association of children with SAF. This action plan will also apply to its proxy groups [i.e. the Janjaweed].[61]

---

[60] Developments in Sudan (Information based on the UN Secretary-General's report on children and armed conflict in Sudan (5 July, 2011)).

[61] UN Secretary-General's report on children and armed conflict in Sudan (Executive Summary) (5 July, 2011, p. 14, para 61, emphasis added).

It seems justified to regard with scepticism the notion advanced by the UN Secretary-General that a national armed force rigidly and hierarchically organized such as the SAF; one that has so long recruited and used children for active participation in armed conflict as has the SAF, does not have a policy supporting such exploitation of children (sexual and non-sexual). It is not at all clear on what basis the Secretary-General would hold that the SAF does not have at a minimum a *de facto* policy of recruiting and using children in armed conflict given: (1) the SAF pattern and practice in this regard and especially (2) the SAF's involving children in the perpetrating of mass atrocity and grave international crimes during the time period relevant to the Al Bashir ICC case (further "...internally displaced peoples interviewed in May 2006 following Sudan government-backed Janjaweed militia attacks on villages near Kartum, northern Darfur, said that many armed child soldiers were amongst those who attacked them and Janjaweed were known to have recruited child soldiers from Sudanese refugee camps in Chad in 2006").[62] Note that the Comprehensive Peace Agreement (CPA) that had been signed in 2005 between the then ruling National Congress Party and the Sudan People's Liberation Movement/Army (SPLA) required that all armed groups join either the Sudan Armed Forces (SAF) or the SPLA by 9 January, 2006.[63] The Sudan Armed Forces conceded that child soldiers were absorbed into the integrated units that were created as per the 2005 CPA and that in 2006 "the SAF estimated that there were approximately 19,000 soldiers in these units and it was thought that a significant number were under 18."[64]

It appears the GoS has discussed with UN representatives an action plan to end recruitment of children by the SAF. Notwithstanding such discussions, however, the UN Secretary General noted in his 2011 report that "steps must ...be taken as a matter of urgency to address the continued presence of children in SAF and its associated forces" and he urged the GoS to "... accelerate its dialogue with the United Nations with a view to developing a concrete time-bound plan, in line with UN Security Council resolution 1612 (2005)".[65] Resolution 1612 states in part that the Security Council:

> *Calls upon* all parties concerned to ensure that the protection, rights and well-being of children affected by armed conflict are specifically integrated into all peace processes, peace agreements and post-conflict recovery and reconstruction planning and programmes;
>
> *Calls upon* all parties concerned to abide by the international obligations applicable to them relating to the protection of children affected by armed conflict as well as the concrete commitments they have made to the Special Representative of the Secretary-General for Children and Armed Conflict, to UNICEF and other United Nations agencies and to cooperate fully with the United Nations peacekeeping missions and United Nations country teams...

---

[62] Child Soldiers Global Report 2008, p. 4.

[63] Child Soldiers Global Report 2008, p. 2.

[64] Child Soldiers Global Report 2008, p. 4.

[65] UN Secretary-General's report on children and armed conflict in Sudan (5 July, 2011, pp. 17–18, para 83).

> *Urges* Member States, United Nations entities, regional and subregional organizations and other parties concerned, to take appropriate measures to control illicit subregional and cross-border activities harmful to children, including . . .abduction of children and their use and recruitment as soldiers as well as other violations and abuses committed against children in situations of armed conflict in violation of applicable international law. . .[66]

Despite the fact that there are reasonable and compelling grounds to believe (based in part on NGO and UN reports and even SAF reports such as the aforementioned) that: (1) there were large numbers of child soldiers in the SAF by at least 2006 and in the Janjaweed and that (2) these children participated in grave international crimes at the behest of SAF and Janjaweed commanders during the time period covered by the Al Bashir case; the ICC Prosecutor did not charge Al Bashir, commander in chief of the SAF, with international crimes relating to the child soldier issue (i.e. the war crimes of recruiting and/or using children under 15 for active participation in hostilities and genocidal forcible transfer of children (persons under 18) to a genocidal armed group to serve as child soldiers/sex slaves or in some other capacity).

In June of 2009 it was reported that the ICC Prosecutor was "looking closely at charges child soldiers have been used by militias [including the Al Bashir government forces and allied Janjaweed militia] in Sudan's conflict-torn western Darfur region."[67] The previous December "the United Nations children fund UNICEF said that up to 6,000 child soldiers, some as young as 11, have been recruited by rebels and government forces in Darfur."[68]

> "We are monitoring the child soldier crimes," ICC chief prosecutor Luis Moreno-Ocampo told Reuters in an interview. "That's a big deal and it's possible that parties to the (Darfur) conflict use child soldiers." Moreno-Ocampo said he had not yet decided whether to press for further indictments in Darfur related to allegations of child soldier recruitment.[69]

In his 2011 report on Darfur to the UN Security Council, there was still no talk by the ICC Prosecutor Moreno-Ocampo of anticipated additional charges against Al Bashir or against Sudanese government allied militia commanders based on the available credible evidence of their recruitment and use of children in their armed forces (the SAF or Janjaweed militia). Further, no ICC charges were anticipated against rebel armed group political and 'military' command leadership for their recruitment and use of child soldiers. This though both the SAF and pro-government militias as well as the rebel belligerents perpetrating mass atrocity engaged large numbers of children in these grave international crimes as child soldiers. Rather, the ICC prosecutor simply reiterated his 2009 pledge to *monitor* the situation (presumably with a view to potentially laying charges at some indeterminate time):

> According to the 5 July [2011] report of the Secretary-General on children and armed conflict in the Sudan, there has been a ***"continued presence of children" in various forces including the SAF, its associated forces, Sudanese police forces and various armed***

---

[66] UN Security Council Resolution 1612 (S/RES/1612) (2005).

[67] Relief Web (2009).

[68] Relief Web (2009).

[69] Relief Web (2009).

> ***movements in Darfur.*** More specifically, between February 2009 and February 2011, 1,041 former child soldiers were registered in Darfur. The Prosecution will continue to ***monitor*** *the alleged use of child soldiers by both governmental forces and armed movements.*[70]

Note that in 2011 Amnesty International reported that large numbers of children were being recruited and used in the hostilities by the Justice and Equality Movement:

> The Justice and Equality Movement (JEM), a Sudanese [rebel] armed group, has been particularly active in recruiting children. Children in refugee camps and in Internally Displaced Persons (IDP) sites in eastern Chad have frequently gone missing and later been found in the ranks of armed groups. JEM recruitment campaigns for fighters continued in refugee camps and IDP sites in eastern Chad in 2010.
>
> Thousands of children are believed to have been involved with these fighting forces.
>
> According to UN figures in 2007, between 7,000 and 10,000 children may have been used as fighters or associated with Chadian and Sudanese armed opposition groups and the Chadian army.[71]

JEM (The Justice and Equality Movement) had signed an agreement with UNICEF in 2010 promising to protect children caught in the armed conflict in Darfur which agreement included a pledge to cease and desist JEM's recruitment and use of children for active participation in hostilities in Darfur and to release to UNICEF all members male and female aged under 18 of the JEM armed group in Eastern Chad and Darfur.[72] Some progress has been made in regards the release of child soldiers from the SPLA (Sudan People's Liberation Army in Southern Sudan; now an independent State) into the custody of UNICEF to enter re-integration programs though many children still remain in the ranks.[73]

Note that as early as 2005 (if not before) there was credible evidence that children were part of rebel armed groups in Sudan:

> *Inquiries made by the Commission indicate that both JEM and SLA have recruited children as soldiers*...These children have been seen in uniforms and carrying weapons in and around the rebel camps. Independent observers confirmed the presence of child soldiers in areas of conflict... the Commission cannot rule out their participation in combat...
>
> In its meetings with leaders of both rebel groups, the Commission did confront them with these allegations. Both groups deny the use of children in armed combat. The SLA leadership does not deny that children are living in some of their camps. However, they deny that these are child soldiers or take any part in armed hostilities. According to them, these children were orphaned as a result of the conflict and the SLA takes care of them. *The Commission does not find this explanation convincing.* As stated above, different sources have confirmed that the children are in uniform and carry weapons. *The Commission, therefore, cannot rule out their engagement in combat.*[74]

---

[70] Moreno-Ocampo, L. (ICC Prosecutor). Fourteenth Report of the ICC Prosecutor to the UN Security Council Pursuant to Resolution 1593 (15 December, 2011, emphasis added).

[71] Amnesty International (2011). 'A Compromised Future: Children recruited by armed forces and groups in Eastern Chad.'

[72] Robert F. Kennedy Centre for Justice and Human Rights (2012). 'Child soldiers JEM Rebels.'

[73] SOS Villages (2012).

[74] UN Commission of Inquiry on Darfur (2005, pp. 106–107, para 415–416, emphasis added).

The fact that no charges have been forthcoming by the ICC Prosecutor against Al Bashir or pro-government militia commanders or against rebel group commanders regarding 'child soldier' recruitment and the use of children for active participation in armed hostilities and none appear to be contemplated inadvertently undermines the perceived gravity of these crimes under international law for the international community.[75] Grave violations of international law must be prosecuted consistently across cases. Yet, there is a lack of consistency in ICC prosecution of international crimes regarding the recruitment and use of children under 15 for active participation in armed conflict (i.e. prosecution of international crimes relating to child soldier recruitment and use in *Lubanga* but not in the Al Bashir case when in fact credible evidence of child soldier recruitment and use by the SAF and allied militia was provided by NGOs, and UNICEF among other NGOs on the ground in Sudan and was available also from other sources). As discussed, both pro-government and rebel groups in Darfur were also responsible for horrendous sexual violence against children during the relevant period; such crimes also constituting, it is here argued, the 'genocidal forcible transfer of children' (such children sexually violated and any offspring that resulted are most often considered outcasts by their home communities). Nevertheless, no charges of the genocidal forcible transfer of children have been brought against any of those most responsible for these grave crimes perpetrated against children that transformed these children into pariahs in their own communities.

5.3 The Interests of Justice and a Judicial Remedy for Child Victims in Darfur

The ICC Prosecutor Moreno-Ocampo indicated, as previously mentioned, that he would continue to "monitor" the situation in Darfur with respect to the presence of child soldiers. This notwithstanding credible UN reports in 2011 regarding the continued presence of child soldiers in the SAF, in pro-government militias, and in rebel militias in the Darfur region. Monitoring the child soldier matter in Darfur is in fact something that the ICC OTP claims it has been doing also for the 2 years prior to 2011 but yet no perpetrating of child soldiering charges are pending.[76] Note that the ICC Prosecutor Moreno-Ocampo has been criticized for a lack of *on-site investigations* in Darfur which fact he justified at the time with reference to the ongoing conflict and concerns for victim safety.[77] It is however vital, on the view

[75] Recall that in 2005 the UN Commission of Inquiry on Darfur reported that: "There are also allegations of the use of child soldiers by the rebels. However, it should be noted that the number of reported violations allegedly committed by the Government forces and the Janjaweed by far exceeds the number of cases reported on rebels." (p. 55, para 190).

[76] Moreno-Ocampo, L. (ICC Prosecutor). Fourteenth Report of the ICC Prosecutor to the UN Security Council Pursuant to Resolution 1593 (15 December, 2011).

[77] Flint and de Waal (2009).

here, that additional charges against Al Bashir and any co-perpetrators be advanced based on the abundance of available credible evidence which exists regarding: (1) the recruitment and use of children under 15 for active participation in armed hostilities by the SAF and allied militia (conduct constituting war crimes) and (2) the use by the SAF and allied militia of children as child soldiers to perpetrate mass atrocities and genocide and the use of child sex slaves (conduct constituting the genocidal forcible transfer of children). The same charges appear justified against various rebel group commanders leading diverse armed groups in the Darfur conflict (i.e. SPLA and the JEM) during the relevant time period. It remains to be seen whether the new ICC Prosecutor Ms. Fatou B. Bensouda will pursue child soldiering related charges or any other additional charges (such as charges pertaining to sexual violence against child soldiers by their compatriots) in existing and/or new cases arising from the situation in Darfur.

It is here contended that not to investigate as best the OTP can (given the constraints posed by the security situation in Darfur) the UN allegations regarding the recruitment and use of child soldiers in Darfur during the time period covered by the Al Bashir case (and the continued alleged presence of child soldiers in the SAF, Janjaweed and in rebel armed groups in Darfur) is contrary to the interests of justice. Further, the fact that: (1) the SAF and certain rebel groups have indicated they are willing to release child soldiers from their ranks (a promise not yet fully met by the rebels while the SAF has yet to finalize a concrete action plan with UNICEF in this regard) and that (2) the SAF and various pro and anti-government armed groups have suggested they will no longer recruit or engage child soldiers in combat should *not* confer immunity on those most responsible in the first instance for: (1) the children's recruitment and use for active participation in armed conflict and (2) the use of the children to perpetrate mass atrocities and, in respect of the SAF and pro-government militia, the use of so-called child soldiers to contribute to genocide directed at targeted ethnic groups (nor should there be immunity for ongoing international crimes perpetrated against children in this regard in the region).

Since the use of child soldiers to perpetrate mass atrocities and genocide is, on the analysis here, itself a form of genocide (the 'genocidal forcible transfer of children') as explained, it is imperative that the ICC Prosecutor prosecute the recruitment and use of child soldiers (*persons under 18)* in armed conflict in genocidal contexts such as Darfur (in addition to prosecuting for war crimes those most responsible for the recruitment and use of *under 15s* for active participation in armed conflict). Anything less would not be consistent with the UN Guidelines that require prosecutors to "protect human dignity and uphold human rights"[78] (which would include, of course, protecting the human dignity and rights also of children 15 and over caught up in armed conflict). There is no indication that those most responsible for the recruitment and use of child soldiers in the conflict either in the north or south of Sudan are being investigated or prosecuted domestically. This is not surprising in that the government

[78] Amnesty International (2005, p. 5).

in the North (the Al Bashir regime) relies on the SAF and allied militia (i.e. Janjaweed) while the new government in the South has the SPLA as its national army. In each case the governments are relying on forces and armed groups known to have recruited and used children in combat and which still have large numbers of children in their ranks. Given the ongoing insecurity in the region; particularly but not exclusively in the border between North and South Sudan, and the instability of both governments (one a fledging institution in a new independent State); the respective governments appear reticent to prosecute high ranking military commanders from forces and armed groups upon which they heavily rely for such security as is present in the region. It is imperative therefore that the ICC Prosecutor hold the perpetrators most responsible to account for their grave victimization of children in Darfur.

5.4 The Standard of Proof in Regards to Establishing the Offence of Genocide in Its Various Forms

5.4.1 The Struggle to Confirm Genocide Charges in the Al Bashir Case

It will be recalled that ICC Pre-Trial Chamber 1 originally confirmed only the charges against Al Bashir relating to 'war crimes' and 'crimes against humanity' but not the three counts of 'genocide' the ICC Prosecutor had advanced. The majority of the Pre-Trial Chamber had held that the test (standard of proof) was that the *only* reasonable inference to be drawn from the evidence be that of genocide as opposed to there simply being "reasonable grounds to believe" that genocide had occurred. As the Pre-Trial Chamber held that the Prosecutor had not evinced evidence that would show that genocide was the *only* reasonable inference to be drawn; the Chamber declined to confirm the genocide charges.[79] The Prosecutor endorsed the view of the dissenting judge of the *Al Bashir* Pre-Trial Chamber and, in part, argued that view before the ICC Appeal Chamber:

> But, as observed by Judge Usacka in her dissenting opinion, if the *only* reasonable inference available is that the suspect intended to commit genocide, then the mental element has been effectively proved beyond a reasonable doubt. *Thus, the Majority in fact applied a standard of beyond reasonable doubt, instead of the appropriate standard of 'reasonable grounds to believe' that is applicable to the assessment of warrant applications.*[80]

[79] *Prosecutor v Omar Hassan Ahmad Al Bashir*, Prosecution's Application for Leave to Appeal the "Decision on the Prosecution's Application for a Warrant of Arrest against Omar Hassan Ahmad Al Bashir", (2009, p. 4, para 13).

[80] *Prosecutor v Omar Hassan Ahmad Al Bashir*, Prosecution's Application for Leave to Appeal the "Decision on the Prosecution's Application for a Warrant of Arrest against Omar Hassan Ahmad Al Bashir" (2009, p. 5, para 15, emphasis added).

The Prosecutor also argued before the ICC Appeal Court that the Pre-Trial Chamber, while not finding Al Bashir criminally responsible for genocide, had yet established/entered all the factual findings which supported the reasonable inference that Al Bashir possessed the specific intent to commit genocide and that he had carried out acts to that end using the State's apparatus.[81]

5.5 The Standard of Proof in Regards to Establishing the Offence of the Genocidal Forcible Transfer of Children (Warrant Stage)

Genocidal intent is evidenced in regards to the recruitment and use of children by the GoS and its allied militias in that the intention was that the child soldiers participate in perpetrating mass atrocity and genocide and such participation of the children did in fact occur. This then would lead, as previously discussed, inevitably to enormous mental suffering for these child soldiers[82] and the likelihood of great difficulty in a post-conflict period in re-integrating if they did so at all into the home community. The end result then is an indefinite forcible transfer to the genocidal GoS and allied militia forces due to the perception of the community and the children themselves that they are 'children of the enemy'[83] and in many instances also through re-recruitment of children who were not accepted back into their home communities. On the view here then genocide can also be perpetrated by members of one's own ethnic, national, religious or so-called racial group by those belonging, for instance, to an armed force or group (adult members of the GoS and Janjaweed) against other members of the same 'protected group' (defined along the dimensions set out in the Genocide Convention)[84] i.e. so-called 'Arab' children targeted for genocidal forcible transfer to the SAF or Janjaweed via their recruitment and active participation in perpetrating mass atrocity and genocide. The current author holds then that genocide cannot be reduced in all cases to "extreme racism" that is directed to only those the perpetrators consider the inferior 'other' contrary to what has been argued by some scholars:

---

[81] Prosecutor v Omar Hassan Ahmad Al Bashir, Prosecution Document in Support of Appeal against the "Decision on the Prosecution's Application for a Warrant of Arrest against Omar Hassan Ahmad Al Bashir" (2009, p. 7, para 18).

[82] This point is not intended in any way to downplay or disregard the unspeakable mental and physical suffering of the civilian victims these so-called child soldiers were commanded to target belonging to particular ethnic groups.

[83] The GoS forces and allied militia have the same ethnicity as the child soldiers of the GoS and Janjaweed but are regarded as tainted and a potential threat to the security of their own communities and in that sense too are 'children of the enemy'.

[84] Genocide Convention (1951).

> …genocide is more akin to extreme racism than extreme conflict – it is organised, *one-sided violence* on a massive scale, and civilians, not combatants, are the prime target.[85]

It is here argued that the so-called 'Arab' children recruited and used by the genocidal forces of Al Bashir to participate actively in the armed hostilities (whether recruited and used by the Sudan Armed Forces or by the Sudanese government proxy armed group; the Janjaweed militia) are a protected child civilian group. There was then a two-sided element to the violence perpetrated by the Al Bashir *genocidaires* against children; in particular involving the targeting of *both* 'Arab' and 'non-Arab' child victims. On the analysis here, such violence constitutes also the genocidal forcible transfer of the children who are of the same ethnicity as the perpetrator group but who were nonetheless targeted with genocidal intent (i.e. knowing what a devastating effect appropriation of these children as child soldiers would have on the viability of the so-called Arab peoples of the Darfur region). At the same time, the perpetrator group of *genocidaires* targeted the children of the perceived 'African' groups in Darfur (mostly Fur, Masaalit and Zaghawa) for other forms of genocidal forcible transfer; for example:

> Various sources reported widespread rape and other serious forms of violence committed against women and girls in all three states of Darfur.[86]
>
> women and girls were abducted, held in confinement for several days and repeatedly raped during that time.. rape and other forms of sexual violence continued during flight and further displacement… ***Some women and girls became pregnant as a result of rape***.[87]
>
> In March 2004, Janjaweed and 150 soldiers reportedly abducted and raped 16 young girls in Kutum, North Darfur. … The Commission's findings confirmed the above reported pattern. … During the attack on Mallaga village, West Darfur, in October 2004, the
>
> Janjaweed abducted four girls, one of them only twelve years old. The girls were held for three days, raped and then released.[88]
>
> The Commission interviewed several eyewitnesses who confirmed that following the joint attacks by Government soldiers and Janjaweed in the area, up to 30,000 people were confined in Kailek, South Darfur, for about 50 days. Women and children were separated from the men, confined in an area around the Mosque, and later taken away by their captors to be raped. *They were subjected to gang rapes which lasted for protracted periods of time.* ***Girls as young as 10 years old were raped***.[89]
>
> In one instance, the Commission interviewed two young girls, 12 and 14 years old, who had gone to collect wood with another five children in November 2004 outside the Abu [IDP] Shouk camp. The soldiers raped the two girls, called the children daughters and sons of "Tora Bora," beat the other children and threatened to kill them.[90]
>
> ***It is apparent from the information collected and verified by the Commission that rape or other forms of sexual violence committed by the Janjaweed and Government soldiers in Darfur was widespread and systematic and may thus well amount to a crime against***

[85] Smith and Walker (2004).

[86] UN Commission of Inquiry on Darfur (2005, p. 87, para 333).

[87] UN Commission of Inquiry on Darfur (2005, p. 87, para 334, emphasis added).

[88] UN Commission of Inquiry on Darfur (2005, p. 89, para 341–342).

[89] UN Commission of Inquiry on Darfur (2005, p. 90, para 343, emphasis added).

[90] UN Commission of Inquiry on Darfur (2005, p. 92, para 348).

> ***humanity [on the analysis here also 'genocidal forcible transfer of children' where children were the amongst the prime targets***].[91]

It is here argued that intentionally and systematically involving children in perpetrating mass atrocity and/or genocide (recruiting them for this purpose) is a marker for genocidal intent; specifically the intent to perpetrate the 'genocidal forcible transfer of children' to a murderous armed entity that stands outside of regular society. Genocidal intent, on the view here, is in fact arguably the only reasonable inference to be drawn from the evidence of child soldier recruitment and the pattern of use by pro-government forces and militias under Al Bashir. This is the case since the outcome for these children in terms of being forever perceived as children of the enemy (i.e. the enemy of Sudan in fuelling ethnic hatred and genocide) is entirely foreseeable given what on the view here and that of the ICC Pre-Trial Chamber was/is Al Bashir's genocidal campaign.[92] Thus, this singular reasonable inference (the presence of genocidal intent) to be drawn on the evidence, if accepted as such, would meet a standard of proof beyond a reasonable doubt to believe that the 'genocidal forcible transfer of children' to the SAF and allied militias had occurred (this then in addition to the counts of genocide so far charged in *Al Bashir*).

The SAF and Janjaweed to date have failed to release all child soldiers from their ranks. Instead, they hold these children enslaved to continue to participate in the continued violence and grave human rights abuses perpetrated against civilians in remaining conflict zones such as Abyei (and to risk their own life and limb fighting SPLA-North rebels and other opposition). Al Bashir's regime thus, on the view here, continues to perpetrate the genocidal forcible transfer of children to an armed force and allied militia engaged in systematic mass atrocities (even post establishment of South Sudan as an independent State).[93] In this regard note also that the Sudanese Armed Forces and pro GoS militias in Darfur were again listed as 'persistent violators' on the U.N. Secretary-General's most recent annual report on children and armed conflict (26 April, 2012) in terms of recruiting and using children in armed conflict.[94] So too a number of opposition armed groups in Sudan were listed in the U.N. Secretary-General's 2012 annual report on children and armed conflict in relation to their recruitment and use of children in hostilities and a number of these as persistent violations of children's rights in this regard (i.e. JEM and various factions of the SLA) thus evidencing the GoS failure to protect children in this regard also. In addition, verified 2011 incidents of rape in Sudan (Darfur) perpetrated on

---

[91] UN Commission of Inquiry on Darfur (2005, p. 95, para 360, emphasis added).

[92] Prosecutor v Al Bashir Second warrant of arrest for Al Bashir (Pre-Trial Chamber I) (12 July, 2010).

[93] Currently, UNICEF estimates there are 2000 child soldiers in South Sudan associated with militias that are being integrated into the national army of South Sudan (SPLA) (InterPress Service 15 April, 2012).

[94] U.N. Secretary-General's annual report on children and armed conflict (26 April, 2012, Annex I, p. 50).

girls ranging in age from 6–17 were also reported in the U.N. Secretary-General's 2012 annual report on children and armed conflict with perpetrators including, amongst others, SAF and pro-government militia members.[95]

5.6 On Identifying Genocide in Darfur

The ICC Prosecutor at the warrant stage in the Al Bashir case had *not* tried to argue before the Pre-Trial Chamber that the evidence regarding genocidal intent rendered the latter the *only* reasonable inference (a 'beyond a reasonable doubt' standard that is *not* required at the warrant stage). While the Prosecutor's strategy at the warrant stage was entirely appropriate; it is disconcerting, to say the least, that the Pre-Trial Chamber would contend that genocidal intent may not have been the only reasonable inference to draw concerning evidence which included but was not limited to: (1) Al Bashir's denial of humanitarian assistance to members of the targeted Sudanese victim groups who managed to reach IDP camps, and (2) the heinous war crimes and crimes against humanity perpetrated by the SAF and allied militias i.e. forcible transfer of large numbers of civilians into "the most inhospitable terrain . . . at times combined with the destruction of basic means of survival, such that death of a significant number was all but inevitable" (thus at times also amounting to genocide).[96]

Note that the genocide[97] in Darfur can in general be considered an autogenocide since the perceived *ethnic* differences between the "Arab" *genocidaires* and so-called "African" victim groups in Darfur are largely, if not entirely, arbitrary and subjective distinctions. Consider in regards to the latter point the historical context of the arbitrary distinctions referred to between so-called "Arabs" and "Africans" in Darfur:

> *The racialization of identities in Darfur has its roots in the British colonial period.* As early as the late 1920s, the British tried to organize two confederations in Darfur: one "Arab" the other "Zurga" or black. Racialized identities were incorporated in the census and provided the frame for government policy and administration.[98]

The scholarly controversy about whether the situation in Darfur constitutes genocide (a matter now settled in the affirmative as far as the ICC is concerned at least at the Pre-Trial stage) is largely related to the subjective nature of the alleged ethnic distinctions between the perpetrator and victim groups in Darfur:

---

[95] U.N. Secretary-General's annual report on children and armed conflict (26 April, 2012, p. 21, para 111).

[96] Prosecutor v Omar Hassan Ahmad Al Bashir, Prosecution Document in Support of Appeal against the "Decision on the Prosecution's Application for a Warrant of Arrest against Omar Hassan Ahmad Al Bashir" (2009, p. 13, para 35).

[97] That genocide occurred in Darfur is the view of the current author and, for instance, the ICC Prosecutor and the Pre-Trial Chamber in the Al Bashir case though there are no doubt some who would still argue the matter.

[98] Mamdanai (2009, p. 86, emphasis added).

> The central issue around which most of the controversy hangs is whether the evidence establishes 'reasonable grounds' on which to believe that Al Bashir intended to destroy, in part, national, ethnical, racial or religious groups as such in Darfur. *Related to this is the threshold issue of whether there are reasonable grounds to believe that the three tribes targeted in Darfur each constitute '... a national, ethnical, racial or religious group, as such'.*[99]

The ICC Prosecutor in *Al Bashir* importantly noted that there is no universal accepted definition of 'ethnic group' but that in the context of Darfur; the Fur, Masalit and Zaghawa could nonetheless be considered on the analysis of the OTP as ethnic groups distinct from the perpetrator so-called Arab group in Darfur:

> The Fur, Masalit and Zaghawa each constitute an ethnic group within the meaning of Art. 6. ***In the absence of a generally accepted definition of an ethnic group, an assessment must be made on a case by case basis,*** taking into account both objective and subjective criteria, in light of the particular political, social, historical and cultural context.[100]

The Prosecutor in Al Bashir argued that the objective markers of distinct ethnicity in respect of Fur, Masalit and Zaghawa were the fact that: (1) they each speak a different dialect of Arabic and (2) the distinct land areas each group occupies.[101] The subjective markers he held were the self-perceptions of the group members and their identification as distinct groups by the diverse and numerous other perceived 'ethnic' groups (tribes) in Darfur.[102] At the same time, it is noteworthy that the ICC Prosecutor conceded that "Zaghawa culture is closer to the Arabs than to the Fur and the Masalit."[103] The ICC Prosecutor also acknowledged that ethnic distinctions between attackers and attacked in Darfur based on traditional means of subsistence of the various groups (tribes) were also not entirely consistent i.e. "The Prosecutor acknowledges ... that both the Zaghawa and Arabs engage in similar farming practices."[104]

The vagueness of the notion of 'protected group' as incorporated in the Genocide Convention[105] is reflected in the fuzzy definition assigned by the ICTR in *Kayishema and Ruzindana* to 'ethnic group' as a protected group:

> An ethnic group is one whose members share a common language and culture; ***or***, a group which distinguishes itself, as such (self-identification); ***or*** a group identified by others, including perpetrators of the crimes (identification by others).'[106]

---

[99] Cayley (2008, p. 830, emphasis added).

[100] Prosecutor v Omar Hassan Ahmad Al Bashir, Public Redacted Version of the Prosecutions' application under Article 58 (2008, ANNEX p. 26, para 77).

[101] Prosecutor v Omar Hassan Ahmad Al Bashir, Public Redacted Version of the Prosecutions' application under Article 58 (2008, ANNEX p. 27, para 83).

[102] Prosecutor v Omar Hassan Ahmad Al Bashir, Public Redacted Version of the Prosecutions' application under Article 58 (2008, ANNEX p. 27, para 84).

[103] Prosecutor v Omar Hassan Ahmad Al Bashir, Public Redacted Version of the Prosecutions' application under Article 58 (2008, ANNEX p. 27, para 81).

[104] Cayley (2008, p. 832).

[105] Genocide Convention (1951).

[106] Kayishema and Ruzindana (ICTR-95-1-T), Trial Chamber Judgment, 21 May 1999, para 98, emphasis added.

It is here argued that there are insurmountable problems with the *restrictive interpretation* of 'protected group' generally adopted in regards to Article 6 of the Rome Statute[107] (where protected group is restricted to a national, ethnic, religious or racial group). The problems with the foregoing restrictive interpretation include but are not limited to the fact that: (1) there is no accepted universal definition of 'ethnic group' (i.e. Are the Fur, Masalit and Zaghawa different 'tribes' or different 'ethnic groups or are these terms equivalent for legal purposes in considering ethnic groups as protected groups?). Subjective perceptions of 'ethnicity' may not always accord with any objective grounds for distinguishing different groups as ethnically different; (2) the concept of 'race' no longer has scientific, logical or philosophical legitimacy, (3) what constitutes a 'religion' as opposed to a cult is arguable in at least some instances. In addition, so-called different religions may be arbitrarily distinguished according to certain differences that do not in fact negate their fundamentally shared roots, tenants and world view making it difficult if not impossible to draw bright lines between the two in any useful way for certain purposes; (4) in respect of 'nationality'; what of persecution and conduct with genocidal intent directed against the de facto or *de jure* stateless (targeted on the basis of being perceived as "outsiders" despite having lived in a region over many centuries). Furthermore, one's religious and national group may change as may other's perception of one's ethnicity or even one's own self-identified ethnicity such that not all the protected groups listed in the Genocide Convention[108] may be considered as stable. Hence, stability of group membership may not necessarily be one among other defining characteristics of a protected group under the Genocide Convention.[109]

Given that: (1) the definition of 'protected group' is so ambiguous but that nevertheless the Genocide Convention is part of international customary law[110] and (2) most importantly; the fact that the prohibition against genocide is a *jus cogens* norm,[111] it is apparent, on the analysis here, that all distinguishable groups targeted for annihilation in part or in whole as a group (carried out by direct or indirect means *as per the modes of genocide listed in Article 2 of the Genocide Convention*) must be considered to fit the criteria for 'protected group' under the Genocide Convention.[112] In fact, it is here suggested that, from an international law perspective, what groups in actuality meet the criteria for 'protected groups' in any particular case/situation cannot be determined *a priori*. Rather, the protected groups are defined/created using one or both of the following: (1) *arbitrarily selected objective criteria* i.e. the Fur, Masalit and Zaghawa *emerge* as 'protected groups' as per the Genocide Convention[113] based on the objective criteria of the lands in the

[107] Rome Statute (2002).

[108] Genocide Convention (1951).

[109] Genocide Convention (1951).

[110] Kayishema and Ruzindana (ICTR-95-1-T), Trial Chamber Judgment, 21 May 1999, para 88.

[111] Kayishema and Ruzindana (ICTR-95-1-T), Trial Chamber Judgment, 21 May 1999, para 88.

[112] Genocide Convention (1951).

[113] Genocide Convention (1951).

region they traditionally have occupied, the manner in which these peoples have traditionally made their livelihood; the Arabic dialect each group speaks (where each dialect arguably may or may not be considered a different language or simply a variant on the same language) and/or (2) *subjective criteria* (self-identification of the targeted group as a distinct group distinguishable from others along some dimension and/or the perceptions of the perpetrator group). The current author thus finds it irrelevant whether the *genocidaire's* arbitrarily selected criteria for defining the targeted victim group (i.e. *perceived* ethnicity etc.) has a basis in reality or not; a view that seems to differ from that implicitly expressed in the quote that follows:

> It is the genocidaire who usually determines the victim's status as a member of a particular ethnic group. Examining evidence of the mindset of the perpetrator not only helps to determine his view of the status of the victim, but also is valuable in establishing genocidal intent. ***Difficulties arise****, however, where a perpetrator believes that a group of people constitutes an ethnic group whereas in fact no objective existence of that group supports this belief.*[114]

The current author is in accord with the ICC Prosecutor's proposition in *Al Bashir* that what constitutes an 'ethnic group' must be decided on a case-by-case basis looking at various contextual factors and would extend this approach to assessing what constitutes a 'protected group' in general. Genocide afterall is fundamentally irrational; ultimately counterproductive for peoples residing in any particular region and for humanity as a whole. Definitions of 'protected group' thus cannot easily be generalized and must take account of the realities on the ground in any particular case.

It is here contended then that where the notion of 'protected group' is so restrictively interpreted as to preclude a charge of genocide where any identifiable group has been targeted for annihilation in whole or in part by any means identified in the Genocide Convention,[115] an injustice inconsistent with the spirit and intent of the Genocide Convention[116] is the result. Indeed, the Genocide Convention[117] anticipates controversy in the interpretation of its terms and Convention application. Thus, there is no definitive interpretation/definition that can be assigned to the notion of 'protected group' in any abstract; out-of-context fashion by virtue of the (ambiguous) Genocide Convention[118] text. Rather, in practice, the interpretation of 'protected group' as per the Genocide Convention[119] is and must be made, it is here argued, in context and on a case-by-case basis. Indeed, controversies in interpretation were contemplated by the drafters given Article 9 of the Genocide Convention which states:

[114] Cayley (2008, p. 831, emphasis added).

[115] Genocide Convention (1951).

[116] Genocide Convention (1951).

[117] Genocide Convention (1951).

[118] Genocide Convention (1951).

[119] Genocide Convention (1951).

> *Disputes between the Contracting Parties relating to the interpretation…of the present Convention*, including those relating to the responsibility of a State for genocide or any of the other acts enumerated in Article 3, shall be submitted to the International Court of Justice at the request of any of the parties to the dispute.[120]

Note that the International Commission of Inquiry on Darfur held that no genocidal common plan had been pursued by Al Bashir and his co-perpetrators while the ICC Pre-Trial judgment in *Al Bashir* reflects an opposite conclusion on the same evidence. Further, the International Commission of Inquiry on Darfur challenged the notion of ethnic difference in the Darfur situation relevant to the question of genocide:

> The International Commission of Inquiry on Darfur ('UNCOI'), the UN body charged with establishing 'facts relating to possible violations of international humanitarian law and human rights law in Darfur', concluded that no objective basis existed for distinguishing between members of the three targeted tribes and their attackers.[121]

However, not even such an august body as the International Commission of Inquiry on Darfur[122] can define away the fact that certain victim groups were perceived as distinct by the Al Bashir perpetrator group in Darfur and specifically targeted for annihilation in whole or in part *en masse* based on those perceived distinguishing characteristics. In short, the reality of genocide on the ground including autogenocide (i.e. autogenocide having occurred on the view here in Darfur) cannot be defined away. Thus, we cannot alleviate our responsibility collectively for preventing genocide in the first instance nor potentially diminish the perceived gravity of the crimes perpetrated by classifying them as non-genocidal based on overly restrictive interpretations. Clearly the International Commission of Inquiry on Darfur had concerns in regards to the latter point given that it included the following cautionary note in its report:

> The conclusion that no genocidal policy has been pursued and implemented in Darfur by the Government authorities, directly or through the militias under their control, should not be taken in any way as detracting from the gravity of the crimes perpetrated in that region. International offences such as the crimes against humanity and war crimes that have been committed in Darfur may be no less serious and heinous than genocide.[123]

The International Commission of Inquiry on Darfur, it should be noted, also reported that attacks on targeted villages by Al Bashir forces and allied militia were most often accompanied by statements (statements that would, on the analysis here, suggest genocidal intent and a combination of motives relating to a desire in part to appropriate the land and means of livelihood of the targeted victim groups):

> Other witnesses referred to statements made by their aggressors during some of the attacks, such as 'you are *Tora Bora*, the SLA are your families', ***'the Fur are slaves,* we *will kill them', 'we are here to eradicate blacks (nuba)'***, 'we will drive you into poverty', 'this is not your land' or 'you are not from here'.[124]

---

[120] Genocide Convention (1951).

[121] Cayley (2008, p. 831).

[122] International Commission of Inquiry on Darfur to the UN Secretary-General (25 January, 2005).

[123] International Commission of Inquiry on Darfur (2005, p. 4).

[124] International Commission of Inquiry on Darfur (2005, p. 65, para 245).

It is the case that neither the ICC Prosecutor nor the International Commission of Inquiry on Darfur recognized or acknowledged the occurrence of the genocidal forcible transfer of thousands of children which had in fact taken place in Darfur over a number of years including during the time period covered in the Al Bashir case. That genocidal forcible transfer of children had been carried out by the SAF and allied militias as well as by various rebel armed groups. This genocidal forcible transfer of children in Darfur was accomplished by means of various modalities including but not limited to: (1) recruiting and using the children as so-called child soldiers to perpetrate systematic mass atrocity and, in regards to some forces (i.e. the SAF and Janjaweed) arguably also genocide and (2) sexual victimization of the children (child soldiers and other child targets).

5.7 The Genocidal Forcible Transfer of Children in Darfur

It is here argued that genocidal intent; specifically the intent to commit the crime of 'genocidal forcible transfer of children' is the *only* reasonable inference based on evidence pertaining to: (1) *the mass rape of children*[125] (mostly female some as young as five of the Fur, Masalit and Zaghawa groups as well as in the Darfur situation the rape of the so-called female Arab children targeted and recruited as child soldiers); (2) *the children born of these mass rapes* who are also stigmatized as children 'of the group perpetrating mass atrocity and genocide' and generally rejected by the home communities and often by the immediate family; (3) *the recruitment and use of children to carry out mass atrocities and genocide* (where the genocidal forcible transfer is to a genocidal group perceived as separate and distinct from mainstream civilized society and comprised of various elements: Al Bashir crony politicians, the SAF, the Janjaweed militia, the Sudanese police under Al Bashir control to mention a few[126]) and (4) *forcible displacement of children*: (a) forcible displacement of the Fur, Masalit (and Zaghawa child groups from their home territories and communities while under the effective control of the Al Bashir forces or militia and use of these children as sex slaves and (b) forcible displacement of "Arab" child soldier recruits taken from their home communities and territories to fight in some distant hot conflict zone within Darfur with pro-Al Bashir forces or militia. In all the aforementioned cases the child victims were separated and alienated from their families and communities and rendered victims of genocidal forcible transfer to the perpetrator self-defined so-called 'Arab' group.

[125] The International Commission of Inquiry on Darfur (2005) reported witness accounts of the attack on, for instance, the Fur village of Adwa by pro-government forces on 23 November, 2004. Witnesses alleged that: "Young girls were taken by the attackers to another location and many were raped in the presence of other women."(p. 69, para 253).

[126] Recall that such genocidal forcible transfer of 'child soldier 'recruits has also occurred in respect of children transferred to anti Al Bashir rebel groups to be used to help perpetrate mass atrocities.

The so-called 'Arab' children recruited and used as child soldiers by Al Bashir forces or the allied militia (Janjaweed), regardless the initial alleged mode of recruitment, also can be properly considered to have been the victims of genocidal forcible transfer. This in that they were/are not free to leave the Al Bashir forces and allied militias and were taken from their home territory and communities to serve in the armed conflict wherever commanded and used to perpetrate atrocity and arguably also genocide. The fact that the so-called Arab children so 'recruited' to the Al Bashir forces share the same *perceived* ethnicity (one arbitrarily distinguished as different from the so-called 'African' tribes of Darfur) as those responsible for their forcible transfer does not, on the analysis here, negate the reality of the children's genocidal forcible transfer (In Darfur, on the analysis here, the situation equates to an autogenocide perpetrated by Al Bashir SAF forces and allied militia using a variety of genocidal means covered under Rome Statute Article 6[127]).

The International Commission of Inquiry on Darfur had concluded in part the following in regards to the issue of genocidal intent by the Al Bashir forces and allied militia:

> The extensive destruction and displacement have resulted in a loss of livelihood and *means of survival* for countless women, men *and children*... The vast majority of the victims of all of these violations have been from the Fur, Zaghawa, Massalit, Jebel, Aranga and other so-called 'African' tribes.[128]
>
> The Commission concluded that the Government of the Sudan has not pursued a policy of genocide...Generally speaking the policy of attacking, killing and forcibly displacing members of some tribes does not evince a specific intent to annihilate, in whole or in part, a group distinguished on racial, ethnic, national or religious grounds. Rather, it would seem that those who planned and organized attacks on villages pursued the intent to drive the victims from their homes, primarily for purposes of *counter-insurgency warfare*.[129]

The argument here is, in contrast, that: (1) all of the aforementioned grave violations of children's basic human rights amount to the genocidal forcible transfer of children and (2) that Al Bashir was *not* acting as a rogue individual within the regime expressing his own idiosyncratic genocidal intent but rather acting in his official capacity as President and Commander-in-Chief and with the cooperation and complicity of key others in his political and military leadership and commanders in the allied militia to implement an agreed upon State common plan of perpetrating genocide and crimes against humanity and war crimes against the targeted groups (Note that the International Commission of Inquiry on Darfur had taken the position that in some cases *individuals* including government officials may be found to have acted with genocidal intent though the Commission did not make any such determination in respect of Darfur as such a matter must be determined on a case by case basis by the Courts).[130]

---

[127] Rome Statute (2002).

[128] International Commission of Inquiry on Darfur (2005, p. 3).

[129] International Commission of Inquiry on Darfur (2005, p. 4).

[130] International Commission of Inquiry on Darfur (2005, p. 4).

On the view here then the genocidal forcible transfer of children in Darfur by the Al Bashir group was accomplished in a variety of ways including through the mass rape of the children; forcible displacement of the children from villages identified as those belonging to perceived '*African' Darfurians*[131] with the children often to be used as sex slaves and by way of 'Arab' children being recruited as child soldiers to the SAF and Janjaweed. In each case the perpetrators knew at the outset the devastating impact these acts would have on the children's group of origin and on the child group itself. Such a genocidal forcible transfer of the children as, on the view here, occurred in Darfur amounts to destroying their groups of origin in whole or in part whether those groups of origin are of the same or a different perceived ethnicity as the perpetrator's group (i.e. the group of origin loses reproductive capacity, and incurs great mental suffering from the loss of the children transferred to the perpetrator group etc.).

The children (so-called Arab children) forcibly transferred as child soldiers to the murderous and genocidal armed force or group suffer physically, and psychologically as a result of their separation from family and home communities, gruelling training and involvement in perpetrating atrocity against targeted civilians etc. Further, children of all ages in Darfur, including the very young and those children lacking the physical and/or psychological capability to participate in a so-called counter-insurgency (due to age and/or a combination of factors) were amongst the victims of the genocidal forcible transfer of children (including via rape, forcible displacement and use as child soldiers). In each case children of perceived ethnic groups were targeted by Al Bashir forces and pro-government militia (i.e. so-called Arab children for child soldiering and purportedly non-Arab children in the main used as sex slaves though undoubtedly the girl soldiers were also sexually victimized to some extent given what we know of patterns in armed forces or groups that use child soldiers and engage in perpetrating systematic widespread grave international crimes). The latter fact and the heinous injuries inflicted in particular on masses of children by the Al Bashir perpetrator group indicate, on the analysis here, that (contrary to the claims of the International Commission of Inquiry on Darfur) the activities of the Al Bashir SAF and allied militias (in regards to children but not exclusively in regards to children) cannot be reduced to a counter-insurgency effort without genocidal intent. In any case in launching any alleged counter-insurgency the Al Bashir government of Sudan had the obligation under the Additional Protocol II to the Geneva Conventions; Article 4(3)(e) to evacuate children to a safe location. That Article states the following:

> (e) measures shall be taken, if necessary, and whenever possible with the consent of their parents or persons who by law or custom are primarily responsible for their care, to ***remove children temporarily from the area in which hostilities are taking place to a safer area within the country*** and ensure that they are accompanied by persons responsible for their safety and well-being.[132]

[131] International Commission of Inquiry on Darfur (2005, pp. 55–56, para 192).

[132] Additional Protocol II to the Geneva Conventions (1977, emphasis added).

Instead of doing everything feasible and necessary to ensure the safety of children (i.e. evacuating the children along with other civilians before attacking rebels thought to be located in villages), the Al Bashir SAF and allied militia made children of all ages, even the very young, prize targets for various grave human rights violations as defined under international humanitarian law. This is, on the analysis here, one indicia of genocidal intent especially when combined with the fact that attacks on villages by the Al Bashir forces and allied militia (even putting aside for the moment the horrific atrocities committed during those attacks) could not be justified based on military necessity:

> Except in a few cases, these incidents [widespread attacks on villages] are reported to have occurred ***without any military justification*** *in relation to any specific activity of the rebel forces.*
>
> This has strengthened the general perception amongst observers that the civilian population has been knowingly and deliberately targeted to achieve common or specific objectives and interests of the Government and the Janjaweed.[133]

According to the Commission of Inquiry's interpretation of international humanitarian law; the purported presence of non-civilians (rebels) in villages did not provide military justification for the attacks on the civilians carried out by the pro-government forces and militia in Darfur:

> Therefore, even if it were proved that rebels were present in a village under attack or that they generally used the civilian population as a 'shield'; nothing would justify the murder of civilians who do not take part in the hostilities.[134]

Further, note the International Commission of Inquiry on Darfur finding of the 'failure to protect' civilians, including child civilians, as a special protected subgroup that:

> . . .even if rebels, or persons supporting rebels, were present in some of the villages – which the Commission considers likely in only a very small number of instances – *the attackers* ***[Al Bashir SAF and allied militia] did not take precautions to enable civilians [including children] to leave the villages or otherwise be shielded from attack***. Even where rebels may have been present in villages, the impact of the attacks on civilians shows that the use of military force was manifestly disproportionate to any threat posed by the rebels.[135]

For the ICC Prosecutor to: (1) fail to acknowledge these various groups of child civilians in Darfur as victims of the *genocidal forcible transfer of children* and to: (2) decline to charge the perpetrators of this forcible transfer (whether Al Bashir forces or rebel forces) with the aforementioned genocide offence is, on the view here, to deny these children the international justice to which they are entitled; and, tragically, to do so in respect of one form of the 'crime of crimes'.

---

[133] International Commission of Inquiry on Darfur (2005, p. 55, para 187, emphasis added).

[134] International Commission of Inquiry on Darfur (2005, p. 78, para 291).

[135] UN Commission of Inquiry on Darfur (2005, p. 3, emphasis added).

Literature, Materials and Cases

Literature

Alfredson L (2002) Child soldiers, displacement and human security. Disarmament Forum 3:17–27

Cayley AT (2008) Editorial Comments: Recent steps of the ICC prosecutor in the Darfur situation: Prosecutor v. President (The prosecutor's strategy in seeking the arrest of Sudanese president Al Bashir on charges of genocide). J Int Crim Justice 6:829–840

Grover S (2012) Child soldier victims of genocidal forcible transfer: exonerating child soldiers charged with grave conflict-related international crimes. Springer, Berlin

Mamdanai M (2009) The International Criminal Court's Case against the president of Sudan: a critical look. J Int Aff 62(2):85–92, Spring/Summer

Parmar S, Roseman MJ, Siegrist S, Sowa T (eds) (2010) Children and transitional justice: truth-telling, accountability and reconciliation. Human Rights Program Harvard University, Cambridge

Materials

Additional Protocol II to the Geneva Conventions (8 June, 1977) http://www.icrc.org/ihl.nsf/full/475?OpenDocument. Accessed 26 Feb 2012

Amnesty International (2011) A compromised future: children recruited by armed forces and groups in Eastern Chad. http://www.amnesty.org/en/library/asset/AFR20/001/2011/en/1cf0816b-12e1-4c15-b055-26f18b5d5201/afr200012011en.pdf. Accessed 26 Feb 2012

Amnesty International (2005) Open letter to the Chief Prosecutor of the International Criminal Court: Comments on the concept of the interests of justice (dated 17 June, 2005). www.iccnow.org/documents/AI_LetterOTP_Interests_Aug05.pdf. Accessed 26 Feb 2012

Charbonneau L (2009) Interview-ICC looking at child soldier issue in Darfur (2 June, 2009). http://www.reuters.com/article/2009/06/02/idUSN02522068. Accessed 16 Feb 2012

Coalition to Stop the Use of Child Soldiers (2008). Child Soldiers Global Report (2008). http://www.childsoldiersglobalreport.org/content/sudan-0. Accessed 18 Feb 2012

De La Sablière, Jean-Marc. Letter dated 1 December 2006 from the Chair of the UN Working Group on Children and Armed Conflict to the President of the UN Security Council. http://daccess-dds-ny.un.org/doc/UNDOC/GEN/N06/659/71/PDF/N0665971.pdf?OpenElement. Accessed 17 Feb 2012

Developments in Sudan (Information based on the UN Secretary-General's report on children and armed conflict in Sudan) (2011). http://www.un.org/children/conflict/english/sudan.html. Accessed 17 Feb 2012

Flint J, de Waal A (2009) Case closed: a prosecutor without borders. World Affairs (Spring 2009). http://www.worldaffairsjournal.org/article/case-closed-prosecutor-without-borders. Accessed 26 Feb 2012

Genocide Convention (Convention on the Prevention and Punishment of the Crime of Genocide) (1952) Entered into force 12 January, 1951. http://www.preventgenocide.org/law/convention/text.htm#II. Accessed 23 Feb 2012

Green A (2012) (for InterPress Service 15 April, 2012) Returning Sudanese child soldiers their childhood. http://www.globalissues.org/news/2012/04/15/13345. Accessed 16 Jun 2012

ICC Charges (Counts) against Omar Hassan Ahmad Al Bashir (International Criminal Bureau, 15 July, 2010). http://www.internationallawbureau.com/blog/?p=1561. Accessed 23 Feb 2012

International Commission of Inquiry on Darfur (25 January, 2005). http://www.un.org/news/dh/sudan/com_inq_darfur.pdf. Accessed 25 Feb 2012

Moreno-Ocampo L (ICC Prosecutor). Fourteenth Report of the ICC Prosecutor to the UN Security Council Pursuant to Resolution 1593 (15 December, 2011)

Optional Protocol to the Convention on the Rights of the Child on the involvement of children in armed conflict (OPCRC-AC) (2002) Entry into force 12 February 2002. http://www2.ohchr.org/english/law/crc-conflict.htm. Accessed 19 Feb 2012

Relief Web Sudan: Interview – ICC looking at child soldier issue in Darfur. http://reliefweb.int/node/311888

Robert F (2012) Kennedy Centre for Justice and Human Rights. Child soldiers JEM Rebels. http://rfkcenter.org/child-soldiers-jem-rebels. Accessed 25 Feb 2012

Secretary-General's report on children and armed conflict in Sudan (2011) http://daccess-dds-ny.un.org/doc/UNDOC/GEN/N11/388/76/PDF/N1138876.pdf?OpenElement. Accessed 15 Feb 2012

Smith JM, Walker B (2004) Darfur: Blueprint for genocide (Report for the Aegis Trust) http://www.genocideeducation.ca/SMITH.pdf. Accessed 21 Feb 2012

SOS Villages (2012) Child soldiers given goats in South Sudan http://www.soschildrensvillages.ca/news/news/child-protection-news/child-soldier-news/pages/child-soldiers-given-goats-south-sudan-153.aspx. Accessed 25 Feb 2012

Statement of the Spokesperson of the ICC, Laurence Blairon (4 March, 2009). http://www.icc-cpi.int/NR/rdonlyres/4EB62BF7-30A7-46BC-B6D9-B9953AD4CA49/279981/Statement_spokes_person_ENG.pdf. Accessed 15 Feb 2012

UN Office for the Coordination of Humanitarian Affairs (IRIN) Sudan: Children still victims of war (23 August, 2006) http://www.irinnews.org/printreport.aspx?reportid=60437. Accessed 13 Jun 2012

U.N. Secretary-General Annual Report on children and armed conflict (including annex 1 and II) (26 April, 2012) http://www.un.org/children/conflict/_documents/A66782.pdf. Accessed 16 Jun 2012

UN Security Council Resolution 1612 (S/RES/1612) (Adopted by the Security Council 26 July, 2005). http://www.unrol.org/files/SecurityCouncilResolution1612_en.pdf. Accessed 18 Feb 2012

Women's Refugee Commission (2009) Refugee girls: the invisible faces of war (In memory of Mary Diaz 1964–2004) http://www.womensrefugeecommission.org/docs/refugee_girls_book.pdf. Accessed 13 Jun 2012.

Cases

ICC Charges (Counts) against *Omar Hassan Ahmad Al Bashir* http://www.icc-cpi.int/Menus/ICC/Situations+and+Cases/Situations/Situation+ICC+0205/. Accessed 15 Feb 2012

Kayishema and Ruzindana (ICTR-95-1-T) Trial Chamber Judgment, 21 May 1999 http://www.unhcr.org/refworld/docid. Accessed 23 Feb 2012

Office of the Prosecutor. Situation in Darfur: Summary of the Case (Prosecution application for warrant of arrest under Article 58 against Omar Hassan Ahmad Al Bashir) http://www.acicc.org/1-2%20english.pdf. Accessed 13 Jun 2012

Prosecutor v Omar Hassan Ahmad Al Bashir, Prosecution's Application for Leave to Appeal the "Decision on the Prosecution's Application for a Warrant of Arrest against Omar Hassan Ahmad Al Bashir" (10 March, 2009) http://www.icc-cpi.int/NR/exeres/CC751CCC-B58D-49A8-8073-83E0D06D3717.htm

Prosecutor v Omar Hassan Ahmad Al Bashir, Prosecution Document in Support of Appeal against the "Decision on the Prosecution's Application for a Warrant of Arrest against Omar Hassan Ahmad Al Bashir" Source: Office, 6 July, 2009. http://www.icc-cpi.int/NR/exeres/F288BDBB-4E80-443D-A043-C9CB837C8A51.htm. Accessed 23 Feb 2012

Prosecutor v Omar Hassan Ahmad Al Bashir, Public Redacted Version of Prosecution's Application under Article 58 filed on 14 July 2008. http://www.icc-cpi.int/iccdocs/doc/doc559998.pdf. Accessed 23 Feb 2012

Prosecutor v Al Bashir Second warrant of arrest for Al Bashir (Pre-Trial Chamber I) (12 July, 2010) http://www.un.org/children/conflict/_documents/A66782.pdf. Accessed 16 Jun 2012

Part IV
Conclusion

Chapter 6
The Genocidal Forcible Transfer of Children: A Crime Well Established in International Law; Yet Still Not Prosecuted by the ICC

6.1 Introduction

As the selected ICC case law here previously discussed illustrates, there is a continuing failure to acknowledge and prosecute the recruitment of children (persons under age 18) ***and/or*** their use for active participation in hostilities *by armed groups or forces (State or non-State) that perpetrate mass atrocities and/or genocide* as the 'genocidal forcible transfer of children'. Rather, such recruitment and/or use *when involving under 15s* is classified exclusively in terms of war crimes for the first time under international criminal treaty law (the Rome Statute).[1] The latter war crimes are regarded by some as a novel category of international crime though, as previously discussed here, this category of war crimes was already reflected in customary international law.[2] For instance, Schabas states "...the Rome Statute does recognize some *new crimes* that were probably not covered by the earlier instruments, such as the recruitment of child soldiers ..."[3]

The failure to acknowledge and prosecute the occurrence of the 'genocidal forcible transfer of children' to serve as so-called child soldiers in armed groups or forces perpetrating mass atrocities and/or genocide serves arguably to unjustly: (1) *undermine the perceived gravity of these crimes* (i.e. the recruitment and use of under 15s to participate actively in hostilities are not classed as grave breaches of the Geneva Conventions in an international armed conflict but rather only as "Other serious violations of the laws and customs applicable in... armed conflict... within the established framework of international law")[4]; (2) *limit the scope of protection for children to those under 15* as per the relevant Rome Statute Article 8 war

[1] Rome Statute (2002).

[2] The rules of war as encoded in the Additional Protocols I and II to the 1949 Geneva Conventions (1977).

[3] Schabas (2010, p. 213, emphasis added).

[4] Rome Statute (2002, Article 8(2)(b)(xxvi) and Article 8(2)(e)(vii)).

S.C. Grover, *Humanity's Children*, DOI 10.1007/978-3-642-32501-4_6,

crimes provisions[5]; (3) *limit protection for girls (i.e. girl soldiers are often excluded as victims of the recruitment and use war crimes in many instances* where these girls serve dual functions as fighters or bodyguards or some other combat related function and are, at the same time, sexually enslaved by the perpetrator armed group or force or serve exclusively i.e. as bush wives in a forced so-called marriage); and (4) *cloud the integral relationship between the use of children as child soldiers by armed groups or forces perpetrating mass atrocities and/or genocide and the targeted cruel and inhuman treatment of children in particular.* In addition, this obscuring and negating of the occurrence of the grave international crime of 'genocidal forcible transfer of children' to armed groups or forces perpetrating mass atrocities and/or genocide eliminates the possibility of accountability for this form of genocidal crime.[6] ICC prosecution on any count involving the targeting of children in particular in the manner here described by such armed groups or forces perpetrating mass atrocities and/or genocide in practice then is limited to consideration of the child soldiering issue (specifically recruitment and use of *under 15s* for active participation in hostilities in a context of widespread use of child soldiers and a common plan to perpetrate these Article 8 Rome Statute[7] war crimes as described at Article 8(2)(b)(xxvi) and/or Article 8(2)(e)(vii); respectively referring to an international and a non-international armed conflict situation).

Genocidal forcible transfer of children is a crime that is likely to meet the Prosecutors gravity test regardless the specific number of victims involved. Unlike the Rome Statute specifications regarding ICC jurisdiction over war crimes, the offence of genocide as set out in the Rome Statute[8] does *not* imply that ICC jurisdiction is *in particular* triggered based on the "large-scale" number of victims[9] or the existence of a common plan. A common plan is in any case an inherent feature of State-sponsored genocide and generally present in non-State instances of genocide as well though there may be exceptions with regards to the latter in cases yet to be tried by an international criminal judicial forum such as the ICC.

[5] Rome Statute (2002, Article 8(2)(b)(xxvi) and Article 8(2)(e)(vii)).

[6] The genocidal forcible transfer of children in such instances as here discussed involves the children in forced service as child soldiers and/or sex slaves or in some other capacity in support of the armed group or force or is accomplished via children's sexual violation even if the children are not transferred physically to be a member of and travel with the armed group or force as child soldiers or sex slaves etc. (even if allegedly enlisted the children are not free to leave). The deeper purpose is to establish control over the targeted population via alienating children from their families and communities and appropriating them fully and indefinitely to the perpetrator group (a political/military entity) represented by the armed group or force committing systematic mass atrocities and/or genocide.

[7] Rome Statute (2002).

[8] Rome Statute (2002).

[9] For instance the Rome Statute Elements of the Crime regarding the genocidal forcible transfer of children in part includes the following: "The perpetrator forcibly transferred *one or more persons*". [Rome Statute (Elements of the Crime) (2002)].

It has been noted that:

> In practice, the [ICC] Pre-Trial Chambers have virtually ignored [Rome Statute] article 8(1)[10] in their decisions on issuance of arrest warrants and confirmation of charges. *The threshold established by article 8(1) [regarding a common plan and large scale commission of the war crimes committed] has proven to be more important to the Office of the Prosecutor.*[11]

In discussing the issue of a threshold criteria in the selection of war crimes cases for ICC prosecution; the ICC Prosecutor Moreno-Ocampo has stated:

> For war crimes, a specific gravity threshold is set down in Article (8)(1), which states that 'the Court shall have jurisdiction in respect of war crimes *in particular* when committed as part of a plan or policy *or* as part of a large scale commission of such crimes. This threshold is not an element of the crime, and the words 'in particular 'suggest that this is not a strict requirement. *It does, however, provide Statute guidance that the Court is intended to focus on situations meeting these requirements. ...*[12]

The prosecution of recruitment and use of children for active participation in hostilities thus faces barriers when pursued exclusively as war crimes under Rome Statute[13] Article 8 in terms of but not limited to the following: (1) the threshold criteria likely to be imposed by the ICC Prosecutor relying on Article 8(1) and (2) the likelihood that States will rely on the complementarity principle of the Rome Statute to argue that they are or will in due course as sovereign States address war crimes specifically classed as serious violations of the customs and laws of war occurring in their territory (as are the Article 8 Rome Statute[14] child soldiering related offences). This becomes a particular problem in instances where, for instance: (1) the State is not a party to the Rome Statute and the perpetrators are not nationals of a State Party and further the UN Security Council is not prepared to refer the case to the ICC in a timely manner if at all (i.e. Somalia situation) or (2) the ICC Prosecutor is unwilling to *investigate in depth* the situation in a State with respect to child soldiering and is loathe to initiate cases to prosecute regarding child soldiering in a timely manner if at all i.e. child soldiering in Darfur, Sudan (though the State has been referred by the UN Security Council as has Sudan or is otherwise potentially under the jurisdiction of the ICC with respect to Rome Statute[15] Article 8 war crimes pertaining to child soldiering). The 'genocidal forcible transfer of children' (which, on the analysis here, occurs also when children are appropriated as child soldiers and/or sex slaves or in some other capacity by armed groups or

---

[10] Rome Statute Article 8 (1): "The Court shall have jurisdiction in respect of war crimes *in particular* when committed as part of a plan or policy or as part of a large-scale commission of such crimes." (Rome Statute, 2002).

[11] Schabas (2010, p. 201, emphasis added).

[12] Office of the Prosecutor, Letter concerning communication on the situation in Iraq (9 February, 2006, p. 8, emphasis added).

[13] Rome Statute (2002).

[14] Rome Statute (2002).

[15] Rome Statute (2002, Article 8(2)(b)(xxvi) and Article 8(2)(e)(vii)).

forces committing mass atrocities and/or genocide) *properly framed* as such, however, is more difficult to ignore or discount. It becomes more difficult to claim that the State is actively and sincerely pursuing domestic judicial remedies in a timely manner when in fact there have already been innumerable child victims of genocide in a certain situation (particularly given the stigma attached to the crime of genocide[16] which is not necessarily attached to other classes of international crimes to the same degree). We will consider this latter point shortly in a later section of this conclusion (a final note) with reference to the mass atrocities being committed *against children in particular* in Syria at the time of the current author's writing.

To date there is no indication that the suffering of children as child soldiers and victims of mass rape and forced marriage consequent to international crimes perpetrated by armed groups or forces committing mass atrocities and/or genocide is *in itself* sufficient to: (1) trigger a referral of the situation by the UN Security Council to the ICC in instances where a non-State Party to the Rome Statute is involved; to whit the example of Somalia (to be discussed here in a later section)[17]; or (2) cause the Prosecutor to initiate an investigation *proprio motu* (with the permission of the Pre-Trial Chamber the latter having considered jurisdictional and admissibility issues and the Prosecutor's preliminary information) regarding the situation in a State over which the ICC does have jurisdiction (i.e. Darfur, Sudan was investigated as a consequence of the referral by the UN Security Council and no charges relating to child soldiering or the genocidal forcible transfer of children have been laid to date in the cases that were developed relating to the Darfur conflict). Despite the widespread and grave international crimes being perpetrated against children in both countries (Somalia and Sudan), and the use of child soldiers in both; only Sudan was referred to the ICC by the UN Security Council. Sadly, and on the view here, incorrectly; notwithstanding the referral of the Darfur (Sudan) situation to the ICC by the UN Security Council; no cases regarding the situation in Sudan have led to charges related to: (1) the recruitment and use of child soldiers (under 15s) for active participation in hostilities or (2) the genocidal forcible transfer of children (persons under 18) to serve as child soldiers or in other

---

[16] Wagner (2003, p. 424).

[17] Arguably the UN Security Council referral to the ICC of a situation in a non-State Party to the Rome Statute does imply an obligation on all States to: (1) abide by international legal principles and (2) take all necessary and feasible measures towards ensuring that the international crimes listed in the Rome Statute do not occur on their territory and are not perpetrated by their nationals in any territory. This in that such referral would not be likely to lead to Pre-Trial authorization for an investigation of the situation (given the Court's reliance on the principle of complementarity) where the non-State Party was willing and able to address the situation internally and had established it was taking or had taken active measures in that direction. Thus, though the Rome Statute deals with criminal responsibility only in respect of individuals and not States, State obligations are nonetheless indirectly incorporated through the Rome Statute complementarity principle. Others such as Wagner (2002, pp. 489–490) take the view that any suggestion that the ability of the ICC to potentially consider situations in non-State Parties does *not* create an obligation on non-State parties and that any theory to the contrary is a "novel theory."

capacities with armed groups or forces committing mass atrocities and/or genocide (i.e. the Sudanese Armed Forces, the pro Al Bashir Janjaweed militia, the rebel Justice Equality Movement etc.).

It remains an open question whether if facts *in particular cases* are framed also as evidence of the unfettered 'genocidal forcible transfer of children' (to serve as child soldiers to perpetrate atrocity and/or serve as sex slaves and in other capacities with armed groups or forces perpetrating systematic widespread grave international crimes as part of a common plan)[18] there will be: (1) intense international outrage regarding the occurrence of this form of genocide targeting in particular children and (2) a greater willingness to ensure ICC jurisdiction (i.e. through the necessary referrals of situations) and a willingness by the ICC OTP to exercise jurisdiction over the crime of genocidal forcible transfer of children (persons under age 18) such that cases will be developed for ICC prosecution.

The suggestion is here that the ICC is well positioned to consider the appropriation of children as child soldiers by armed groups or forces committing mass atrocities and/or genocide as meeting the criteria for the 'genocidal forcible transfer of children'. Note that the Rome Statute Elements of the Crimes[19] legal text is non-binding on the ICC[20] as set out in Article 9 of the Rome Statute:

Rome Statute Article 9

Elements of Crimes

1. Elements of Crimes shall *assist* the Court in the interpretation and application of articles 6, 7 and 8. . .[21]

Thus, the Court has some discretion in terms of judicial interpretation. It is here suggested that article 6(e) of the Rome Statute[22] regarding the genocidal forcible transfer of children is an applicable classification of international crime regarding instances of the appropriation of children as child soldiers and/or sex slaves etc. by armed groups or forces committing mass atrocities and/or genocide[23] as will be explored further with reference to the situation in Somalia to be discussed. To consider children appropriated for so-called soldiering by armed groups or forces

[18] See Grover (2012).

[19] Rome Statute Elements of the Crime (2002).

[20] Wagner (2003, p. 417).

[21] Rome Statute, 2002, Article 9, emphasis added.

[22] Rome Statute (2002).

[23] For example, such appropriation of children as child soldiers: (1) reduces the future reproductive capacity of the group of origin by removing children from their midst, (2) causes immense physical and psychological suffering for the children and their groups of origin reducing the vitality of both; (3) often involves sexual violence with respect to girl child soldiers reducing their reproductive capability as a member of their original group should they return to their home communities, (4) destroys the children's personal identity and links to their communities with this ultimately contributing to the physical and psychological destruction of the original communities/groups from whence the children were transferred etc.

committing atrocities and/or genocide as constituting the genocidal forcible transfer of children requires the ICC OTP to engage in a deeper analysis of : (1) what is involved in child soldiering for such armed groups and forces and how this reflects genocidal intent for those individuals most responsible for the transfer of the children from their original group and (2) what constitutes a protected group in such contexts and how this yet meets the requirements in regards to protected group as set out in Article 6(e) of the Rome Statute[24] (generally children of one or more particular ethnic groups and the same nationality are targeted within a territory for child soldiering though, in some instances, children from neighboring States who may differ in nationality or even ethnicity from the perpetrators of the transfer of these children to the armed group or force may also be appropriated). It is here contended that the interpretation of Article 6(e) "Forcibly transferring children *of the group to another group*" must be interpreted so as not to lead to the unreasonable conclusion that children of the same perceived ethnicity, religion, nationality and/or so-called racial group appropriated as child soldiers (or otherwise forcible transferred with genocidal intent) as the perpetrator group cannot be considered transferred to 'another group' (consistent with the definition of the genocidal forcible transfer of children) when in fact: (1) the bonds between the children and their original community/group of origin have in fact been broken and (2) the armed group or force perpetrating mass atrocities and/or genocide is perceived as outside the margins of the rest of society and an entity unto itself; separate and apart. The Vienna Convention on the Interpretation of Treaties Article 31 in fact, by implication, suggests that the interpretation of the terms/text of a treaty must not lead to unreasonable conclusions.[25] The current author contests the notion that a literal interpretation of the terms of Article 6 of the Rome Statute (duplicating the Genocide Convention wording) is even possible given the ambiguity of some of the text[26] i.e. there is no consensus on the meaning of 'ethnic' group and how the term applies in various instances nor is the term 'race' considered to have any legitimate (scientific) or objective meaning independent of perpetrator perceptions. Recall the problems encountered in attempting to distinguish Hutu and Tutsi along ethnic or so-called racial lines on any objective and/or stable criteria:

> [there is a] widespread presence of "mixed marriages," the social mobility from "Hutu" to "Tutsi" upon acquiring cattle, the fact that both groups speak exactly the same language, and the unreliable dependence on eugenic-related notions of nineteenth century
> Europe (where do tall Hutus or short, squat Tutsis fit into the racialist categories?)
> ...It is exactly the racial categorizations of the Germans, and later the Belgians, that constructed the indelible nature of "ethnic" or "tribal" identification for Rwandans ...According to this instrumental theory, this closed ethnic caste system is not of Rwandan making.[27]

[24] Rome Statute (2002).

[25] For a discussion on this issue see Wagner (2003, p. 423).

[26] Wagner (2003, p. 423) takes the opposition view to that of the current author.

[27] Afflito (2000, p. 82)

Note that Rome Statute[28] Article 6(e) does not specify the means by which the genocidal forcible transfer of children might occur and has thus left open the possibility for the Court to consider various forms of transfer to another group as constituting the genocidal forcible transfer of children. Though the means may vary, they all constitute the same act of genocidal forcible transfer of children. It is here contended that such transfer need not be a physical transfer to the other group but can be accomplished via stigmatizing the child as having been transferred as when the child is raped even though not physically with the perpetrator armed group or force on an ongoing basis; travelling with them etc. Thus, the interpretation of what constitutes the means for the genocidal forcible transfer of children to "another group" is open to interpretation and arguably also so is what constitutes a protected group on the facts in a particular situation (even if the group is referenced in terms of the vague group monikers listed in Rome Statute[29] Article 6(e) itself). The Rome Statute[30] Article 8 war crimes provisions regarding child soldiering, however, are equally controversial regarding a number of their terms though this may not seem obvious on its face. For instance, as previously discussed, there has been controversy about: (1) whether or not child soldiers in the midst of armed conflict, separated from family, in dire poverty etc can be truly regarded as voluntary enlistees especially to an armed force or group that is terrorizing the general population (such that the distinction between enlisted and conscripted may not always be meaningful in every situation); (2) what constitutes 'active participation' in armed hostilities (for instance whether sex slaves and other children forcibly transferred to the armed group or force to perform non-combat related functions are also active participants in the hostilities) and (3) whether children used by armed groups committing mass atrocities and/or genocide to participate in hostilities are in any sense child soldiers (something other than civilians taking part in the hostilities).[31] The question arises then, given the ambiguity of terms in both the Rome Statute[32] provisions concerning the recruitment and use of under 15s in hostilities and that dealing with genocide (including genocidal forcible transfer of children), whether or not these grave international crimes are being vigorously prosecuted by the ICC where the State, for whatever reason, has not met its burden in this regard.[33] We will consider this question next with reference to the situation in Somalia but first need to consider a few key points regarding ICC case admissibility criteria and how ICC case selection must take into account the interests of justice.

---

[28] Rome Statute (2002).

[29] Rome Statute (2002).

[30] Rome Statute (2002).

[31] It has been noted here in a previous section that the term 'child soldier' is not a term to be found in international treaty or convention instruments. This author has argued here and elsewhere that so-called child soldiers under 15 are in fact civilians as are so-called child soldiers (persons under 18) participating with unlawful armed groups or forces perpetrating mass atrocities and/or genocide as part of a common plan (Grover 2008, 2012).

[32] Rome Statute (2002).

[33] This assuming of course that all ICC jurisdictional and admissibility requirements are met in regards to the cases developed.

6.2 Gravity of the Crime as an ICC Admissibility Criterion

The ICC Prosecutor Moreno-Ocampo has explained the significance of the gravity assessment in relation to the International Criminal Court's mandate as follows:

> Crimes within our jurisdiction are by definition grave crimes of international concern. ***But gravity in our Statute is not only a characteristic of the crime, but also an admissibility factor***; which seems to reflect the wish of our founders that the ICC should focus on the gravest situations in the world. [Referring here to Article 17(d) of the Rome Statute[34] which requires that the case, among other things, be of "sufficient gravity" in order to be ruled admissible].[35]

In considering the issue of gravity we will take account of the factors highlighted in the decision of ICC Pre-Trial Chamber II to authorize an investigation into the situation in the Republic of Kenya (hereafter referred to as *Kenya*). That decision included some guidelines in assessing gravity. Pre-Trial Chamber II in *Kenya* cited with approval the position of Pre-Trial Chamber I in *Lubanga* that: "...the fact a case addresses one of the most serious crimes for the international community as a whole is *not sufficient* for it to be admissible before the Court."[36] The Pre-Trial Chamber in *Kenya* held further that: (1) the: "...gravity assessment is a mandatory component for the determination of the question of admissibility"[37] and that (2) at the preliminary stage of examination of the situation by the ICC Prosecutor; gravity will be assessed; not in reference to a concrete case; but rather "against the backdrop of the likely set of cases or "potential cases(s)" that would arise from investigating the situation."[38] The Pre-Trial Chamber in *Kenya* stated further that in making gravity assessments (of the situation and the cases developed) there should be note taken of the: "...interplay between the crimes and the context in which they were committed (the incidents)" such that "...the gravity of the crimes will be assessed in the context of their *modus operandi*."[39] The Pre-Trial Chamber in *Kenya* explained that gravity assessments properly have both a qualitative and quantitative dimension:

[34] Rome Statute (2002, Article 17(d)).

[35] Statement by Luis Moreno-Ocampo, Prosecutor of the ICC, Informal meeting of legal advisors of Ministries of Foreign Affairs, New York, 24 October, 2005 Cited in Schabas (2008, p. 738, emphasis added).

[36] Prosecutor v Lubanga Pre-Trial Chamber I, Decision on the Prosecutor's Application for a warrant of arrest. Article 58, ICC-01/04-01/06-8-Corr, para. 41 Cited at para 56 of the Pre-Trial Chamber decision to authorize an investigation into situation in the Republic of Kenya (*Kenya*) 31, March, 2010, emphasis added).

[37] Pre-Trial Chamber decision to authorize an investigation into situation in the Republic of Kenya (*Kenya*) 31, March, 2010, para 57.

[38] Pre-Trial Chamber decision to authorize an investigation into situation in the Republic of Kenya (*Kenya*) 31, March, 2010, para 58.

[39] Pre-Trial Chamber decision to authorize an investigation into situation in the Republic of Kenya (*Kenya*) 31, March, 2010, para 61.

> In making its assessment, the Chamber considers that gravity may be examined following a quantitative as well as a qualitative approach. Regarding the qualitative dimension, it is not the number of victims that matter but rather the existence of some aggravating or qualitative factors attached to the commission of crimes, which makes it grave. When considering the gravity of the crime(s), several factors . . .could provide useful guidance in such an examination. These factors could be summarized as: (i) the scale of the alleged crimes (including assessment of geographical and temporal intensity); (ii) the nature of the unlawful behaviour or of the crimes allegedly committed; (iii) the employed means for the execution of the crimes (i.e., the manner of their commission); and (iv) the impact of the crimes and the harm caused to victims and their families. In this respect, the victims' representations will be of significant guidance for the Chamber's assessment.[40]

In discussing the situation in Somalia in a later section, we will consider the qualitative and quantitative aspects (as outlined above in *Kenya)* of the international crimes involved in perpetrating child soldiering. We will consider the implications of the contextual qualitative and quantitative aspects of the crimes for considering child soldiering not only in relation to particular Rome Statute Article 8 war crimes; but framed also as the 'genocidal forcible transfer of children' as per Article 6(e) of the Rome Statute.[41] We will rely on a 2012 report by Human Rights Watch for information regarding the situation on the ground with respect to child soldiering in Somalia.

6.3 The Interests of Justice: Insights from the ICC Pre-Trial Judgement in *Kenya*

The Pre-Trial Chamber in *Kenya* explains that while the ICC Prosecutor is duty bound to establish that an investigation is warranted based on the gravity of the situation (i.e. more specifically that the investigation is warranted based on the gravity of the crimes committed and the nature of the cases that may develop based on such an investigation), no such affirmative obligation exists with respect to the matter of the "interests of justice." That is, the Prosecutor is *not* required "to establish that an investigation is actually in the interests of justice."[42] ("Indeed, the Prosecutor does not have to present reasons or supporting material in this respect.")[43] It is only when the ICC Prosecutor decides *not* to do an investigation that, according to the Pre-Trial Chamber in *Kenya*, the Prosecutor must provide reasons for such a decision.[44] Note that the ICC Prosecutor may on his or her own

[40] Pre-Trial Chamber decision to authorize an investigation into situation in the Republic of Kenya (*Kenya*) (31, March, 2010, para 61).

[41] Rome Statute (2002).

[42] Pre-Trial Chamber decision to authorize an investigation into situation in the Republic of Kenya (*Kenya*) (31, March, 2010, para 63).

[43] Trial Chamber decision to authorize an investigation into situation in the Republic of Kenya (*Kenya*) (31, March, 2010, para 63).

[44] Trial Chamber decision to authorize an investigation into situation in the Republic of Kenya (*Kenya*) (31, March, 2010, para 63).

motion attempt to obtain Pre-Trial Chamber approval to launch a formal investigation having concluded that, based on a preliminary examination, such is warranted. That move on the part of the Prosecutor is independent of the question of whether any particular cases developed will ultimately in fact be ruled admissible.

Let us then consider the situation in Somalia involving the widespread use of child soldiers by armed groups or forces perpetrating mass atrocities where there has been, to date, no referral of the situation or ICC cases opened to allow for prosecution of the crimes of appropriating and using children for child soldiering. (The situation in Somalia has *not* been referred by the UN Security Council to the ICC (as is required in that Somalia is a non-State Party to the Rome Statute) and the Prosecutor has not therefore opened a preliminary investigation).[45] We will consider specifically whether the child soldiering situation in Somalia warrants referral to the ICC and prosecution of cases (the latter likely to be developed subsequent to analysis by the Office of the Prosecutor (OTP) of this situation) given: (1) the gravity of the crimes committed in Somalia in respect of children appropriated for child soldiering and/or victimization through sexual violence and (2) considering the interests of justice.

6.4 The Somali Situation[46] and the Matter of Impunity for Perpetrating 'Child Soldiering'

6.4.1 Introduction

The child soldier situation in Somalia is an example, on the analysis here, of the fact that the international crimes involved in perpetrating widespread child soldiering (even when occurring in the context of massive grave other human rights abuses against children) are unlikely to lead to U.N. Security Council referral to the ICC of a non-State party where crimes against children are a central issue in the situation underlying any referral:

> Children in war-torn Somalia face horrific abuses, including forced recruitment as soldiers, forced marriage and rape, and attacks on their schools by the parties to the conflict. *Those responsible are never held to account.*[47]

It is important to note in the context of this discussion that according to Human Rights Watch (hereafter 'HRW'): "Children, defined as anyone under age 18, have suffered disproportionately from the ongoing conflict."[48] Hence, any referral of the Somali situation to the ICC by the UN Security Council would presumably in large part incorporate a focus on child victims.

---

[45] Ratifications to the Rome Statute.

[46] Somalia is a non-state party to the Rome Statute and the Somali situation has not as yet been referred to the ICC by the UN Security Council.

[47] Human Rights Watch (2012a, p. 1, emphasis added).

[48] Human Rights Watch (2012a, p. 1).

6.4.2 *Background to the Somali Situation and Child Victimization*

In fact there are now several parties to the 21-year conflict in Somalia including Kenya which is a State Party to the Rome Statute:

> Fighting between the Transitional Federal Government (TFG), the African Union Mission in Somalia (AMISOM), and TFG-aligned militias on one hand and al-Shabaab, the Islamist armed group that now controls much of the country, on the other, intensified in the capital, Mogadishu, and other parts of south-central Somalia in mid-2010 and early 2011. In October 2011 the conflict in the southern regions escalated further with the incursion of Kenyan armed forces against al-Shabaab, followed shortly after by the arrival of Ethiopian forces.[49]

The 2012 Human Rights Watch (HRW) report on Somalia focuses on the international crimes being perpetrated by al-Shabaab against children in Somalia; particularly "al-Shabaab's targeting of children for recruitment as soldiers, forced marriage, and rape, with a focus on abuses in 2010 and 2011."[50] In addition, the report focuses on attacks on schoolchildren, teachers and schools, the use of students (schoolchildren) as "human shields" while using schools as firing positions without regard to the risk of injury or death to the students inside the school.[51] HRW notes that child soldiers also serve with the Transitional Federal Government (TFG) armed forces and the pro-government militias:

> Children continue to also be found within the TFG armed forces and TFG-affiliated militias; the TFG has ... failed to ensure that all its recruits, including those formerly associated with aligned militias, undergo effective age vetting to prevent the recruitment of children [under 15s].[52]

HRW reports that to date despite the TFG alleged commitment (promise) to enter into a UN plan to end its use of child soldiers, children continue to serve in the TFG armed forces and allied militias and there is no system of age vetting in place to ensure children are not members of the aforementioned armed forces.[53]

> The TFG has on several occasions publicly committed to ending the use of children by its forces but has to date not sufficiently acted on all these commitments.[54]

The U.N. Secretary-General's annual report on children and armed conflict of 26 April, 2012 listed Somalia as one of the worst offenders in terms of violations of children's rights during armed conflict in that agents of both Al Shabaab and the Transitional Federal Government continue to kill and maim children and recruit and use children for active participation in hostilities. The 2012 annual report listed the TFG as a persistent offender in that it has been listed as an offender on recent

---

[49] Human Rights Watch (2012a, p. 1).

[50] Human Rights Watch (2012a, p. 1).

[51] Human Rights Watch (2012a, p. 1).

[52] Human Rights Watch (2012b) World Report 2012: Somalia.

[53] Human Rights Watch (2012a, p. 4).

[54] Human Rights Watch (2012a, p. 44).

previous such annual reports. No action plan has been entered into to date with the U.N. by either of these armed entities to end these practices constituting international crimes perpetrated against children.

Thus, there appears indeed for many children in Somalia to be no place for them to turn for safety as the State too has for the most part failed them in terms of protecting them from child soldiering, sexual violence, attacks on education and from famine (there is a UN declared famine[55] throughout the South-Central region of Somali). HRW reports that to date no one in the TFG has been held responsible for the recruitment and use of children in hostilities and for the failure to screen recruits regarding age.[56]

HRW describes the data base for their 2012 report "No place for children" as follows:

> ...164 newly arrived Somali refugees in the Dadaab refugee camps and in Nairobi in May and June 2011. Interviewees included more than 81 girls and boys who were under age 18 at the time. Human Rights Watch also interviewed TFG officials, officials of United Nations (UN) agencies and the African Union, members of nongovernmental organizations, and members of the diplomatic community.[57]

HRW in 2012 reports that though there have always been child soldiers involved in the Somali conflict "there has been an unprecedented upsurge of al-Shabaab forced recruitment of children since mid-2010; attacks on students, teachers, and schools have also been prevalent in the last two years."[58] Al-Shabaab, according to HRW, is relying primarily on abduction (forced recruitment) of children rather than on more indirect forms of coercion (abducting children while they are at school or on their way to or from school appears to be a favoured al-Shabaab child soldier 'recruitment' strategy though children have been abducted from any place they tend to congregate).[59]

Cruel and inhuman treatment intended to result in both physical and psychological suffering appears to be a hallmark of Al Shabaab 'military' training:

> Life for children in al-Shabaab training camps is harsh: *boys undergo grueling physical combat training*, weapons training, and religious and political teaching during which some describe being *forced to watch videos of suicide bombings. Boys also described witnessing brutal physical punishments and executions of those accused of spying for the TFG, and those attempting to escape or merely failing to obey orders.*[60]

As with other armed groups or forces perpetrating mass atrocities and/or genocide, Al-Shabaab also sends children into combat with very little training:

---

[55] Human Rights Watch (2012a, p. 1).
[56] Human Rights Watch (2012a, p. 3).
[57] Human Rights Watch (2012a, p. 2).
[58] Human Rights Watch (2012a, p. 2)
[59] Human Rights Watch (2012a, p. 2).
[60] Human Rights Watch (2012a, p. 2, emphasis added).

> Children, mostly boys, said they were sent to the front lines from the training camps, often with *minimal training*.[61]
>
> *Al-Shabaab militants send children to the front lines, often with little training*. Several witnesses spoke of children serving effectively as "human shields" for more experienced fighters during some of the most intense fighting in Mogadishu [with the children in front of the more experienced adult al-Shabaad fighters].[62] Others, including children too young to carry military weapons, were aggressively coerced and threatened into serving as *suicide bombers*.[63]

The fact that the children are so ill-prepared by their brief military training in Al-Shabaab to be effective fighters is consistent with the view that the recruitment and use of child soldiers by armed groups or forces committing mass atrocities is less about effectively reinforcing the strength of their armed units in any meaningful way and more about the genocidal forcible transfer of children and its correlated propaganda value (i.e. communicating that the perpetrators have unlimited power and have a fathomless well-spring of young devotees who will grow to be loyal adult members of the perpetrator group or force).

Also as is characteristic of armed forces perpetrating mass atrocities and/or genocide, girl children recruited and used by these perpetrators (for instance Al-Shabaab) are generally raped and forced into becoming bush wives for these adult fighters:

> Abducted girls are assigned cooking, cleaning, and other domestic duties in the camps. Al-Shabaab uses girls and young women not only for support for combat operations, but also for rape and forced marriage to fighters.[64]

Such mass rape of child soldiers is, it is here contended, another vehicle for ensuring that the children are tainted and no longer acceptable to their home communities (as is having the children participate in committing atrocities). Sexual victimization in this context then becomes a vehicle for the genocidal forcible transfer of children to the perpetrator group.

Parents generally have no choice but to surrender their children to Al-Shabaab when this is demanded of them and any resistance by parents has often led to the parents' murder.[65] So too any resistance from children targeted for 'recruitment' and use by Al-Shabaab can and often does lead to summary execution:

> Al-Shabaab said to my elder brother, "Come with us." He refused and they beheaded him. He was 16. They took him and put his head in front of our house. (Deka R. (not her real name), 13-year-old girl whose brother was killed in El Ashabiya, Somalia, around Ramadan 2010, June 5, 2011).47
>
> Children repeatedly told Human Rights Watch that they felt powerless to resist recruitment by al-Shabaab. Witnesses spoke of "children who had refused recruitment having their hands cut off" or in some instances beheaded. Knowing that refusal would mean being taken by force

[61] Human Rights Watch (2012a, p. 30).

[62] Human Rights Watch (2012a, p. 31).

[63] Human Rights Watch (2012a, p. 2, emphasis added).

[64] Human Rights Watch (2012a, p. 3).

[65] Human Rights Watch (2012a, p. 3).

or possibly killed, children recounted the fear they felt as al-Shabaab fighters entered their schools and homes and the desperate measures they would take to escape detection.[66]

Several children said they witnessed brutal physical punishments and executions at the camps, sometimes involving other children. The reasons for execution varied from not obeying orders and attempting to escape to accusations of being a TFG spy.[67]

Clearly, to describe what al-Shabaad and other armed groups and forces perpetrating mass atrocities and/or genocide are doing in respect of child solders as simply "recruitment" and "use" of children for active participation in hostilities—even if described as forced recruitment-does not begin to capture the brutal reality. These groups have fully appropriated these children as human beings not just their labor.

School attacks are a major feature of Al-Shabaab's assault on the children of Somalia. Such attacks serve Al-Shabaab in various ways in successfully implementing a strategy of 'genocidal forcible transfer of children' in that:

(i) The schoolchildren congregated at the school are easy victims for transfer to Al-Shabaab (i.e. through abduction or lures to serve as child soldiers, and in the case of girls transferred, to serve as sex slaves and/or combat supports etc. and often also to function as forced 'wives');
(ii) Through the attacks on and destruction of schools, and attacks on teachers and students; Al-Shabaab has successfully engendered great fear amongst children and weakened resistance;
(iii) Due to the ongoing assault on schools, teachers and students by Al-Shabaab "Many Somali children are no longer in or have never been to school. Somalia has one of the lowest rates of enrolment in the world."[68] This then means that these children have little if any hope for the future in terms of any remote possibility of extricating themselves from absolute destitution and this increases their view that membership in Al Shabaab is the only means for survival (at least in the short-term);
(iv) The only schools free from attack are those schools in Al-Shabaab controlled territory which follow meticulously Al-Shabaab dictates directed to instilling the armed group's ideology and re-making the children's personal identity and collective identity in the image of Al-Shabaab devotee. All this is then a tool for 'recruitment' of the children:

They [Al-Shabaab] have threatened and even killed teachers who resist their methods, lectured students on jihad and war as a recruitment tool, and placed their own teachers in schools. Lessons have been left devoid of substance. . .[69]

Several children told Human Rights Watch that al-Shabaab brought their members into schools to teach subjects such as "jihad," where children were lectured on their duty to join the jihad and promises of "entry into paradise" if a child died as a martyr. The classes, which ranged from daily to weekly classes, were also used as a way for al-Shabaab to gain entry into the school and recruit children. Children described being lectured on the virtues

---

[66] Human Rights Watch (2012a, pp. 24–25).

[67] Human Rights Watch (2012a, p. 28).

[68] Human Rights Watch (2012a, p. 3).

[69] Human Rights Watch (2012a, p. 3).

> of jihad, shown Islamist propaganda videos, and given weapons demonstrations.... Other children also described a mix of propaganda and force that led them and their classmates to join[70]

It is, on the view here, simply inadequate and unjust to expect that children should continue to attend schools in hot conflict zones on the promise that they will be provided adequate protection (a promise yet to be realized and considering that protection cannot be guaranteed in any case)[71]; thus risking abduction to al-Shabaab or life and limb in the process should the school come under attack. Yet, such a proposition is incorporated in the recommendations contained in the 2012 Human Rights Watch report on the situation for children in Somalia:

> **Key Recommendations**
>
> **To Foreign Parties to the Conflict: AMISOM and the African Union, Kenya, and Ethiopia**
>
> Ensure that schools are identified and protected and that students, teachers, and school administrators are able to safely leave school buildings during military operations where they may be at risk.
>
> Map out key civilian infrastructure, including schools, with the assistance of relevant agencies, including the Education Cluster, in order to ensure that schools *in areas of military operations are identified and protected.*[72]

Genocidal forcible transfer of children to serve as so-called child soldiers in armed groups or forces perpetrating mass atrocities and/or genocide involves grave maltreatment of the child recruits at every stage; a breaking down of the children's original identity and links to family and community; and a conditioning toward witnessing, accepting as inevitable and often themselves perpetrating atrocities. The latter approach is quite unlike the situation in which a child of 15 or over is recruited into an armed group or force that is expected by the command structure to abide by the customary rules of war, and the Geneva Conventions[73] in respect of the humane treatment[74] of all children including child recruits to their own or the adversary's forces.

Let us turn now to an examination of the gravity of the international crimes committed by Al-Shabaab in its appropriation and use of children. We do so by

---

[70] Human Rights Watch (2012a, pp. 23–24).

[71] Grover (2011).

[72] Human Rights Watch (2012a, pp. 7–8).

[73] See the Additional Protocols I and II to the 1949 Geneva Conventions (1977).

[74] The current author holds as does the ICRC that the use of children (persons under age 18) by armed groups or forces (State or non-State) for direct or indirect participation in armed hostilities is in fact an inhumane practice. However, the straight 18 position with respect to protection of children from direct or indirect participation in hostilities as members of armed groups or forces has not as yet been incorporated into international humanitarian or criminal law (though prohibitions on States using persons under 18 in their armed forces to take a *direct* part in hostilities and on armed groups recruiting or using children (persons under age 18) in hostilities under any circumstances does appear in the Optional Protocol to the Convention on the Rights of the Child on the involvement of children in armed conflict (2002)).

considering various factors held to be essential to the assessment of gravity according (as previously discussed) to the Pre-Trial Chamber in *Kenya*[75]:

6.5 Gravity of the International Crimes Perpetrated by Al Shabaab Against Children

Consider the qualitative and quantitative aspects of the international crimes perpetrated by Al Shabaab against children:

(i) *Scale of the Crime:* Recruitment and use of children in armed conflict and attacks on/abductions of schoolchildren are being perpetrated by Al Shabaab on a systematic and widespread basis;

(ii) *Nature of the Unlawful behaviour*: The crimes committed against children by Al Shabaab include both those construed as serious violations of the laws and customs of war and grave breaches of the Geneva Convention as well as crimes against humanity (and, on the analysis here, also the genocidal forcible transfer of children); thus they include highly egregious violations causing much mental and physical suffering to the children and their families

(iii) *Manner of Commission of the Crime*: The recruitment of children by Al-Shabaab is carried out in a most vicious and inhuman manner i.e. through abductions, by ripping children from their parents and murdering parents before the children's eyes should the parents resist and murdering children who resist etc. The children are then subjected to cruel and inhuman treatment during their training with no regard whatsoever for the children's well-being only to be put into combat with minimal training and expected to commit atrocities; to perform suicide missions if commanded to do so etc.

(iv) *Context of the Crimes*: The recruitment and use of children for active participation in armed conflict by Al-Shabaab and by TFG armed forces and allied militia is occurring in the context of mass atrocities that variously can be construed in terms of: (1) *crimes against humanity* perpetrated against the children so recruited and other children in Somalia (i.e. mass rape,[76] forced marriage to al-Shabaad fighters, sexual slavery, inhumane acts causing great suffering etc.) or (2) *war crimes* carried out with a plan and on a widespread basis (i.e. murders of children and parents who fail to comply with Al-Shabaab dictates, attacks on schools and school personnel as well as schoolchildren, deprivation of the necessities of life in famine stricken regions (as a form of cruel treatment and violence to life) (3), using children as human shields (a violation of customary law in an internal conflict) etc.) or sometimes multiple

---

[75] Pre-Trial Chamber decision to authorize an investigation into situation in the Republic of Kenya (*Kenya*) 31, March, 2010, para 61.

[76] HRW reports that: "... sexual and gender-based violence in Somalia is widespread and perpetuated not only by combatants but also by civilians." Human Rights Watch (2012a, p. 59).

categories of crime (i.e. crimes against humanity and war crimes) on the same facts.

(v) *The impact of the crimes and the harm caused to victims and their families*: There are innumerable psychological and anthropological field studies and investigations by NGOs, UNICEF and other bodies concerning ex child soldiers and their families. The findings attest to the enduring devastating after-effects for many ex child soldiers of having served with an armed group or force that perpetrated mass atrocities and/or genocide i.e. alienation from family and community; longer term trauma after-effects, poor mental health, loss of schooling opportunities, poor physical health, debilitating injury, (for girls, in some instances, lasting physical injury due to enduring repeated rape/gang rape and contraction of HIV etc.)[77] Girls who are raped by al-Shabaad fighters (as part of the armed group's widespread campaign of rape as a tool of war) are often rejected by their communities, and thought of as now belonging to Al-Shabaad:

> Victims of rape and, at times, their families may also face severe stigma and repercussions in their communities.[78]

It is here contended; furthermore, that the recruitment and use of children by an armed group such as Al-Shabaad (which is engaged in perpetrating mass atrocities) is a '*continuing crime*'[79] under the Rome Statute (i.e. the children tend to stay alienated from their families and communities and vice versa and suffer long-term the adverse physical and mental health effects of their recruitment to and use by such an armed group or force. *Most importantly; the children tend to be forever identified with the perpetrator group in the eyes of the community even if they manage to leave the group; thus perpetuating their genocidal forcible transfer to the perpetrator group and putting the children at high risk of re-recruitment*). This author would thus dispute the view that the recruitment and use of children for active participation in hostilities, when perpetrated by a murderous armed group such as Al Shabaab and when framed as genocidal forcible transfer, ends when the children turn 15 or physically leave the armed group or force. The suffering for these Al-Shabaad ex child soldiers continues in that they can never really leave the group even if they do so physically; they are forever stigmatized by their association with Al Shabaab and generally mistrusted by their families and/or communities. As noted as well; armed groups such as Al Shabaab (perpetrators of mass atrocity) generally do *not* release their child soldiers or do so in highly limited fashion to perpetrate a sham on the international community when under pressure then only to re-recruit many if not

[77] For instance See Schauer and Elbert , T. (2009).

[78] Human Rights Watch (2012a, p. 60).

[79] There is dispute as to whether or not the Rome Statute (2002) contemplates the notion of 'continuing crimes'. This author maintains that the Statute should be interpreted as doing so and that this is consistent with the purpose of the Statute and its mandate to hold accountable those who commit the gravest of international crimes which generally are continuing crimes. Arguably the prohibition against appropriation and use of other people's children has been a part of customary law for some time. For a discussion of the matter of continuing crimes under the Rome Statute (2002) see Nissel (2004).

most of the children "released" (the returnees). The framing of the recruitment and use of children (persons under 18) by armed groups or forces such as Al Shabaab also in terms of the 'genocidal forcible transfer of children' is more consistent with an appreciation of the fact that the crime is a continuing one (the children continue to be perceived as members of the perpetrator group even if they are no longer physically with the group and are now15 or older).

6.6 Pursuing the Accountability of Somali Perpetrators

Human Rights Watch in its 2012 report on Somalia makes the following poignant, well-intentioned (and on the view here) almost sure to be ineffectual plea:

> Al-Shabaab should publicly order its commanders to end the recruitment and use of children, and immediately hand over children within its forces to a civilian protection body, cooperating with the United Nations Children's Fund (UNICEF) and child protection actors to ensure their safe release. It should also immediately end targeted attacks on students, teachers, and schools.[80]

Armed groups or forces with an agenda of genocidal forcible transfer of children, as is here contended is the case with Al-Shabaab, will never voluntarily surrender the children *appropriated* to their 'cause'. The appropriation of children in such instances is an integral part of the genocidal common plan and not a mere strategy for increasing troop strength. Hence, such armed groups or forces generally intend for the most part to continue to enslave the child soldiers amongst them indefinitely (this notwithstanding any sham demobilization orders that may be issued or releases of small numbers of children for propaganda purposes that may occur in some situations such as was the case with the UPC/FPLC in the Democratic Republic of Congo conflict as earlier discussed).

Human Rights Watch in its 2012 report laments that:

> There remains no accountability in Somalia for violations of international human rights and humanitarian law. The TFG and AMISOM have not taken action against commanders responsible for laws-of-war violations or the conscription of children. Al-Shabaab has to date been impervious to all calls to end human rights abuses. Governments supporting the TFG and AMISOM have largely failed to recognize that al-Shabaab atrocities are counter-productive and no excuse for abuses by the Somali government.[81]

Despite pro-children's rights rhetoric by key State players on the international stage and by the UN; in practical terms; there has been little in the way of concrete steps taken by the international community to end the grave widespread abuses against children in Somalia. Those abuses include widespread recruitment and use of children by an armed group committing mass atrocities (on the view here genocidal forcible transfer of children, persons under age 18, to Al-Shabaab as

[80] Human Rights Watch (2012a, p. 5).

[81] Human Rights Watch (2012a, p. 3).

child soldiers to enter into combat, perpetrate atrocities and/or serve as sex slaves and perform a variety of other functions) and by the forces of the Transitional Government (both of which have under 15s in their forces and do not use age screening to exercise due diligence not to violate in this regard the customary rules of war and the Additional Protocols to the Geneva Conventions)[82]:

> The TFG has come under too little pressure to improve its record on children's rights, or human rights more generally, by key international actors who, by offering political and financial support to Somalia, are in a position to demand progress...***The "Roadmap" signed in September 2011 under the auspices of the UN Political Office for Somalia*** *(UNPOS), which is seen by international partners of the TFG as the main instrument through which to hold the TFG to account,* ***vaguely refers to ending recruitment of children but fails to include clear benchmarks that would enable monitoring compliance. While the UN and US have recently called on the TFG to end the use and recruitment of children, to date they have not sought to condition support to TFG forces on this basis.***[83]

It is here maintained that the UN Security Council should refer the Somalia situation to the ICC with respect to (1) the recruitment and use of children for active participation in hostilities amounting to both war crimes and genocidal forcible transfer of children in the case of Al Shabaab and in respect of various other armed parties to the conflict; and with respect to (2) widespread sexual violence crimes and other grave crimes perpetrated by armed groups or forces against children which, on the facts, constitute crimes against humanity and/or war crimes committed against children. (In the case of Al Shabaab sexual victimization of children also serves as a vehicle for the genocidal forcible transfer of children to the perpetrator group). It is here argued that the failure of the U.N. Security Council to refer the Somalia situation to the ICC (a situation involving such egregious violations of international law as perpetrated by Al-Shabaab) is tantamount, under the circumstances, to a *de facto* immunity for the perpetrators. It must not be allowed to be the case that with respect to child-specific international crimes[84]; that the international political calculus is such that UN intervention in terms of a referral of the situation (such as with the Somalia situation) to the ICC by the UN Security Council is not deemed prudent (i.e. that the alleged peace versus justice balance in such instances is *a priori* pre-weighted in favour of the U.N. *not* making the ICC referral).[85] Clearly, after 21 years of armed conflict and the ongoing grave human rights abuses/international crimes perpetrated against children in Somalia (perpetrated in particular but not exclusively by al-Shabaad) purported political

---

[82] Additional Protocols I and II to the 1949 Geneva Conventions (1977).

[83] Human Rights Watch (2012a, pp. 4–5, emphasis added).

[84] The child-specific international crimes referred to are those involving the genocidal forcible transfer of children (persons under 18) and the recruitment and use of under 15s for active participation in hostilities.

[85] Note that the OTP of the ICC has made it clear that "there is a difference between the concepts of the 'interests of justice' and the 'interests of peace' and that the latter falls within the mandate of institutions rather than the Office of the Prosecutor." [Office of the ICC Prosecutor. Policy paper on the interests of justice (September 2007, p. 1)].

rationales for non-referral seem particularly vacuous. Further, it seems wholly inadequate that instead of demands for a referral of the Somalia situation to the ICC, there should be instead a call (such as that by Human Rights Watch) only for a UN Commission of Inquiry on Somalia.[86]

The women and children of Somalia and other victims are entitled to justice through the ICC for the grave violations of their fundamental human rights; justice that is long overdue. A UN Commission of Inquiry that takes considerable time to further document the suffering of the Somali people; in particular women and children[87] is no substitute for a referral of the situation to the ICC. Once a situation is referred to the ICC Prosecutor, he or she is duty bound-in theory at least-to set politics aside. Further, there is a checkpoint in this regard in that any Prosecutorial decision not to proceed with a full investigation is subject to review by the Pre-Trial Chamber which will scrutinize the available evidence to determine whether this decision (not to further pursue the matter and develop cases) is warranted or whether the reverse is in fact in the interests of justice:

> It is true that the Prosecutor, when exercising his discretion under Article 53 of the Statute, may take into account the concept of the "interests of justice", which gives some elbow room for him to decline to become involved in certain circumstances.... However, as he has made clear... ***where there is a basis to believe that crimes under the jurisdiction of the Court have been committed, prosecution is meant to be the default option.... Furthermore, as has been said by the Prosecutor, the interests of justice are not necessarily the same as the interests of peace.***[88]

Moreno-Ocampo (as of June 2012 former ICC Prosecutor[89]) has commented as follows in respect of the issue of politics on the one hand versus the interests of justice and its relation to ending impunity on the other:

> The Statute provides a clear framework to select situations and cases to investigate. [...] I have to apply the law. Nothing more, nothing less. The decision that ending impunity will endure lasting peace and security was taken in Rome. I should not, and I will not take into account political considerations.[90]

The failure of the U.N. Security Council to refer Somalia to the ICC (i.e. for the extreme human rights abuses against children occurring there; many in the context of recruiting and using children as child soldiers for active participation in hostilities) clearly serves to *in effect*, at least to some considerable degree, undercut, in the *perceptions* of key players in the international community and/or the region,

---

[86] Human Rights Watch (2012a, p. 6).

[87] "Children have suffered both from the conflict generally and because they have been specifically targeted for recruitment, rape, forced marriage, and other grave violations of international law by the parties to the conflict." Human Rights Watch (2012a, p. 11). Children have also succumbed in record numbers due to the drought conditions with most affect regions in south-central Somalia and given al-Shabaad's blocking of much of the attempted international humanitarian assistance.

[88] Cryer (2009, pp. 71–72, emphasis added).

[89] Moreno-Ocampo only recently ended his term as ICC Prosecutor replaced by Prosecutor Fatou Bensouda who took her oath of office 15 June, 2012.

[90] Cryer (2009, p. 71).

the gravity of the crimes against children being committed in Somalia. It is imperative that such situations are referred to the ICC for investigation and possible prosecutions in as much as the child victims are otherwise not properly regarded as victims. In the latter regard, note also that children "associated" with al-Shabaad are detained by the TFG merely due to their so-called association. Thus the transitional government is not fully regarding these children as victims of Al Shabaab. Human Rights Watch has the following to say on the issue of the detention of children captured as members of al-Shabaab:

> It should... ensure that captured children alleged to have been formerly associated with al-Shabaab are promptly transferred to civilian rehabilitation and reintegration programs. Children should not be detained solely for their association with armed opposition groups.[91]
>
> ***Reports suggest that a proportion of escaped and captured children are sent to different TFG camps and detention facilities that fail to meet basic international standards.*** [some captured children said to be part of al-Shabaad have been sent to adult prisons, are not in separate quarters and have been maltreated including being malnourished].[92] ***This has raised concerns as to whether the TFG is taking into account the best interests of the children, including how to rehabilitate and reintegrate them into society.***[93]

It is here contended that until and unless children who are members of armed groups or forces perpetrating mass atrocities and/or genocide are properly regarded as the victims of the 'genocidal forcible transfer of children', these children will not be viewed fully as the victims that they are in fact.[94] While it is here understood that the term 'children associated with armed forces' is intended to be more inclusive such that it covers, for instance, also girl soldiers who may be used for the most part though not exclusively as sex slaves, the term is in some respects 'sanitized'. This is the case since, as discussed, children recruited and used by armed groups or forces committing mass atrocities and/or genocide are, regardless of gender, the victims of genocidal forcible transfer. Thus, their so-called 'association' with those groups or forces generally continues in that: (1) these armed groups or forces are reluctant to release the children even in alleged post-conflict periods after peace agreements are at least signed and (2) the children, for the most part, even if rescued or otherwise escaped or released from the perpetrator armed group or force; remain highly stigmatized and *are generally still considered by a large proportion of their home communities as belonging to; being the children of, the perpetrator armed group or force*. Thus, the children's "association" so-called with the armed perpetrator group continues indefinitely in the latter sense.

It is necessary, but by no means sufficient, to simply have the UN monitor and report on the situation for children in Somalia and to put international pressure on the TFG in the Somalia to end the so-called recruitment and use of child soldiers by

[91] Human Rights Watch (2012a, p. 5).

[92] Human Rights Watch (2012a, p. 50).

[93] Human Rights Watch (2012a, p. 49, emphasis added).

[94] See for example Drumbl (2012) who argues that child members of armed groups or forces committing mass atrocities do not always hold victim status or victim status exclusively. For the opposing view see, for instance, Grover (2012).

the TGF and al-Shabaab (and other armed groups in Somalia). After such longstanding impunity for grave violations of women and children's fundamental human rights in particular, it is time to refer the Somalia situation to the ICC. This, furthermore, is an urgent situation not in small part as the children of Somalia are at increasing risk of transfer to al-Shabaad in particular given: (1) the growing power of al-Shabaad and (2) the tremendous increase in numbers of unaccompanied children on the street, in refugee camps and in child-headed households in Somalia:

> The numbers of abandoned, orphaned, or separated children and children living and working in the streets has skyrocketed over the course of the last four years.[95]
>
> Children are also among the most vulnerable groups of internally displaced persons and refugees for both protection and health reasons. The number of unaccompanied minors and child-headed households among the displaced person and refugee population has increased over the course of the conflict, particularly since 2007.[96]
>
> ... ***as of July 2011 al-Shabaab still controlled eight of the sixteen districts of the capital. In al-Shabaab-controlled areas, there was virtually nowhere that children could be assured of their safety***. While families sought shelter in their homes during periods of intense fighting between al-Shabaab and AMISOM forces, homes offered no protection from the ongoing forced recruitments by al-Shabaab. Children told Human Rights Watch how al-Shabaab approached homes where families were known to have boys considered old enough to fight and demanded that families hand them over to join their forces.[97]

Thus it is argued that referral of the Somalia situation by the U.N. Security Council to the ICC is a human rights imperative given both the gravity of international crimes being committed and their widespread nature and considering what is in the interests of justice for the children of Somalia in particular. Measures that involve conditioning military and peacekeeping assistance on human rights improvements (such as reducing the recruitment and use of children for active participation in hostilities by the TFG and progress in ending al-Shabaad's recruitment and use of child soldiers) are recommended by Human Rights Watch.[98] Such measures in the abstract seem reasonable but whether they would in fact reduce the recruitment and use of child soldiers by the TFG at least or positively impact the besieged civilian population or worsen their situation is an open question. In any case, the Transitional Federal Government of Somalia continues to receive military aid from the US despite the TFG's continued use of child soldiers and failure to implement a system for age screening. That aid is provided through the State Department's peacekeeping account.[99] In any case, such measures *cannot* be considered a substitute for ICC prosecution of those most responsible for grave violations of the basic human rights of children (violations that constitute grave

---

[95] Human Rights Watch (2012a, p. 17).

[96] Human Rights Watch (2012a, p. 17).

[97] Human Rights Watch (2012a, p. 17, emphasis added).

[98] Human Rights Watch (2012a, p. 102).

[99] Lobe (2011).

international crimes under the Rome Statute).[100] This is especially the case since perceived national security interests appear unjustifiably to trump the fundamental human rights of children over or under age 15 recruited and use for active participation in hostilities by national armed forces and rebel armed groups in Somalia. Hence, on the analysis here, a referral by the U.N. Security Council of the Somalia situation to the ICC appears more than justified and long overdue.

Unfortunately, when it comes to prosecuting individuals via the ICC mechanism for their widespread appropriation and use of children as child soldiers, there appears to be little consistency in the way various State situations are handled by the international community. Another example of *de facto* immunity *to date* for the genocidal forcible transfer of masses of children to various parties committing atrocities in an armed conflict is to be found in the situation in Chad[101] to be discussed next.

6.7 The Situation in Chad and the Matter of Impunity for Perpetrating 'Child Soldiering'

6.7.1 Reports by Amnesty International and the UN on the Situation in Chad

Although the former ICC Prosecutor Moreno-Ocampo has in the past issued statements that he was monitoring and conducting a preliminary examination of the situation in Chad,[102] there is yet to be a formal investigation opened and approved by the Pre-Trial Chamber or cases pursued for prosecution relating to grave international crimes already committed against children by various armed parties in Chad including the State national armed forces (i.e. in relation to mass rape of women and girls and/or the recruitment and/or use of child soldiers for participation in hostilities). A Human Rights Watch 2011 report no longer listed Chad as one of the States under consideration for possible formal investigation of the situation after preliminary examination of the evidence was complete.[103] Though a State party to the Rome Statute[104] since 2006, Chad has not, in pursuit of accountability for the perpetrators of grave international crimes, self-referred to the ICC atrocities committed on its territory. This despite the fact that as late as

[100] Rome Statute (2002).

[101] Chad ratified the Rome Statute 1 November, 2006. Chad is providing the ICC access to Darfurian refugees to assist in the ICC prosecution of cases relating to Darfur, Sudan but would not assist in the apprehension and transfer of President Al-Bashir of Sudan to the ICC.

[102] Coalition for the International Criminal Court (n.d.).

[103] Human Rights Watch (2011, p. 1).

[104] Rome Statute (2002).

April 2012; the U.N. recognized that serious human rights concerns remain regarding Chad and that Chad is lacking in "judicial capacity":

> A senior United Nations human rights official has acknowledged that the political will exists in Chad to improve human rights, but noted that the country has a difficult task ahead, having to address problems that range from food shortages[105] to violence against women, ***impunity and limited judicial capacity***.[106]

Amnesty International's 2011 report: "A compromised future: Children recruited by armed forces and groups in Eastern Chad"[107] details the fact that children in Eastern Chad were/are being recruited and used in the armed conflict in that country. Especially at risk for such recruitment and use are the internally displaced child refugees from Darfur; some 're-settled' at refugee camp sites:

> All parties involved in the conflict in eastern Chad recruited and use children – the Chadian army (Armeé Nationale Tchadienne, ANT) as well as Chadian and Sudanese armed opposition groups. Community leaders from different ethnic groups use children to participate in violent communal conflicts and unrest. The Chadian government has said that it has no policy of recruiting children but has admitted to the presence of children within the army. Until moves towards normalizing relations at the beginning of 2010, both the Chadian and Sudanese governments actively supported armed groups opposed to each other despite evidence that these groups were actively recruiting children. The Justice and Equality Movement (JEM), a Sudanese armed group, has been particularly active in recruiting children. Children in refugee camps and in Internally Displaced Persons (IDP) sites in eastern Chad have frequently gone missing and later been found in the ranks of armed groups. JEM recruitment campaigns for fighters continued in refugee camps and IDP sites in eastern Chad in 2010.[108]

According to U.N. sources in 2007, between 7,000 and 10,000 children were estimated to have been used as fighters and/or recruited by Chadian and Sudanese armed opposition forces and the Chadian national armed forces.[109] As of December 2010, only 850 of these children had received rehabilitation services from UNICEF.[110] Although the Chadian government has participated in developing action plans to end the recruitment and use of child soldiers, organized checks for children at military camps; and met with UN officials to discuss the issue; Amnesty International reported in 2011 that the prevention of child soldier recruitment and use by rebel groups, and demobilization and re-integration efforts regarding child soldiers have been rather ineffectual due to a number of factors including instability and insecurity in the region.[111] There are currently in 2012 in Chad an estimated 264,000 Sudanese refugees; 64,000 refugees from the Central African Republic and

[105] UNICEF (2012):Food shortages in Chad have reached to the point in 2012 of creating life threatening conditions for many civilians with children being especially vulnerable.

[106] All Africa UN (News Service) (4 April, 2012).

[107] Amnesty International (2011).

[108] Amnesty International (2011, p. 5).

[109] Amnesty International (2011, p. 5).

[110] Amnesty International (2011, p. 5).

[111] Amnesty International (2011, p. 6).

approximately 130,000 IDPs with only a comparatively small segment of the IDPs having been reintegrated back into their areas of origin.[112] The high number of refugees and IDPs; the return of large numbers of Chadians from Libya combined with severe droughts have led to acute food shortages in parts of Chad in 2012. These factors strain Chadian government resources and its ability to effectively address other matters such as the demobilization of child soldiers and prevention of recruitment and use of child soldiers in hostilities thus no doubt contributing to the inadequate human rights situation which still prevails in Chad.[113] Refugees and IDPs are particularly vulnerable to attack and the children amongst them to sexual violence and recruitment[114] into Chadian rebel groups in 2012 as in years past.

Amnesty International in its 2011 report notes that for years the Sudanese and Chadian government supported each others' armed opposition groups.[115] In 2010, relations normalized somewhat between the two countries and the two countries now jointly monitor the common border to repel any attempted rebel incursions.[116] However, these rebel groups (such as the Sudanese rebel group the Justice Equality Movement[117]) are notorious for the recruitment and use of child soldiers (often 'recruiting' in refugee camps)[118] and for the commission of atrocities including sexual violence directed against women and girls. Note, in addition, that some of the sexual violence against women and girls has also been committed by members of the Chadian national armed forces.[119]

In a 2011 report the UN Secretary-General on children and armed conflict reported that:

> During the period under review [July 2008 to December 2010], the country Task Force on Monitoring and Reporting in Chad documented grave violations against children, including: recruitment and use of children by armed forces and groups [most of the children being between 14 and 17 but some being as young as 12][120]; killing and maiming of children, principally from unexploded ordinance; and sexual and gender-based violence. In addition access to adequate humanitarian services was limited owing to attacks on humanitarians.[121]

---

[112] UNHCR (2012).

[113] All Africa UN (News Service) (4 April, 2012).

[114] Report of the Secretary-General on children and armed conflict (9 February, 2011, p. 5, para 11).

[115] Amnesty International (2011, p. 10).

[116] UNHCR (2012).

[117] Chad was accused by Sudan of supporting a JEM attack on Omdurman 10 May, 2008 in which children participated as child soldiers. About 109 of those children were captured by the Sudanese and at least 8 were tried and sentenced to death in contravention of international law [See Amnesty International (2011, p. 11)].

[118] Report of the Secretary-General on children and armed conflict (9 February, 2011, p. 6, para 18).

[119] Report of the Secretary-General on children and armed conflict (9 February, 2011).

[120] Report of the Secretary-General on children and armed conflict (9 February, 2011, p. 5, para 12).

[121] Report of the Secretary-General on children and armed conflict (9 February, 2011, pp. 4–5, para 10).

On the 23 February, 2012, the annual United Nations report documenting conflict-related sexual violence around the world noted that sexual violence in Chad threatened security and peace-building efforts in that State.[122]

A recently released report by 'Child Soldiers International' (formerly the 'Coalition to Stop the Use of Child Soldiers') observed that:

> ...***although the [Chadian] government does not appear to recruit children as a matter of policy, the security environment remains conducive to the recruitment and use of children.*** Despite the lull in conflict, incidents of children associated with the armed forces were still reported – albeit at significantly reduced levels – in 2011, demonstrating that effective prevention mechanisms are still lacking.[123]
>
> ...government control over the child RRR [release, recovery and reintegration program in Chad] has resulted in a focus being put on screening armed opposition groups; the same level of scrutiny was not applied to the ANT [Chadian National Army (*Armée nationale tchadienne*/ANT)], as ***only five per cent of the children registered as demobilized were released from the army. Finally, the recruitment and use of children, although illegal, has not yet been criminalized, and the government has failed to investigate reported allegations of unlawful child recruitment and use and sanction those found responsible***. In some cases, alleged perpetrators have been given amnesties or even high-level appointments. ***To date, no member of the national army is known to have been held accountable for recruiting or using children – a failure that is symptomatic of a broader inability or unwillingness to hold members of the army accountable***.[124]

If respect for international criminal and humanitarian law is to be upheld; those most responsible must be held to account for their grave international crimes in Chad (such crimes notably in large part involving the recruitment and use of children in armed conflict and widespread sexual violence against women and girls) As the Chadian government is either unwilling and/or unable to address these issues effectively (perhaps due in part to its less than robust judiciary)[125]; it is imperative that: (1) Chad make a self-referral to the ICC regarding international crimes relating to child soldiering and the systematic and widespread sexual violence being perpetrated against women and children in Chad; or alternatively, (2) if such a self-referral is not forthcoming, that the ICC Prosecutor on his own motion pursue a preliminary investigation hopefully to be followed up (with the Pre-Trial Chamber's permission) by an in-depth investigation of the grave human rights abuses that have occurred in Eastern Chad and which continue to this date. This with a view to developing cases for prosecution. That ICC investigation must consider both: (1) the activities of rebel armed groups in Chad and (2) the Chadian national army's conduct (in respect to perpetrating the recruitment and use of child soldiers and the sexual violation of women and girls) if the ICC is not to be accused of political partisanship and instead maintain a general perceived moral legitimacy.[126]

---

[122] UN News Centre (23 February, 2012) UN report on sexual violence during conflict singles out worst offenders.

[123] Child Soldiers International (2012, p. 2, emphasis added).

[124] Child Soldiers International (2012, p. 2, emphasis added).

[125] All Africa UN (News Service) (4 April, 2012)

[126] For further discussion and debate regarding the issue of politics and the ICC see, for instance, Nouwen and Werner (2011).

6.7.2 *Chad and the U.S. 'Child Soldiers Prevention Act of 2008'*

Chad is one of the countries to which President Obama in 2011 for the second year in a row granted a waiver regarding a U.S. law (the U.S. Child Soldiers Prevention Act of 2008)[127] that entered into force in 2010. The latter statute prohibits, with a few exceptions, U.S. military assistance (i.e. military training and financing etc.) from being given to countries that recruit and use child soldiers.[128] Chad was granted the waiver as:

> In Chad, according to the White House, the government had issued an "action plan" to halt child recruitment and demobilise child soldiers and taken some steps towards its implementation. It said a U.N.-led task force charged with monitoring the problem had not verified any cases of recruitment during 2011 and that the government had turned over some 1,000 children to UNICEF and NGOs for re-integration programmes.[129]

However, Human Rights groups are unsure to what degree Chad will follow through to ensure full demobilization of child soldiers in the State national armed forces and work toward the end of child soldier recruitment by all armed entities in its territory.[130] Further,

> *... several activists noted that the United Nations and State Department both kept Chad on their list of countries violating international standards for child recruitment this year* [2011], and that international monitors' limited access in Chad calls into question anybody's ability to verify whether the government has stopped using child soldiers.[131]

Note that Chad was listed on the U.N. Secretary-General's annual report on children and armed conflict[132] as one of the worst offenders in violating children's rights during armed conflict in that: (1) the *Armée nationale tchadienne*, including newly integrated elements, and the Justice Equality Movement (JEM) in Chad still recruit and use children for active participation in hostilities and (2) both armed forces were listed in the aforementioned report as persistent offenders in this regard. The Chadian national army has, however, entered into an action plan agreement with the U.N. to end this conduct but it remains to be seen if its' promises are kept.

Somalia also receives varied military assistance from the U.S. despite the fact that child soldiers are still found in the ranks of the national forces of the Transition Federal Government (TFG) and there are no age screening mechanisms in place to ensure that when militias are integrated into the TFG forces, for example, more child soldiers will not be amongst them. This is the case since the U.S. provides military financing to Somalia through a peacekeeping account.

---

[127] U.S. Child Soldiers Prevention Act (2008).

[128] Lobe (2011). The other countries granted the waiver as well were the Democratic Republic of Congo (the DRC received a partial waiver only given its restance to fully demobilizing child soldiers), Yemen and the newly independent nation of South Sudan.

[129] Lobe (2011).

[130] Patel (2011).

[131] Rogin (2011).

[132] Report of the U.N. Secretary-General on children and armed conflict (26 April, 2012).

Child soldier is defined in the U.S. 'Child Soldiers Prevention Act' as follows:

CHILD SOLDIER.—Consistent with the provisions of the Optional Protocol to the Convention of the Rights of the Child,[133] the term "child soldier"—
(A) means—

(i) any person under 18 years of age who takes a direct part in hostilities as a member of governmental armed forces;
(ii) any person under 18 years of age who has been compulsorily recruited into governmental armed forces;
(iii) any person under 15 years of age who has been voluntarily recruited into governmental armed forces; or
(iv) any person under 18 years of age who has been recruited or used in hostilities by armed forces distinct from the armed forces of a state; and
(B) includes any person described in clauses (ii), (iii), or (iv) of subparagraph (A) who is serving in any capacity, including in a support role such as a cook, porter, messenger, medic, guard, or sex slave.[134]

It is noteworthy that the U.S. includes sex slaves as child soldiers if they meet the definition of child soldier as set out in the statutory provision cited above. The above cited provisions of the U.S. 'Child Soldiers Prevention Act'[135] do not include as child soldiers children over age 15 who allegedly volunteered for service in a State national armed force and did not take direct part in hostilities. Note that there are no distinctions made in the aforementioned U.S. law in regards to whether or not the national State armed force in question was committing mass atrocities and/or genocide. If the State national armed force was perpetrating grave international crimes as part of a common plan then, on the analysis here: (1) child members of such a force (persons under 18) would be the victims of genocidal forcible transfer to that perpetrator group and (2) *any* child member would be considered a *forced* 'child soldier' (where child refers to persons under 18).

The four countries granted the waiver regarding compliance with the U.S. 'Child Soldiers' Prevention Act "are slated to receive a total of more than 200 million dollars in military aid in 2012."[136] Human Rights Watch decried the decision in the following statement:

Countries that keep using child soldiers aren't going to get serious about ending the practice until they see the U.S. is serious about withholding the money. The Obama administration has been unwilling to make even small cuts to military assistance to governments exploiting children as soldiers. Children are paying the price for its poor leadership. (Quote from Jo Becker, head of HRW's children's rights division).[137]

[133] The U.S. ratified the Optional protocol to the Convention on the Rights of the Child on the involvement of children in armed conflict 23 December, 2002 (the U.S. has signed the CRC but not ratified that Convention).

[134] U.S. Child Soldiers Prevention Act (2008).

[135] U.S. Child Soldiers Prevention Act (2008).

[136] Lobe (2011).

[137] Cited in Lobe (2012).

We must be highly self-conscious in our actual practice in respect of abiding by international norms in armed conflict not to return to a time when the *purported* legitimacy of the recruitment and use of child soldiers was determined by the parties to the conflict alone.[138] States fighting terrorism (domestic or international) then, on the view here, gain no legitimated right to recruit or use child soldiers whether over or under age 15 for active participation in hostilities. The use of children in hostilities is an inhumane practice (as the ICRC has long pointed out) violating the special protected status of a highly vulnerable group (a group with little if any political power generally and which is not a party to any international treaty, convention or other international agreement and which, in most contemporary situations of armed conflict, does not benefit regardless which party to the armed conflict is the ultimate victor).

6.8 Acknowledging Existing International Norms that Protect Children from Genocidal Forcible Transfer

Notwithstanding the complexities of national security interests for the West and whether the West deems it appropriate to provide some sort of military assistance in any particular situation where the State assisted is not in full compliance with relevant international law, at a minimum, respect for international humanitarian law demands that: (1) those most responsible for the recruitment and/or use of children under age 15 for active participation in hostilities be prosecuted for war crimes and that (2) those most responsible for the 'recruitment' and/or use of children (persons under age 18) for participation in any respect in a State or non-State armed force or group perpetrating mass atrocities and/or genocide be prosecuted for the 'genocidal forcible transfer of children' (in addition to any war crimes charges relevant to the matter of child soldiering).

The charge has been made explicitly by some scholars and implied by others that:

> A major challenge for human rights and humanitarian groups is that they strive to create new universal norms, rather than to reflect existing ones. Sometimes dubbed "norm entrepreneurs" such groups have a vested interest in developing and expanding the scope of international law. At the same time, these groups are dependent upon sovereign States to sign, ratify and implement the treaties that encode human rights and humanitarian concerns into international law.[139]

[138] For example Rosen points out that "... Protocol Additional I permitted guerrilla movements engaging in wars of national liberation to recruit and enlist children below the age of fifteen by categorizing wars of national liberation as international conflicts rather than as internal conflicts. This was particularly significant since virtually all insurgent forces in twentieth century wars of national liberation recruited vast numbers of child fighters." (Rosen, D.M., p. 93).

[139] Rosen (2009).

The argument has been made here, however, that children's privileged status during times of armed conflict is well-established in customary law and international humanitarian law (i.e. as incorporated in the Additional Protocols to the 1949 Geneva Conventions)[140] and is not a novel norm in the new millennium. Furthermore, the Additional Protocols to the 1949 Geneva Conventions[141] arguably have themselves attained the status of customary law. Furthermore, the prohibition on the 'genocidal forcible transfer of children' was incorporated into the Genocide Convention of 1951[142] and duplicated in the Rome Statute[143] of 2002. Thus, considering the foregoing; this book has not been about "new universal norms" but about the obligation to implement an existing *jus cogens* norm (the prohibition against the genocidal forcible transfer of children). That well established norm is critical to the protection of children against recruitment and use in any manner or for any purpose by State or non-State armed forces or groups committing mass atrocities and/or genocide.

As to the issue of human rights advocates being "dependent upon sovereign States to sign, ratify and implement the treaties that encode human rights and humanitarian concerns into international law"[144]; it is to be noted that State sovereignty in fact does *not*, in principle at least, extend so far as to afford any State a discretionary choice to violate *jus cogens* norms such as the prohibition against genocide. This is the case notwithstanding whether or not the State in question is a party to a treaty that codifies these violations as grave international crimes. That is; State sovereignty does *not* provide immunity in respect of endorsing, facilitating, orchestrating and/or tolerating grave international crimes on the State's territory or perpetrated by its nationals outside of its territory. That the international community may potentially intervene where the State is unwilling and/or unable to prevent and end these grave international crimes (genocide, crimes against humanity and war crimes) is reflected, for instance, in the mechanism that provides for referral of a non-State party to the ICC (that is, the Rome Statute[145] permits referral by the UN Security Council to the ICC for non-State parties to the Rome Statute[146]). The violation of *jus cogens* norms (relating to prohibitions against genocide, crimes against humanity and war crimes) are viewed as ultimately being a threat to peace and hence of concern to humanity as a whole.

[140] Additional Protocols I and II to the 1949 Geneva Conventions (1977).

[141] Additional Protocols I and II to the 1949 Geneva Conventions (1977).

[142] Convention on the Prevention and Punishment of the Crime of Genocide (Genocide Convention) (1951).

[143] Rome Statute (2002).

[144] Rosen (2009).

[145] Rome Statute (2002).

[146] Rome Statute (2002).

6.8.1 Gaps in Children's Access to International Justice

How the international community deals with the perpetrators most responsible for the recruitment and use of children (persons under age 18) for active participation in hostilities is itself a test of the moral legitimacy of the 'gravity' and 'interests of justice' assessments made by the UN Security Council, the ICC Prosecutor, the judicial panels of the ICC, individual States Parties to the Rome Statute[147] and the international community as a whole. Respectfully, we have seen in what has here been discussed that ICC jurisprudence is flawed and inconsistent in many respects in meting out justice to perpetrators when it comes to 'child soldiering'; even in respect of so-called 'child soldiering' which occurs in the most horrendous of contexts (that is, where the children are recruited and/or used for active participation in hostilities by armed State or non-State forces or groups perpetrating mass atrocities and/or genocide). Thus, we have the following selected examples, for instance, of the failure to deliver international justice in a fulsome and consistent manner regarding the child soldiering issue: (1) In *Lubanga*; sexual violence (rape, forced pregnancy etc.) was not charged in terms of separate war crimes nor as a form of genocidal forcible transfer of the children sexually victimized to the perpetrator group. Further, child sex slaves of the FPLC were not clearly declared by the Lubanga Trial Chamber to be child soldiers actively participating in hostilities; (2) no referral has to date been made by the UN Security Council to the ICC of the Somalia situation (there has been no such referral with a view to ultimately allowing for the prosecution of, for instance, Al-Shabaab commanders who continue to commit unspeakable atrocities against children in Somalia including against children who attempt to resist their own recruitment and use as child soldiers by the Al-Shabaab. There has also been thus a failure to prosecute Somali national army commanders who recruited and used child soldiers on a widespread basis); (3) there has been a failure to charge Al Bashir (as commander-in-chief) with crimes relating to the recruitment and use of child soldiers for active participation in hostilities by government armed forces and regarding his complicity with respect to his allied militia (the Janjaweed) and their use of child soldiers, (4) there has been also a failure to charge the genocidal forcible transfer of children in cases where children are appropriated indefinitely by an armed group or force committing mass atrocities and/or genocide (i.e. the Janjaweed and the SAF both have been reluctant to release the child soldiers from their ranks and continue to use these children, for instance, to perpetrate atrocities as so-called child soldiers and as sex slaves).

While one can appreciate the enormous constraints under which the ICC Prosecutor Moreno-Ocampo was operating in pursuing investigations and prosecutions (constraints that the new ICC Prosecutor Fatou Bensouda will have to contend with as well since taking office in June 2012);[148] one can yet justifiably contend that, to date, in many instances, in particular insofar as child victims are concerned:

---

[147] Rome Statute (2002).

[148] Several States have insisted on zero increase in the ICC budget (see Human Rights Watch 2011, p. 2). There are also constraints on ICC investigations due to volatile country security situations and concerns regarding the safety of potential witnesses and victim participants that hamper progress in prosecuting cases etc.

> . . .the ICC's investigations and prosecutions have failed to demonstrate coherent and effective strategies for delivering meaningful justice. . .[149]

It is clear that many of the situations involving the widespread recruitment and use of children for child soldiering/sex slavery by armed forces or groups have not been formally investigated by the ICC (i.e. Somalia and Chad). Further, cases that have been developed have not always addressed the child soldiering/child sex slavery issue when in fact child soldiering/child sex slavery is a prominent feature on the facts of the case and in terms of the broader particular situational context (i.e. the Al Bashir case, Darfur, Sudan). These glaring gaps in ICC prosecutions and investigations exist though the international community is well aware of decades long human rights abuses against children in particular occurring during armed conflict in these specific cases and situations and the unwillingness and/or inability of the national government to hold those most responsible to account. Human Rights Watch holds; and most would, given the ICC mandate, likely not disagree that:

> Identification of . . .cases should emerge. . .with a focus on perpetrators and incidents that match up with underlying crime patterns, and with particular attention given to those cases—whether because they are the most complex or because they target high-level defendants—least likely to be effectively pursued by national authorities.[150]

Clearly, there is no consistency in regards to the willingness[151] or capacity of the ICC[152] to prosecute those most responsible for perpetrating child soldiering/sex slavery during armed conflict even in a context in which these children are appropriated indefinitely as members of the armed group or force (as victims of the 'genocidal forcible transfer of children'). What is clear is that the ICC Prosecutor's selection of cases must be made on an impartial and non-political basis. Further, the Pre-Trial Chamber's decisions regarding (1) authorizing or not authorizing formal investigations of situations and (2) confirming charges in particular developed cases from those situations must be apolitical in nature. These features are part and parcel of what is required to ensure the independence of the ICC:

> Rather than provide "victor's justice," the ICC should investigate and prosecute crimes committed by all sides within its jurisdiction, even where doing so is politically inconvenient or otherwise difficult.[153]

---

[149] Human Rights Watch (2011, p. 2).

[150] Human Rights Watch (2011, p. 4).

[151] For instance, consider the situation in Chad and the impunity existing for international crimes perpetrated during armed conflict against children and women in Chad; impunity in part due to inaction at the national level regarding prosecution of those most responsible. Chad ratified the Rome statute 1 November, 2006 and it entered into force 1 January, 2007. There has yet been no self-referral by the State of the situation in Chad to the ICC nor had the former ICC prosecutor taken steps to begin a preliminary examination on his own motion of the situation in Chad regarding child soldiering and child sex slavery.

[152] For instance, consider the failure of the U.N. Security Council to refer Somalia to the ICC *versus* the referral of Darfur, Sudan despite the grave abuses of children and women occurring on a systemic basis in Somalia as well and the failure of the Transitional Federal Government (TFG), for a variety of complex reasons, to vigorously prosecute those most responsible.

[153] Human Rights Watch (2011, p. 5).

The former ICC Prosecutor Moreno-Ocampo has been criticized for not charging government officials also responsible for participation directly or indirectly in the perpetration of grave international crimes falling under ICC jurisdiction (i.e. in the Uganda situation to date only LRA commanders have been charged but no members of the State army; the UPDF (Uganda People's Defence Forces) or government officials responsible in some way for grave international crimes committed during the relevant period).[154] This situation has arguably created an *appearance* of ICC OTP political bias in the minds of some whether such a perception is warranted or not.

6.8.2 Genocidal Context and the Recruitment and Use of Child Soldiers

Human Rights Watch (HRW) suggests that:

> The concern to do meaningful justice should guide the prosecutor in his choice of cases to pursue. In practice, this means that the ICC should try those most responsible for the most serious crimes on ***charges representative of the underlying patterns of ICC crimes***.[155]

Consider the above quote from HRW and the fact that recruitment and use of children (persons under age 18) for active participation in hostilities by armed groups or forces (State or non-State) committing mass atrocities and/or genocide does in fact involve a pattern of activity consistent with the 'genocidal forcible transfer of children'. The 'recruitment' and use of child soldiers in such circumstances involves a pattern of varied crimes against children that include all manner of atrocity including but not limited to sexual violence such as rape, sexual enslavement, cruel and inhuman treatment (i.e. compelling the children to participate in atrocities against their own families and/or communities, executing children who resist committing atrocity or attempt to escape etc.), forcible transfer away from family and community for an indefinite period, and systematic crimes against humanity in regards any child or family who dare resist the child's appropriation by the armed group or force. The broader context of crimes in which the recruitment and use of child soldiers occurs, as perpetrated by an armed group or force that systematically engages in mass atrocities and/or genocide, distinguishes this perpetrating of child soldiering as a vehicle for the genocidal forcible transfer of children (unlike the situation where children aged 15 and over are recruited and used for active participation in hostilities by armed groups or forces that abide by international humanitarian law).[156]

The current author is in accord then with the view that generally the acts that constitute genocide (although ultimately committed by individuals working as cogs

---

[154] Human Rights Watch (2011, p. 27).

[155] Human Rights Watch (2011, p. 4, emphasis added).

[156] The current author holds that children's direct or indirect participation in armed hostilities is in any circumstance an inhumane practice regardless the motives behind the military campaign.

in an overall scheme) reflect a *collective* genocidal intent and conduct and hence occur in a certain characteristic overall context:

> the Court [referring to the International Court of Justice judgment in Bosnia and Herzegovina v. Serbia and Montenegro), Judgment of 26 Feb. 2007][157] should have made it clear that, under normal circumstances, ***the genocidal intent of the individual perpetrator presupposes his or her knowledge of a collective genocidal act.***[158]

A *collective genocidal intent*, it is here argued, is present when an armed group or force (State or non-State) that systematically engages in mass atrocities and/or various forms of genocide appropriates and uses children as so-called child soldiers and/or sex slaves or in any other capacity. The collective genocidal intent of such armed groups or forces (State or non-State) in appropriating and using children is to: (1) alienate the children from their families and home communities and vice versa and to (2) physically remove the children from these communities thus destroying in part or in whole the children's groups of origin/home communities as well as reshaping the children's identities such that the children's personal and collective identity is nothing more nor less than 'FPLC' or 'LRA' or 'SAF' or that of whatever armed group or force (State or non-State) to which they have been appropriated. The targeted victims of the 'genocidal forcible transfer of children' then include both: (1) the targeted families, group of origin/communities, however identified, from whence the children come and (2) the children as a special protected group under international humanitarian and human rights law who are transferred to the armed group or force that is operating outside the margins of civilized society and committing widespread grave violations of international law. In the perception of the perpetrators of the 'genocidal forcible transfer of children' both of the aforementioned categories of victims are the intended direct victims.

The armed groups or forces committing mass atrocities and/or genocide generally target children of a particular ethnic and/or perceived 'racial' group[159] for appropriation and use as a child soldiers and/or sex slaves (children who may or may not share the same ethnic; perceived 'racial', religious, or national characteristics as the perpetrator group). The 'military training' of these children as 'child soldiers' (once transferred to the perpetrator group) typically involves cruel and inhuman treatment designed, in practice, to strip the children of all loyalty and identification other than to the perpetrator armed group or force. This is the case regardless the rhetoric that some of these commanders may use regarding nationalism and alleged national liberation movements (as did *Lubanga* in meeting with child soldier new 'recruits' at FPLC 'military' camps). The children 'recruited' and used by these murderous armed forces or groups are well indoctrinated to participate in mass atrocities which in fact weaken the nation State considerably as does the children's appropriation in the first instance.

---

[157] Case concerning the Application of the Convention on the Prevention and Punishment of the Crime of Genocide (Bosnia and Herzegovina v. Serbia and Montenegro), Judgment of 26 Feb. 2007.

[158] Kreß (2007, p. 623, emphasis added).

[159] The concept of race has no scientific validity according to the general consensus in the scientific community.

Hence such appropriation and use of children by these armed groups or forces is not in any respect consistent with a genuine expression of or motivation related to nationalism.

There is then, on the view here, a disheartening and legally insupportable failure to acknowledge as the 'genocidal forcible transfer of children': (1) the recruitment and use of children as child soldiers *by armed groups or forces perpetrating mass atrocities and/or genocide* or (2) the systematic sexual violation of girl soldiers in the aforementioned armed ranks and of the girls of other groups targeted by such armed groups or forces. The failure to acknowledge the 'genocidal forcible transfer of children' in such contexts as described is striking in that the children are appropriated by and to the perpetrator group in a most intimate fashion both symbolically and also often in terms of their physical transfer to the perpetrator group as child soldiers and/or sex slaves for an indefinite period.[160] Such appropriation of children leads to the social *and* physical destruction in part of the groups/communities from whence the children were transferred. This is the case given the reduction in the birth rate as a consequence of the children's transfer out of the home group and the loss of a segment of the next generation to whom to impart cultural tradition (in some instances such as in the DRC and Uganda very large segments of the child population were transferred ('recruited') to rebel militia as child soldiers).

The drafters of the Genocide Convention[161] understood that the genocidal forcible transfer of children to another group is about the *appropriation in the fullest sense* of children by another group and not simply about the removal *per se* of a segment of a group (some or most of the children). In regards to the appropriation of children to the perpetrator group; recall the typical reluctance of these perpetrator armed groups or forces (engaged in mass atrocities and/or genocide) to allow the child soldiers in their ranks to be demobilized at any time; including during transitional or actual post-conflict periods. Further, children who are demobilized are most often also targets for re-recruitment if left unprotected (i.e. in camps for refugees or IDP's). Where demobilization decrees have at times under international pressure been issued by, for instance, rebel leaders such as Lubanga,[162] as discussed, there is evidence that these are often largely sham orders though some small number of children may be released and turned over to UNICEF or NGOs for appearances sake.

While it is the case that Lubanga was only charged with the recruitment and use of children under 15 in armed hostilities, it is to be recalled that evidence as to the cruel and inhuman treatment of the FPLC child soldiers and the sexual violation of girl soldiers in the FPLC was entered into the court record as well as presented

[160] The removal of these children from their original group/communities reduces the birth rate in the groups/communities from whence the children were transferred (a marker for genocide) while forced pregnancies of girl child soldiers and the addition of the children recruited to the perpetrator group as child soldiers often increases substantially the perpetrator group's overall numbers.

[161] Genocide Convention (1951).

[162] HRW notes that after the charges against Lubanga were confirmed " children were hidden or chased from the [militia] ranks, and some were abandoned rather than being brought to the demobilization ceremonies." (Human Rights Watch, 2011, p. 11 FN 17).

orally by the Prosecution witnesses and experts and by victim participants through their legal representatives. That testimony which was cross-examined appears to have been accepted by the Trial Court as reflected in its judgement of 12 March, 2012.[163] Yet, disappointingly (on the view here) W.A. Schabas commenting on the *Lubanga* case and ICC prosecutorial discretion stated:

> It is difficult to reconcile the prosecutorial discourse about gravity with the decision to proceed against Lubanga.[164]

Schabas frames his argument for the alleged lack of comparative gravity of child soldier recruitment and use by armed groups such as the FPLC (which were spreading terror and committing mass atrocities) in terms of the Prosecutor declining to pursue a case against those most responsible for the invasion of Iraq and the grave violations of international law alleged in that situation perpetrated by Westerners.[165]

The topic of whether or not the ICC Prosecutor should have pursued a formal investigation and development of cases for prosecution regarding the situation in Iraq pursuant to the invasion by the U.S. and British is beyond the scope of this book. The current author would only point out that the nature and impact of the conduct involved in the crime of the 'genocidal forcible transfer of children' (as occurs when an armed group or force *perpetrating mass atrocities or genocide* on a civilian population recruits and or uses children for active participation in the fighting and/or for sexual purposes or other purposes) meets the ICC gravity test as an admissibility criterion. Such cases involving those most responsible are amongst the most serious of cases that, on the analysis here, fall under the material jurisdiction of the Court pertaining to the gravest of international crimes as contemplated by the drafters of the Rome Statute.[166] The appropriation and use of children by armed groups or forces perpetrating mass atrocities and/or genocide destroys in part the children's home communities/group of origin, undermines peace and stability in the region, contributes to the continued and varied persecution of a highly vulnerable protected group; children; and undermines the human dignity of children (persons under age 18) generally.[167] Note in this regard that Lubanga was allegedly being investigated domestically, according to the DRC, for genocide and crimes against humanity at the time of the ICC indictment for the recruitment and use of under 15s for active participation in hostilities. In 2008, Schabas wrote on this point:

---

[163] Prosecutor v Thomas Lubanga Dyilo, Final Trial Judgement Pursuant to Article 74 of the Rome Statute (14 March, 2012).

[164] Schabas (2008, p. 741).

[165] Schabas (2008, pp. 742–743). Schabas states that there have been more combat-related deaths in Iraq than in the DRC and Uganda combined in relation to the conflict in the latter territories for instance. However, the number of victims is not the only criterion to be considered. Whether cases against those most responsible for any alleged atrocities in Iraq connected to the U.S. and British invasion should have been developed by the OTP for prosecution by the ICC (assuming the ICC formalities allowing for the same were in place) is a topic beyond the scope of this book.

[166] Rome Statute (2002).

[167] For a discussion of the internationalization of crimes see Slye and Van Schaack (2009, pp. 107–119).

> It would appear that the ICC has removed Thomas Lubanga from jeopardy before the criminal tribunals of his own country *for crimes that are more serious than those for which he is being prosecuted in The Hague*. To be fair to the Prosecutor, his position was that the courts of the DRC were not prosecuting adequately. There were also concerns that Lubanga might soon be released...But perhaps if the Prosecutor would agree that if the Congolese justice system is working, then it would be better for Lubanga to stand trial at home for genocide and crimes against humanity than to stand trial in The Hague for recruitment of child soldiers. As for Lubanga he must be delighted to find himself in The Hague facing prosecution for relatively less important offences concerning child soldiers rather than genocide and crimes against humanity.[168]

The current author takes the view, on the analysis of the facts and circumstances of the situation in the DRC, and Lubanga's involvement in: (1) the FPLC appropriation and use of child soldiers; (2) the cruel and inhuman treatment accorded these child soldiers; (3) the sexual exploitation and abuse of FPLC girl child soldiers in particular though not exclusively, (4) the perpetrating of systematic and mass sexual violence and other atrocities against Lendu and Ngiti girls that Lubanga should have been charged with the genocidal forcible transfer of children as well as with war crimes and crimes against humanity that cover the full scope and pattern of the grave international crimes committed by the UPC/FPLC under the command leadership of Lubanga and his co-perpetrators. These charges would have been in addition then to the war crimes charges relating to the recruitment and use of children under 15 for active participation in hostilities which were filed against Lubanga by the OTP and confirmed by the Pre-Trial Chamber. Prosecution of Lubanga on this expanded set of charges before the ICC (rather than in his home country or before the ICC only on the war crime charge related to child soldiering that was in fact the only charge lodged and confirmed) would have been, on the view here, the more legally supportable approach given: (1) the pattern of conduct of the FPLC under the leadership of Lubanga and his co-perpetrators and given (2) the fact that the Pre-Trial Chamber appeared to have accepted the notion that the DRC was not actively pursuing an investigation of Lubanga.[169] It will be recalled that ultimately the President of the DRC at the time referred the situation in the DRC to the ICC for investigation and adjudication regarding international crimes committed in the DRC during the relevant time period.

As to just how "delighted" (to use Schabas' terminology)[170] Lubanga is to have been charged with and tried by the ICC for the war crime of recruitment and use of children under 15 for active participation in hostilities (as opposed to crimes against humanity and genocide in his home country) is an open question. However, the ICC sentence imposed of 14 years is, on the view here, quite meagre given the facts of the case and Lubanga's involvement as co-perpetrator. In any case, the current author is wholeheartedly, though respectfully, disagreed with Schabas that:

---

[168] Schabas (2008, p. 744, emphasis added).

[169] See Schabas (2008, p. 744) discussing the fact that the Pre-Trial chamber noted the Prosecutor's allegation regarding the DRC not pursuing an investigation against Lubanga.

[170] Schabas (2008, p. 744).

> The impression remains that in the *Lubanga* case, the exercise of prosecutorial discretion had more to do with the fact that this was an accused who was accessible to a court starved for trial work rather than any compelling analysis based upon either gravity or complementarity.[171]

Instead, on the current analysis, the prosecution of Lubanga fell squarely into the ICC material jurisdiction to prosecute only the most serious of conduct taking into consideration various factors, both qualitative and quantitative, in the gravity assessment as an aspect of the test for admissibility of the case.

6.8.3 Genocidal Forcible Transfer of Children Through Sexual Victimization

The current author suggests that one of the reasons for the gaps in access to international criminal justice for the child victims of recruitment and use in hostilities by armed groups or forces (State or non-State) perpetrating mass atrocities and/or genocide is the failure to charge (consistent with the facts and gravity of the crime in any particular ICC cases or situations as discussed) genocidal forcible transfer of children (in addition to war crimes relating to the recruitment and use of under 15s for active participation in hostilities.). The failure to also charge genocidal forcible transfer of children has resulted, on the view here, in the denial of justice through the ICC for: (1) child soldiers 15 and over and (2) in some instances, as in *Lubanga*, the denial of access to justice for girl soldiers sexually enslaved and violated by various armed forces and groups (these girl soldiers not being considered to have actively participated in the hostilities as per the relevant war crimes provisions dealing with recruitment and use of children under 15 in armed hostilities and the latter being the only category of charge pursued by the ICC Prosecutor in the case at issue).

A pattern of rape of children carried out in a widespread and systematic manner, is, on the analysis here, a form of genocidal forcible transfer of children as has been previously here discussed.[172] Hence, charging genocidal forcible transfer of children would have provided a framework for prosecuting the systematic and extreme and varied sexual violence crimes, including mass rape, which targeted children in particular and were carried out by various parties to the conflict in the DRC for the period covered in the various cases developed and which crimes appear to be continuing.[173] There was then, it is here contended, a failure of the ICC Prosecutor to properly address sexual violence crimes as a separable issue in *Lubanga* and to ensure that this was reflected in the charging. This is inconsistent with the objective of

[171] Schabas (2008, p. 744).

[172] This author concurs with those who maintain that mass rape of women (and girls) during armed conflict is a form of genocide intended to alienate these women from their communities and reduce the reproductive capacity of their communities (See for example, Mackinnon 2007).

[173] Human Rights Watch (2011, p. 9). This is not at all to suggest that sexual violence should not also have been charged as *war crimes and/or crimes against humanity* should the facts substantiate such a charge in any particular case developed in the context of the situation of the DRC.

the OTP to select incidents for trial [and charge them in such a manner] as to highlight: "...the gravest incidents and the main types of victimization."[174]

The ICC Prosecutorial approach in *Lubanga* in regards to sexual violence international crimes contributes to the culture of denial in the DRC in regards to: (1) any general acknowledgement that this category of grave international crime was and is occurring on a widespread basis in the DRC (and that there was and is special targeting of children, including girl child soldiers, for sexual violence) and (2) acknowledging the fact that sexual violence was and is perpetrated in the DRC by varied armed groups and the national State forces such that the perpetrators include both Hema and Lendu amongst others:

> Among the Hema, opinion leaders claim that the absence of other charges [such as co-perpetrating mass rape] against Lubanga (and, by implication, Ntaganda) shows that the Office of the Prosecutor was not able to find evidence of other crimes, thus implying their innocence.[175]

There has been some inconsistency in the ICC charging of sexual violence crimes across and within the cases emerging from various situations:

> the limited charges brought against Lubanga and Ntaganda as compared to those brought against Katanga and Ngudjolo [For example, Katanga and Ngudjolo were charged with rape and sexual slavery both as war crimes and crimes against humanity while Lubanga and Ntaganda were not] continue to raise questions about the impartiality of the court.[176]

Perhaps sensitive to some of the aforementioned criticisms, Moreno-Ocampo had announced that he *planned* to add rape as well as murder charges to the indictment of Bosco Ntagnada, one of Lubanga's former senior commanders who now shockingly holds the rank of General in the State's national army.[177] Ntagnada, who has been under indictment by the ICC and is still at large in the Congo, was initially charged only with the war crimes of recruitment and use of children under 15 for active participation in hostilities. In July 2012, however, additional charges including, amongst others, rape and sexual slavery as both war crimes and crimes against humanity were affirmed by the Pre-Trial Chamber as part of a second warrant of arrest.

LRA leader Joseph Kony and certain of his co-perpetrators were charged in regards to the situation in Uganda[178] (for the period covered by the charges) with sexual enslavement and mass rape as crimes against humanity and mass rape as a war crime. Again, although the LRA is notorious in large part for the extreme systematic and widespread sexual and other violence, such as mutilations, it perpetrates against children in particular, these sexual violence and other crimes targeting children were not charged also as a form of 'genocidal forcible transfer of children'. This was the

[174] Office of the ICC Prosecutor. Prosecutorial Strategy 2009–2012 (February 1, 2010, para 18–21).

[175] Human Rights Watch (2011, p. 21).

[176] Human Rights Watch (2011, p. 20).

[177] Radio Netherlands Worldwide (International Justice Desk) 'ICC Prosecutor seeks long sentence for Lubanga' (15 March, 2012).

[178] The LRA has now left Northern Uganda but is implicated in mass atrocities against civilians in northeastern DRC, CAR, and South Sudan (Human Rights Watch, 2011, p. 23).

case though, as previously discussed, this charge is fitting where an armed group such as the LRA (which is perpetrating mass atrocities) is intent on appropriating children to itself through, for instance, mass abduction of children for child soldiering, mass sexual violence perpetrated against girls and other atrocities targeting children and destroying targeted communities through this genocidal forcible transfer of the children (sometimes this being a physical transfer of the children to the LRA ranks to serve as 'child soldiers' or in other cases a strictly symbolic transfer through the rape and killing of girls such that the murdered child is first defiled through rape transforming the child in the perception of the community as now a child 'of' the perpetrator group; the LRA).

Systematic and widespread sexual violence and other mass atrocities specially targeting children are, on the analysis here, highly symbolic and not just a means of gaining compliance from the civilian population. The latter perspective is then more nuanced (in that it contemplates that the LRA has specific motives for targeting children *in particular* for the most extreme sexual and non-sexual violence) as compared to the following Human Rights Watch view:

> In Uganda, the LRA has abducted thousands of children, and carried out countless acts of wilful killing, torture, and mutilation *as part of its strategy to enforce compliance on the civilian population through terror...*[179]

The LRA, now operating outside of Uganda, continues to be a significant perpetrator group of grave international crimes especially against children and continues to abduct children for use as LRA child soldiers and/or for sexual enslavement:

> In 2005 and 2006, renewed Ugandan military campaigns compelled the LRA to relocate its forces from Uganda and southern Sudan to the remote region of the Garamba National Park in northeastern Congo. The LRA has since become a regional threat operating in the remote border areas between South Sudan, DRC, and CAR...Since September 2008 [to 2011], the LRA has killed [at least] nearly 2,400 civilians and abducted about 3,400 others, according to documentation by Human Rights Watch and the UN. These atrocities are continuing in northern DRC, eastern CAR, and South Sudan. In the first four months of 2011, the LRA carried out at least 120 attacks, killing 81 civilians *and abducting 193, many of them children.*[180]

To date there has been no ICC Prosecutor initiatives to address these new LRA mass atrocities committed along the borders or in northern DRC, eastern CAR, and South Sudan despite demands from civil societies, and victims.[181] The current author is in accord with HRW urging that additional charges, supported by the evidence, be brought[182] against the LRA commanders most responsible including any additional such persons[183] not currently under indictment by the ICC.

---

[179] Human Rights Watch (2011, p. 23, emphasis added).

[180] Human Rights Watch (2011, p. 29).

[181] Human Rights Watch (2011, p. 29).

[182] Human Rights Watch (2011, p. 30).

[183] "According to Ugandan army officials, Lt. Col. Charles Arop commanded the group of LRA combatants that attacked the town of Faradje on December 25, 2008, killing at least 143 people, mostly men, and abducting 160 children and dozens of adults." (Human Rights Watch, 2011, p. 30).

On the view here; these grave international crimes reflect the LRA's genocidal agenda that properly should be acknowledged through the charging (i.e. the correct charging strategy, it is here contended, would include the charge of genocidal forcible transfer of children). It is here contended that: (1) the lack of consistency of the OTP (Office of the Prosecutor of the ICC) in charging regarding sexual violence (i.e. as in the Lubanga case) and (2) the failure to recognize that this crime, in many instances, targets children (even very young children and babies) in particular (though not exclusively) for the most heinous of sexual crimes (as with the LRA) and constitutes the genocidal forcible transfer of children: (a) undermines the perceived gravity of mass sexual violence crimes perpetrated against children in times of armed conflict and (b) works against a genuine understanding of the ultimate *genocidal* objective of the perpetrators in committing this type of grave international crime involving child victims in particular.

6.8.4 ICC independence and Impartiality and Prosecuting Grave International Crimes Perpetrated Against Children

Human Rights Watch in its 2011 report on factors to be considered in the selection of ICC cases highlights the importance not only of the Court's independence but the appearance of independence in the perception of the international community:

> At a certain point… the prolonged absence of any investigation of government officials alleged to have committed abuses—or adequate explanation as to why these cases are not being pursued—risks jeopardizing the court's independence.
>
> The need to rely on states' cooperation [i.e. re execution of arrest warrants, and investigations etc.] makes it all the more important for the ICC prosecutor to manage investigations, and public information about those investigations, in a manner that signals clearly the court's independence. Given the many global challenges to the ICC's legitimacy, this is the best, and a necessary, antidote to allegations of political interference or influence.[184]

Certainly, when it comes to the situation in Chad, for example, the quote immediately above is highly relevant. This is the case when one considers that the Chadian army itself has long been accused by NGOs and UN investigators of perpetrating systematic rapes as a pattern and practice (as have other armed parties in that State) during armed conflict in that State in contemporary times (post Chad's ratification of the Rome Statute[185]). Yet Chad appears to have been dropped from the list of countries in which a potential application for a formal investigation to be presented by the ICC Prosecutor to the Pre-Trial Chamber might be considered.[186] Such an investigation might have allowed for development of cases against:

---

184 Human Rights Watch (2011, p. 7).

185 Rome Statute (2002).

186 Human Rights Watch (2011, p. 1).

(1) Chadian government officials that may have, at a minimum, been complicit in some way in, for example, mass rapes and other acts of sexual violence perpetrated on girls and women in Chad as well as other crimes; and (2) rebel Chadian commanders and those of other armed groups or militia crimes (such as the Sudanese Justice and Equality Movement) operating in the territory at the relevant period perpetrating grave international crimes such as the recruitment and use of child soldiers in armed hostilities.

The current author is, of course, certainly agreed that government officials most responsible for international crimes in cases that meet all ICC jurisdictional and admissibility requirements ought to be prosecuted.[187] She is *not* agreed, however, that the same crimes when perpetrated by commanders of State national armies as opposed to non-State entities led by rebels should automatically take priority for the OTP in terms of case selection and prosecution targets.[188] Much if not most recruitment and use of children as child soldiers is in contemporary times perpetrated by rebel armed groups, including in respect of under 15s, and on a systematic and widespread basis. In most instances, the State has been ineffectual in prosecuting these rebel leaders for this particular grave crime not in small part as: (1) the States in these situations generally also recruit and use child soldiers (including under 15s) as has here been previously discussed,[189] and/or (2) the States in which child soldiering has been widespread during armed conflict (sometimes for decades) do not generally, on their own initiative, in the midst of civil strife and mass atrocities, prioritize child soldiering as something that must be prevented with the perpetrators held accountable.

Yet in the post-conflict period some State governments have co-operated with international criminal tribunals or the ICC in this regard (holding to account at least some of those most responsible for the recruitment and use of children under 15 for active participation in hostilities).[190] The latter is an indication, at least on its face, that these States do not accept child soldiering (especially child soldiers as part of an armed group or force perpetrating mass atrocities and/or genocide or recruitment and use of children under 15 as child soldiers) as a feature of acceptable or *bona fide purported* "regional custom."[191] This is also reflected in the fact that African States

[187] Schabas points out that States will be *unlikely* to self-refer situations to the ICC if they think that, in practice, some of their own leaders have a high probability of being prosecuted by the ICC thus putting the ICC Prosecutor, who needs State cooperation, in a difficult bind (Schabas 2008, p. 753).

[188] For the contrasting view see (Heller 2009, p. 14).

[189] For instance, a 2005 judgement of the ICJ held that the Republic of Uganda trained child soldiers as well as committing a range of other grave crimes against the Congolese civilian population (Democratic Republic of Congo v Uganda, ICJ, 2005, p. 280, para 3).

[190] Sometimes such States also set up Truth and Reconciliation Commissions as in Sierra Leone some of which can make referrals to the Courts.

[191] Osiel (2009) discussed the difficulties of defining what should be taken as indicators of "social alarm" in the international community regarding certain conduct such as child soldiering which he states is "regarded as 'regional custom' in much of Africa" (p. 5).

were heavily involved in the drafting of the Rome Statute[192] and many such States are a party to the Statute as well. That statute sets out a universal standard for peaceful coexistence of all segments of the human family and a mechanism for accountability in regards to grave violations of that standard [including also in regards to the recruitment and use of children under 15 for active participation in hostilities and the genocidal forcible transfer of children (persons under 18)]. Consider in regards to this matter an important fact sheet titled "Africa and the International Criminal Court" released by the Coalition for the International Criminal Court in response to allegations made by some following the issuance of the ICC arrest warrant for Sudanese President Omar Al-Bashir that the "ICC is a Western Tool."[193] That fact sheet includes the following informational points amongst others:

> African countries have been actively involved in the establishment of the International Criminal Court and the Rome Statute since negotiations for the Court began . . .47 African states were present for the drafting of the Rome Statute. . .at the Rome Conference in July 1998. . .Of the 47 African countries involved in the drafting of the Statute, the vast majority voted in favour of adopting the Rome Statute and establishing the ICC.
>
> Africa [is] the most heavily represented region in the Court's membership. . ..In the 2004–2007 Strategic Plan of the African Union, one of the AU's five commitments was to secure the ratification of the ICC treaty by all countries.[194]

At present, 33 Africa States have ratified the Rome Statute including Chad, Uganda, the DRC, Sierra Leone, and Liberia where child soldiering has been a major phenomenon; many more are signatories.[195]

6.8.5 The ICC and the Interests of Child Victims of Genocidal Forcible Transfer

In the final analysis, this book has been fundamentally about the interests of child victims; specifically: (1) those children appropriated for use as child soldiers and/or for sexual violation by armed groups and forces (State and non-State) perpetrating mass atrocities and/or genocide and (2) other child civilian groups subjected to mass rape and other forms of sexual violence who are not physically transferred to and travelling with these armed groups or forces. It has been argued that not recognizing: (1) mass rape and other widespread sexual violence against children in particular and (2) the appropriation and use of children as child soldiers by armed

[192] Rome Statute (2002).

[193] Coalition for the International Criminal Court (n.d.) Africa and the International Criminal Court (p. 1).

[194] Coalition for the International Criminal Court (n.d.) Africa and the International Criminal Court (p. 1–2).

[195] International Criminal Court, States Parties to the Rome Statute (2012).

groups and forces (State and non-State) perpetrating these mass atrocities and/or genocide as genocidal forcible transfer of children (along with other categories of crime which the facts might sustain) does a great disservice to the interests of justice for these child victims. It is important to recognize and appreciate the import of the fact that, as the ICC Prosecutor has pointed out:

> ***The Office [the ICC Office of the Prosecutor] also assesses the victims' interests as part of its determination of interests of justice under Article 53***. . .Finally the interests of victims are also at the heart of victims' participation in judicial proceedings pursuant to the Statute.[196]

The interests of the child victims of grave international crimes and of justice are not being fully and adequately addressed by the ICC in all instances, it is here argued, in that international crimes targeting children in particular and perpetrated by armed groups or forces committing mass atrocities and/or genocide,[197] are not being properly acknowledged as a form of the "crime of crimes" (namely the 'genocidal forcible transfer of children'). This failure to charge genocidal forcible transfer of children in regards to the aforementioned grave international crimes (along with any additional charges supported by the same facts) is, on the analysis here, in fact an unwitting violation of one of the fundamental principles of the prosecutorial strategy as set out by the ICC's Office of the Prosecutor (OTP); namely "to maximize the impact of the activities of the Office [Office of the ICC Prosecutor]"[198]:

> [To maximize the impact of the OTP is a prime objective given that] as noted in the Preamble of the Statute, the Court's goal is to end impunity to contribute to the prevention of future crimes.[199]

It is here argued that maximizing the impact of the OTP of the International Criminal Court regarding preventing and punishing the grave international crime of the 'genocidal forcible transfer of children' requires: (1) communicating through ICC/OTP information releases and by prosecutorial practice that: (a) recruitment and use of under 18s in any capacity in hostilities when committed by armed groups or forces (State or non-State) perpetrating mass atrocities and/or genocide and/or (b) systematic and widespread rape and other sexual violations of children perpetrated by such State or non-State actors are construed by the ICC to be acts constituting the 'genocidal forcible transfer of children' and, that (2) the ICC Prosecutor, whoever that may be, in the judicious and proper exercise of his or

---

[196] Office of the ICC Prosecutor. Prosecutorial Strategy 2009–2012 (February 1, 2010, para 22, p. 6, emphasis added).

[197] The grave international crimes referred to here include but are not delimited to recruitment and use of children for active participation in hostilities, and mass sexual victimization of children as part of a common plan.

[198] Office of the ICC Prosecutor. Prosecutorial Strategy 2009–2012 (February 1, 2010, para 23, p. 7).

[199] Office of the ICC Prosecutor. Prosecutorial Strategy 2009–2012 (February 1, 2010, para 23, p. 7).

her discretion under the Rome Statute,[200] will, if need be, on his/her own motion where feasible: (a) seek Pre-Trial Chamber authorization for formal investigation of all such situations involving crimes of such extreme gravity (the genocidal forcible transfer of children) and (b) having received authorization, develop select cases for prosecution pertaining to the most grave instances of such violations of the Rome Statute.[201] Thus, such cases of the genocidal forcible transfer of children as here specified (but not limited thereto) will automatically be considered by the OTP to be of sufficient gravity for prosecution and such prosecution viewed as consistent with the interests of justice in the normal course.[202] There are instances then; it is here contended, as with the genocidal forcible transfer of children, where the consideration of gravity and the interests of justice do *not* in fact allow for 'enormous space for highly discretionary determinations' in terms of whether or not certain cases will be developed.[203] That is, all cases of the 'genocidal forcible transfer of children' where ICC jurisdiction has been triggered must be pursued against those most responsible since all cases of the genocidal forcible transfer of children are equally grave in terms of: (1) the nature of the crime and (2) its' symbolic and actual impact on children as a special protected group, the children's groups of origin and in terms of the implications for humanity more generally. When it comes to the genocidal forcible transfer of children then it is the nature and impact of the crime (i.e. the fact that it victimizes children; a most vulnerable specially protected group under international law; causes very long term damage to families and the community at large (for instance, reproductive capacity of the group is greatly diminished and the children are often permanently alienated from the group), causes great emotional suffering for the children and their families; often involves great physical harms to the children forcibly transferred as child soldiers and/or sex slaves etc.); quite apart from the number of victims (though this may also be considered perhaps even as an aggravating factor) that results in fulfillment of the gravity assessment as an additional admissibility criterion and creates the necessity for prosecution. In this regard, note that the ICC Prosecutor Moreno-Ocampo, in explaining ICC prosecutorial strategy, described the OTP policy of choice regarding cases to be pursued as follows:

> ...***cases inside a situation are selected according to gravity***, taking into account factors such as the scale, *nature*, manner of commission, and *impact* of the alleged crimes.[204]

---

[200] It has been noted that the Prosecutor of an international criminal tribunal [and by implication then also the OTP of the ICC] has a great margin of discretion in selecting cases for prosecution and that "the criteria upon which prosecutorial discretion is to be exercised are ill-defined and complex." (Statement of Justice Arbour, L., 8 December, 1997 to the Preparatory Committee on the Establishment of an International Criminal Court at 7–8). Cited in Schabas (2008, p. 735, FN 16).

[201] Rome Statute (2002).

[202] There may be a few exceptions as when a perpetrator is deathly ill.

[203] See Schabas (2008, p. 735) for a general discussion of issues of gravity and interests of justice and the ICC Prosecutor exercising his or her proprio motu powers.

[204] Office of the ICC Prosecutor, "Prosecutorial Strategy 2009–2012," (February 1, 2010, p. 6, para 20, emphasis added).

As certain of the ICC cases in Darfur illustrate; namely those in which defendants were charged in relation to, amongst other conduct, attacks on UN peacekeepers in which there were very few direct victims; the scale of the crime is not one of the ultimate determinative factors in assessing gravity of the crime in all instances.

In sum then some situations involving the 'genocidal forcible transfer of children' (both under and over age 15) as child soldiers and/or as victims of systematic and widespread sexual violation are not being formally investigated (i.e. the situation in Somalia involving the al-Shabaab recruitment and use of children as child soldiers and sexual violation of abducted girl children) due, in the first instance, to non-referral by the UN Security Council of a non-State party. In other situations involving State Parties (i.e. Chad); there has been no self-referral nor exercise of the Prosecutor's *proprio motu* powers to go through the steps that might allow for a formal investigation and development of cases related to that situation and the recruitment and use of children under age 18 for child soldiering as well as systematic widespread sexual violence perpetrated against children in that State. Both the Chadian national army and rebel armed groups have been implicated in these grave offences though the extent of involvement may vary for each party.

It is here contended that situations such as Somalia and the activities of al-Shabaab are more likely to be referred to the ICC by the UN Security Council if legally characterized properly as involving the genocidal forcible transfer of children and not just war crimes (the recruitment and use of children under 15 for active participation in hostilities).[205] This is the case in that in the common imagination (public perception of the international community) and arguably so in international criminal law, in practice, genocide in all its forms is considered a more serious international crime than are war crimes.[206] The UN Security Council in turn does sometimes, though not generally in a timely way, consider and react to significant pressure from the international human rights community and the general public's crisis of conscience to act in situations of perceived genocide.

Note that while it is correct to say that the Rome Statute[207] does *not* explicitly rank order genocide, crimes against humanity and war crimes in terms of level of gravity; it is also the case that:

> ...there is implicit evidence in the ICC statute that war crimes are less serious than genocide and crimes against humanity. States may accept the treaty but opt out of the subject matter jurisdiction over war crimes, and the defences of superior orders and defence of property are available with respect to war crimes but not genocide and crimes against humanity.[208]

---

[205] Once the Somalia situation were referred to the ICC by the UN Security Council, the ICC Prosecutor would be obligated also to examine the facts relating to other parties to the conflict such as the TFG and its use of child soldiers.

[206] Recall Schabas' comment: "As for Lubanga he must be delighted to find himself in The Hague facing prosecution for relatively less important offences concerning child solders rather than genocide and crimes against humanity." (Schabas 2008, p. 744).

[207] Rome Statute (2002).

[208] Schabas (2008, p. 743)

Thus, in certain respects at least, the Rome Statute's formulation of gravity in relation to various international crimes under ICC jurisdiction is consistent with the common perception of the international community (that war crimes are less serious than genocide and crimes against humanity).

Further, in situations where a State Party to the Rome Statute[209] has been ineffective in holding to account: (1) those most responsible for the genocidal forcible transfer of children within its territorial jurisdiction and/or (2) its nationals perpetrating this grave crime and other mass atrocities in some other bordering or nearby jurisdiction; the State Party caught up in the midst of these and other mass atrocities and civil and/or cross-border war may be less able to deflect from the necessity of a self-referral to the ICC given the perceived gravity of the situation (where the crime alleged is 'genocidal forcible transfer of children' as opposed to only the war crimes of recruitment (conscription or enlistment) and use of children under 15 for active participation in hostilities). It is the case that neither: (1) rebel propaganda regarding the recruitment and use of children for combat in an alleged war of national liberation; nor (2) State propaganda[210] regarding the purported legitimate use of children for active participation in hostilities in an alleged justified defence of the self-proclaimed righteous State will serve well as a smokescreen where the international community conceptualizes the situation as one involving the 'genocidal forcible transfer of children'.[211] In the latter circumstance, the chances for an ICC formal investigation either subsequent to State self-referral of the situation or on the Prosecutor's own application and authorization by the Pre-Trial Chamber for a formal investigation (or subsequent to UN referral of the situation to the ICC where applicable) likely will be enhanced. The OTP further points out that: "...the ICC and a territorial State incapacitated by mass crimes may agree that a consensual division of labour is the most logical and effective approach."[212]

Respectfully, on the view here, there has been to some extent, a significant failure to properly legally characterize certain facts and circumstances in ICC cases and situations such as discussed here involving: (1) the recruitment and use of under 18s in any capacity in armed hostilities when perpetrated as part of a common plan

---

[209] Rome Statute (2002).

[210] To date, the State self-referrals of 'situations' to the ICC (Uganda, DRC and the Central African Republic) have led only to 'cases' involving international crimes being perpetrated by rebel armed groups in those States. This has led to some criticism of the OTP on this very point. However, it must be understood that States that self-refer situations contemplate the possibility of cases being developed regarding State officials understanding that the ICC Prosecutor is duty bound under the Rome Statute to objectively and impartially consider the activities of all parties to the conflict.

[211] As when both State and non-State armed forces are using children to participate in perpetrating mass atrocities and the child soldiers are being subjected to sexual violation and various types of cruel and inhuman treatment by all sides to the conflict.

[212] Office of the ICC Prosecutor (2003). Informal expert paper: The principle of complementarity in practice [The complementarity regarding prosecutions refers here to national (domestic) prosecutions of some perpetrators as well as ICC prosecutions in respect of certain State or rebel leaders where domestic prosecutions of the latter individuals may contribute to civil unrest].

by armed groups or forces (State or non-State) committing mass atrocities and/or genocide and/or (2) systematic and widespread rape and other sexual violations of children perpetrated by State or non-State armed groups or forces as part of a common plan. That is, these facts and circumstances have *not* been properly characterized as constituting also the crime of 'genocidal forcible transfer of children'.[213] These child victims have the right to have the facts and circumstances surrounding the international crimes perpetrated against them correctly legally characterized under international criminal law (i.e. the Rome Statute[214]) so as to allow the international community to fully understand and appreciate the nature and gravity of the fundamental rights violations they have suffered (i.e. the facts legally characterized as substantiating a charge of 'genocidal forcible transfer of children' in addition to any other charges that might apply such as sex slavery as a crime against humanity and recruitment and use of children under 15 for active participation in hostilities as war crimes etc.). Further, where cases of the 'genocidal forcible transfer of children' are not properly acknowledged as such by the OTP; by the Court, and even by the legal representatives of the victim participants themselves; the conduct of such cases before the ICC (i.e. the analysis of the facts and circumstances); and/or the sentencing regarding grave crimes involving: (1) the recruitment and use of children for child soldiering by armed groups or forces perpetrating genocide and/or mass atrocities and/or (2) the mass sexual violation of child victims in particular (including girl soldiers) by such armed groups or forces cannot, it is here contended, in actual fact deliver the full quality and measure of justice to which these child victims are entitled under the Rome Statute.[215]

6.9 PostScript: The Syrian Regime's Genocidal Targeting of Children in Particular

This author would be woefully remiss if she did not comment on the Syrian regime's brutal targeting of children in particular for extreme violence in the recent months and weeks. On the 11 June, 2012, the U.N. Special Representative for Children and Armed Conflict (SRSG) issued a press release which stated in part:

> New crises have caused enormous suffering for children and continue in 2012. In Syria, children were victims of killing and maiming, arbitrary arrest, detention, torture and ill-treatment, including sexual violence, by the Syrian Armed Forces and the Shabbiha militia.

---

[213] Recognizing that the same facts may, in addition, meet the criteria for war crimes and/or crimes against humanity and that the crimes should then also be charged as such in addition to the charge of the genocidal forcible transfer of children.

[214] Rome Statute (2002).

[215] That is, assuming cases (falling under ICC jurisdiction and meeting admissibility requirements) involving the genocidal forcible transfer of children are brought before the ICC for adjudication in the first instance which assumption, as we have seen, is too often in fact incorrect.

> Children between 8 and 13 were forcibly taken from their homes and used by soldiers as human shields, placing them in front of windows of buses carrying military personnel into the raid on villages. Schools have been regularly raided, used as military bases and detention centres. In detention, girls and boys were beaten, blindfolded, subjected to stress positions and to electric shocks, as well as whipped with heavy electrical cables.[216]

The Special Representative of the Secretary-General stated in the same press release that: "The world is keeping a detailed account of the violence against civilians in Syria and I am confident that these crimes will not go unpunished."[217] The latter, of course, is not nearly a fully adequate U.N. response to the crisis situation.

The Secretary-General in his annual report of 26 April, 2012 on children and armed conflict reported the following:

> There is no evidence of Government forces formally conscripting or enlisting children under the age of 18 years. However, the Syrian Armed Forces and its associated Shabbiha militia used children as young as 8 years on at least three separate occasions within the reporting period [January-December, 2011).[218]
>
> At least one witness said that he had seen a young boy of approximately 15 years of age succumb to his repeated beatings. Children were detained and tortured because their siblings or parents were assumed to be members of the opposition or FSA, or they themselves were suspected of being associated with FSA.[219]
>
> The United Nations has received some credible allegations of the recruitment and use of children by armed opposition, including FSA and other armed groups, although FSA has a stated policy of not recruiting any child under 17 years of age.[220] [There does not appear to date to be any allegations of widespread use of children by the opposition as far as the current author could determine and no opposition group is listed as a perpetrator group on the 'list of shame' annexed to the U.N. Secretary-General's annual report on children and armed conflict (the latter dated 26 April, 2012].
>
> Several witnesses stated that the intelligence forces and the Shabbiha militia had gun emplacements installed on the roofs of schools while students were attending. Accounts also indicated that, on a number of occasions, children were killed or injured by Government forces during military operations on school grounds, and schools were looted and burned as retribution by Government forces in response to student protests.[221]

The Syrian Arab Republic was listed as a perpetrator of violations of children's fundamental human rights in the U.N. Secretary's-General's annual report on children and armed conflict (26 April, 2012) in relation to agents of the State

---

[216] Special Representative of the Secretary-General for Children and Armed Conflict (SRSG) Press Release 11 June, 2012.

[217] Special Representative of the Secretary-General for Children and Armed Conflict (SRSG) Press Release 11 June, 2012.

[218] U.N. Secretary-General's annual report on children and armed conflict (26 April, 2012, p. 23, para 122).

[219] U.N. Secretary-General's annual report on children and armed conflict (26 April, 2012, p. 23, para 123).

[220] U.N. Secretary-General's annual report on children and armed conflict (26 April, 2012, p. 23, para 124).

[221] U.N. Secretary-General's annual report on children and armed conflict (26 April, 2012, p. 23, para 125).

(members of the Syrian government forces including the Syrian Armed Forces, the Syrian intelligence forces and the Shabbiha militia) killing and maiming children and in regards to their attacks on schools and hospitals.

On 1 June, 2011 UNICEF spokesperson Patrick McCormick commented on the torture death of 13-year-old Hamzah al-Khateeb allegedly at the hands of pro-government forces:

> I have no idea why anybody would brutalize a young boy like that, adding "we want to get to the bottom of it".[222]

On the view here; the victimizing of *children in particular* for extreme violence by President Bashar al-Assad's regime (as reported by UN sources, NGOs and other credible sources[223]) is a marker for the occurrence of genocide in Syria.[224] This is in addition to such child victimization constituting 'crimes against humanity' that likely are substantiated also prima facie based on some of the same facts i.e. persecution as a 'crime against humanity' where:

> Such targeting was based on political [grounds i.e. the perceived political affiliation of the children's family]. . .gender [grounds i.e. girls being targeted for sexual violence] as defined in article 7, paragraph 3, of the Statute, *or other grounds* [age; targeting persons under age 18 in particular for extreme violence] that are universally recognized as impermissible under international law (Rome Statute (2002), Article 7 (1) (h), Crime against humanity of persecution).[225]

Note that 'crimes against humanity' are widespread attacks on the civilian population.[226] The atrocities perpetrated (according to the UN and other observers) by the al Assad regime against children in particular can properly be viewed through the lens of 'crimes against humanity' (for instance persecution as a 'crime against humanity' perpetrated against a group based on young age; being a child) as that legal characterization appears also to fit the Syrian situation. At the same time, legal characterization of the crimes being perpetrated by the al Assad regime against children in particular as genocide (for instance via genocidal forcible transfer of children of the targeted group to the perpetrator group to serve as human shields and through sexual victimization) is appropriate on the analysis here and captures in no uncertain terms that children of the opposition in Syria were/are being targeted in particular for extreme violence with a *genocidal intent*.

---

[222] United Nations News and Media. Statement of UNICEF spokesperson Patrick McCormick (1 June, 2011).

[223] Save the Children (2012). Untold Atrocities: The stories of Syria's children.

[224] Such targeting of children in particular for varied atrocities generally occurs alongside sexual violence against girls and women as well.

[225] Rome Statute Elements of the Crime (2002, emphasis added).

[226] Schabas (2000) states that: "There are several definitions of crimes against humanity, but they share the common denominator of persecution of individuals or groups in a widespread and systematic fashion."

For the reasons here previously discussed in detail; the fact that it is children of the opposition that are being targeted does *not* negate the characterization of the violence against children in particular as also government perpetrated 'genocide;' even if arguably an autogenocide. On the issue of autogenocide note that, on the analysis here, the targeted group need not be a national, religious, ethnic or religious *minority:*

> The Genocide Convention does not explicitly mention or address the situation in which perpetrators target their own group or parts of it...auto-genocide in this sense is merely a descriptive term. The travaux préparatoires of article II of the Genocide Convention are not instructive on this issue, either. The matter was not considered and debated as such.[227]
>
> In his UN study of genocide, Whitaker noted that ***article II of the Genocide Convention imposes no requirement of the victims having to be of a different group from that of the perpetrators.***[228]

In any case, the Syrian regime does not perceive the targeted opposition group as of the same group as the perceived majority but rather as an extraneous element to be eradicated. Children are to be regarded as a protected group in this context (one subjected, in violation of international law, to genocidal attack) in that: (1) international humanitarian law sets out that children are a special protected group during armed conflict; (2) the contemporary view is that of children as persons in their own right with inherent human dignity and certain fundamental human rights legal entitlements and (3) children in particular are regarded as a protected group in relation to the prohibition on the genocidal forcible transfer of children to another group (i.e. as per Article 6(e) of the Rome Statute).[229] According to W.A. Schabas, the provision of the Genocide Convention[230] regarding the 'genocidal forcible transfer of children' introduces the notion of 'cultural genocide' into the Genocide Convention:[231]

> ...the drafters of the [Genocide] Convention quite expressly excluded cultural genocide, with one exception, the forced transfer of children from one group to another.[232]

Arguably then one could argue that the al Assad regime's attempt to destroy the children of the opposition (in whole or in part) in Syria is to some extent an attempt to destroy democratic cultural norms by eliminating the possibility for transmission of such norms from adults in the opposition to their offspring (the potential next generation of opposition). Thus even Schabas, who argues for a restrictive textual reading of the Genocide Convention,[233] found he had to take a more expansive view in considering how the Genocide Convention[234] addresses the genocidal targeting of children in particular. Respectfully, on the view here, Schabas at the same time,

---

[227] Forster (2011, pp. 141–142).

[228] Forster (2011, p. 142, emphasis added).

[229] Rome Statute (2002).

[230] Genocide Convention (1951).

[231] Genocide Convention (1951).

[232] Schabas (2000, pp. 291–292).

[233] Genocide Convention (1951).

[234] Genocide Convention (1951).

in inconsistent fashion, maintains that a strict textual interpretation of the Genocide Convention[235] is possible implying *in effect* that there is little if any ambiguity in its terms to stand in the way of such an approach. The current author would dispute Schabas' contention that restrictive interpretation is possible (as was discussed in detail earlier). This is evidenced in that, in practice, it seems that the Article 2 Genocide Convention[236] provisions as incorporated into various international criminal law statutes (such as that of the ICTR) are interpreted on a case-by-case basis with judicial interpretations informed by particular historical, socio-cultural, political and other contextual factors specific to the broader situation and the cases emerging from that particular situation.

It is the child group that is the target of genocide *also* in and of itself in the Syrian situation and not simply as an alleged extension of the targeted political opposition group (comprised of adults with whom the children are affiliated or perceived to be affiliated). The children of the perceived opposition are then the victims of a genocidal campaign as a distinct child group separate and apart from any other that may be targeted. The political motivations of the perpetrators[237] in attempting to destroy, at least in part, this objectively speaking *apolitical* child group[238] are irrelevant to the genocidal quality of the conduct in targeting children in particular.

The children of the opposition are being targeted for torture and massacres[239] thus causing the children themselves and their surviving family members great suffering. These children are, furthermore, being *appropriated* by the perpetrator group in various ways including: (1) by their use as human shields (essentially thus being forced to function as child soldiers playing this role (as human shields) in support of the military activities of the pro-government forces) and (2) through their being sexually victimized. This no longer amounts simply to the Bashar al-Assad regime fighting opposition groups, if it ever did, but rather to genocide; an intent to destroy in whole or in part the targeted child group itself through: (1) Killing members of the child group; (2) Causing serious bodily or mental harm to members of the child group; and (3) Forcible transfer of members of the child group to another group[240] (the perpetrator pro-government forces and allied militia engaged in perpetrating mass atrocities). To date, the forcible transfer of members of the

[235] Genocide Convention (1951).

[236] Genocide Convention (1951).

[237] The political motivation is, of course, on the view here, to quash opposition to the Bashar al-Assad's regime by setting as the price of opposition the cost of losing one's children in a most horrific way.

[238] Very young children have been targeted for torture, massacre and abduction and used as human shields (See Special Representative of the Secretary-General for Children and Armed Conflict (SRSG) Press Release 11 June, 2012) Thus, though there may have been some children who have been victimized by the regime who participated in the opposition this is not generally the case nor have children targeted been selected on such a basis.

[239] The majority of persons killed in the Houla massacre were women and children (49 children were victims in that massacre).

[240] See Article 6 (e) of the genocide provision in the Rome Statute (2002).

child group to the perpetrator group has occurred through the children's abduction (forced recruitment) and use as human shields and through sexual victimization of the children. Such forcible transfer attempts to eliminate the children's personhood and personal identity and reduce the children to but tools of the perpetrator group.[241] This author is thus fully in accord with UN High Commissioner for human rights Navi Pillay's call for the Security Council to refer Syria to the International Criminal Court considering the mass atrocities being perpetrated against the opposition; adults and children alike.[242] It is long past due the time for the UN Security Council to take the necessary action in this regard in the face of the egregious mass atrocities being perpetrated in Syria including, on the view, here the genocidal campaign being waged without mercy by the Bashar al-Assad regime against children in particular. If no action is taken in this regard then the UN Security Council might as well be added to the Secretary-General's 'list of shame' normally reserved for armed groups and forces perpetrating grave international crimes against children during armed conflict[243] in that the members of the Security-Council blocking the referral to the ICC will have been complicit in the ongoing indescribable suffering of the children of Syria.

Literature, Materials and Cases

Literature

Afflito FM (2000) Victimization, survival and the impunity of forced exile: a case study from the Rwandan genocide. Crime Law Soc Change 34:77–97

Cryer R (2009) Prosecuting the leaders: promises, politics and practicalities Göttingen. J Int Law 1:45–75

Drumbl MA (2012) Reimagining child soldiers in international law and policy. Oxford University Press, New York

Forster TK (2011) The Khmer Rouge and the crime of genocide: issues of genocidal intent with regard to the Khmer Rouge mass atrocities. http://www.cambodiatribunal.org/sites/default/files/reports/KHMER%20ROUGE%20AND%20THE%20CRIMES%20OF%20GENOCIDE.pdf. Accessed 18 Jun 2012

Grover SC (2008) 'Child Soldiers' as 'Non-Combatants': the inapplicability of the refugee convention exclusion clause. Int J Hum Rights 12(1):53–65

Grover SC (2011) Schoolchildren as propaganda tools in the war on terror: violating the rights of Afghani children under international law. Springer, Berlin

Grover SC (2012) Child soldier victims of genocidal forcible transfer: exonerating child soldiers charged with grave conflict-related international crimes. Springer, Berlin

[241] See Article 6 of the Rome Statute (2002).

[242] Tamil Guardian Refer Syria to ICC – Navi Pillay (13 December, 2011).

[243] Secretary-General's annual report on children and armed conflict with appended list of shame at annex I (26 April, 2012).

Heller KJ (2009) Situational gravity under the Rome Statute. In: Stahn C, van den Herik L (eds) Future directions in International Criminal Justice. T.M.C Asser Press, The Hague, http://papers.ssrn.com/sol3/papers.cfm?abstract_id=1270369. Accessed 15 Apr 2012
Kreß C (2007) The International Court of justice and the elements of the crime of genocide. Eur J Int Law 18(4):619–629
Mackinnon CA (2007) Are women real people and other international dialogues. Harvard University Press, Cambridge
Nissel AT (2004) Continuing Crimes in the Rome Statute. Mich J Int Law 25(653). http://papers.ssrn.com/sol3/papers.cfm?abstract_id=2070212. Accessed 16 Jun 2012
Nouwen SMH, Werner WG (2011) Doing justice to the political: the International Criminal Court in Uganda and Sudan: a rejoinder to Bas Schotel. Eur J Int Law 22(4):1161–1164
Rosen DM (2009) Who is a child? The legal conundrum of child soldiers. Conn J Int Law 25:82–118
Schabas WA (2000) Problems of international codification Paper presented at the conference. International Jurisdiction: Myths, Realities and Prospects. New England School of Law November 3, 2000. http://www.nesl.edu/userfiles/file/lawreview/Vol35/2/schabas.PDF. Accessed 18 Jun 2012
Schabas WA (2008) Prosecutorial discretion v. Judicial activism at the International Criminal Court. J Int Crim Justice 6:731–761
Schabas WA (2010) The International Criminal Court: a commentary on the Rome Statute. Oxford University Press, New York (Oxford Commentaries on International Law)
Slye RC, Van Schaack B (2009) Essentials: International Criminal Law. Aspen Publishers, New York
Wagner M (2003) The ICC and its jurisdiction-Myths, misperceptions and realities. Max Planck Yearbook United Nations Law 7:409–512

Materials

All Africa (UN News Service) (2012) Chad: UN Official Highlights Human Rights Concerns, Praises readiness to address them. http://allafrica.com/stories/201204041085.html. Accessed 10 Apr 2012
Amnesty International (2011) A compromised future: children recruited by armed forces and groups in Eastern Chad. http://www.amnesty.org/en/library/asset/AFR20/001/2011/en/1cf0816b-12e1-4c15-b055-26f18b5d5201/afr200012011en.pdf. Accessed 10 Apr 2011
Child Soldiers International (2012) Better than cure: preventing the recruitment and use of children in the Chadian national army. http://www.child-soldiers.org/Better_than_cure.16April2012.pdf. Accessed 18 Apr 2012
Coalition for the International Criminal Court (n.d.) Africa and the International Court. http://www.iccnow.org/documents/Africa_and_the_ICC.pdf. Accessed 15 Apr 2012
Coalition for the International Criminal Court: Cases and Situations http://www.iccnow.org/?mod=casessituations. Accessed 10 Apr 2012
Convention on the Prevention and Punishment of the Crime of Genocide (1951) Entry into force 12 January, 1951. http://www.preventgenocide.org/law/convention/text.htm. Accessed 8 Apr 2012
Human Rights Watch (2012a) No place for children: child recruitment, forced marriage, and attacks on schools in Somalia. www.hrw.org/sites/default/files/reports/somalia0212ForUpload.pdf. Accessed 4 Apr 2012
Human Rights Watch (2012b) World Report 2012: Somalia (Events of 2011). http://www.hrw.org/world-report-2012/world-report-2012-somalia. Accessed 4 Apr 2012
Human Rights Watch (2011) Unfinished Business: closing gaps in the selection of ICC cases. http://www.hrw.org/sites/default/files/reports/icc0911webwcover.pdf. Accessed 10 Apr 2011

International Criminal Court, States Parties to the Rome Statute (2012) http://www.icc-cpi.int/Menus/ASP/states+parties/. Accessed 15 Apr 2012

Lobe J (2011) Obama Waives Aid Curbs on Militaries Using Child Soldiers. http://www.ipsterraviva.net/UN/news.asp?idnews=105356. Accessed 7 Apr 2012

Office of the ICC Prosecutor (2003) 'Informal expert paper: the principle of complementarity in practice'. http://www.iclklamberg.com/Caselaw/OTP/Informal%20Expert%20paper%20The%20principle%20of%20complementarity%20in%20practice.pdf. Accessed 15 Apr 2012

Office of the ICC Prosecutor, Letter concerning communication on the situation in Iraq (9 February, 2006, p. 8). Cited in W.A. Schabas (Oxford Commentaries on International Law) The International Criminal Court: A commentary on the Rome Statute. New York: Oxford University Press, 2010, p. 201

Office of the ICC Prosecutor (2007) Policy paper on the interests of justice. http://www.icc-cpi.int/NR/rdonlyres/772C95C9-F54D-4321-BF09-73422BB23528/143640/out.html. Accessed 15 Apr 2012

Office of the ICC Prosecutor (2010) Prosecutorial Strategy 2009–2012. http://www.icc-cpi.int/NR/rdonlyres/66A8DCDC-3650-4514-AA62-D229D1128F65/281506/OTPProsecutorial-Strategy20092013.pdf. Accessed 12 Apr 2012

Optional Protocol to the Convention on the Rights of the Child on the involvement of children in armed conflict (2002) Entry into force 12 February, 2002. http://www2.ohchr.org/english/law/crc-conflict.htm. Accessed 5 Apr 2012

Osile M (2009) How should the ICC Office of the Prosecutor choose its cases? The multiple meanings of 'Situational Gravity'. http://www.haguejusticeportal.net/Docs/Commentaries%20PDF/Osiel_ICC_EN.pdf. Accessed 7 Apr 2010

Patel A (2011) Obama Waives Child Soldier Ban in Yemen and Congo. http://abcnews.go.com/Blotter/obama-waives-child-soldier-ban-yemen-congo/story?id=14663930#.T4O0HtX1lko. Accessed 9 Apr 2012

Radio Netherlands Worldwide (International Justice Desk) 'ICC Prosecutor seeks long sentence for Lubanga' (15 March, 2012). http://www.rnw.nl/international-justice/article/icc-prosecutor-seeks-long-sentence-lubanga. Accessed 15 Apr 2012

Ratifications to the Rome Statute (n.d.) http://www.icc-cpi.int/Menus/ASP/states+parties/. Accessed 2 Apr 2012

Report of the Secretary-General on children and armed conflict (9 February, 2011) http://www.crin.org/docs/Children_and_armed_conflict_in_Chad.pdf

Rogin J (2011) Congress strikes back against Obama's child soldiers' waivers (5 October, 2011) http://thecable.foreignpolicy.com/posts/2011/10/05/congress_strikes_back_against_obama_s_child_soldiers_waivers

Rome Statute Elements of the Crime (2002) http://www.icc-cpi.int/NR/rdonlyres/9CAEE830-38CF-41D6-AB0B-68E5F9082543/0/Element_of_Crimes_English.pdf. Accessed 18 Jan 2012

Save the Children (2012) Untold Atrocities: The stories of Syria's children. http://www.savethechildren.org.uk/sites/default/files/images/untold_atrocities.pdf. Accessed 21 October, 2012

Schauer E and Elbert T (2009) The psychological impact of child soldiering. http://www.forensiktagung.ch/index.cfm?action=act_getfile&doc_id=100518. Accessed 7 Apr 2012

Secretary-General's annual report on children and armed conflict with appended list of shame at annex I (26 April, 2012). http://www.un.org/children/conflict/_documents/A66782.pdf. Accessed 16 Jun 2012

Special Representative of the Secretary-General for Children and Armed Conflict. Press release (11 June, 2012) http://www.un.org/children/conflict/english/pr/2012-06-11290.html. Accessed 19 Jun 2012

Tamil Guardian. 'Refer Syria to ICC – Navi Pillay' (13 December, 2011). http://www.tamilguardian.com/article.asp?articleid=4084. Accessed 17 Jun 2012

UNHCR (United Nations High Commission on Refugees) (2012) 2012 UNHCR country operations profile – Chad. http://www.unhcr.org/cgi-bin/texis/vtx/page?page=49e45c226. Accessed 10 Apr 2012

UNICEF (2012) Children in Chad face life-threatening malnutrition. http://blog.unicef.ie/2012/03/children-in-chad-face-life-threatening-malnutrition/. Accessed 11 Apr 2012

United Nations News and Media. Statement of UNICEF spokesperson Patrick McCormick (1 June, 2011) http://www.unmultimedia.org/tv/unifeed/d/17745.html. Accessed 17 Jun 2012

UN News Centre (23 February, 2012) UN report on sexual violence during conflict singles out worst offenders (presented to the UN Security Council by Margot Wallström (Special Representative to the Secretary-General)) http://www.un.org/apps/news/story.asp?NewsID=41344&Cr=sexual+violence&Cr. Accessed 11 Apr 2012

Cases

Case concerning the Application of the Convention on the Prevention and Punishment of the Crime of Genocide (Bosnia and Herzegovina v. Serbia and Montenegro) (International Court of Justice)(ICJ), Judgment of 26 Feb. 2007. http://www.icj-cij.org/docket/files/91/13685.pdf. Accessed 13 Apr 2012

Democratic Republic of Congo v Uganda,(Case concerning armed activities on the territory of the Congo) (International Court of Justice) (ICJ) 2005 judgement. http://www.icj-cij.org/docket/files/116/10455.pdf. Accessed 15 Apr 2012

Pre-Trial Chamber decision (ICC) to authorize an investigation into situation in the Republic of Kenya (*Kenya*) 31, March, 2010. http://www.icc-cpi.int/iccdocs/doc/doc854287.pdf. Accessed 4 Apr 2012

Prosecutor v Lubanga Pre-Trial Chamber I, Decision on the Prosecutor's Application for a warrant of arrest. Article 58, ICC-01/04-01/06-8-Corr, para. 41.

Prosecutor v Thomas Lubanga Dyilo, Final Trial Judgement Pursuant to Article 74 of the Rome Statute (14 March, 2012). http://www.icc-cpi.int/iccdocs/doc/doc1379838.pdf. Accessed 20 Mar 2012

Index

A
Additional Protocol I, Geneva Convention
  Article 74, 181
  Article 77(2), 94–95, 151
Additional Protocol II, Geneva Convention
  Article 4(3)(e), 255
  Article 4, 181
  Article 4(3)(c), 95, 151, 180, 188
African' Darfurians, 255
African Union Mission in Somalia (AMISOM), 271
African Union Mission in Sudan (AMIS), 58–61
Amnesty International, 241, 285
Armed Forces of the Democratic Republic of the Congo (FARDC), 144–146
Autogenocide
  Darfur, 224–225
  genocidal forcible transfer of Hema children, 87, 190

B
British Military Court, 71

C
Chad
  Amnesty International and UN reports
    armed forces and groups, 284
    grave international crimes, 283
    IDPs, 285
    judicial capacity, 284
    sexual violence, 286
    State national armed forces, 283
  U.S. Child Soldiers Prevention Act of 2008
    Human Rights groups, 287
    military assistance, 287
    purported legitimacy, 289
    State national armed force, 288
    TFG forces, 287
Child bodyguards, 100–101
Child soldiers
  cruel and inhuman treatment, FNI/FRPI
    armed attacks, 215
    civilian population, 217
    heinous injuries, 215
    Hema ethnic group, 215
    mortality rates, 216
    protected persons, 214
    PTSD, 216
    war crimes, 214
  genocidal forcible transfer of children, FNI/FRPI
    armed hostilities, 208
    combatants, 213
    conscription/alleged enlistment, 211
    criminal responsibility, perpetrators, 208
    DRC conflict, 213
    grave international crimes, 209
    ICRC, 211
    international law, 210
    Katanga and Chui case, 212
    military training, 212
    protected group, 210
    recruitment, 209
    war crimes, 213
  ICC victim participant status, 64–66
  Lubanga case (*see Prosecutor v. Thomas Lubanga Dyilo*)
  mens rea and appropriation of children, 217
  nationality and protected status of children, 218

S.C. Grover, *Humanity's Children*, DOI 10.1007/978-3-642-32501-4,

Child soldiers (*cont.*)
outrages on personal dignity, 218–220
State criminal liability
failure to protect children, 76–77
genocide, 74–76
truth and reconciliation processes
Article 75 of Rome Statute, 68–69
TRC, 67–68
victims of genocidal forcible transfer
Essen Lynching case, 71
Hadamar case, 71
international criminal tribunals, 73
military tribunal prosecutions, 72–73
Rome Statute, 69
Zylon B case, 71–72
Comprehensive Peace Agreement (CPA), 239
Convention on the Rights of the Child (CRC)
Article 1, 187
Article 2, 187
Article 4, 187
Article 5, 180
Article 6, 45–46
Article 8, 29, 180
Article 9, 29, 180
Article 15, 46–47

D
Darfur
Arab' children, child soldiering, 228–232
autogenocide, 224–225
child victims, 242–244
genocide identification
African victim groups, 248
arbitrary distinctions, 248
case-by-case basis, 251
ethnic group, 249
International Commission of Inquiry on Darfur, 252
protected group, 249
religious and national group, 250
restrictive interpretation, 250
ICC case selection and gravity
attack on AMIS peacekeepers, 58–61
children as protected groups, 60–61
child victims, 61
Democratic Republic of Congo (DRC), 202
Article 23, CCPR, 180
child soldiering, 144–146
ICC case selection and gravity
Article 17(d), Rome Statute, 55–56
Article 33, Rome Statute, 57
genocidal forcible transfer of children, 56–58
ICC Appeal Chamber judgment, 56

E
Essen Lynching case, 71
Ethnic cleansing, 26, 88, 233

F
Forced pregnancy, 107, 130, 233
Fur community, 234, 235, 249, 250

G
Gender-based crimes
sex slaves, procurement of, 109–110
sexual violation of girl recruits, 107–109
Women's Initiatives for Gender Justice, 110–113
Geneva Convention
Additional Protocol I
Article 74, 181
Article 77(2), 94–95, 151, 153
Additional Protocol II
Article 4(3)(e), 255
Article 4, 181
Article 4(3)(c), 95, 151
Genocidal forcible transfer of children
Al Shabaab against children
international crimes, 276–277
recruitment and use of children, 277
armed groups/forces, 262
Chad
Amnesty International and UN reports, 283–286
U.S. Child Soldiers Prevention Act of 2008, 287–289
child soldiers as victims of
Essen Lynching case, 71
Hadamar case, 71
international criminal tribunals, 73
military tribunal prosecutions, 72–73
Rome Statute, 69
sex slaves, 263
Zylon B case, 71–72
controversy, 267
FNI/FRPI
armed hostilities, 208
combatants, 213
conscription/alleged enlistment, 211
criminal responsibility, perpetrators, 208

DRC conflict, 213
grave international crimes, 209
ICRC, 211
international law, 210
Katanga and Chui case, 212
military training, 212
protected group, 210
recruitment, 209
war crimes, 213
foreseeability, perpetrator accountability and Rome Statute Article 6(e)
armed group/force, 34
Convention on the Rights of the Child, 29
families and home communities, 28
international criminal law treaties, 35
interpretation of treaties, 36–37
jus cogens norm, 28
nullum crimen principle, 30–34
political groups, 35
pre-existing knowledge, 28
Vienna Convention on the Law of Treaties, 36
grave international crimes, 264
civilian population, 9
discriminatory intent, 10
ethnicity, 10
Genocide Convention, 11
political affiliation, 11
gravity assessment
Article 5, Rome Statute, 54
Article 6(e), Rome Statute, 54, 57
Article 33, Rome Statute, 57–58
legal characterization of facts, 63
ICC admissibility criterion, 268–269
ICC prosecution, 262
international norms, 289–291
children's access, 291–293
child soldiers, 293–298
ICC and child victims interests, 303–308
ICC independence, impartiality and grave international crimes, 301–303
sexual victimization, 298–301
judicial interpretation, 265
Kenya, ICC Pre-Trial Judgement, 269–270
Lubanga case (*see Prosecutor v. Thomas Lubanga Dyilo*)
mass rape and forced marriage, 264
protected group
Additional Protocols I and II, 17
Al Bashir forces and allied militia, 20
child-specific provisions, 12, 16
customary law, 12
genocidal intent, 19
grave child-specific international crimes, 15
homosexual parents, 14
human rights law, 11
identifiable group, 15
international criminal law, 12
international humanitarian law, 11
perceived political affiliations, 21
political dissidents, 14
Preparatory Working Group, 18
Pre-Trial Chamber, 21
racial group, 13
special protection, 13
targeted group, 19
textual interpretation, 18
traditional interpretation, 16
UN Commission of Inquiry on Darfur, 20
racial lines, 266
recruitment and hostilities, 267
restrictive interpretation
ambiguous terminology, 24
armed conflict, 25
Aryan qualities, 27
international humanitarian and human rights law, 22
Nazi Lebensborn program, 26
physical destruction, 26
political opposition, 23
racial group membership, 22
reproductive capacity, 25
rights of children, 27
Rome Statute Article 6 Protected Group
atrocity, 42
civilized international community, 44
Convention on the Rights of the Child, 45–47
counter-insurgency, 42
cultural genocide, 40
future generations, 41
genocidaires, 38
LRA, 43
marginalized child groups, 40
membership, 39
perpetrator group, 38
political groups, 37
pregnant women, 45
sexual violence, 41
spared children, 43
Rome Statute elements of crimes, 265
Somalia
child soldier situation, 270
child victimization, 271–276
perpetrators, 278–283
Syrian regime
crime against humanity, 310

democratic cultural norms, 311
pro-government forces, 310
protected group, 311
restrictive interpretation, 312
torture and massacres, 312
targeted children
armed hostilities, 8
child soldiers, 6
forced mental and physical enslavement, 7
German children and youth, 5
Hitlerjugend, 6
ICC, 4
indoctrination, 5
international crimes, 3
mass atrocity, 3
Nazi anti-Semitic propaganda, 5
obscurantism, 7
racial/national identity, 4
special protected group, 8
suicide bombers, 9
terrorist groups, 9
UN Security Council, 263
war crimes, 261
Girl soldiers
sex slaves, 109–110
sexual violation
forced pregnancy, 107
gang rape, 108
mental and physical harm, 108
protected group, 108–109
in recruitment process, 107
Trial Chamber judgement in *Lubanga* case, 161–164
Women's Initiatives for Gender Justice, 110–113
Government of Sudan (GoS), 223
Gravity and interests of justice
Article 53, Rome Statute, 78–79
Article 58(1), Rome Statute, 53–54
children's right to justice and legal empowerment
definition of, 64
ICC victim participant status, 64–66
child soldiers
State criminal liability, 74–77
truth and reconciliation processes, 67–69
victims of genocidal forcible transfer, 69–73
in Darfur
attack on AMIS peacekeepers, 58–61
children as protected groups, 60–61
child victims, 61
Democratic Republic of Congo
Article 17(d) of Rome Statute, 55–56
Article 33 of Rome Statute, 57
genocidal forcible transfer of children, 56–58
ICC Appeal Chamber judgment, 56
genocidal forcible transfer of children, 54
ICC Prosecutor policy paper, 79–80
legal characterization of facts
genocidal forcible transfer of children, 63
war crimes and armed conflict, 61–62

H

Hadamar case, 71
Hitlerjugend, 6
HIV/AIDS, 108, 112, 139
Humanitarian Aid Commission (HAC), 223
Human Rights Watch (HRW), 117, 270, 271

I

International Committee of the Red Cross (ICRC), 95, 211
International Covenant on Civil and Political Rights (CCPR), 180
International Criminal Court (ICC)
gravity and interests of justice (*see* Gravity and interests of justice)
Lubanga case (*see Prosecutor v. Thomas Lubanga Dyilo*)
International Military Tribunal (IMT), 5
International norms
child soldiers
armed group/force, 293
collective genocidal intent, 294
cultural tradition, 295
ethnic and perceived racial group, 294
FPLC, 295
HRW, 293
ICC gravity test, 296
customary law and international humanitarian law, 289
human rights, 290
ICC and child victims interests
fundamental rights violations, 308
grave international crimes, 304
mass rape and sexual violence, 303
physical harms, 305
Pre-Trial Chamber, 307
UN Security Council, 306
ICC independence, impartiality and grave international crimes, 301–303
international justice, 291–293

military assistance, 289
sexual victimization, 298–301
UN Security Council, 290

J
Justice and Equality Movement (JEM), 223

L
Latin maxims, 33
Lord's Resistance Army (LRA), 43
Lubanga case. *See Prosecutor v. Thomas Lubanga Dyilo*

M
Masalit community, 234, 235, 249, 250
Mistake of law, 95–96

N
National Intelligence and Security Service (NISS), 223
Nazi Lebensborn program, 90
Nullum crimen principle
armed group/force, 30
international criminal law provision, 31
mass atrocities and genocide, 30
Rome Statute
Article 21(3), 32–34
Article 22, 34
substantive justice considerations, 32
Nuremberg Charter, 5

O
Omar Hassan Ahmad Al Bashir
Arab' children, Darfur
child soldiers, 231
GoS forces, 229
humanitarian aid, 229
IDP camps, 229
inhumane treatment, 231
international community, 230
Janjaweed militia, 230
Pre-Trial Chamber, 228
autogenocide, 224–225
children and armed conflict
child soldier recruitment, 237
concrete time-bound plan, 239
CPA, 239
grave international crimes, 240
ICC charges, 240
JEM, 241
Lubanga, 242
re-integration programs, 241
Sudanese Armed Forces and allied militias, 238
UN Secretary General's report, 237
motive, genocide and child soldiering
armed groups/forces, 225
child soldiers, 228
grave international crimes, 226
international criminal law community, 227
recruitment/use of children, 225
Rome Statute war crime, 226
State or non-State armed forces, 227
recruitment and use of child soldiers, 236
sexual violence
armed opposition groups, 232
Fur, Masalit and Zaghawa communities, 234
GoS/pro-government militia members, 234
home communities, 235
inter-ethnic conflicts, 233
international criminal law, 235
military encampments, 233
UNICEF, 234
women and girls, 232
Optional Protocol to the Convention on the Rights of the Child on the involvement of children in armed conflict (OP-CRC-AC), 70, 144, 145, 151
Article 1, 148–149, 187
Article 2, 187
Article 4, 151, 187
child soldier, definition of, 288

P
Patriotic Forces for the Liberation of Congo (FPLC) child soldiers. *See also Prosecutor v. Thomas Lubanga Dyilo*
common plan
child bodyguards, recruitment of, 100–101
component of, 98–99
objective of, 97–98
Prosecution closing brief, 98–99
Rome Statute Elements of the Crime, 99
continuous nature of international crimes in DRC, 144–146
genocidal forcible transfer of children, 138–141
lack of criminal culpability, 141–143

Patriotic Forces for the Liberation of Congo (FPLC) child soldiers. (*cont.*)
  gendered crimes
    sex slaves, procurement of, 109–110
    sexual violation of girl recruits, 107–109
    Women's Initiatives for Gender Justice, 110–113
  genocidal forcible transfer of childern
    Hema children, 87–90
    prosecution closing statement, 92–94
    protected groups, Genocide Convention, 89
    recruitment, 89–91
  manifestly unlawful appropriation of children
    knowledge and genocidal intent, 101–104
    under 15s as child soldiers, 105–106
  short-term training, 137–138
Post-traumatic stress disorder (PTSD), 216
Prosecutor v. Germain Katanga and Mathieu Ngudjolo Chui
  confirmed charges
    crimes against humanity, 201
    Pre-Trial Chamber, 201
    war crimes, 201
  FNI/FRPI
    cruel and inhuman treatment, 214–217
    genocidal forcible transfer of children, 208–214
    mens rea and appropriation of children, 217
    nationality and protected status of children, 218
    outrages on personal dignity, 218–220
  prosecution opening statement, 202–203
  sexual violence crimes
    armed group, 205
    child soldiers, 207
    conscription and active participation in hostilities, 206
    domestic and sexual services, 205
    FNI/FRPI perpetrators, 203
    Lendu girl sex slaves, 206
    Lubanga case, 205
    military camps, 204
    Ngiti girl sex slaves, 206
    Pre-Trial Chamber, 204
    psychological and physical harms, 207
    women and girls, 203
Prosecutor v Omar Hassan Ahmad Al Bashir
  Arab' children, Darfur, 228–232
  autogenocide, 224–225
  children and armed conflict, 237–242
  child victims, Darfur, 242–244
  counter-insurgency campaign, 224
  genocidal forcible transfer of children
    armed hostilities, 246
    Darfur, 253–256
    extreme racism, 245
    mental sufferings, 245
    perceived African groups, 246
    pro-government forces and militias, 247
    systematic mass atrocities, 247
  genocide charges, 244–245
  genocide identification
    African victim groups, 248
    arbitrary distinctions, 248
    case-by-case basis, 251
    ethnic group, 249
    International Commission of Inquiry on Darfur, 252
    protected group, 249
    religious and national group, 250
    restrictive interpretation, 250
  motive, genocide and child soldier, 225–228
  recruitment and use of child soldiers, 236
  sexual violence, 232–236
Prosecutor v. Thomas Lubanga Dyilo
  armed conflict
    Additional Protocols I and II, Geneva Convention, 94–95
    ICRC, 95
    mistake of law defence, 95–97
    Pre-Trial Chamber, 96–97
  children's special protected status, 150–161
  common plan
    child bodyguards, recruitment of, 100–101
    component of, 98–99
    objective of, 97–98
    Prosecution closing brief, 98–99
    Rome Statute Elements of the Crime, 99
  confirmation of charges, 85–86
  continuous nature of international crimes in DRC, 144–146
    genocidal forcible transfer of children, 138–141
    lack of criminal culpability, 141–143
  gendered crimes
    sex slaves, procurement of, 109–110
    sexual violation of girl soldiers, 107–109

Women's Initiatives for Gender Justice, 110–113
genocidal forcible transfer of child soldiers
Hema children, 87–90
prosecution closing statement, 92–94
protected groups, Genocide Convention, 89
recruitment, 89–91
in Rwanda, 89
ICC Trial Chamber judgement
"active participation" in hostilities, 165–171
child soldiers as UPC/FPLC mascots, 164–165
child soldiers, recruitment of, 171–172
girl soldiers, sexual violence of, 161–164
ICC Trial Chamber's analysis of
Article 31, Vienna Convention on the Law of Treaties, 178–185
children associated with armed conflict, 191–195
child soldiers, demobilization of, 195–196
child soldiers over 15, protection of, 185–188
common plan as intrinsically criminal, 188–191
Odio Benito's view, analysis of, 172–178
legal re-characterization of facts and circumstances
active participation in armed hostilities, 124–125
Article 61(9), Rome Statute, 115
Article 74, Rome Statute, 114–115
ICC Appeal Court, 114–115
ICC Trial Chamber, 115–116
Pre-Trial Chamber Decision on the Confirmation of Charges, 116–123
sexual slavery, 116
sexual violence, Ocampo's view of, 126–137
victim participant group, petition of, 113–114
manifestly unlawful appropriation of children
knowledge and genocidal intent, 101–104
under 15s as child soldiers, 105–106
recruitment of child soldiers, 146–150
short-term training to child soldiers, 137–138

R
Rome Statute
Article 5, 54
Article 6, 104
Article 6(e), 54
Article 8(2)(b)(xxvi), 85
Article 8(2)(e)(vii), 85
Article 17(d), 55–56
Article 21(3), 186
Article 22(2), 173
Article 30, 103
Article 33, 57
Article 53, 78–79
Article 58(1), 53–54
Article 61(9), 115
Article 74, 114–115
Article 75, 68–69
Elements of the Crime, 99, 173

S
Sex slaves, 109–110, 130–131
Sexual violence
Lubanga case
forced pregnancy, 107
gang rape, 108
mental and physical harm, 108
protected group, 108–109
in recruitment process, 107
sex slaves, 109–110
Trial Chamber judgement, 161–164
Women's Initiatives for Gender Justice, 110–113
Omar Hassan Ahmad Al Bashir
armed opposition groups, 232
Fur, Masalit and Zaghawa communities, 234
GoS/pro-government militia members, 234
home communities, 235
inter-ethnic conflicts, 233
international criminal law, 235
military encampments, 233
UNICEF, 234
women and girls, 232
Somalia
child soldier situation, 270
child victimization
children's rights, 271
cruel and inhuman treatment, 272
forced recruitment, 274
grave maltreatment, 275
home communities, 273
HRW, 272

    military training, 273
    school attacks, 274
    TFG, 271
  perpetrators
    HRW, 278
    human rights improvements, 282
    impunity, 282
    international political calculus, 279
    national security interests, 283
    pro-children's rights, 278
    Prosecutorial decision, 280
    recruitment and use of child soldiers, 281
    transitional government, 281
    UN Security Council, 279
    women and children, 280
Special Court of Sierra Leone, 97
Sudanese Liberation Movement/Army (SLM/A), 223

T
Transitional Federal Government (TFG), 271
Truth and Reconciliation Commissions (TRC), 67–68

U
Uganda People's Defence Forces (UPDF), 293
UN Commission of Inquiry on Darfur, 20
U.N. Convention on Genocide, 87–88
UN Security Council, 224
U.S. Child Soldiers Prevention Act of 2008, 287–289

V
Vienna Convention on the Law of Treaties, 18, 36
  Article 31, 36–37, 178–179
  Article 32, 18

W
Women's Initiatives for Gender Justice, 110–113

Z
Zaghawa community, 234, 235, 249, 250
Zylon B case, 71–72

Printed by Printforce, the Netherlands